THROUGH THE VALLEY OF THE SHADOW OF DEATH

The Civil War Manuscript Collection of
Captain Harvey Alexander Wallace
5th South Carolina Infantry and
19th Texas Infantry
Walker's Texas Division

Edited by
Stephen R. Skelton

HERITAGE BOOKS
2009

HERITAGE BOOKS
AN IMPRINT OF HERITAGE BOOKS, INC.

Books, CDs, and more—Worldwide

For our listing of thousands of titles see our website at
www.HeritageBooks.com

Published 2009 by
HERITAGE BOOKS, INC.
Publishing Division
100 Railroad Ave. #104
Westminster, Maryland 21157

Copyright © 2004 Stephen R. Skelton

All rights reserved. No part of this book may be reproduced or transmitted in any form or by any means, electronic or mechanical, including photocopying, recording or by any information storage and retrieval system without written permission from the author, except for the inclusion of brief quotations in a review.

International Standard Book Numbers
Paperbound: 978-0-7884-3134-0
Clothbound: 978-0-7884-8119-2

The Lord is my shepherd: I shall not want.

He maketh me to lie down in green pastures: He leadeth me beside the still waters.

He restoreth my soul: He leadeth me in the paths of righteousness for His name's sake.

Yea, though I walk through the valley of the shadow of death, I will fear no evil: for thou art with me; thy rod and thy staff they comfort me.

Thou preparest a table before me in the presence of mine enemies: thou anointest my head with oil; my cup runneth over.

Surely goodness and mercy shall follow me all the days of my life: and I will dwell in the house of the Lord forever.

Psalm 23

Contents

Illustrations	vi
Acknowledgements	ix
Editor's Note	xi
Editorial Methods	xv
Introduction	xvii
Letters	
1861-On the Eve of A Bloody War	1
1862-A Soldier's Life Is A Hard One	147
1863-Hard Fighting	203
1864-Prisoners Of Us All	257
1865-Homeward Bound	265
Prison Diary	274
Journals	
The Different Camps of Company-H, 19th Texas Infantry	294
Writings of Captain Harvey A. Wallace, C.S.A	306
Moves of the 19th Texas Infantry From Jan., 1865	309
Epilogue	311
Appendix-I - Deaths in Capt. H. A. Wallace's Company-H 19th Texas Infantry	321
Appendix-II - Muster Roll-The Catawba Light Infantry (Company-H, 5th S.C. Infantry)	327
Appendix-III - Muster Roll-Company-H, 19th Texas Infantry	333
Bibliography	345
Index	357

Illustrations

Cover - Captain Harvey Alexander Wallace - The Ruby Lee (Beall) Stevens Collection
Cover Background - Walker's Texas Division Battle Flag - Courtesy of the Texas State Archives

Page

xviii   Congress Street, Yorkville, South Carolina - Courtesy of the Historical Center of York County
xix   Railroad Depot, Yorkville, South Carolina - Courtesy of the Historical Center of York County
xxii   First Lieutenant Harvey Alexander Wallace, - The Ruby Lee (Beall) Stevens Collection
xxviii   Letter of May 9, 1861 - The Harvey Alexander Wallace Manuscript Collection
2   Aaron Wood "Bud" Wallace - The Ruby Lee (Beall) Stevens Collection
5   Achsah (Wood) Wallace - The Ruby Lee (Beall) Stevens Collection
19   Colonel Micah Jenkins - Courtesy of the Library of Congress
22   The Floating Battery - From the Americana Image Gallery/ U. S. Army Military History Institute
42   Samuel Watson Wallace - The Ruby Lee (Beall) Stevens Collection
79   U.S.S. Niagara - Courtesy of the U. S. Naval Historical Center
92   James and Margaret (Barnett) Wallace - The Ruby Lee (Beall) Stevens Collection
138   Samuel L. "Blind Sam" Campbell - The Ruby Lee (Beall) Stevens Collection
146   Letter of November 29, 1862 - The Harvey Alexander Wallace Manuscript Collection
150   Dempsey Cook - The Ruby Lee (Beall) Stevens Collection
170   William Marcellus Wallace – The Ruby Lee (Beall) Stevens Collection

176	Colonel Richard Waterhouse, Jr. - Courtesy of the Hill College Confederate Research Center
191	Brigadier General Henry E. McCulloch - Courtesy of the Hill College Confederate Research Center
202	Letter of May 20th, 1863 - The Harvey Alexander Wallace Manuscript Collection
206	Samuel L. "Blind Sam" Campbell #2 - The Ruby Lee (Beall) Stevens Collection
212	Colonel William B. Ochiltree - Courtesy of the Hill College Confederate Research Center
225	Letty - The Ruby Lee (Beall) Stevens Collection
229	Major General John George Walker - Courtesy of the Hill College Confederate Research Center
230	General Edmund Kirby Smith - Courtesy of the Hill College Confederate Research Center
242	Major General Richard Taylor - Courtesy of the Hill College Confederate Research Center
251	*U.S.S. Carondelet* - Courtesy of the U. S. Naval Historical Center
256	Letter of June 2nd, 1864 - The Harvey Alexander Wallace Manuscript Collection
266	Major General John Bankhead Magruder - Courtesy of the Hill College Confederate Research Center
275	March 14, 1864 map of Fort DeRussy, Louisiana - From the Image Archives of the Historical Map & Chart Collection/ Office of Coast Survey/National Ocean Service/NOAA
278	*U.S.S. Fort Hindman* (Gunboat #13) - Courtesy of the U. S. Naval Historical Center
279	Major Augustus C. Allen - Courtesy of the Hill College Confederate Research Center
292	Prison Diary Entry - The Harvey Alexander Wallace Manuscript Collection
301	*U.S.S. Carondelet* # 2 - Courtesy of the U. S. Naval Historical Center
302	Brigadier General William Scurry - Courtesy of the Hill College Confederate Research Center
304	Brigadier General Wilburn H. King - Courtesy of the Hill College Confederate Research Center

310	Journal Entry - The Harvey Alexander Wallace Manuscript Collection
316	William Thomas and Aaron Wood Wallace - The Ruby Lee (Beall) Stevens Collection
317	Aaron Wood Wallace on mail route, Minden, Texas - The Ruby Lee (Beall) Stevens Collection
318	William Thomas and Aaron Wood Wallace #2 – The Ruby Lee (Beall) Stevens Collection
320	Duncan and Achsah (Wallace) Poovey and Family - The Ruby Lee (Beall) Stevens Collection

Acknowledgements

This compilation would have been impossible without God's divine hand working in every part and I give thanks to Him for allowing me to take part in this task. I am also deeply indebted to many others who have helped in ways too numerous to mention. Many thanks go to my wife, Pam, who assisted with research, inspiration, motivation, editing, indexing, proofreading, typing, formatting, photo editing, and countless other tasks. This work would also have been impossible without her assistance and perseverance.

I wish to thank Captain Wallace's Great-Granddaughter, Mrs. Ruby Lee (Beall) Stevens, who has been so gracious to provide complete access to the Wallace collection, along with copies of family photographs. Mrs. Stevens also assisted by relating family history handed down through oral tradition and provided copious personal genealogical research notes and material. She and her husband, Mr. Tommy Dean Stevens, hosted numerous interview and research sessions with patience and warm, friendly hospitality. I pray that God richly blesses this wonderful Christian couple.

I am also indebted to Ms. Virginia Knapp, a first class Historian with the Rusk County Historical Commission, whose help was instrumental in tracking down the location of the Wallace Collection. Ms. Knapp also assisted with her vast knowledge of Rusk County history, people, and places. She provided inspiration, friendship, and wisdom from years of experience. She is an honor to her profession.

A word of thanks also goes to Mr. Sam Thomas, Curator of History at the Historical Center of York County, South Carolina. Mr. Thomas, along with Historical Research Assistant Heather South guided me through the historical collections and materials at their facility and provided information to locate related historical sites in York County. I also wish to thank Mr. Steve Mayeux, Historian, and Chairman of the Friends of Fort DeRussy Association, who assisted with research on Fort DeRussy and the soldiers who served there.

Much gratitude also goes to Susan R. Black, Research Librarian at the Longview, Texas Public Library, for her assistance with locating numerous reference materials from sources across America.

Finally, thanks to everyone who provided help or encouragement of any kind along the way. May God richly bless you all.

Editor's Note

No period in American history holds our attention as that of the years spanning the Civil War. It was a monumental event that touched almost every citizen of the nation. It drew into its awful grasp people of every class, gender, and race represented in America at the time. As a result, many of us can trace one or more of our relatives who were involved in the conflict in some way or another. The war is distant in time from us now, yet very near and personal because of this. We want to know what part our relatives played; how they lived; where they served; what they did. In essence, we strive to find answers to questions of why and how in order to come to know our ancestors in a more personal way. What most of us would give to have a time machine that could take us back and deposit us in another place and time, but no such machine exists; or does it?

Many who participated in the American Civil War had a sense that they were making history. Some saw their own impending death with each coming battle or skirmish, or with ever present sickness. In addition, many considered the war an adventure of a lifetime. As a result, they recorded their experiences, convictions, and emotions in diaries and letters that have somehow survived the ravages of time and the elements, carefully preserved by successive generations who perceived their intrinsic value. These documents provide windows in time that allow us to step through into the world and lives of the participants. We must turn to these original manuscripts to answer the questions that we cannot now ask of those who walked before us. The Captain Harvey Alexander Wallace Manuscript Collection is a marvelous time machine that allows us to experience the Civil War by walking beside those who endured it.

The Wallace Collection consists of approximately one hundred-nine letters, three personal journals, a chronological prison diary, an original muster roll, and a casualty list, along with several records of Confederate Army supply and subsistence. Other documents existing with the collection but not included in this work are various plantation records and letters dated before and after the time of the war. The collection has been cared for and handed down through several generations of Wallace descendants. It currently resides with Captain Wallace's Great-Granddaughter, Mrs.Ruby Lee (Beall) Stevens, of Jacksonville, Texas.

With many Civil War letters, journals, and diaries being discovered and published in recent years, one may ask why these are any different from the rest. The Wallace Collection can be considered unique in several ways, one of which is its completeness. Even with some letters missing, the collection contains enough material from different sources to tell a continuous story in detail through the course of the war. Each document is thorough and descriptive of people, places, and events. Captain Wallace and many others record their thoughts, feelings, and emotions as if they were speaking directly to us. We can come to know them in an almost personal way. Another unique aspect is found in the fact that so many letters sent to Captain Wallace from his family and friends survived. Because of such harsh conditions in the field and exposure to the elements, literally hundreds of letters sent to soldiers of both sides were lost or destroyed. With Captain Wallace's attention to preserve and bring home the letters sent to him, we have a marvelous record of a Confederate family and extended family at war. Also unique to this collection is Wallace's intuition that he was making history and his drive to record it as it happened. So many participants of the war missed this important point, only to recall those youthful events through dim memories in recollections recorded in the waning years of their lives. A final unique aspect is the historical value of the collection. In his manuscripts, Captain Wallace relates a concise history of his company and many of the soldiers who served with him. As a result, Wallace's Company-H, 19th Texas Infantry can be considered one of the most chronicled Texas Infantry units of the Trans-Mississippi.

The historical and genealogical value of the Wallace collection is easily recognized, but there is an underlying message that transcends time which the reader should not miss. Through Captain Wallace's example, we can see that a relationship with God through His son Jesus Christ brings peace and an understanding that God is in control, even in the midst of a terrible war. This is as true in today's trying times as it was in the dark days of the Civil War. Through a relationship with God, we can face our own trials and troubles with a peace that passes all understanding, so that we can say with the Psalmist, "Yea, though I walk through the valley of the shadow of death, I will fear no evil; for thou art with me" (Psalm 23:4). This is the assurance that Harvey Wallace and his family found and that this editor hopes you will seek for and find as well.

Editorial Methods

The documents included in this work represent all existing handwritten material of the Captain Harvey A. Wallace Civil War Manuscript Collection dated between the years 1861 and 1865, with the exception of one letter that was excluded because its condition rendered it unreadable. All material is presented in chronological order starting with the earliest date and divided into chapters with headings supplied by the editor. Footnotes are provided for explanation and clarity whenever possible. An attempt was made to identify every person included in the manuscripts. This proved nearly impossible due to the extensive number of people mentioned and lack of information available for some. All information that could be found on an individual is provided. If nothing at all could be located, the individual is listed as unidentified. Bibliographical references are provided with footnotes for reference or further study. If no reference is listed, the source is the editor.

An effort was made to present the documents exactly as written with little or no editorial intervention. Some editorial problems were encountered that precluded this in its entirety. Many documents were found to be in a very good state of preservation, but some were not. In some instances, text was faded and unreadable and pages torn or missing. The grammar, punctuation, and spelling were found to be either nonstandard or missing to the point that many documents were incomprehensible without some editorial intervention. All nonstandard grammar has been left original in order to give the reader a sense of the personality of each writer. Spelling errors are corrected silently in modern form except in most proper names. For readability purposes, punctuation and capital letters have been silently added where none originally existed. In cases where text is missing or illegible, or pages torn in the originals, statements to the effect are added in brackets. Several other minor additions or corrections were made in the transcription process for the sake of clarity. These have also been enclosed in brackets to distinguish them from original text. Some letters contain material enclosed in parentheses or written in large capital print for emphasis in the originals. These have been left as found in the original document.

Throughout the editing and transcription process, the intent has been to provide a work that is as close to the original as possible, yet easily read and understood by a wide general audience. The editor believes that this purpose has been accomplished without detracting from any original historical content. An exhaustive bibliography of sources is provided for the reader or researcher who desires further information.

Introduction

The spring of 1861 broke across South Carolina with the fury of an approaching storm. A cry of war was in the wind and the people of the Carolina back country were standing ready, as they had been for years past, to fight for their liberties. In York District, nestled among the rolling hills of upstate South Carolina, excitement was electrifying. The militia companies were forming and preparing to move after being called up by Governor Francis Pickens. The Catawba Light Infantry was counted among several York District companies preparing for duty. The Catawba consisted primarily of farmers from the plantations of the northeastern portion of the county along and near the Catawba River. They were a light-hearted group. After all, it was going to be a short fight and they would all be back home soon to celebrate the victory, but First Lieutenant Harvey Wallace had a feeling to the contrary. Deep inside Wallace harbored a foreboding premonition that the coming conflict would be long and costly. He was right, and York District would soon pay the price with the lives of almost a complete generation of its young men[1].

A Rich Heritage

Harvey Alexander Wallace was born in York District on April 15, 1829, the seventh of twelve children of James and Margaret Ewart (Barnett) Wallace. The Wallaces were descendants of Scots-Irish immigrants who originally settled in Maryland, Pennsylvania, and Virginia, then migrated south down the Great Wagon Road into the Carolina Piedmont region during the early and mid-seventeen hundreds. The Scots-Irish came seeking fertile land to farm, and peace in which to live and raise their families in their staunch Calvinistic Presbyterian beliefs. They were peaceful but would fight like mad hornets when provoked, as the British experienced in York District at King's Mountain and Huck's Defeat during the Revolution. By the middle of the nineteenth century, the Wallaces

---

[1] York District suffered the highest casualty rate of any South Carolina county during the war.

Yorkville, South Carolina – Congress Street looking north

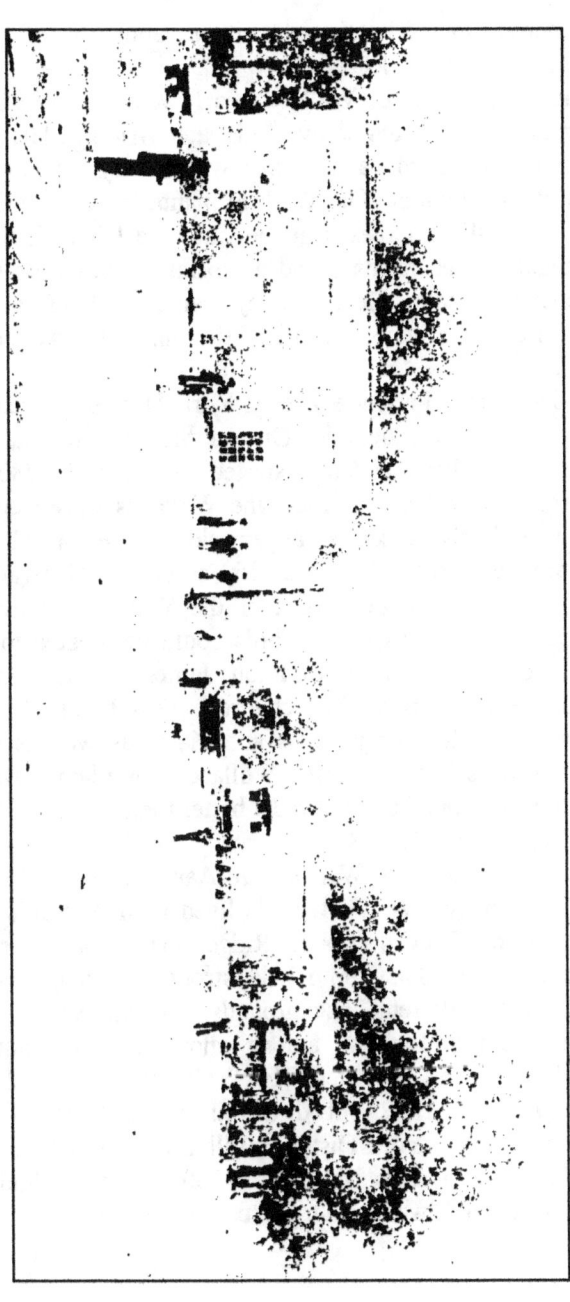

Railroad Depot – Yorkville, South Carolina

were numerous in York District, with a reputation of being good farmers and community leaders.

An account of Harvey Wallace's early years must be taken from family tradition, and from study of his later writings. His father was a predominantly self-educated farmer with a very active presence in the lives of his children. The Wallace plantation consisted of about 325 acres on Allison Creek near the Catawba River. It was typical of the medium sized farms found in upstate South Carolina during the antebellum years. Here Harvey came to love farming and learned to manage a successful plantation under the watchful eye of his father.

The Scots-Irish Presbyterians of York District placed a strong emphasis on formal education. One of the earliest schools in the area was the Bethel Academy, started in the mid 1780's by the Bethel Presbyterian Church where the Wallaces were members and where James Wallace served as an elder. The Bethel Academy named, among some of its earlier students, General Andrew Jackson. It is possible that some of the Wallace family attended Bethel Academy, although no records could be located to establish the fact. According to family tradition, James Wallace took care of the formal education of his children himself at the family's plantation. From the war journals and diary, as well as numerous plantation records left by Harvey Wallace, it is plainly evident that he enjoyed writing and had received a better than average education.

On December 31, 1851, Harvey married Achsah Wood, daughter of Revolutionary War veteran Aaron Wood and his second wife, Matilda (Mayhew). The couple lived with Achsah's widowed mother on Aaron Wood's "Locust Ridge" plantation, where Harvey served as manager. They both held strong Christian convictions, although from different backgrounds. In time, Harvey was persuaded to join the Baptists, among whom the Wood family had a long tradition in York District. The Wallace's first child, Matilda Jane, was born in 1852 but died four years later. Three more children were born in York District: William Thomas (1855), Aaron Wood (1857), and Martha Margaret (1860). Another child, Harvey Alexander Jr. (1864), was born to the couple in Texas.

Gone for A Soldier

In antebellum South Carolina, service in the militia was compulsory for every male eighteen to forty-five years of age. The local militia units at that time consisted of infantry, cavalry, artillery, and light infantry or rifle companies. These were organized into battalions, regiments, brigades, and divisions in the same manner as the organizational structure of the United States Army. Between 1820 and 1868, the South Carolina Militia consisted of 46 line regiments, 10 brigades, and five divisions[2].

Prewar records of the Catawba Light Infantry indicate that the company existed in the early 1850's. Its organization may date to an earlier period but this cannot be verified with existing information. The company was assigned to the North Battalion, 46th Regiment, 9th Brigade, 5th Division of the South Carolina Militia until February 1861. Most likely, Harvey Wallace served in the militia since conscription age, but it is uncertain whether all of his service was with the Catawba Company. What is clear, however, is that Harvey had the qualities and personality of a good leader and military officer. His training and service through the years in the militia helped him develop and hone his leadership skills to the point that those who served with him were confident of his abilities. Wallace's Christian background and southern antebellum heritage helped to instill a sense of duty that could not be broken. As he saw it, his duty was first to God, then to his family, then to those who served under him, and finally to his state and country. Harvey's duty to family, as opposed to his duty to his soldiers and country, caused an internal conflict that dogged him through the course of the war. On one hand, his family needed him at home, and on the other his men, whom he also had responsibility for, needed his leadership. To top it all off, his country required him to fight a war that he would really rather not have to fight, and to do it with little or no support for him, his soldiers, or their families at home.

---

[2] Michael Stauffer, *South Carolina's Antebellum Militia* (Columbia: South Carolina Department of Archives & History, 1991), 2-15.

**First Lieutenant Harvey Alexander Wallace
Catawba Light Infantry**

The families of the members of the Catawba Light Infantry watched with apprehension as the events of December climaxed with the secession of South Carolina from the Union. This could only mean that war would soon follow. After the Ordinance of Secession was adopted, South Carolina's General Assembly passed an "Act to Provide an Armed Military Force." The act called for companies of volunteers to be organized into ten regiments of ten companies each. The term of enlistment would be for twelve months state service. When it was learned that one of these regiments was to be raised from York, Spartanburg, and Union Districts, the men of the existing militia companies met together and volunteered their services with the new regiment; among them stood almost every member of the Catawba Light Infantry.

As circumstances deteriorated politically in South Carolina, the ten new volunteer infantry regiments were hastily organized, the members of each casting votes for their officers. Micah Jenkins, a graduate of the Citadel Military Academy in Charleston, was nominated and elected Colonel of the regiment containing the York District companies. Colonel Jenkins served as Captain of the Jasper Light Infantry, a militia company from Yorkville, before his election. Jenkins, along with his friend and partner, Asbury Coward, owned and operated the Kings Mountain Military Academy in Yorkville. The academy prepared young boys for college or military schools. Colonel Jenkins' new regiment was officially designated the Fifth South Carolina Volunteer Infantry.

Originally, the Fifth Infantry consisted of twelve companies: five from Spartanburg District, three from Union District, and four from York District. The York companies included the Catawba Light Infantry, the Jasper Light Infantry, the Kings Mountain Guards, and the Whyte Guards. The Catawba Company was initially assigned as Company-H. When the regiment was reorganized in April 1862 its designation changed to Company-B, by which it was known through the remainder of the war.

The volunteers of the Fifth South Carolina Infantry would not wait long before being called to service. Even as the first of the big guns thundered at Charleston Harbor against Fort Sumter in the early morning hours of April 12, 1861, word came to Colonel Jenkins to assemble his regiment at Columbia as soon as possible.

The Catawba Light Infantry left Yorkville by train the following morning and reported in at Columbia the same afternoon. From Columbia the regiment was ordered to Charleston and then on to Sullivans Island in Charleston Harbor, where it would guard against any attempt by the Federals to retake Fort Sumter. For nearly two months the volunteers worked on the island defenses and watched the sea for signs of an impending invasion. Meanwhile, Colonel Jenkins became increasingly more impatient. He feared the war would pass him and his regiment by before they had a chance to see action.

The fighting at Fort Sumter did not bring a quick and glorious victory as most of the men of the Fifth Infantry believed. The next major threat to the new Confederacy emerged in Virginia and the Old Dominion State quickly called for assistance from the Confederate government. On May 23, Governor Pickens held a review on Sullivans Island for the troops stationed there. Afterwards, he asked the soldiers to convert their state enlistments to the Provisional Confederate States Army with the stipulation that they would be sent to Virginia. This request was met with angry opposition from some of the members of the Fifth Regiment, who claimed their duty was to the State of South Carolina and their families. Each man was then given the choice to volunteer or to remain in state service. The decision was not easy for Lieutenant Wallace, but he eventually decided to stay in state service so he could be near his family. In all, about three hundred men out of twelve hundred chose not to convert their enlistments. On June 4, 1861, the Fifth South Carolina Infantry was mustered into the Provisional Confederate States Army at Orangeburg, South Carolina. They left by train for Virginia the next day. Those who did not volunteer were left on Sullivans Island as reserve state troops until June 8, when they were discharged and sent home. Most of these men eventually re-enlisted in other companies and regiments as the war continued.

West to Texas

Harvey Wallace arrived back home an anxious man. Before secession Wallace was urged by relatives to move to Texas, where good fertile farming land was plentiful and cheap. By the time of the

Civil War, land in York District was worn out from years of cotton and corn farming. Land prices in South Carolina were also becoming very costly due to an increasing population. Because of this, most farms and plantations were small subsistence operations. In the 1850's, many families migrated out of York District in search of better farming. Some went northwest to Tennessee and Arkansas, and others southwest into Mississippi, Louisiana, and Texas. By the time South Carolina seceded, three of Harvey's brothers and two of his wife's sisters, along with other extended family members, were living in Texas. They advised Harvey that the war would cause land prices in Texas to rise drastically very soon. Wallace knew he could have a profitable farming business with the right amount of good land, so by the time he came home from Sullivans Island his mind was made up to head for Texas. Harvey sold the family's plantation to Achsah's cousins, Dempsey and Polly Cook, and loaded everything else that he could take on wagons and ox carts. The slaves that Wallace owned who wished to stay in York District were either sold or given to neighboring plantation owners. The remainder left with the family for Texas sometime near the First of October, 1861. The group traveled the southern route through Georgia, Alabama, Mississippi, and Louisiana. According to Harvey's record, they arrived in Rusk County, Texas on December 1.

With a harsh Texas winter coming, Harvey quickly located and rented a farm near his relatives in the little settlement of Minden. Many other settlers from York District relocated to Minden and Mount Enterprise between 1850 and 1860. The rolling hills and scattered plantations of the area were much like the country they left behind in South Carolina. After their move, the Wallace family settled in and Harvey began preparations for spring planting. The family also became acquainted with their new neighbors and spent time with family and old friends. Harvey Wallace's dream had finally been realized, but it faded away in just a short time.

Duty Calling

By the early months of 1862, the war fever that swept the south at the outbreak of hostilities ended. Enlistments began to dwindle and the volunteers who enlisted in early 1861 would be discharged in April 1862. To avert critical manpower shortages, the Confederate Congress enacted a conscription act on April 16. The act required military service of every able-bodied white male between the ages of eighteen and thirty-five unless exempted by special provision. In order to give men an opportunity to avoid conscription, the act allowed thirty days for volunteer companies to be raised. In Texas, the conscript act caused a tide of volunteers who wished to choose which branch of service they would serve in, or with whom they would serve with. Many wanted to enlist with their friends and relatives in a locally recruited company. During this time, Harvey Wallace started recruiting an infantry company at Minden. Wallace already held a reputation as a good orator and he gave recruiting speeches in the neighboring towns and villages of Rusk, Panola, and Nacogdoches counties. He had no problem enlisting volunteers and initially took 114 men ranging from seventeen to fifty years of age. Many of these were related and most listed their occupations as farmers. Included in the enlistments were Harvey's brother, William, his brother-in-law Duncan McCallum, and several other distant relatives. Captain Wallace's nephew, Leonard Wood, enlisted in the company later in the war after he reached conscription age. Almost every family in Minden, and many of the Mount Enterprise community had one or more members serving with Wallace's company. He knew and acutely felt the heavy responsibility that he carried for these men and their families. They were his relatives, friends, and neighbors.

In May of 1862, Harvey and his men volunteered to join a new infantry regiment being formed at Jefferson, Texas under Colonel Richard Waterhouse Jr. The regiment was mustered into Confederate service on May 13, 1862 as the Nineteenth Texas Volunteer Infantry. Harvey Wallace accepted the rank of Captain and was left in charge of his company, which was designated Company-H. Apparently, Wallace took this designation in honor of his old Company-H, the Catawba Light Infantry. Company-H drilled in Rusk County under Captain Wallace's instruction through June and July 1862. The company was ordered to assemble at Jefferson in late July to prepare to move for Arkansas. Captain Wallace and his men went into camp at Jefferson about the First of August, where they began preparing for a long march to Little Rock.

The regiment was later divided into two battalions of five companies each. The First Battalion left for Little Rock on August 6 after a flag presentation ceremony. On August 19, the Second Battalion formed into columns with Company-H leading and swung out into the narrow, dusty road heading north out of Jefferson. Harvey Wallace knew that this was just the beginning of a long and dangerous road. They marched that day into history and would, in time, come to carry the renowned name of "Walker's Greyhounds" from their service in General John G. Walker's Texas Division. Now, here is their story in their own words.

My Beloved wife I   Sullivans Island
have rose this morning   Thursday morning May the 9, 61
and commenced the
pleasant task of writing you a few lines the
men are just rising to have been oil and washed
sometime ago I am up first mostly I am well the
company is all able to bee up some of them still
have Diorhea but none so bad as they have been
Achsah I expected a letter yesterday but got none
none of our Company got letters on yesterday I got
one Monday that you wrote Saturday so I hope I will
get one this evening I allow to write three times to
you a week at least I suppose you have seen
cousin Peter and got all of the news before this
time I sent you lots of Sea Shells I have no doubt
you would bee glad to get them I have not much
news to write to you wee are still here on the Beach
wee were Inspected yesterday by the Adjutant General
Jones Col Jenkins has got us swords so iff wee had
our uniform wee would bee fixed off have not got
sashes yet they cant be had in Charleston Achsah I
cont recollect whether I have ever written to you how
many of us stay in our room it is Twenty feet
long about Twelve wide their is 15 of us sleep in it
keep all of our concerns in it Capt Glenn Campbell
Thompson myself Col Bone Uncle Aitken Mason Ja Tate
lies that straight Gid patrick R Patrick Jo McIngvie two Sims

1861

On the Eve of A Bloody War

" It does appear to me that we are on the eve of a bloody war."

Lieutenant Harvey Wallace to his wife
April 26, 1861

York District, So. Ca.
April the 4th, 1861

Dear Harvy,
I seat myself down to write you a few lines. The morning we have just eat breakfast. The sun is just up. The children is all sleeping. They sleep this morning a hour or two. Willy[3] is very lazy. He does not care about doing. Mack[4], he musters; hunts eggs. He and Bud[5] fight some times. I'm trying to break them. Uncle Rease[6] makes them whips. Bud wants all and cries for them. Bud says he wish you would come home. He knows you would make him some. Matty[7] has got pretty well. She is getting quite mischievous; wants to be out all the time. Harvy she very often wants on a petty coat and I have to keep them hid from her. Well, I have wrote you about the children; must say something else. We are all well. Mother[8] is not well. She has a bad cold. You know she can't stand trouble. [illegible] lays her up.

Aaron Wood "Bud" Wallace

---

[3] William Thomas Wallace (1/2/1855-10/23/1929) was Harvey and Achsah Wallace's eldest son.

[4] Mack Wood, son of Addison Wood, was a young slave.

[5] Nickname for Harvey and Achsah's second son, Aaron Wood Wallace (5/14/1857-10/4/1948).

[6] Reason (Reece) Mayhew (1797-?), son of William and Charity Mayhew, was a brother of Achsah's mother, Matilda (Mayhew) Wood. Uncle Reece lived with the family, assisting with chores around the plantation.

[7] Martha Margaret Rebecca Wallace (2/12/1860-9/25/1866). Harvey's infant daughter, "Matty", was the apple of his eye.

[8] Matilda (Mayhew) Wood (5/8/1799-7/2/1876), daughter of William and Charity Mayhew, was the widow of Revolutionary War veteran Aaron Wood (1757-1834). The Wallace family lived on Matilda Wood's plantation where Harvey served as manager.

Nothing can please her like you [illegible] the worse. She says it appears like you have been gone three months. Says people is foolish to think you will be back in a month or two, for she is afraid you will not get home until your time is out.[9] Harvey, your men differ in opinions. Captain Glenn[10] says you will be at home in five or six weeks. Someone else says you will be taken to Virginia, so we do not know how to take it. But I trust God will provide for you to come back before your time is out. Your Pa[11] was here yesterday evening. They are well. He brought your shirt home. Your buttons was in it. It is dirty. It looked like you had done nothing but cook. Harvy we have got our ambrotypes. I will send them by Mr. Wright[12]. Marion[13] went to York yesterday; got his watch fixed. He says he will send it down by Mr Wright if it keeps good time. Andy[14] has offered to find his. I will send your clothes. I want to send a pair of drawers and fine shirt if I can get them took. I bought a silk handkerchief. I will send it to you if you want it. There is nothing I can do, but what I would do for you if I can . Sorry I can not do no more. I would like to send you some cakes by Mr.

---

[9] Wallace's enlistment was for state service for a period of one year.

[10] Captain Robert Henry Glenn (11/2/1829-6/16/1893), son of William and Eliza M. (Boyd) Glenn, commanded the Catawba Light Infantry. Captain Glenn was discharged in June 1861 after choosing not to go to Virginia with the regiment. He later organized Co.-H, 18th S. C. Infantry in York District.

[11] James Wallace (4 /28/1793-5/18/1863), husband of Margaret Ewart (Barnett) Wallace (9/24/1798-11/18/1886).

[12] James L. Wright (10/2/1804-3/24/1876), a neighbor and very wealthy plantation owner ($142,000 net worth per 1860 census), was instrumental in carrying supplies and mail for the company while they were stationed near Charleston. He may also have contributed financially to help outfit the Catawbas. His son, James S. Wright was serving with the Catawba Company at this time.

[13] Daniel Marion Wood (6/15/1831-2/1/1892), Achsah Wallace's nephew and son of Rezin and Mariah Wood. Marion took Harvey's place as overseer of the Wood plantation when Harvey was sent to Charleston with his company. Marion and his wife Mary (Harper), and son Martin, moved to Mississippi in late 1861. He later enlisted in Co.-G, 46th Mississippi Infantry as a private.

[14] Andrew (Andy) Wood (c.1829-?) was a slave born in South Carolina as stated in the 1870 York District, South Carolina census.

Wright if he would take them. Your mother and Rebecca[15] says they want to send some. They are making their men some checked shirts. I suppose you won't want yours or I would send it to you. I am sorry you did not know my provision. I could [have] marked them very easy. I put them in a poke and wrote your name on them but took them out at Mr. Simril['s][16]. Marion marked the butter. They did [illegible] him to do that, but he would. If I cook any more provisions I intend to write your name on it. I sent some coffee. Enough to done you two weeks; never thought [illegible] you would get them. Harvey we do not want you to [illegible] yourself about them shawls. I expect they would be [illegible]. We can do without them. I do not want to buy anything [illegible] can help. I want you to buy all you need. If you [illegible] anything you see you get it, for you know we can get [illegible] that is good if we want it. And as for the wearing, we [illegible]. I am sorry you have such bad water. I am afraid you [illegible] had better buy the water you drink than drink [illegible]. Tresvan[17] is getting well. They say he still wants to go with [illegible]. [illegible] seen him but once since you left. I have not been off the place but once a visiting since you left. Harvey you said you have got no letter from me. I do not know how it is that you don't. I wrote last Saturday evening and finished it Monday morning. Did not get put in the mail that morning, and wrote one a Wednesday evening and sent it to office that night. This makes three letters I have wrote you this day; never got but one letter from you since last Saturday night 'til yesterday morning. You see we don't get them regular. Marion says

---

[15] Reference here is to Harvey's sister, Margaret Rebecca (Wallace) Campbell (7/12/1825-6/26/1894). Rebecca was married to Samuel Campbell, who was a member of the Catawba Company.

[16] Hugh H. Simril (3/12/1804 -12/26/1863) farmed a large plantation in the Bethel community. His sons Samuel and John were members of the Catawba Company.

[17] Dempsey Tresvan Cook (11/12/1842-1/28/1878), Achsah's second cousin and son of Dempsey and Mary (Gibson) Cook, lived with his elderly aunts, Mahala, Harriet, and Eleanor (Nelly) Gibson and helped them work their farm. Tresvan is listed on the February, 1861 militia roster of the Catawba Light Infantry but does not appear on any subsequent muster rolls of the company.

Achsah Wood Wallace

he will write you soon. They have run [illegible] the corn and talking about harrowing the cotton to make it come on. The flour is holding out very well. I won't eat so much as I did. [illegible] won't eat and think you have got nothing fit to eat. Mother, it does her no good to eat. Uncle Rease say howdy; to do the best you can. I must close. The children says howdy. Mother joins [illegible] in well wishes [illegible]. The Lord spare us to meet again and do better by each other. And to Him [illegible]. So farewell.

A. [Achsah] Wallace

State of Texas
Panola County
Apr. 7th, '61

Dear friends,
I take this opportunity to answer your kind letter which came to hand. It was delayed some time on the way. Our mails are so very irregular this spring. As to news, I have none that will interest you but I will do the best I can. This has been a remarkable wet winter and spring, the worst I ever seen in my life. Just one flood of rain after another, and about the time the ground gets so it will plow it comes a big rain. And last Wednesday night, Thursday, and Friday it rained all the time as hard as it could fall all the time. Had we not the promise God would never deluge the world again with water, we might have thought there was going to be another flood. Hollows that hardly run in the winter would swim an elephant almost. It has tore our lands where it could wash all to pieces where it would wash at all. I have only about 16 acres of corn planted yet. Ten acres of that is large enough to plow. The other six I planted over about a week ago. Now it is as bad as ever. When I will get done planting I don't know. You said you had a great deal of rain. I have no idea you know anything. I have seen cows bog down in height upland this winter. In riding, if you turn out of the trail you are down sure the minute you leave it. Well Harvey, I am not trying to work a big crop this year. I am planting only about forty acres of crop. I have about twenty in small grain. People here don't think wheat can do any good this year on account of the wet, though it looks fine yet. It is now heading out. It has some rust in it. Some think if it will turn off dry it won't injure it. If wheat fails, I tell you, there won't be much bread stuff in Texas till corn comes in. How your friends are getting along I don't know. I have not seen any of them, nor heard from them in near amount. I have been looking for Thomas[18] up this week but he has not come. There has been so much rain is the

---

[18] Thomas Stanhope Wallace (11/21/1821-3/1/1886), Harvey's older brother, was married to Achsah's younger sister, Martha (Wood) Wallace (4/29/1832-7/26/1870). Thomas and Martha moved to Texas from York District earlier in the year.

reason I suppose. I was down at the river last week and brought him some corn. I have been looking for him after it. The last corn I bought at 80 cts. but it cost about $1.50 cts. the kind of road we have to haul it over and the time it takes us to do it. I was working on the road yesterday; will have to work two or three days more, the rains has tore them up so. Well Harvey, from what I see, you have got possession of Fort Sumter without a fight.[19] The enlistment has cooled down here since the state has went out, but the people are determined to stand firm in what they have done. Our great Governor and hero of San Jacinto, SAM HOUSTON, has refused to take the oath of allegiance to the Southern Confederacy.[20] They swore in the Lieutenant Governor[21] and turned him out of office. How I hate his principles. This leaves us all well, in hopes it may find you all enjoying a like blessing. The health of this country is good. I am in hopes times will get settled so you will get to Texas next fall.[22] It is the opinion there will be a great migration to Texas and Arkansas from the border slave states. Land speculators are beginning to watch it already and talk of land rising, though I don't think land will rise much for a year or two. Last year was a heavy

---

[19] McCallum apparently based his observation on misinformation or rumor, as Fort Sumter did not fall until April 13, and certainly not without a fight.   See Robert Hendrickson, *Sumter: The First Day of the Civil War* (Chelsea, Mi.: Scarborough House Publishers, 1990).

[20] Houston refused on grounds that it violated his oath to the United States. He fought to have the vote for secession overturned before being thrown out of office. Sam Houston died a heartbroken man in July 1863 at the age of 71.

[21] Edward Clark was elected Lieutenant Governor on the Houston ticket in 1859. After losing a bid for a full term to Francis Lubbock later in 1861, Clark organized the 14th Texas Infantry and served as its Colonel. Clark was wounded at Pleasant Hill, La. and finished the war at the rank of Brigadier General.   Ross Phares, *The Governors of Texas* (Gretna, La.: Pelican Publishing Co., 1976), 97-98.

[22] Presumably, Harvey had been planning to relocate to Texas in the fall of 1862. Four of his brothers (James, Thomas, Joseph, and William) and two of his wife's sisters (Martha Wallace and Matilda Jane McCallum) had moved to Northeast Texas between 1859 and 1861.

blow on the people of Texas. It will take them a long time to get over it. I will close for the present. So good bye.

D. A. McCallum[23]

Well Achsah,
As Duncan is written a few lines, I shall for the first time lately. Achsah you said you were making clothes for Harvy. I hope they will get leave to stay at home. I have been down to see Martha['s] home and I don't like it as well as our county. Achsah I have been to a big wedding; one of our neighbors, a widow lady's daughter; Miss Mary F. Neel[24] to John Reed[25]; a large crowd. I left the children at home with Jo[26]. I let Mary[27] go that morning to help them. Mother you ought to see my boy baby. As I have got nothing but boys,[28] I reckon it is best so. I have a rude set of boys. Jimmy can whip Ren in fair fight. He is wearing Dow's[29] old pants and says he won't wear a frock. Tell Willy that Willy has no school to go to. He runs about and stumps his toe nails off. Dow follows the hens and gathers eggs. I have received your cabbage seed you sent me. I was glad of them. Our gardens look well before the rain. I have to keep sewing all the time to keep up with my set I have. I have yarn ready to commence making fringe for my counterpin[30]. I don't know

---

[23] Duncan A. McCallum (c.1832-11/11/1862), son of Peter (Cousin Peter) and Violet McCallum, was married to Achsah Wallace's sister, Matilda Jane (Wood) McCallum (2/3/1834-4/12/1912). The McCallum family moved to Texas sometime in the late 1850's and settled in Panola County near the town of Pine Hill.

[24] Mary F. Neal (c.1842-?), daughter of Eliza C. Neal of Panola County, Texas.

[25] John M. Reid (c.1831-?) was a farmer from the Mount Enterprise community. He served later as a Private in Harvey Wallace's Co.-H, 19th Texas Infantry.

[26] Unidentified, but most likely a slave

[27] Mary McCallum (c.1830-?), a slave born in South Carolina as stated in the 1870 Rusk County, Texas census.

[28] The McCallum children were: William- age 12, Aaron (Ren)- age 6, James- age 3, and infant "Buddy".

[29] Unidentified

[30] A bedspread

whether I will ever get it done. Cooking and eating is all that get done. I dreamed the other night of talking to you and showing you and Mother little Buddy. Achsah I wish I could see your little girl. Well, I think it is time to quit scribbling as you will have to spell and guess at the [illegible]. So no more at present, but remains your sister,

Jane M. McCallum

Letters – 1861

Camp Jenkins
Columbia, S.C.
April the 14, 1861

Well Achsah, we left York on yesterday morning; arrived here at 1 o'clock without any accident, all in good spirits. We were on duty from the time we landed until 4 o'clock. We marched from the Charlotte & So. Ca. depot to the Charleston depot. There we met the Union and Spartanburg companies[31]. We went through the center of the city, the Catawbas leading; hundreds of the citizens crowding the streets and cheering. We marched back from the depot through the town and then went in to camp on the fair grounds. We posted out sentinels; are keeping up regular camp duty; have good quarters in the buildings. There is ten companies of us in all; nine or ten hundred men. Our company gets the right of the regiment. I must say, our boys have behaved noble so far. They take the praise in the regiment. The Union & Spartanburg companies are far behind the York companies. No man is allowed to go outside of the encampment without a permit. G. W. Mason[32] is the only one of our men that have been out of the encampment. He is our commissary; goes out & buys what we need, him and Mr. Wright. So Fort Sumter has been taken at last. They attacked on Friday morning at 4 o'clock. He hung out his white flag on yesterday. We lost no man at all; one or two wounded slightly. One report says Anderson[33] lost ten.

---

[31] The 5th S. C. Volunteer Infantry consisted of twelve companies at this time; three from Union District and five from Spartanburg District. York District contributed four companies, which included Lieutenant Wallace's Catawba Light Infantry. James J. Baldwin III. *The Struck Eagle: A Biography of Brigadier General Micah Jenkins, and a History of the 5th South Carolina Volunteers and the Palmetto Sharpshooters.* (Cambridge: White Mane Publishing, 1996), 41.

[32] 6th Corporal George Washington Mason (8/29/1825-5/30/1861) was the son of William and Nancy (Pegram) Mason.

[33] Major Robert Anderson commanded the U. S. military installations in Charleston Harbor, including Fort Sumter. A Kentuckian by birth, the fifty-five year old Anderson was a career army officer loyal to his country. His father, Major Richard Clough Anderson, won fame as a defender of Fort Moultrie in Charleston Harbor during the Revolutionary War. Major Anderson was brevetted Major General after Fort Sumter fell for his gallant defense. He was in poor health and

The news this morning says he lost none. As we came on yesterday we expected to go right through. Every train we met would say they were fighting. The vessels tried to come in to Anderson during the fight but they soon drove them back. Anderson surrenders today. He goes out and goes in the United States vessels. We expect to stay here a few days drilling. We don't know how long. We don't know where we may be ordered to. I think as we have had one fight now we may expect to have plenty of fighting. So my dear wife, it is very uncertain where we may be in a few days. We can make no calculation at all. We will be certain, I think, to stay in camp until things are settled, if that is done soon. Fort Pickens in Florida was reinforced night before last[34] so they will have bloody work there. I expect they are fighting there now. We have preaching in camp today at eleven o'clock. We are keeping our duty today. The boys are all in fine spirits, enjoying themselves fine; sadly disappointed about not getting on to Charleston yesterday to see the fight. Some of them was very tired last night. We were on duty so long on yesterday. All the way down on the railroad the ladies were out waving their handkerchiefs. In this place they crowded the pavement & windows; cheered us all the time as we went through. Get along as well as you can. I will write soon again when I have more time. Send me a letter by the return mail. My love to you all.

H. A. Wallace

Marion you will have to take things as you find them. Do the best you can. Your watch is just like it was; won't do no good. If we stay here a few days I will get it fixed.

---

died in 1871, still broken and despondent over his role in the opening battle of a war that would rend the country that he so loved.   Hendrickson, 35-39 and 234.

[34] Fort Pickens stood sentinel on Santa Rosa Island in Pensacola Bay. When the governors of Florida and Alabama demanded the surrender of the fort on January 12, 1861, Lieutenant Adam Slemmer refused, declaring, " A governor is nobody here". Slemmer and his ragtag band of forty-six soldiers and thirty sailors tenaciously held the fort until they were reinforced in April. Fort Pickens never saw the "bloody work" that Wallace predicted. Union forces held the fortress until the end of the war without a shot fired.   Hendrickson,162-163.

Race Paths, Charleston
10 o'clock
April the 16, 1861

Dear Wife,
I send you a few lines. We are all well and in good spirits. We received orders Sunday at 12 o'clock to be ready to move here Monday morning. We rose at two o'clock; had everything pack[ed] up and sent to the cars before day; marched to the cars by day. We landed here at half past 8. Got orders for to march to the arsenal, get arms, and march to the wharf and take a boat for Morris Island[35]; that they were fighting. Our boys appeared in fine spirits when they got the orders. We marched to the arsenal 3 miles; stood there 'til in the night. Only three of our companies got arms. It came on a heavy rain. We then got orders to move here. It was a false report about the fight. We marched here through rain and mud, wet; did not even have a blanket. They had been sent to the wharf; wishing they had got them here before we got here. It was so dark we had to hold to one another to keep from getting lost; 10 o'clock when we got here; after 12 before we got to bed. It is still raining. We do not know when nor where we may have to move. It is raining so we never have went back for our arms. Our regiment has 1100 hundred men in it. People are excited here. There [is] a large force of soldiers about the forts. The vessels are said to be maneuvering around; have soldiers on board. Don't expect us back soon. We will be sure to have to fight now. Keep in good spirits. Trust to God for the best. Send this to Father, & give Cousin Peter Mc[Callum][36] word their boys are well and in good spirits, ready to do their duty. Farewell. I don't have time to write much, we are pretty busy. Kiss the children for me. H. A. Wallace

---

[35] Morris Island, a long barrier island stretching south from the mouth of Charleston harbor, contained several batteries of heavy artillery that fired on Fort Sumter. Less than a mile away from Sumter stood the Cummings Point battery, built and manned by cadets and their instructors from The Citadel Military Academy in Charleston. Hendrickson, 43 and 93.

[36] Peter McCallum (born c.1808 in Scotland) and his wife, Violet, lived in the Zeno community of York District. They were the parents of Duncan A. and William Augustus McCallum.

York, South Carolina
April the 16, 1861

Harvey,
I seat myself down to tell you how we are getting along. We are well at present, and all friends so far as I know except Tresvan. He is bad but not dangerous. He has the catarrh fever.[37] The[y] goes to see him every day. He says he will follow when he gets well. Ward[38] sent him word to go by and he would go with him. Your Father was here yesterday. He looks pale and bad. He is badly hurt about you boy[s] going away. He said he wanted to see you once more before you left. We have had a great deal of rain last night and today. I do not know why you did not take your overcoat along. I think you will need it when it is so cold and wet. We were planting cotton yesterday. The wind blew so hard that they had to sew them so very thick. Marion says they very scarce to sow the balance. Willie says to tell Pa that [he] harrowed one row and held the line for Aunt Cintha[39] 'til dinner. He went out about nine o'clock. Cousin Peter Mc[Callum] sent down a note Sabbath evening that Fort Sumter was taken and they had Anderson a prisoner of war in Charleston. We heard today that you were gone to Charleston. Well Harvy, you say you were sadly disappointed. I do not think it was sadly, I think it was happy. I am glad to hear of you getting the praise, but I do not want you to get too sassy and forget your God. You must prepare to die as well as live and fight. Harvy, I want you to buy you a Bible and read it and talk to the boys. You have a

---

[37] Catarrh fever was an infection of the respiratory tract with symptoms resembling those of influenza or bronchitis, (fever, cough, aches and pains, loss of appetite). At the time, catarrh was attributed to exposure to dampness and cold. During the war, epidemics were reported in commands that occupied low-lying, damp campsites. Deaths were common, especially among new recruits and prisoners. Catarrh was more prevalent in the Confederate Armies due to the lack of clothing and shelter suffered by many of the troops.   Joseph K. Barnes and J.J. Woodward, *The Medical and Surgical History of the War of the Rebellion 1861-65*, Vol-6. (Washington D.C.: U.S. War Department, 1870-1888), 719-726.

[38] Unidentified

[39] Aunt Cintha was a slave.

pretty wild set. Bud sits by me, cries, and says he wants Pa to come back. He is afraid the mans will shoot you. Sissy is playing about. She won't let Frank[40] leave her a minute. We ask, "where is Pa?" She looks at Marion and says nothing. Mother says she don't know whether you had money enough or not. She says she would send you some if you need it. You never said whether you had to get the other suit or not. You never told how long your provision lasted, nor what you get to eat. The Negroes appears to be very that you are gone. They are very kind to children. Marion was at a meeting at the store yesterday morning. Says the people all throwed in 10 cents and sent for a daily paper. We get the mail every day. So nothing more at present, but remains your ever affectionate wife. So goodbye. Write as soon as you get this.

Achsah Wallace

Editors note: There were several inches cut off the letter and the following note was written on that piece of paper.

Uncle Harvy,
I will send you a line or two and anything you want done, if you can instruct me, I will take a pleasure in doing all in my power. Peter Mc[Callum] said something about putting some money out. You can write instruction regarding that. Achsah says Matty's shoes werevery pretty & fits her very neat. It is raining at this time hard. It commenced with a shower of hail as big as bird eggs. The ground is very wet. The bottoms will be wet for some time. The boys is gone to Cousin Nelly's[41] to roll some logs[42] this evening. We shelled

---

[40] Frank Wallace (c.1830-?) was a slave born in Virginia, as stated in the 1870 Rusk County, Texas census.

[41] Eleanor "Nelly" Gibson (11/13/1802-8/14/1878), a niece of Matilda Wood, managed her farm with her two sisters, Mahala, and Harriet (5/16/1807-6/10/1886) Gibson and their nephew, Tresvan Cook.

[42] Log rolling was a festive custom practiced throughout the South on many plantations. When newly acquired land needed to be cleared of timber for planting, neighbors and their slaves would cut the trees and roll the logs into huge piles. When the work was finished, the piles of logs and brush were set on fire. The plantation owner provided food and drink and the participants sang and danced by

some corn, fixed some fence, and built a pig pen. Achsah says she would send you some provision if you are in need of it if she knew where to send them to. I will close. Yours as ever,

D. M. Wood

---

the fire with music provided by slaves scratching skillet lids, beating bones together, and playing homemade instruments.   Elizabeth Silverthorne. *Plantation Life In Texas*. (College Station, Tx.: Texas A&M University Press, 1986), 127, 132.

Camp Butler
Charleston, So. Ca.
April the 18th, 1861
9 o'clock at night

My dear Wife,

I this night send you a few lines to let you know how we are getting along. I am well & have been so since I left home. Our company are all well except Green Finly[43]. He has been sick ever since we came here. He is up and about again. Achsah, a soldier's life is a hard one, but if God only gives us health we can put up with hardships and rough usage. This is a bad place for a sick man. There is eleven hundred men all living in one building. Our quarters here is a room forty feet long and twenty five wide; have straw on the floor; 80 men to sleep; keep all of their baggage; & from before day until after nine at night you can't hear your own voice for talking, hollering, singing, and swearing; all kinds of men in camp. We are all camped in a long house; one half of the company upstairs. We are quartered downstairs. We cook out before the doors; very much hampered about cooking. You ought to see me, Sam Campbell[44], & Lawson Thompson[45] cooking; so many fires the smoke nearly puts our eye out. Col. Bone [Bowen],[46] Capt. Glenn, Campbell,

---

[43] Private William Green Finley (12/1822-6/17/1883), son of Robert Finley, was discharged in June 1861 after choosing not to go to Virginia with the regiment. He later served as a private in Co.-H, 1st S. C. Cavalry.

[44] 2nd Lieutenant Samuel Leroy Campbell (8/26/1829-6/16/1898), son of Isaac A. and Elizabeth (Waller) Campbell, was married to Harvey's older sister, Margaret. Sam was discharged in June, 1861 and later enlisted in Co.-H, 18th S. C. Infantry as 1st Lieutenant.

[45] 3rd Lieutenant William Lawson Thompson (c.1834-6/30/1862), son of Ephraim D. and Mary (Gingles) Thompson, was killed during the Battle of Frayser's Farm, near Richmond, Va. while serving with the Catawba Company.

[46] Private William James Bowen (2/28/1818-4/23/1906), son of Andrew Bowen, took command of the Catawba Light Infantry when it was mustered into Confederate service on June 4, 1861, replacing Captain R. H. Glenn who declined to go to Virginia. In 1851, Bowen served as Colonel of the 46th Regiment S. C. Militia, thus his title of Colonel. *Samuel Leroy Campbell Papers 1862-65.* York, S. C.: Historical Center of York County.

Thompson, and me mess together. We have determined to hire a cook. Col. Bone [Bowen] has sent for six of the Catawba Indians[47] to come down and cook for our company. If they come we will get one of them for our mess. If they do not come, Col. Bone [Bowen] is going to try to get us a cook in Charleston. We have not time to cook. We have to muster four times a day.[48] They give us plenty to eat; bakers bread, light bread, ham shoulders, & beef. Our men do not like the beef much. We get plenty of rice, sugar, & coffee. The men can't near eat the provisions they get. Us officers are allowed as much as two men but we have not got any provisions but a little for our mess yet. The men get more [than] they can eat so we have eat off them. We are allowed the privilege to buy ours and choose what we please. If we don't draw our rations they will pay us for them.

---

[47] The Catawba were an ancient tribe that inhabited the regions around the Catawba River, which winds through the eastern portion of York District. They were a proud people and fierce warriors who were friendly toward the white settlers that poured into the Carolinas beginning in the 1660's. War and disease devastated the tribe through the years until only 55 men, women, and children remained in York District by the time the Civil War began. They survived by doing day labor and menial jobs for the neighboring settlers. Nineteen Catawbas, almost every adult male of the tribe, joined the ranks of the Confederate Army. Nearly all were killed, wounded, or captured during the war.
Laurence M. Hauptman, *Between Two Fires:American Indians in the Civil War* (New York: The Free Press, 1995), 87-102; Louise Pettus, *Catawba Indians in the Civil War*,[http://www.rootsweb.com/~scyork/louise.htm]; Lee Sultzman, *Catawba History*, [http://www.dickshovel.com/Catawba.html].

[48] Colonel Jenkins knew he had very little time to whip his new regiment into fighting prime. A rigorous training schedule was invoked, consisting of: 5:30-6:30 a.m. squad drill; 9:00-10:00 a.m. officers drill; 10:30-11:30 a.m. squad drill; 2:00-3:00 p.m. company drill; 5:00-6:00 p.m. battalion drill and dress parade. Roll call was taken four times throughout the day. Although the young Colonel was a strict disciplinarian, his men loved and respected him. Their time of "breaking in" would soon prove invaluable in Old Virginia. Baldwin, 43.

Colonel Micah Jenkins
5th South Carolina Infantry

We have orders to move from here in the morning to Sullivans Island[49], so if there is any fighting to do here we will get a share of it. I am glad to move from here. I don't like this place. We are so crowded; so much filth about here. This place would be very sickly. People all say that Sullivans Island is one of the healthiest places in the state. We expect to have to go to work and throw up breastwork to fight behind. They say the water over there is good. Our boys are all in good spirits; seem to enjoy themselves fine. The cadets[50] have been drilling us the last two days. The Colonel[51] don't allow any drinking in camp. There has not been one of the Catawbas the least tight[52] since we left York. Achsah I never went out of the camp in Columbia only to march through the street to the depot. I never have been outside of the camp since I have been here. Jenkins don't let out only them that are oblige to go. Us officers have to buy our own swords. We never have got a chance to go out to buy them yet. It may be they will let us get them tomorrow as we go through the city. We have to buy us a uniform. We expect to have it bought and sent to York to make. Achsah, my humble opinion is we will be here for a time. It will not surprise me if we have to serve our

---

[49] Sullivans Island is a long, slender barrier island that courses north by northeast from the mouth of Charleston harbor. In 1861, Fort Moultrie was the prominent landmark on the island. It dated to the time of the American Revolution and was captured by the British in 1780. To the south of the fort lay the little summer resort town of Moultrieville, where many wealthy Charleston residents owned cottages. The town boasted a large hotel on the beach called The Moultrie House, and a steamboat wharf with a horse railway connecting the two. Hendrickson, 46-48.

[50] Reference here is to cadets of the Kings Mountain Military Academy, a preparatory school for young boys located at Yorkville, S. C. Micah Jenkins and his business partner and friend, Asbury Coward, organized the academy in 1854 and served as its headmasters and instructors. A large portion of the student body abandoned their studies and enlisted in Confederate service, to the extent that the school was forced to close after the first term of 1861. Baldwin, 12-19.

[51] Colonel Micah Jenkins (12/1/1835-5/6/1864) was the son of Captain John and Elizabeth (Clark) Jenkins of Edisto Island, S. C. and a graduate of The Citadel Military Academy. Jenkins organized and commanded the Fifth S.C. Volunteer Infantry Regiment in April 1861, and the Palmetto Sharpshooters Regiment in April 1862. He was promoted to the rank of brigadier general July 22, 1862 on the recommendation of Gen. Robert E. Lee. Micah Jenkins died of wounds suffered from friendly fire during the Battle of the Wilderness.

[52] Drunken

time out if we live. We get the papers every day from Charleston. The news is warlike. We got the news this evening that old Virginia has seceded. We won't have but twelve months to serve from the time we volunteered, so we are told here. We had a sermon tonight from Mr. Adams[53] of York. Lots of the York people are here every day. Stillwell & Sam Moore[54] sent us a bushel of apples this evening. Achsah, do the best you can. Take care of our boys & Matty, dear little things. You do not know how much good it would do me to see them & you, but I trust that it is God's will that I will be spared to get back and find you all alive and well. We have to go through dangers from disease and accident, and perhaps on the battlefield, but pray for us. We have a just cause and should look to God for strength to do our duty. That is my intentions, to try to do my duty. John and Samuel, Gustis, & Leroy[55] all stand camp life first rate. Send me word what news you get from Texas. Give my love to your Mother & Uncle Reece, Marion, and all Negroes. Tell Marion to do the best he can. I have no time to think about the farm. Tell Willy and Aaron I want them to know all about mustering when I get home. Your husband,

H. A. Wallace

---

[53] Rev. James M. H. Adams (12/25/1810-3/31/1862) was a respected and popular Presbyterian minister from York District.
[54] Alfred Stillwell (9/20/1822-2/2/1872) served as York District Sheriff, and Samuel E. Moore (c.1822-?) as Court Clerk at the time of this letter.
[55] John Wallace, Samuel Wallace, Augustice McCallum, and Samuel Leroy Campbell.

The Floating Battery at its mooring on Sullivan's Island, April 16, 1861

Sullivans Island
April the 20th, 1861

Well Achsah, I again send you a few lines to let you know how I am getting along. I am still well with the exception of bad cold. The whole company are bad off with cold. I have just come in from drilling one hour in squad drill. We took up our march from our camp in Charleston Friday morning at daylight. Marched five miles to the wharf carrying our blankets, knapsacks, haversacks, canteens, and tins on our backs, and what bread & water we got to eat till near sundown. We had not got much breakfast, our cooking utensils having been packed up the night before. We got to the wharf at ten o'clock. Our regiment has been recruiting all the time. We have 122[56] men in our regiment. Our men all tired. Some of them nearly give out. We all got on two steamboats against half past eleven and steamed for Sullivans Island. We passed near Castle Pinckney[57]; left it to our left; passed close by the famous Fort Sumter. Landed near the Floating Battery[58] about one o'clock; formed our regiment on the

---

[56] Wallace is mistaken or has entered this figure in error as Colonel Asbury Coward, who succeeded Micah Jenkins as regimental commander, states that the 5th Regiment consisted of approximately 560 men when it was initially formed. Natalie Bond and Osmun Coward, *The South Carolinians: Colonel Asbury Coward's Memoirs* (New York: Vantage Press, 1968), 69. See also the *Yorkville Enquirer* (April-June, 1861) and the *Carolina Spartan* (May 16, 1861).

[57] Castle Pinckney stood on Shute's Folly Island in Charleston Harbor, less than three-quarters of a mile from the Charleston wharves. This large, half-moon shaped masonry fort, named after South Carolina patriot Charles Pinckney, was built in 1811 and mounted 27 pieces of heavy artillery. One U. S. Army officer and his young daughter manned Pinckney in 1861. The fortress was surrendered to the Confederates after the fall of Fort Sumter and was later used to confine Federal prisoners of war. Hendrickson, 49.

[58] The Floating Battery was a barge approximately 100 feet long by 25 feet wide constructed of pine timber. It was armored with two layers of one-inch thick railroad iron and a layer of palmetto logs. The vessel mounted four heavy cannon, two-42 pounders and two-32 pounders, firing through gun ports at the bow. It also contained a small hospital in an attached shed on the stern. From it's mooring at Cove Inlet on Sullivans Island, the Floating Battery pounded Fort Sumter during the siege. It was afterward nicknamed "The Boomerang" for its tendency to deflect cannonballs that struck the sloping roof of the shed that protected its guns. Hendrickson, 134-135 & 260.

beach; took a rest; marched about a mile; got a house for our company. It has five rooms. We are camped between Fort Moultrie & a sandbag battery. I tell you, old Anderson give Fort Moultrie a heavy pounding. He knocked off two of their guns. There is a considerable town here[59]. He riddled the houses with his balls. The house we are [in], he shot one of the posts out of the piazza, the ball passing through the corner of the house. We are posted right on the beach. The ocean is nearly up to our door at this time, high tide. Achsah I had no idea what the ocean was like. It is a continual roar. The island is a complete sand bank. The ground all along the ocean is as level as the floor; some very pretty large houses. The Moultrie House has over one hundred rooms in it. It is full of soldiers. The yards are all piled up and some of the pilings the sand has drifted up against them until they are covered up. People say when there comes a big storm of wind they have to go in the houses and stay; shut the doors to keep from being covered up. Achsah I have been on the famous Floating Battery. It is a strong piece of work. Anderson tried his guns on it but there never was but one ball went through. They have lots of hands at work on Sumter & Moultrie repairing them. Achsah I received your kind letter since I began to write this. You say that you want me to buy a Bible and read it. I bought one in York and I don't get much time to read it, but I hope I will soon get more time if we get stationed for some time. I don't know how long we may stay where we are. Our provisions lasted us 4 or five days. In fact, most of the dinner I eat today was biscuit that came from home. We have been drawing hams & shoulders; drawed beef one time but it was not good. They did not want any more of it. Bakers bread, you know I don't like it, but hunger is good sauce. If you had have see[n] how I could eat it yesterday by itself. Plenty of sugar & coffee, rice, salt, we get very plenty, but we are not fixed for cooking; have to cook out on the sand. Here it [is] shoe mouth deep; get smoked and burnt and half cook our victuals. I would like to just eat one good mess with you now, but so it is. If God gives me health I will not grumble. I have not bought any sword yet. I never have been outside of the camp since I left home only when we were

---

[59] The town of Moultrieville

moving from one place to another. Never got in to Charleston nor Columbia only as we marched through. Colonel Jenkins told me today he would let me go to Charleston tomorrow to buy a sword & uniform but I won't go on Sunday. I am mustering without a sword. We will have to buy a uniform too. I expect we will buy it and send it to York to get it made. The charge in Charleston is so high for making. They charge us high for everything we get. It will take more money than I have to get a sword and uniform, but I can get it from some of the rest. Mr. Wright speaks of starting home tomorrow. If he does and I have need of any more, I will get him to bring it to me. He says he will not stay longer than a week or two. We fare worse about lying than anything else. Last night we just had to take the hard floor. I have only two blankets that I bought in York. You know that is a bad chance to lie on and cover with too. Some of the men say they most freeze. They are all bad off with cold & sore throat. James H. Glenn[60] is in bed today with sore throat. This is said to be a very healthy place. Good cistern water, if it only holds out. The pump water is just like the water that was on the plantation Marion lived on when we were in Mississippi[61]. You know I won't like it. The sand hurts our eyes. Achsah I am burnt nearly black with the sun wearing nothing but my cap. If I ever get a chance I will get a hat and wear it only when I am mustering. Our boys all are sunburnt but keep in good spirits. John Barnes[62] makes one of the best soldiers we have. He never grumbles at nothing. I don't know how the thing may turn out, but think there will be a

---

[60] Private James Henry Glenn (2/20/1820-6/8/1865), son of John F. and Sarah (Johnston) Glenn, joined Co.-H, 18th S. C. Infantry later in the war as a private. Glenn died at Farmville, Va. of wounds received on March 29, 1865 during skirmishing at Gravelly Run near Petersburg.

[61] Daniel Marion Wood lived in Smith County, Mississippi before moving back to York District sometime in late 1860 or early 1861. No evidence was found to prove that Harvey Wallace lived in Mississippi as well. He may have been there on a visit.

[62] Private John O. Barnes (c.1820-5/12/1864) was discharged in June 1861 after voting not to go to Virginia with the regiment. He later joined Co.-A, 12th S. C. Infantry as a private and was killed during fighting at the Salient or "Mule Shoe" during the Battle of Spotsylvania.

bloody war. But I don't think we will have much fighting to do here. I think now the fighting will be done in Virginia & Maryland. They were fighting in Baltimore last night[63]. This place is well fixed for to give them a warm fight. We are completely armed and equipped. My dear wife, do write often. Remember me to the dear little children. You don't know how my heart beats when I think about them and you and the rest, but take care of yourself and them. I trust to God I will be restored to you again. I have seen a great many sights. Tell Marion to do the best he can. Take care of the horses & other stock. I can't give him any directions. All the little time I have I write to you. I want to write to Father and will as soon as ever I can. Tell the Negroes all howdy. Tell them to do the best they can. I am glad to hear they are good to my little children. I could write more if I had time. So farewell my dear wife & mother- in -law.

H. A. Wallace

Written upside down at top of first page:
Achsah if you could get to York and get your likeness & Matty's taken and send them to me I would be glad to have them. Your ring has never been off my finger since I left home.

---

[63] Wallace is referring to a clash between pro-secessionist citizens of Baltimore and Federal troops of the 6th Massachusetts Infantry, which were passing through the city enroute to Washington. Nine civilians and four soldiers were killed and the incident brought Maryland to the brink of secession. E. B. Long, *The Civil War Day By Day: An Almanac 1861-1865* (Garden City, N. Y.: Doubleday, 1971), 62.

Sullivans Island
Camp Beauregard
April the 23, 1861

My dear Wife,
I this morning, after one hours drill and a little breakfast, turn my thoughts to you and my little children & the rest at home whom I delight to think about. I am well except cold & sore throat, but I have not lost a meal since I left home. The company is all pretty well. Most of them have bad colds. Some have boils on them. Brother John[64] has a bad boil on his neck but is knocking about this morning. Achsah we are kept very close; scarcely ever see any person but soldiers. There is no person but soldiers lives on this island. Achsah I looked anxiously for a letter on yesterday but got none. I have got but one since I left home. If you could know how much good it done me to get a letter you would write every few days, if it was a task for you to write. I don't get much time to write but I will, while able, try to write to you every few days. I wrote five letters Sunday. Went to preaching, prayer meeting, & mustered some too, but I sent one to Father, one to J. L. Watson[65], one to Brother James[66]. I wrote the other two for the other men. Capt. Glenn & Col. Bone [Bowen] got leave to go to Charleston yesterday morning to buy our swords & uniforms. They did not get back last night and won't before ten today. Our swords will cost us twenty dollars. Our uniforms will cost us some forty or fifty dollars. So you see it will take all the money I have & more too to get my equipments. Capt. Glenn has just returned & brought our swords.

---

[64] 1st Corporal John Rufus H. "Ruff" Wallace (8/22/1838-6/28/1862), son of James and Margaret Ewart (Barnett) Wallace, died of wounds received during the Battle of Gaine's Mill near Richmond, Va. while serving with the Catawba Company.
[65] John L. Watson was a planter and the local storekeeper and postmaster at Clay Hill.
[66] James Adams Wallace (12/10/1818-11/4/1895) was the eldest child of James and Margaret (Barnett) Wallace. James, his wife Margaret Elizabeth (Farris), and their eight children immigrated to Rusk County, Texas in 1859. The family settled near the town of Mount Enterprise.

He paid $20.20 cts. for swords that I would as leave have my old one. They are not to be had in Charleston. I am down on them and won't have the one he got for me. If I can get it took back I will send home and have my old one brought down. He could not get cloth in Charleston to make our coats so we will have to send to York. It looks like they would just rob us of what we have. Everything we have to buy we have to pay two prices for it. I have sent today with Grier[67] for a watch. I am oblige to have one. I would be glad you would send me $25 with Mr. Wright when he comes down as he will get home today. He will tell you how we are getting on. I sent my best fine shirt & buttons with him as I have no chance to take care of it here and will get colored ones. I have not been out of the encampment since I left home only in moving from one place to another. I don't want to be running about. I came here to do my duty. I intend if we have to stay here to try to get off to go home in 2 or 3 months on a visit. Capt. Glenn is going to try to get off in a month or so to go home a while. Achsah we had lots of muster on yesterday, and then the officers of us had to go out and be drilled by the Colonel until after nine o'clock. I don't feel at any loss about drilling. There is lots of green officers here. Our company does fine. We get along in peace; have not had a quarrel in the company since we left home; not a tight man. You ought to see me cooking; in the smoke making coffee, cooking rice, frying meat, washing the dishes. I don't get but little rest. What time I have I write or read. We have sent for some free Negroes to cook for us. If they come I will get more time. Tell the children to be good boys. Kiss them for me. I dreamed about them on my hard bed last night. Tell your Mother I would like to have a good mess of pancakes. I don't get any butter at all but I live well enough. If I have health I won't grumble. Do write often, and may God bless you all. I would like to have your prayers. So farewell. Get your ambrotype & send

---

[67] Private Thomas Grier (c.1825-?) voted to go to Virginia with the regiment in June 1861, where he served until he joined the Palmetto Sharpshooters as Orderly Sergeant in April 1862. Grier was transferred to an unlisted unit on January 31, 1863.

it to me. I have to go to the Colonel to answer questions on tactics[68].

Your husband,

H.A. Wallace

---

[68] Colonel Jenkins established an officer's school in order to instruct his officers in drill and tactics. Jenkin's officers proved themselves good students by their capable leadership in combat. The officer's school idea was repeated by Colonel Jenkin's successor, Colonel Asbury Coward when he took command of the regiment in October 1862. Coward states in his memoirs, "I also established a night school for officers in tactics and bugle calls for skirmish drills". Bond and Coward, 69.

S. C., York
April the 24, 1861

Harvy,
I send you a few lines to let you know how we are getting along. We are all well at present. Matty is better than she was. She still has a little fever. She has a very sore throat. It is swell very bad. I keep it poulticed. I gave her some blue mass[69] today. It is operated. She is playing about. Mary and Martin[70] is here. They are going home this evening. Mr. Z.D. Smith[71] was to dinner with us today. He saw Mr. Wright. He said you were all well except cold. We were glad to hear that he said North Carolina and Maryland had come off. Harvy, I tried to send your pants and shirt but could not. We have not been to York yet. I do not care much about going as you are not here to go with us. If we thought you would come home soon we would not go. We talked about going this week but Sis is not well enough. I can hardly write for Sis is pulling at me to get up. They finished the bottom this evening. Is gone to replanting the field next to Mr. Mason's[72]; is come up very bad. We had a nice shower this evening. There is meeting at Mill Creek[73] Saturday and Sabbath. We want to go there if we are spared. Mr. S[imril] says Mr. Nic Orr[74]

---

[69] Blue mass, also known as blue pill, was a soft, pliable, blue colored mercury mass that could be formed into pills. It was a standard medication used for many ailments of the time.

[70] Marion Wood's wife, Mary (Harper) Wood (1/30/1831-11/24/1919) and son, Martin Ward Wood (8/28/1858-7/15/1931)

[71] Zadoc Darby Smith (5/13/1822-11/25/1884), son of Samuel D. and Jane (Darby) Smith, and his wife, Martha Jane (Glenn) were close friends with the Wallaces. Zadoc was a staunch secessionist and well educated, as attested to in later letters (see letters of April 27, 1861 and May 14, 1861). Smith owned a plantation in the Zeno community of York District. He later served as 1st Lieutenant in the 46th S. C. Militia Regiment.

[72] This reference is most likely to Mr. William Mason or his son, George Washington Mason.

[73] Mill Creek Baptist Church was located near the Wallace's residence in northeastern York District.

[74] Unidentified

and Croxton[75] is to be there. Harvy, the blacks is doing very well so far; the horses too. The filly has got a sore eye. It has been sore ever since the Monday night you left. Marion rode her a patrolling[76]; found her eye sore next morning. I wrote this to keep you from being uneasy about Sis. Write soon, for we are glad to hear from you. So goodbye.

A.Wallace

---

[75] Rev. John S. Croxton, a Baptist minister from Fort Mill, S.C.

[76] Since 1721, the South Carolina Militia conducted the slave patrol. The militia's primary duty was to protect citizens from hostile invasion, Indian attack, outlaws, and slave insurrection. All able bodied males between eighteen and forty-five years of age were required to serve. Small groups of men from local militia companies patrolled their respective beats, helping to quiet the growing fear of a slave uprising that gripped the free population of South Carolina early in the war. Stauffer, 2 & 9-11.

Sullivans Island
Camp Beauregard
April the 26th, '61

Dear Wife & family,
I have taken my pen to drop you a few lines in answer to your kind letter of the 22nd, which I received last evening. Achsah if you knew how glad I am to get a letter from you, you would write every time you could. I know you have a bad chance to write, but write as often as you can. I write letters every day. I write to you every other day and write letters for the men most every day. I am well; have got nearly over my cold. My throat is still a little sore. I have to command so much it don't get well fast. I have not missed a meal nor a drill as yet. You never seen a set of men as bad off as the whole regiment was from cold, but they are getting over it. The company is generally well. Some three or four complaining, & Cousin Gustis McCallum[77] has been very sick since last night; appears very bilious[78]; has considerable fever today. Dr. Bratton[79] visited him this morning. He thought he would get along without going to the hospital. If there is any chance on him for the worse I will let his father know. How is Matty? I trust she has got better. Achsah you say the children often speak of me. Well, I am sorry to hear of them being disturbed about me, yet glad to think there is some beings in the world that thinks of me. Tell them to be good

---

[77] Private William Augustus Josephus McCallum (2/20/1840-6/28/1910) was the son of Peter (Cousin Peter) and Violet A. McCallum. William volunteered to go to Virginia with the regiment and was discharged on disability after being wounded on June 27, 1862.

[78] Bilious fever was a disease which medical officers included in a category called "continued fevers". It presented with symptoms closely resembling those of typhoid fever or malaria. These often consisted of fever, jaundice, and headache, and in late terminal stages, stupor and delirium occurred before death. Bilious fever, though rarely fatal, was often a precursor to the dreaded typhoid fever.   Barnes & Woodward, 365-367.

[79] Dr. James Rufus Bratton (11/12/1821-9/1/1897), son of John S. and Harriet (Rainey) Bratton, served as Assistant Surgeon of the 5th S. C. Infantry at the time of this letter.

children. I trust that it is God's will that we may all meet at our happy home together again on this earth. If not, let us try to be prepared for the worst. Times look dark and gloomy indeed. It does appear to me that we are on the eve of a bloody war. I trust that God, in His providence, may yet prevent it. There is a strong talk of sending our regiment to Virginia. Our company I don't think will go, though there is some of them wants to go. Some of the companies in the regiment are anxious to go. If I was a single man I would not mind it, but as it is, I don't think I would be getting too far from my home. This will be a hard place to stay all summer. I will hate very much if there should be a call and our company [is] left here under other officers, for our colonel & major[80] treat their men better than any of the rest of the colonels & majors. Captain Glenn expects to go home in three or four weeks. We can't get off only for 7 days at a time, and then it has to be in bad cases of sickness in one's immediate family. So a man could only be three days at home. And if they think we will have a fight soon, we can't get off atall. So farewell my wife. I have to close as I have to go on duty. May God bless you all is my prayer. Write soon.

H. A. Wallace

---

[80] W. T. Thompson of Union, S. C. served as Major of the 5th S. C. Infantry at this time. Baldwin, 37.

Zeno[81]
April 27, 1861

Bro. Wallace

Dear Sir,
I called last Wednesday to see your family; spent a few hours with them. I found them in good health and spirits. I saw Mr. J. L. Wright. He is in fine spirits; determined to go back to you in a short time. He gave me a good deal of information in regard to the company and matters in Charleston. Your Colonel Jenkins he states, is spoiling for a fight and is bound for Virginia if his regiment will follow him. I am glad to hear that the Catawba Company have resolved to rest satisfied where they are to defend their own native country. I hope you all will stick to this determination to the last. Tell the Colonel go where he pleases. I am satisfied there are other men that can take his place and fill it too, and who will have more feeling and interest for you. Remaining where you are to defend your country will never cast any slur upon your honor or reputation, but I consider that it will greatly add to it. Your state's honor and protection has called you all from your homes and family, not merely a desire of fame and honor. I do not look upon honors that are begged for and chased as any great display of patriotism, but the honor that is gained by fine motives, by meritorious deeds, and with an eye to the welfare of our country I consider will be far more profitable. Charity begins at home; my beloved state, my home and liberty. First, our state is not yet out of danger. She is the most envied by our enemies. She is, and has ever been, and ever will be the first in the defense of her rights. And, like the ancient Roman citizen, he was proud to say, "I am a citizen of the Roman Empire," so every son of South Carolina may proudly say of her, "I am a citizen of that noble state, and by her I will stand to defend to the last extremity the honor she has always borne." I see notices from

---

[81] The Zeno post office operated from 1850 until the end of the Civil War. The community was located in York District near the North Carolina border, northeast of present day Clover, S. C.

Charleston in the Enquirer of other companies but nothing about the Catawbas. Cannot some of you say something for your company? I think you certainly have some in your number that can write something. I had the letter I wrote to the company published to give you a fair showing. And if you or any of the company will give me any item of importance concerning the company at any time I will be very glad, and I will have the same published in the Enquirer. Come pull up, you must not be behind altogether. Give me everything from time to time of any importance as I wish to make a note of the same. I want to give the Catawbas a place in the history of our country. I must close for the present to start to church. I hope you will excuse this hasty epistle at present. I will write again, and write to me soon.

Yrs. rsp.,

Z. D. Smith

PS: W.G. Finly arrived yesterday. He looks very bad.
Z. Smith

York District, So. Ca.
Saturday evening
April the 27th, 1861

Dear Harvy,
I sit down this evening to write you a few more lines to inform you we are all well at present. Sissy is not very well yet but is better. Her gums is inflamed and her throat sore, yet her trouble is nearly through. I think she will get along if I can keep her bowels open. She is very costive. Her kidneys does not act very much. I am trying to write with Sis on my knee. You know I make a bad out at best, but you can read it. You think it a task. It is a pleasure for me to write to you, for I think you are always glad to hear from us. I received two letters from you yesterday evening. I was glad to hear from you. Sorry to hear you having so much to do. Does no person help you to cook or wash the dishes? I am afraid you will get sick. I fear that as much almost as anything else. There are so many men there. If any disease gets there I think you could not stand it, but the Lord will provide. We must put our trust in Him. He is able to do good for us if we ask Him. You asked me to pray for you. I try to do so but I make a bad prayer, but if it comes from the heart it is all that is required. I try to make the two boys say "Now I lay me down to sleep" at night but they are asleep sometimes before I get the chance. I try to get Willy to spell. You know he is hard to get to spell. He has turned over a leave. He learns a little. He says if you would come home you could learn him better than I do. He wants me to tell you to come home to go with us to preaching. Bud has just come in and crying. He fell off the bench. He says he wants you to come home so he can see you and you may sleep with him. Now the Negroes is very anxious for you to come home. They say M[arion] W[ood] is too tight. He wants them [to] be pushing all the time. They are out of work. They are done planting and read[y]ing up. They have finished ditching the spring bottoms. Marion says they go to the bottoms next week. There is a very bad stand on it. The birds have pulled up a great deal of it. The cotton is not coming up yet. We did not get a watermelon patch planted. Uncle Reese has planted his I believe. Uncle was to fishing this morning and has not returned yet. He does not take care of nothing no more than he did

when you were here. He is very good to the children. He do not like M[arion] much, says we could do better without; is vexed about the filly's eye. He says she looks like she will go blind. I think so too. We put white sugar in it. M[arion] rode her over to the store. John Watson told him to give her copperas[82] for the hooks. It might help her. It is blue. The other horses looks well. M[arion] is riding King to Mr. Harper's[83] this evening; going to preaching tomorrow at M[ill] Creek. We did not get to church today. Sis was not well enough. We intend to go tomorrow if it does not rain. Mrs. N. H. Mason[84] came over this morning; brought Marion's watch home. Mr. Wright left it at Mrs. Mason's. She said he did not say anything about your shirt. Said you wanted him to see me. He had brought up something for the men. I wish you had sent you drawers to got washed. I could sent them back. We want to go to York next Wednesday if we can. M[arion] says he will take his watch, get Crave[85] to work on it, and send it back to you if it will do and you will have it. If it will not I will try to get you one. Harvey, Robert Barnett[86] came by here yesterday morning and got your sword. He said you told him to get it; forgot to ask you the price of it. If you want me to keep it I shall do it. Harvey, tell Alexander[87] to write to

---

[82] Copperas, or ferrous sulphate, was a green, crystalline substance made of iron pyrites. It was used in medicines, black dye, and ink.
[83] Robert J. Harper (7/1808-2/19/1892)
[84] Mrs. Nancy Hannah (Stowe) Mason (1/7/1827-4/8/1904), wife of 6th Corp. George Washington Mason.
[85] Dr. Alfred Craven (c.1822-1872) was a popular jeweler and silversmith at Yorkville. Craven also practiced dentistry and advertised as a "Resident Surgeon Dentist" in the Yorkville Enquirer. In the same advertisement he makes the connection between his two professions by announcing, "Artificial Teeth inserted on Gold Plate-from one to a full set". During the war, Craven served as a private in the 34th S. C. Militia (Co.-B, 5th S. C. State Troops). Louise Pettus, "Crystal Palace In Old York", *York County Genealogical and Historical Society Quarterly*, Dec. 1992, 24-25.
[86] Robert A. Barnett (c.1840-7/5/1864), son of James and Eliza (Currence) Barnett and cousin of Harvey Wallace, enlisted as a private in Co.-H, 18th S. C. Infantry. He was killed while on picket duty during the siege of Petersburg.
[87] 2nd Sergeant Alexander Albert Barnett (11/8/1830-2/18/1900) was Harvey's cousin and son of James and Eliza (Currence) Barnett. Alexander volunteered to go

his mother. She has never got a letter from him yet. I will send you the money. Harvey I am sorry to hear you have such a poor bed to lie on. No wonder you have cold and sore throat. I would send you some bed clothes if you could get them. You might get a poke and put straw or leaves in and make a pillow. I hope you have got your provision by this time. We think there is enough to do a few days until you get a cook. What have you got to cook in? I would like to know who you mess with and how you eat; whether on the [illegible] or tables to eat on. I suppose you have not no plates to eat on; nothing but pots to eat out. Harvey, Mother says she would like to have you to eat a mess of pancakes with us. It would be a happy pleasure to see you. She says it appears like you have been gone a month. She says tell you we make lots of butter. Would like to send you some if we had the chance. We do not know when that will [be]. We hate to trouble Mr. W[right] or we would send you some more. We sent the little bucket full down. You get the bucket; it will be some use to you. Harvey you said you were disappointed not getting letter from me. I wrote two letters this week. I thought I was writing often enough. I will try to write twice a week. Write often. We are glad to hear from you. It is not much trouble to you. The Negroes sends you howdy. Cinth says she had rather see you than hear talk of you coming home. Farewell for a while.

Achsah Wallace

Written upside down on page 2:
Miles[88] has just brought up five cows. Got them in the old pasture.

---

to Virginia in June 1861 with the company and is listed on the rolls of those present on April 9, 1865 when the Army of Northern Virginia surrendered at Appomattox.

[88] Miles Wallace (c.1832-?) was a slave born in Georgia as stated in the 1870 Rusk County, Texas census.

Written on a separate scrap of paper enclosed with this letter:

April 27, 1861
Harvey you said something to me about fixing your business. You can do as you like about that. You know what I told you before you left home. I do not know what I would do no how. Harvey I will write again this week. I think I had better send our likeness down by Mr. Wright. So farewell for a while.

A. Wallace

Camp Beauregard
Sullivans Island
Sunday, 12 o'clock
April the 28th, 1861

My beloved Wife,
This beautiful Sabbath day, while I trust you are listening to the Gospel, I feel that I could not spend a few leisure moments better than to write to them nearest my heart. I am quite well. Have got over my sore throat & cold. I was taken off yesterday morning as Captain of the Guard to guard the boat landing and commissaries stores that is our provision. The boat comes from Charleston 3 times a day. We have to let no one pass to the boat nor from it unless they had a permit from General Dunovant[89] to leave the island, or from Beauregard[90] to come on it. It is near one mile from our quarters. I have just been relieved and got to my quarters; washed & put on clean clothes. I have got one shirt washed and done up for 10 cents. I will get some washing done this week. Achsah our provisions came on yesterday. I helped to deliver them so I was not here when they were divided. Washington[91] saved me a bucket of butter and brought me my supper to the guard house. Achsah if you send me anything put my name on it, for it would do me more good to eat if I knew you sent it. You said you had cooked a ham. I did not get any, but we get plenty to eat here. I would have liked you had have

---

[89] Colonel John Dunovant (1825-1864), a native of Chester, S. C., commanded the 1st S. C. Regulars. Dunovant's regiment was stationed on Sullivan's Island with the 5th S. C. Infantry. Colonel Dunovant was dismissed from the service for drunkenness in June 1862 but was appointed Colonel of the 5th S. C. Cavalry by Governor Pickens afterward. Dunovant won promotion to brigadier general on August 22, 1864 and was killed just over a month later on the Vaughan Road near the James River in Virginia.   Ezra Warner, *Generals In Gray: Lives of the Confederate Commanders* (Louisiana State University Press, 1959), 78-79.

[90] Brigadier General Pierre Gustave Toutant Beauregard (1818-1893), A Creole from New Orleans, took charge at Charleston in March 1861. Beauregard directed the attack on Fort Sumter and commanded the Charleston defenses at the time of this letter. Warner, 22-23.

[91] George Washington Mason

marked your cakes for me so they would have been saved for me, but don't bother yourself sending. We get plenty of good meat. I don't like the bread very well but can do very well on it. I have been over to the hospital since I came in to see Gustice & Timberlick[92]. They are both better. Gustice has been very sick and is still quite sick. He is very bilious. I think when the medicine he is taking operates he will be better. It is bowel affection that Timberlick has. That is a complaint we have hard work to guard against here. I had intended to have written to Cousin Peter today but Samuel Campbell is writing to him. Achsah I trust little Matty has got well. Don't let her forget to say Pa. Tell Willy and Aaron to be good boys. If God spares me & them I will come home some day. Achsah there was some excitement on this island night before last. There was some vessels seen off the island, and about 8 or nine o'clock the cannons on Morris Island fired a few rounds. After we had went to bed, about 10 or 11 o'clock, they sent round for the captains to go and get ball cartridges. Capt. Glenn was off on guard duty. James A. Glenn[93] went and got us a box of ammunition. Our company is right on the ocean. I slept perfectly sound. Some of the company loaded their guns and lay with their coats on. We never opened our box of ammunition. Achsah you must excuse some of the letters I write, for sometimes when I write I don't get half time, and the men talking, dancing, bothering every way all around. I do expect we will have to stay here or go to Virginia one for a time. This island is said to be healthy. The sea breeze is splendid but there is three thousand men crowded here on this island. You know there will be so much filth that I am afraid for our health in the heat of summer. Our cistern water is about done. The well water is very bad indeed. You know it can't be good when the island is just a sand bank; no timber but the palmetto tree. It is not more than from 150 to three hundred yards wide. The ocean is nearly as high all around as the island. In high

---

[92] Private John C. Timberlake (c.1818-9/1/1901) enlisted in Co.-C, Gill's Battalion, 4th S. C. State Troops after being discharged in June 1861.
[93] 1st Sergeant James A. Glenn (11/2/1829-8/30/1868), son of William and Eliza Glenn, served as Orderly Sergeant.

**Private Samuel Watson
Wallace
Catawba Light Infantry**

tide the water gets all over the whole island. When the moon filled it was all under our house. It rises and falls twice a day; goes in 100 or 150 yards and then comes out again; keeps up a continual roar, the waves as high as ones head. Achsah we did not have to go to work as we expected to build sand bags. One company went to work yesterday; one at it today. We will have to take it day about. Two of the companies have to camp out a day and night at a time. Achsah we have prayer every night in our house by John Witherspoon[94]. He belongs to the York Company. He is a young son of old Witherspoon of York. He is going to be a preacher. You said you could not send my clothes. You need not send them. I can do without them, and any of the clothes I would have here would be spoilt. I have bought me a hat. Give $1.25 cents for it and put it on today. I don't spend anything I can help. There is some of the boys that are continually buying. I never have been to the city yet, nor don't want to go unless the company was to go. You can tell Father and Mother that John and Samuel[95] are quite well; hold their own very well. So are all of the boys except Gustice and Timberlick. John Cullender[96] stands it prime. So does Robbisson [Robertson][97], James Stewart[98], in fact, all. Achsah I only got 2

---

[94] John Alfred Witherspoon (5/14/1841-10/19/1862), son of Isaac and Ann (Reid) Witherspoon, was discharged in June 1861 and later served as Captain of Co.-C, 17th S. C. Infantry. He died at Warrenton, Va. of wounds suffered during the Second Battle of Manassas.

[95] Private Samuel Watson Wallace (5/10/1841-9/27/1923), the youngest child of James and Margaret Barnett Wallace, served in the Catawba Company with his brothers John and Harvey. Sam was discharged in June 1861 after declining to go to Virginia with the company. He enlisted as a private in Co.-E (The Indian Land Tigers), 17th S. C. Infantry in November 1861. In 1872 Sam, his wife Harriet (Cook), and his widowed mother moved to Rusk County, Texas where they settled near Mount Enterprise.

[96] Private William J. Cullender (c.1835-?), son of Lawrence and Sarah Cullender, declined to volunteer for Virginia in June 1861 and was subsequently discharged.

[97] Private James Robertson Cook (5/18/1841-9/20/1905) was the son of Dempsey and Mary (Gibson) Cook and second cousin of Achsah Wallace. Robertson declined to go to Virginia with the 5th Regiment and later joined Co.-H, 1st S. C. Cavalry. After a brief service with the cavalry, Private Cook enlisted in Co.-H, 18th S. C. Infantry. He was captured at Farmville, Va. on April 6, 1865 during the retreat to Appomattox from Petersburg.

hours sleep last night and I just wrapped up in a blanket; laid down on a billiard table with my coat under my head, James V. Choat[99] & me together. He was all the man I had with me from our company in a house where we lay. My Corporal of the Guard was from Union; Kelly[100], brother to the Presiding Elder Kelly. He is a noble fellow. What little sleeping I done I had a pleasant dream. I dreamed I was at home with you, all safe. How does Uncle Reece come on? I want to hear from him. Tell Marion to write me, but be sure to write twice a week yourself. I would rather get your writing as any one else's a sight. Tell your Mother to cheer up. If God spares me I trust I may come back nothing worsted and a better man, although I am in the midst of wickedness. So farewell my dear wife, children, & friends for this time.

H. A. Wallace

---

[98] Private James A. Stewart (3/4/1840-8/23/1918), son of Joseph B. and Eliza (Tate) Stewart, rejoined Co.-H, 5th S. C. Infantry later in the year after a period of illness. He is listed as present at the surrender of the Army of Northern Virginia at Appomattox.

[99] Private James Van Buren Choate (1829-1898), son of Augustine and Dorcas (Garrison) Choate, was discharged in June, 1861 and later served as Corporal in Co.-E, 17th S. C. Infantry.

[100] 2nd Corporal Joseph Kelly of Co.-E, 5th S. C. Infantry

April the 29, [1861]

Harvy,
I send you a few more lines. We are all well this morning. The friends are all well. I have been to the store this morning to get some lining for your pants. Betsy[101] [illegible] came here Saturday night; went with us to preaching; went home this morning. She took your pants. Said she would make them for nothing. She would do anything for you or the company for nothing. I saw Mr. Choat[102] at the store. He had been over to see his people [illegible] away. Madison Choat[103], Sam Youngblood[104], three [of] Tommy Boyd['s] sons[105], Jo Akins[106], Steven H.[107], D. Wood[108] did not go; got a man going in place. Harvy, we have distressing times here. The is nearly gone. They are making a company up at Union. J. F. Glenn[109] is going. He has drank ever since you left; sober only two days since. Harvy we had good preaching yesterday; no one but Owens[110]. The

---

[101] Unidentified

[102] Mr. Augustine D. Choate (2/27/1798-7/2/1890), father of privates James Van Buren Choate and Robert W. Choate of Wallace's company.

[103] Josina Madison Choate (12/10/1823-4/19/1870), another son of Augustine D. and Dorcas (Garrison) Choate, enlisted in Co.- B, 13th N. C. Infantry as a private. He was later promoted to 1st Sergeant and was discharged July 16,1862 for being overage.

[104] Samuel C. Youngblood (c.1831-11/12/1862) enlisted later in Co.-B, 13th N. C. Infantry as a private. He died at home of unknown causes.

[105] Unidentified

[106] Unidentified

[107] Stephen Huddleston (3/18/1831-11/22/1882), son of William H. and Nancy Huddleston, later served as a private in Co.-H, 18th S. C. Infantry. He is listed on the rolls of those paroled at Appomattox.

[108] Daniel Marion Wood

[109] John F. Glenn (c.1823-12/8/1861), son of William and Eliza (Boyd) Glenn, enlisted in the Gaston Guards (Co.- H, 23rd N. C. Infantry). Glenn died of fever at the Petersburg, Va. hospital.

[110] Rev. William C. Owens was a Baptist minister from the Fort Mill, S. C. area.

people appeared distressed. Mr. O. made a great prayer for you volunteers and their families. Marion and the Negroes are gone to the river to replanting corn. They say it is a very bad stand; going to bed some over. Cotton is not come up yet. Wheat looks fine. Our garden is not doing much as yet. The turnip stand is nice. We have greens every day for dinner; would like you to have some. I think you would like them now. Harvy, I never have wrote to Texas yet. I want you to write to Thomas and Duncan. It takes a good while to write and I must work some. I never have felt much like work since you left here. A good many of the women say they are the same way. Harvy, I got a letter from you Saturday evening. I had to read it last evening to the Negroes. They always want to hear the news from you. I do not want you to go to Virginia. Stay there if you can. I will try to get Sis and my likeness taken and send them to you. Harvy, keep in good spirits. I will try to do the same. I hope to see you again at home, if it should be a long time. I hope they will make peace soon. Mother sends you her best wishes and prayers. Nothing more at present, but remain your affectionate wife. The Negroes say howdy. They are glad for you to say something to them.

[Achsah Wallace]

Camp Beaureguard
Sullivans Island
April the 30th, 1861

My beloved Wife,
I again drop you a few lines to let you know how we are coming on. I am well ready to turn out at the tap of the drum, which will be in a few minutes. The company is all up except Timberlick & Gustice. They are both better this morning. They have both been pretty bad but I trust will get along now. It is a bad place to be sick. The water here don't agree with us. The cistern water is done & we have to drink well water. It is very bad. The cistern water was all full of wiggletails, but it was good to what the well water is. I could just drink hearty of it when I could see them thick in the water. It keeps our bowels always wrong but I trust we will get used to it after while. Achsah there is a talk of taking us to Virginia if we are needed, but we won't go unless we are oblige to. I am not going to put myself any further from you & my little children than I am oblige to. But I trust they won't need us, nor call for us. I fear for our health here but I would rather risk it as to be hauled from one place to another and wore out that way. Achsah, the fighting part is a small matter with a soldier to the other hardships. Tell them to go ahead and make all they can at home. If I am kept here I will try and clear my own expenses against a uniform and buy a sword. I can't do much more. I have no sword yet. Capt. Glenn went to Charleston and bought us one apiece but we sent them back and would not have them. They were no account. The sword cost $15 dollars & the belts $3.20; the belts, no account ordinary thing. We got the money back for the swords but have to keep the belts, so there is just $3.20 throwed away clear. Col. Jenkins told me he would go over and try to get us swords. He would take the belts back and try to get them taken back. He is very kind and obliging with me. I never have been in town as yet. Achsah I never have been outside of our camps only when passing from one place to another, nor don't want to go. Uncle Arthur[111] and me are speaking of going to Charleston as soon as

---

[111] Private Arthur Armstrong "Uncle Arthur" McKenzie (8/15/1809-8/3/1875), son of Joseph McKenzie, was married to Harvey's Mother's sister, Rachel (Barnett).

the rest gets through. One officer and two privates gets to go every day. That is, a corporal or a sergeant, and they are responsible for the men. Every man that gets off has to have a pass signed by General Dunovant and come back the same day. The captain of companies have to give their men their pass and sign it, then Col. Jenkins has to sign it, then Dunovant. So you see we are in a tight place. The steamboats come three times a day and go back. We have guards all around where they land. They look at the passes. If they are [illegible] they let you pass; if not, take you to the guard house. None of our men have been in guard house yet. Achsah, some of the boys that was so keen to come are the sickest men we have to get home. They thought it would be a frolick. They don't get any liquor to drink & don't get to see nothing but men. Some days there is a few ladies & gentlemen come over and ride over the island. But I think they will all become better satisfied after while. How has Trisvan got? Tell him to stay at home and do all he can to help his Aunts. If he has got well he has made a lucky escape, for he could not stand it here. My dear wife, you don't know what a treat the butter you sent me is. I think of you every time I go to eat. That was all the thing I got that you sent that I knowed of. It was all divided out when I was off on duty. Mason saved it for me. We have plenty of the provision that was sent yet. Mason and Campbell brought me my supper that night and a letter from you. I tell you, James Choat & me went it. They brought us pound cake and things that was good. James and me was the only ones of our company that was on guard duty that day. Capt. Glenn got a ham marked to him and a pound cake. Achsah I don't want to trouble you sending, but if we stay and you send anything more, mark what you send in my name. I would rather have what you send as anyone else. I don't think so many sweet good things will be good for us. Thin, well baked biscuits will save the longest and are the best for us. We have got no cook as yet but I hope will have one in a few days. How is

---

Arthur was elected 1st Lieutenant of the Catawba Company when it mustered into the Confederate Provisional Army on June 4, 1861. Lieutenant McKenzie was discharged in 1862, most likely due to being overage.

Matty? I trust she has got well. Kiss her for me, and the boys too. Tell them to be good boys. Their father will come home again if God spares him. If not, trusting to God for grace to help me. I will try to do nothing that will ever cause you, my wife or children, to blush for me. Well Mrs. Wood, I suppose you have a fine chance of chickens by this time. I trust I will get back in time to help you eat some of them. I suppose your garden is beginning to show by this time. I tell you, some vegetables would be a treat. Achsah, if you do go to York and can get your ambrotype, be sure to have it taken and send it to me. I want you to go if you can. Never mind the expense. Write to me often; twice a week at least. If I want any clothing from home I will write for it. Capt. Glenn has the promise of leave to go home in two or three weeks to see his family. Ach, tell the Negroes all howdy. Tell them to [do] the best they know and that will do, and to stay at home close; don't have much company about them at night. Don't let Miles get into the habit of running about. So farewell for the present my wife and family. May God bless you all.

H. A. Wallace
I expect I write so often you will get tired of the same tale over.

The following note was enclosed with this letter:
Well Marion, how are you coming on? I suppose by the time you get this you will be working your corn. Write to me. Tell me if you have good stands. Marion, be sure to thin your corn out to evenly stands. Take care of the stock. Let me know how my hogs are doing, how your corn is holding out, & flour and so on. I suppose you got your watch. I sent it by Mr. Wright. I have none as yet but I need one badly. Give my love to Mary & Martin and any of the friends that think worthwhile to ask for me. Do the best you can for me. I tell you, I can't give you much advice. There is too much confusion here for one to write a letter. So farewell.

H. A. Wallace

Written upside down on page 5:

Tell Uncle Reece I want him to raise some good watermelons, for if I live I trust I will get home to see [illegible].

York District
So. Ca.
May the 1st, '61

Harvy,
I take my pen again to drop you a few lines to let you know we are all well at present except cold. Mother has a very bad cold. The friends are all well so far as I know. Tresvan Cook is getting pretty well again. Well Harvy, I have been at York today; got home at five o'clock. I seen Mr. Wright a few minutes; never passed but few words. He said he never had got his saddle bags yet. I am afraid he never will. I am sorry about the buttons being gone. Harvy, I have not received a letter from you this week. I can say, like you, I feel very much disappointed. I am anxious to get a letter from you every day or two. I send you a letter from Thomas. I want you to write to him. I will try to write him one after while. Harvy, the people says in York you are a suffering there for good water. Your cistern has given out. I think you will all get sick. They say provisions is getting sca[rce]. They say they think you all will co[me] home by the 1 of June. I do hope yo[u] [page torn], if it is the good Lord['s] will. They [page torn] you might come home on a furlough. [page torn].....wanted, I would. You do not know how [page torn] we want to see you. The women all are waiting to see their men and boys come home. Mrs. Cullender[112] is troubled about her boy. We are very dry now. Marion has not worked our corn yet. He is replanting at the river yet. Our wheat is heading out. It looks very well. The cotton is coming up some. Harvy, [I] had no white person with me today but Sis. I got ambrotypes. I will send them by P[eter] McCallum if he goes. Your Pa was at York today after the mail. He went with me down to Mr. Chorl's[113]. Frank carried Matty. Ad[114]

---

[112] Mrs. Sarah Cullender, mother of Private William J. Cullender.

[113] Unidentified

[114] Addison Wood (c.1815-?), known as Add by the family, had been a slave on the Wood plantation for many years. Addison lists his birthplace as South Carolina in the 1870 York District census.

drove me there. So you see I was well set up with Negroes. Believe Ad bought more than I did. I bought nothing hardly. I got Mother [a] dress, some calico for stock curtains, Miles a pair of shoes, some other small article; never bought the children a thing but spelling book. Harvy, do write to me. Do not forget us so quick. So nothing more but yours affectionately,

Achsah Wallace

Sullivans Island
May the 2nd, 1861

My beloved Wife,
I this morning have taken my pen to drop you a few lines to let you know how we are getting on. We are all well except Gustice, Timberlick, and James A. Stewart. Gustice and Timberlick are getting pretty well again. They are both up & about again. Stewart was right sick last evening. Well Achsah, there was 50 letters come to the company last evening and not one for me. Every married man got a letter but me and Tommy Huddleston[115]. It looks a little like you did not think as often of me as I thought you would. But Achsah, I know you have a bad chance to write and I lay it to that, having no doubt but you will write when you can. Achsah, our men are busy packing up their blankets to go in to the tents. It is just sunrise. We have got to go in to the tents at 8 and stay until tomorrow at 8. Two company go in each day. We have to work on the sandbag battery Saturday. Achsah we are kept pretty busy here but get along as well as I expected. I have had no trouble with any man & think our men are all satisfied with me. I try to do the very best I can. This is a very cool place; a continual wind. My fingers are cold writing this morning. If we only had good water here we might do, but our water is miserable. We have nothing but well water. It gets worse every day. We can get a drink of ice water by paying for it five cents. I have had a drink the last two days. I am going over to Charleston today; me, Uncle Arthur, & William Moore[116]. I did not care about going but I have to have a sash and trunk when I get that fine uniform and I have got tired trusting to other men to buy for me. We get off at 9 o'clock boat; have to come back at 3. Well Achsah, I suppose you have got the pants made before you get this. I never seen the trimmings. Capt.Glenn attended

---

[115] Private Thomas J. Huddleston (c.1829-?), son of William Henry and Nancy Huddleston, enlisted as a private in Co.-H, 18th S. C. Infantry after being discharged in June, 1861. Private Huddleston was later promoted to Corporal.

[116] Private William R. Moore (c.1839-?) declined to volunteer for Virginia and later enlisted in Co.-H, 1st Battalion S. C. Cavalry as a musician.

to all of that. Achsah there is lots of reports here of what they will do with us. I have no doubt they will want us to go to Virginia & I expect there will be the most of the men of our regiment that will go. I will not go unless I am oblige to go. If I was a single man it might be different. What I hate, if part of the regiment goes, what of us is left will be hauled about first under one officer then another, and not treated like our officers would treat us. And I have not thought that any of us will get off before our twelve months are out unless peace is made. I will go home to see you sometime if God spares me & I can get off long enough. Achsah try to get Nelly[117] to learn to shell. You don't know how often I think about you & the children and all at home, but it is necessary I suppose, that we have some crosses in this world, that we may be able to appreciate the blessings that we are permitted to enjoy. Tell Marion to write to me. I reckon Uncle Reece has caught lots of fish. Tell your Mother I often think of her and trust she don't forget me in her prayers. Kiss the children for me. May God's choicest blessings attend you all is the pray[er] of your husband.

H. A. Wallace

---

[117] Nelly was a young slave, possibly a child.

Camp Beaureguard
Sullivans Island
Saturday evening, May the 4th, 1861
5 o'clock

My dear Wife,
I have resumed my pen to perform the pleasant duty of writing you a few lines again. I am quite well today. Our company are all pretty well. The boys have all got home from the hospital again. James Stewart & Livingston Laney[118] have both came home this evening & will be able for duty in a few days. I trust we have no new cases today, & I trust we will get on with less sickness than we have had. Our company has been at work today on the sandbag battery. Cousin Peter, Uncle Hamilton[119], & Thomas Greer [Grier] and me rode around the island this morning in a two horse fixin; had a man to drive us. We started at nine, got back at twelve. Cousin Peter can give you a description of the island. I send you a lot of shells by him that I picked up on the beach as we went around. Mr. Wright took some for me. Achsah I am afraid you will not get the shirt I sent by him. It was my best fine shirt. I don't mind the loss of the shirt like I do the buttons. Them buttons feels dear to me the way I got them, but I hope you will get them. Our men have just quit work. I have been with them all evening. I told them at five o'clock we would all go to our quarters, wash and shave, and go to our wife's houses. I tell you, it would be a pleasure to some of us to go, but I hope God will spare us to see that time. Achsah keep in good spirits. I am standing the campaign better than I had expected to do. We fare better too than we expected. Anderson McElwee[120] landed here

---

[118] Private Livingston L. W. Laney (c.1841-2/9/1862), Son of John and Rachel Laney, died of disease in Virginia. Most likely Private Laney died at Centreville, where the 5th S. C. Infantry was quartered through the harsh winter of 1862.

[119] Alexander Hamilton Barnett (4/29/1812-12/29/1893), was the son of Alexander and Rachel Jane (Adams) Barnett, and brother of Harvey's mother.

[120] Samuel Anderson McElwee (2/18/1836-5/20/1903), son of James and Nancy (Wright) McElwee, enlisted as a private in Co.-E, 17th S. C. Infantry after being discharged in June 1861. McElwee later won promotion to Lieutenant.

this morning. He brought Jim Wilson[121], a free Negro, with him. He is to cook for us officers so I will not have to cook if he keeps well. I wrote you a letter last evening and sent it by Hoglen[122]. He said he would leave it at Clay Hill. I will send this by Cousin Peter. The long and cheerful letter you wrote me & the news Cousin Peter brought of you all being in good spirits and doing well makes me feel more at ease. And that you have got your & Sissy's ambrotypes for me. Achsah send me some of your hair with your ambrotype. If I had anything to send you I would send it. When I was in the city I wanted to buy some presents for the children but did not know when I could send them, and knowed I had a bad way of keeping them and did not get them. If I only had them now I could send them right on. We have wind all of the time. It keeps it from being too hot. Capt. Glenn & Washington[123] went to the city this evening to get some boxes of provisions that is there for the company. They did not get them. I suppose we will get them tomorrow. My butter is done. There was some boxes come last evening. I got a good mess of pound cake. Butter is 75 cents a pound in Charleston. If you have a chance, send me some more. I tell you, I am pretty well wore out on coffee. I take sugar in it. This water is too mean to make coffee out of. I will have my clothes washed at home by our Negro. Now I will send the shirt I have on by Cousin Peter. You can send it back by someone. Achsah I have a new check shirt I will put on tomorrow. Both of my home spun shirts are clean. Tell Marion to try to cure up Lucy's eyes. Is it one or both of them? She ought not to be used any he can help, and feed light. I am sorry about you not getting a stand of corn but trust it will be better than you thought it would. People ought to make all they can & spend as little as possible. If this war goes on provisions will be a powerful price. Flour is worth 12 1/2 dollars a barrel in Charleston. I would like, if there is a good season, to see a good crop on the bottom this year. How is the wheat doing? Are you going to have flour enough? I tell you, I would like to have a good mess of cornbread.

---

[121] Seventeen-year-old Jim Wilson was a painters apprentice from Yorkville.
[122] Unidentified
[123] George Washington Mason

Sunday morning
May the 5th, 1861

My beloved Wife,
I did not finish last evening so I give you a few lines this Sabbath morning. The company all appear pretty well, this morning at least. There is none of the company but what is able to be, up and about. It came on a thunderstorm and rain about 3 o'clock this morning; is still raining. I think it will help us lots. It will settle the sand and fill the cisterns with water. I trust you have had rain up your way too. As Cousin Peter says, you need it badly. Him & Uncle Hamilton leave us this evening at five. I hear of a good many coming down to see us. Am glad to see them sure, but if you could come it would be a pleasure indeed. But Achsah, I know it does not suit for you to come & I don't expect it if I keep well. Indeed, this island don't suit for a decent woman. Tell the Negroes all howdy. I often think of them and am glad to hear that they want me to come home, but God only knows when that will be. Tell Uncle Reece howdy. Achsah, the reports you hear about our company & the Yankees fighting is all a lie, every word of it. Our men have had no fights with anyone only one Regular[124]. Cousin Peter can tell you about that. Don't believe half of the reports you hear. James Stewart is about this morning. Do write twice a week. My love to you all. Kiss the children. So farewell my beloved wife. May God bless you all.

H. A. Wallace

The following note was included in the same envelope:
Achsah I send you my epaulets. If anyone wants them, sell them. If Robert Barnett wants the sword let him have it at $3.00, the epaulet at five or five & a half. I send you my [officer's] commission. Take good care of it. I send my satin vest; don't want to use it here. If I

---

[124] This reference is to a soldier of the 1st S. C. Regulars, which was stationed on Sullivan's Island with Wallace's regiment. The 1st S. C. Regulars was formed in January 1861 for state service by orders of Governor Pickens. It held the distinction of being the first infantry regiment from South Carolina to be taken into the Confederate Provisional Army after the Confederate Government was established.

need one I will buy a cheap one. Achsah, Col. Bone [Bowen] is going to send to you for corn. If it is to spare let them have it. He says he left money in the hand of Mr. Caruthers[125] to buy it if he has collected it. It has cleared off beautiful. I have sent a shirt. Do it up and send it back. I would not care you would send one of my other fine shirts down too. Don't forget to write often. So farewell my beloved wife. It is now Sunday, 11 o'clock. May God's choicest blessings rest on you all is my prayer.

H. A. Wallace
May the 5, 1861

---

[125] Hugh Carothers (c.1808-?) was a neighbor of Augustine D. Choat near Clay Hill.

Letters – 1861

York District, So. Ca.
May the 5th, '61

Dear Harvy,
I again drop you a few lines to let you know how we are getting along. We are well at present except colds. Mother and Matty and I have colds. We are getting better. Willy did not rest well last night. He has got poisoned again. Got a snag run in his foot yesterday evening. I had hard work to get it out. Got the end stumped off his little toe so he is in bad fix for traveling. He wants me to tell you that Miles is very [illegible] to him. He run after him. Made him stump his toe and threatens to whip him. Harvy, I am going to tell you about Miles. I do not want you to get vexed. He has taking the horses two Saturday evening when Marion goes away and plows his patches. Says they are watermelon patches. They are next to Mr. Stewart's[126]. Says you told him to have them. He does what he please and says nothing [to] us about it; kept at me to buy a curry comb. I got one; gave it to Ad. He won't have [illegible] old one. Say he will buy him one. Marion say if he tell him do anything, he say that he does as you told. I did not get any hoes. Uncle Reece said you wanted some (43 or 4) got. Miles broke Caroline's[127]. Tell me how many to get. The Negroes has every Saturday evening yet. They are getting along very well. The horses are doing very well. Lucy's eye is not much better. The hogs keep like they were. Some of them are lousy. We gave them copperas and sulphur once or twice. Must gave them some more. We have got three pigs up. Mother tells you the chickens are doing no good. A great many of them died. We have no young ones; no hens sitting. We get good many eggs. We wish you had some of them. Harvy, we are talking about sending down another box of provision. If we do I shall write your name on everything I send. We shall not make a large company mess; just a few of us. I am going Cousin

---

[126] Joseph B. Stewart (c.1790-?), father of Private James A. Stewart, owned a plantation in the Clay Hill Community.
[127] Caroline was a slave born in 1845 in South Carolina, as stated in the 1880 Rusk County, Texas census.

P[eter] McCallum to see about it when he comes home. Harvy, Betsy has made your pants. Your mother brought them over last evening; stayed last night with us. They are well. Rebecca['s] children is not very well. Fair[128] had fever Friday night. She is going to write today to Sam. Cousin Haly[129] and Tresvan was here last night. Tresvan looks bad. I read your letters to them. Cousin Haly says she is much oblige to you for sending that word. Tresvan says he may go down after while but I think he will give it out. He is afraid he will be counted a coward and people say he got sick a purpose to keep from going. Harvy, I want you to be very careful of yourself and not eat or drink anything that will make you sick. You know it would be doing bad without you. You say life is precious to you for us. I felt that long ago. I hope the Lord will spare us to meet and live together again. I know I have done wrong to you. I hope, if God spares us to live, I will never do so no more. It makes me miserable to think of it. Harvy, you get some pain killer and use that. It would be good for your bowels. I hope you have rain enough today to fill your cistern. It is not raining here much but is very cold and cloudy and misting. Harvy, I am going to write to Thomas and Martha today. I got Matty's and my ambrotype taken to send to Texas on oil cloths, for I had to hold her in my lap. I did not think she would sit by herself. Mrs. Schorb[130] come in; help to fix Matty and talked to her. She sat very still. It cost 2 dollars 50 cents for the two. Matty is beginning to say a few words. I cannot hardly get her

---

[128] Samuel Fair Campbell (9/14/1857-5/1/1862) was the son of Samuel and Margaret Rebecca (Wallace) Campbell.
[129] Nickname for Mahala Gibson
[130] In an 1858 issue of the Yorkville Enquirer, Mr. John R. Schorb, a teacher at the Yorkville Female Seminary, advertised that he "takes pictures next door to the Presbyterian Church (in Yorkville) on Saturday between half past eleven to two o'clock". Schorb, a native of Neiderweiler, Germany and graduate of Hamilton College in New York, is recognized as one of the first commercial photographers to practice in the United States. Mary Schorb assisted her husband at the photography studio. Records indicate that John Schorb served as 2nd Sergeant in Yorkville's Home Guard unit during the war. Louise Pettus, *York County Research*, "Downtown Yorkville, 1858", [http://www.rootsweb.com/~scyork/louise.htm] and Louise Pettus, "Daguerrotype Portraits", *York County Genealogical and Historical Society Quarterly*, Dec. 1992, 3-4.

to name you. I fear she has forgotten you. She is getting to be mischievous. Harvy, Mother says she will send you down $15 dollars. I shall send you ten and if you want more you shall have it. I think they ask enormous for the sword and belts. If you want your old one I will send it to you. Marion['s] watch will not run. I will get Andy['s] and send it to you. Jo McClain[131] said he could get a good silver watch second handed if you wanted it for $22. Harvy, you must write to Uncle Jo Stewart how James is. Write to me and give all the particular. Tell what you have to cook in and who mess with you; if you have any plates or table. Samuel Campbell says you officers have to buy your own provision. Why do you have to do that? Do they not allow you none? It is twelve o'clock now; is raining a little faster. We need rain very bad. The potatoes are coming up in the patch but not one is coming up in the bed. I must go to dinner. Would be glad you could dine with us, but not so. Harvy, I wish you would look in the envelope I wrote last Wednesday evening and see if there is any post stamps. I bought six envelopes and stamps. I had them in a envelope and forgot about them. [I] put your letter up in a hurry and expect they are in your envelope. I have lost them no doubt. Harvy, you must tell how many letters you get from me. You must certainly not get all I send you. Harvy, Mr. McCorkle[132] said anything I would send to him he would send it down. If you want anything tell me and I will send it to you. I hear of good many complaining of Jenkins being partial, but the best way is to keep in good friends with him. But do not go to Virginia with him. He is able to take his family with him, and he does not care for the rest of your families, so he gets a big name. I

---

[131] Mr. Joseph A. McLean (c.1831-?) was a store clerk at Adams & McCorkles in Yorkville.

[132] William Hart McCorkle (8/25/1821-2/13/1904), son of Stephen and Jane (Hart) McCorkle and popular York District merchant, organized the Palmer Guards (Co.-A, 12th S. C. Infantry) at Yorkville in August 1861. McCorkle served as Captain of the company until he was elected Major of the 12th Regiment in April 1862. He was subsequently promoted to Lieutenant Colonel of the regiment in September of the same year and was wounded at Second Manassas. Colonel McCorkle resigned in February 1863 due to rheumatism of the heart. After the war, William McCorkle served as York County Judge and as Mayor of Yorkville for eight terms. Robert Krick, *Lee's Colonels: A Biographical Register of Field Officers of the Army of Northern Virginia* (Dayton, Oh.: Morningside Bookshop, 1979), 229.

heard it was him that took you away without much authority, and after you got there your companies had either to fill sandbag or go home. He put you to filling sandbag. They say the company at Union in North Carolina starts tomorrow. Harvy, the Weekly Day Book is stopped so we do not get much news. I want you to send me the news in your letters. I never heard whether you got the Yorkville Enquirer or not. You ought to get the Enquirer. Harvy, the children think the shells you sent is beautiful and wants you to send them some more. I turned the ink bottle over on the other letter I sent you. I do not know whether you can read it or not. I make some very bad spelling but you will have to guess at it. I write sometime and never get to read it over. You must not let no one see my letters, for they are so badly spelt and write. You must tell me when you write to Thomas. Well Harvy, I thought a great deal about you last night. It was so cold and wet. I do not know what you would do. I think you would be very cold lying on the floor with a blanket. Rebe[cca] says some got a mattress. I wish you would get one too. It would be better than the floor. It rained all night and is raining and thundering. Looks like it might rain all day. Tell me if you got chimney in your house or not. I must come to a close. May the Lord bless you is my prayer. I shall not write till the last of the week if nothing happens. So farewell.

Achsah Wallace
May the 6th

The following letter was enclosed in the same envelope:

Monday
May 6th, 1861

Uncle Harvy,
I will write you a few lines to let you know how the crop is at this time as well as I can. It rained all night and is raining yet. You have an idea how much water is afloat at this time. Well, I planted cotton on Monday after you started and rained that evening and settled the ground, and it has not come up as well as what I planted after. It will come now I have no doubt. This is a very cold rain, and it turned off

cold and windy after the other rain and you have no idea how quick the ground got dry and hard. I bedded up and planted all the land you left not planted and it has come up good. And I would have done well to kept right on and bedded up half that you planted, but I waited for it to come up until the ground got so hard I could not plow it without making a lot of clods, so I planted some over and the balance I replanted. Fortunately, the best ground had the best stand on it. Corn looks yellow and little. There has been no warm weather yet to make anything grow. Wheat looks very well. Oats has not started yet. Your hogs look very well. I feed 38 head. I spayed & ottered 13 head. They are doing well. The horses looks as well or better as when you left except Lucy['s] eye. I did not notice anything wrong with her eye for a week after you left, but it looked like it had been sore for some time. I got my watch fixed to send to you by Mr. Wright. It runs very well but it runs too slow. It loses 15 or 20 minutes in a day & night, and I reckon you would not want it without it kept the right time. Mr. Crave [Craven] said it had been strained in winding. There was some cogs bent, and he said there was one wheel left out when Alexander[133] fixed it and he would charge [illegible] 50 cts. for putting in one, but said it would run without it; to be careful in winding. I expect I will tire you writing so much and telling so little. Ad wants me to write a good word for him. I suppose you would guess at Ad['s] notion as well as I can. I suppose he means right. They work very well. I will close. Yours as ever,

D. M. Wood

---

[133] Moses Alexander, a Yorkville jeweler, announced in the Yorkville Enquirer in 1851, "Watches, Clocks and Jewelry repaired in superior style". Louise Pettus, "Crystal Palace In Old York", *York County Genealogical and Historical Society Quarterly*, Dec. 1992, 25.

Well Harvey,
As Marion has got through I will finish it out. Willy keeps at me to tell you howdy for him. He wants to see you bad. I tell him you will come home after while. Bud still cries for you to come home. They still look lost. Andy is going to let me send you his watch. He says for you to sell it if you can for fifteen dollars; must not take less than that when you go to come home. He says you must not wind it tight. Andy sends you howdy; to take care of yourself. Ad says to tell he will be a friend to us and tell us if anything goes wrong. He prays for you every day. Cinth and Candis[134] says howdy. They want you to come back soon as you can. The Negroes all appears hurt about you having to stay away so long. Farewell,

A. Wallace

---

[134] Candis was a slave.

Sullivans Island
May the 7th, 1861

Ever dear Achsah,
I have seated myself this morning to perform the pleasant task of writing to you. The sun is not up. I have been up some time myself; got up first in our camp. Some of our men are just pulling on their clothes to parade. I am quite well this morning. Had the bowel complaint Sunday but feel stout again. Our camp is all afoot and I trust we will get on better now. We have had lots of rain. Last night a perfect storm of rain, wind, thunder, and lightning. The sharpest lightning I ever seen. Achsah, I got a letter from you last evening saying all was well except your Mother. I am sorry to hear she is not well but trust she has got better. You don't know how glad I am to get a letter from you. I got one Sunday evening too. [illegible] sorry and glad both when I get your letters. Glad to hear of all being well and of you, my beloved wife, feeling so for me, but sorry to hear of you grieving about. Achsah we fare well enough here for soldiers, and if it was not for being parted from you and my little children I would not have anything to trouble me in the discharge of my duty to my beloved state. Even as it is, I feel that I am discharging my duty to my God in defending my state. I consider this a just, a holy war. The company got beds yesterday. We can do fine for lying now. We also got two boxes of provisions, one out of the Point[135] and one for Uncle Arthur, so we will have something good for a day or two. My dear wife, do cheer up and don't fret about me. Try and eat as hearty as usual, and trust to our God to return me home safe to you again. I feel like I would get back safe to my loved ones. Achsah you say there is a difference of opinion amongst us about coming back. Well my wife, I don't intend to flatter you in any way; give you the truth as far as I am able. There is none of us here knows any more about how long we may have to stay here than you do. I have little hopes of getting off before our time is up though. I

---

[135] This reference is most likely to the southeastern York District settlement now known as Old Point, located between the Ebenezer Community and Rock Hill.

don't think we will be kept here more than two weeks if there is no fighting. I think they will move us up the country to drill us. That is the talk now, but we don't know what we have to do until ordered. You write about sending my fine shirts. You can send them by Mr. Wright. Send the drawers too if you want. I could do very well without them. Achsah you may send the silk handkerchief if you wish. Not that I need it, but if it comes from you I will be happy to have it. You speak about sending my checked shirt. I have bought one and will not need it. I have plenty of clothing. If [I] have to stay out I will have to have a pair of pants after while. I suppose you have had my uniform pants made. Thompson got his. Anderson McElwee brought them to him. They fit very well. Achsah, tell your Mother not to fret about me. I get plenty to eat and that will do very well. To be sure, we don't just fare like we do at home, but get good enough for soldiers. Tell the boys to be good boys and not fight. Tell Bud he must not have all the whips. I will get home some day and make him whips. Try what little chance you have to learn Willy. Tell Uncle Reece howdy. My love to Marion. Tell him to do the best he can. Tell the Negroes all howdy, & to be faithful & mind the advice I give them before I left. So farewell my beloved wife for the present.

H. A. Wallace

Wednesday
[May] the 8th, [1861]

Harvy,

I drop you few to let you know we are well this morning. Mother and I still have colds yet. Harvey I seen Cousin Peter yesterday evening. I did not stay long with him. He told me about you. I am better satisfied than I was but still keep uneasy. I fear something happens you so many there. Cousin P[eter] told me you gave Mr. Hogelin a letter which I never have got. I got one from him and your shirt and vest and shells. I have washed your shirt and done it up. I wish you would send your clothes home to get washed, for they will be ruined if you don't. I took the buttons out and sewed some on. I sent some provision with Hannah Mason to you. I got your commission; will take care of it. I will send you some of my hair in a letter. I want to fix it up so you can keep it. Harvey, Malancthon Henry[136] came yesterday; got some corn. He said he wanted more. He got 4 1/2; wants 10 bushel more. We will let Mrs. Bowen[137] have some if we can spare it. It is Lucy's left eye that is sore. Her eye is getting better. She has not been [illegible] much. The second corn planting at the river is up nice. The cotton is not coming up very much that was planted the first day. Marion speaks of planting it in corn if it does not better. I gave Mr. Wright twenty five dollars for you but you said not send more so I will take it back. I send two shirts to you. Would send some socks if you want them. I cannot go to see you if you keep well. I would like you to come to see me soon as you can. May the Lord bless you is my prayers. So farewell a while.

A. Wallace

I will write soon. I have not got time [to] write much. It would make you laugh to hear Matty calling Frank.

---

[136] Malancton Henry (c.1825-?) was a farmer from the Clay Hill community.
[137] Mrs. Mary J. Bowen, wife of private William J. Bowen of the Catawba Company

Sullivans Island
Thursday morning
May the 9th, '61

My beloved Wife,
I have rose this morning and commenced the pleasant task of writing you a few lines. The men are just rising. I have been out and washed some time ago. I am up first mostly. I am well. The company is all able to be up. Some of them still have diarrhea but none so bad as they have been. Achsah I expected a letter yesterday but got none. None of our company got letters on yesterday. I got one Monday that you wrote Saturday so I hope I will get one this evening. I allow to write three times to you a week at least. I suppose you have seen Cousin Peter and got all of the news before this time. I sent you lots of sea shells. I have no doubt you would be glad to get them. I have not much new to write to you. We are still here on the beach. We were inspected yesterday by the Adjutant General Jones[138]. Colonel Jenkins has got us swords, so if we had our uniform we would be fixed off; have not got sashes yet. They can't be had in Charleston. Achsah, I don't recollect whether I have ever written to you how many of us stay in our room. It is twenty feet long; about twelve wide. There is 15 of us sleep in it; keep all of our concerns in it. Capt. Glenn, Campbell, Thompson, myself, Col. Bone [Bowen], UncleArthur, Mason, Jas.Tate[139], Grier, Sprat Wright[140], G. A. Patrick[141], R. Patrick[142], Joe McKenzie[143], & two

---

[138] Adjutant General David Rumph "Neighbor" Jones (1825-1863), of Orangeburg District, S. C., served as Chief of Staff to General Beauregard. He is said to have hauled down the U.S. flag on Fort Sumter after its surrender. Jones died of heart disease in Richmond after being promoted to Major General and serving capably in a command position. Warner, 163-164.

[139] 5th Sergeant James B. Tate (3/21/1836-7/28/1874), son of Hugh and Jane (Patrick) Tate, was discharged in June 1861 and later served as 1st Sergeant (Orderly Sergeant) in Co.-H, 18th S. C. Infantry.

[140] Private James Spratt Wright (3/2/1835-4/16/1921), Son of James L. (Mr. Wright) and Martha (Spratt) Wright, was discharged in June 1861. Wright enlisted as a private in Co.-A, 12th S. C. Infantry in August 1861.

[141] Private George Anderson Patrick (7/6/1831-5/25/1902), son of Elias and Susannah (Anderson) Patrick, won promotion to 1st Lieutenant, then to Captain of

Negroes all stretch down in the room. We have very comfortable beds now and sleep very well. We are out of home provisions now, only butter. Some of the boxes that came brought lots of butter. When I have butter I don't eat any meat scarcely, though we get excellent ham. I don't drink any coffee scarcely; drink sweetened water and vinegar. We get lots of coffee. Achsah, be careful of your coffee. It is twenty five cents a pound in Charleston and won't be had long if this war goes on. There is some noble cows on this island. A little girl brings milk to our house twice a day. I bought a pint of sour milk the other evening. They sell at five cents a pint. You don't know how good it drank. I intend to get it every chance. Mason & me will go the milk if we can get it. They brings us water over from Charleston in barrels. It is about two days old when we get it. River water at first, but we are not choice about our water now. We still get water out of the cisterns. Achsah we have prayer most every night. Mr. Witherspoon read the 10 chapter of Romans last night & sung the 453 hymn in the Presbyterian hymn book. He always remembers our absent families & friends in his prayers. Our company give great attention and behave well. Achsah, I am fully satisfied from the news we get that we are to have a bloody war. I

Company-H, (Co.-B after the regiment's re-organization in April 1862) later in the war. Patrick served for a time as color bearer for the 5th S. C. Infantry. The position of color bearer was the most coveted and hazardous duty in the regiment. For instance, Colonel Jenkin's battle report for the Battle of Seven Pines states "In my two color companies, out of 80 men who entered, 40 were killed and wounded, and out of 11 in the color guard, 10 were shot down, and my colors, pierced by nine balls, passed through four hands without touching the ground."   Davis, Major George B. et al. *The War of the Rebellion: A Compilation of the Official Records of the Union and Confederate Armies*. 128 Volumes. Washington D.C.: U.S. War Department, 1880-1901, (hereafter cited as *O.R.*). Part 1, Vol. 11, 950.

[142] Private Robert Vaughn Patrick (6/1/1838-12/12/1861), another Son of Elias and Susannah (Anderson) Patrick, died of disease at winter quarters near Centreville, Va. while serving with the Catawba Company.

[143] Private Joseph Stanhope McKenzie (3/30/1842-6/2/1894), the Son of Arthur A. (Uncle Arthur) and Rachel (Barnett) McKenzie, served in Virginia with the company and was later promoted to 5th Corporal. He was present at Appomattox when the Army of Northern Virginia surrendered.

don't see no other alternative. But I think it will be in Virginia for a while, and if the Yankees are not whipped there they will come out to our state. President Davis telegraphed to our Governor[144] yesterday to keep a look, for he had reason to believe an attack would be made on us here. But I don't think there is any danger of a fight here for a while. There is companies leaving Charleston nearly every day for Virginia. Three companies leave there this morning. Our colonel wants our regiment to go badly but I don't know how they will vote as yet. I think he is waiting to hear of a fight and then bring it to a vote while the men are excited. Achsah I want your advice what to do. It looks like a hard place to stay here this summer but I don't feel like going so far from you unless you want me to go. If we would go the officers would get double pay. My wages would be $100 dollars per month, but I am not willing to go so far from you & my little children unless you think I ought to go, if I was to get five hundred a month. I don't allow money to have any weight with me in regard to duty to my family. Though the big wages will have weight with some of the officers in the regiment, not with our company officers. Achsah I hope Mother has got better. Tell her not to fret about me. I am faring better than I thought I would every way, & if it was not for being separated from you I could enjoy myself fine, for our cause is a just one, a holy one. It does appear to me, if a man has no family he ought to meet our enemies wherever they put their feet on Southern soil. Tell my Father I thought he would write to me. I have written twice to him. John & Sam are well, so is S.L.C.[Samuel Campbell]. Augustis [Gustis] has gone to mustering again. So has James Stewart. John Cullender stands it fine; makes a good soldier. Tell his Mother John will get on without any trouble. Rollisson [Robertson] is well and gets on very well. In fact, the boys are doing fine. Tell Uncle Reece howdy. I would like

---

[144] Governor Francis W. Pickens took office in December 1860 as South Carolina boldly declared herself free from the Union. In a speech to the General Assembly before his inauguration, Pickens declared that he " would be willing to appeal to the god of battles; if need be, cover the state with ruin, conflagration, and blood rather than submit." Baldwin, 34.

to see him down here but I don't know if our friends will get over to see us now or not. They have quit allowing any man to come over here to see even his sons. There was three men come over in the boat yesterday morning that they would not give passes in Charleston, so they could not get over. One of them had a son here. They would not have got over but someone of the officers smuggled them in. I don't know why they are getting so strict. They say when they come to Charleston let them send them word to come over to Charleston to see their friends. Our commissary says that the men will have to be saving of their meat as it is going to be scarce. Tell Marion to take care of the hogs as meat will be an object if this war goes on. Our men have been getting more meat than they could eat. My love to you all. Kiss my little children for me. So farewell my beloved wife. Write soon, write often. May God bless you and enable us soon to meet in peace is my prayer. Your husband,

Harvey A. Wallace

I must now quit to eat as breakfast is ready. I don't have any cooking to do atall. Jim does our cooking & washing. Tell the Negroes howdy.

Clay Hill, So. Car.
May 9, '61

Dear friends,
I received your kind favor by yesterday's mail. Found us all well with the exception of colds, which is common. I can truly say that I am one who feels anxious in your welfare and was delighted to hear from and read your letter with pleasure. There is no way that I can hear from you that gives the same satisfaction that a letter does. It is the next thing to an interview. I am glad to know those reports you alluded to is false, and also that you are doing so well. And it affords me pleasure to hear from other sources how well the Catawbas has behaved; how they are respected. And I am in hopes that there will no one of the boys do anything to cast the least slur on their characters while they remain in the service of their country. I am in hopes you may not be call out up North Carolina, and that before long you may be allowed to return home, but the prospect is rather bad now. One thing is, there must be something done before long. Old Lincoln will have to back down or attempt to carry out his threats, and he will find the latter pretty hard to do. I think if the South had the City [of] Washington & Fort Pickens there would be no more fighting, and from what I can see, neither of them places will be attacked soon. The Confederate troops is not ready and will not be for some time, but I am in hopes when they do undertake they will succeed as well as they did at Sumter. It is exciting times and we are all on tiptoe for news. You ought to see us every evening at Clay Hill waiting for the mail, and see how anxious we are to get letters from you and hear the latest news. We do not hear a great deal lately. We are kept in the dark all right I suppose. I am glad to hear that you have had rain and supplied you with water. We had fine rains at the same time, rather much. And it has been a little cold and windy since and I am afeared it will not do us so much good. Land is baking. Cotton is coming up very slow; a good deal of complaint about bad stands of corn. Your folks is doing very well I think and we are all doing the best we can. I never seen the time when Negroes tried to do better. There is no danger of an insurrection in this neighborhood. I will call at your house soon in

compliance with your request, and I am willing to do them any favor they want and hope they will not be backward in asking. You requested me to give you the news of the country. There is very little local news. The whole topic of conversation is about the boys at Charleston and the condition of our country. Mr. Wright & Simril will give you the news more fully than I can do. I received a letter from S. L. Campbell and have fail to answer it up to this time. He stated that John Timberlake wanted me to send him a substitute. Please say to John that I have made every exertion to get him one but have fail. I will still endeavor to get him one yet but think the chances bad. Tell G. W. Mason that I have not got but one letter from him yet and he must do better. Please excuse this uninteresting letter. Give my love to all the boys. Tell them all to write to me and be certain to do so yourself. I still remain your friend.

T. L. Patton[145]

---

[145] Unidentified

Sullivans Island
May the 11th, 1861

My beloved Wife,
I have taken my pen this morning to answer your kind letters that I got last evening by Mesrs. Simril, Wright, & Finly[146]. They landed here by the 1 o'clock boat. Achsah I had got a letter Sunday and one Monday. Had got none since until they come. Mr. Tate[147] come with them. Achsah you do not know how glad I felt to read your letters and then to get the shirts you had done up with your own hands. The drawers, handkerchief, & last but not least, you & sweet little Matty out of my pants pocket. When I opened the case to have you both looking at me it made me feel very strange indeed. Achsah I will carry that picture next to my heart. I think they are very natural pictures, though I can't help but see you have fell off and got poor. Achsah I am afraid you are fretting about. I don't want you to do that. I am glad for you to think often of me but do not want you to fret. I am well and getting along better than could be expected. Some of our boys are pretty bad off with their bowels. Brother John is pretty bad off with his. He was better on yesterday morning but not so well in the evening. He is still poorly this morning but I have no doubt he will be better in a day or two. Davison Simril[148] is quite sick with his bowels too; several others pretty bad off. None of them have went to the hospital. We have had but one man there this week, Adkins[149]. He is about well again. My bowels are not altogether right but I have come off quite well so far. You say for me to get some pain killer and take it. I got me a bottle of French brandy when

---

[146] Robert Finley, father of Private William Green Finley

[147] Hugh Tate, father of 5th Sergeant James B. Tate

[148] 1st Corporal Samuel Davidson Simril (5/2/1836-3/29/1890), son of Hugh H. and Nancy (Partlow) Simril, was discharged in June, 1861 and later enlisted in Co.-H, 18th S. C. Infantry as a private. Private Simril was disabled when he suffered a severe thigh wound on July 30, 1864 near Petersburg during the Battle of The Crater.

[149] Private S. Randolph Adkins (c.1841-?) was the son of James S. and Jane Adkins of the Fort Mill community. Private Adkins declined to go to Virginia with the regiment and later enlisted in Co.- H, 18th S. C. Infantry.

I was in Charleston. It is very good for our bowels. I take a dram every morning. We are not allowed to have a drop but we slip it in. Some of the men have kept it all of the time and never have been sick any. I do wish I had a bottle of your blackberry wine and one of that corn whiskey, but I will try to get some when I need it. Mason's provision box come last evening. I got a nice poke of provisions out of it. You know I will appreciate them. We all divide our provisions around. I have not eat none of this nasty bread we get but once this week. Boxes have been coming so I could always get biscuits. Achsah you want to know why we have to buy our provisions. Well, the officers don't draw their[s], they buy them where the others get theirs. I am allowed sixty cents a day for board and they sell us provisions at what they cost them. They buy so many they get them cheap. They charge them to us officers. Captains are allowed ninety cents a day. The men get thirty cents worth. It is enough for them to eat. We have a better chance by buying. They always get hams for the officers. We can buy molasses. We lay out about all of our allowance and let the men have anything we have they want. The men get more coffee than they can use. Some of the messes have 20 pounds of coffee so we don't buy any coffee. You want to know what we have to cook in. I thought I had written. We have a coffee pot, kettle, a big pot like your deep stove pot to every 12, wash pan, dish pan, tins & spoons, tin plate, a knife and fork apiece. Capt. Glenn, Campbell, Thompson, Col. Bone [Bowen] & me mess together. I don't do any cooking at all since Jim Wilson come. He does all of our cooking. We will have him to do all of our coarse washing too. He does fine. You say for me to send home my washing. Achsah you may rest assured I would rather send it home but I don't see how I can. I will take care of my fine shirts and make them do me two weeks if I live. I have a checked shirt I never have had on yet. Achsah our quartermaster went over to Charleston and brought over three or four women to wash for the regiment. They said they would wash for twenty men at seventy five cents to the man. I told our boys they should not wash for me. None of our men would have them. They have been here about a week. Night before last there was said to be a perfect row where they were. They were bad women. The men got to running there. They say they used pistols but nobody was hurt. But one man, they say, got three balls in him. So yesterday they were sent back to the city. Achsah, such people can't wash for me if I know it. There is some of the Regulars have their wives. They wash for some of the men. Achsah I sent my white handled knife to you by Cousin Peter. You never said whether you got it or not. You must get it and keep it. I sent you a lot of shells wrapped up in a paper with your name on them. I wrote your name in the inside of some of them, & your Mother's & the children's. I hope you got them all. I sent my epaulets and satin vest by Uncle Hamilton. He said he would take them to you. I got Andy's watch. Tell him I am glad to have it if it keeps good time. I will take care of it. I am glad to hear they all think of me. Tell them all howdy, and to do the best they can. Achsah I am sorry to hear of Miles doing as you say he is. I never allowed him to take a horse without leave. Tell Marion to stop him, and anything he wants him to do make him do it. He is master there now, not me. I am sorry to hear that he is not good to Willy. If he won't do without hickory, I want Marion to make him do. Achsah, get whatever hoes they need. I can't say how many. I am glad to hear of our flour holding out. Take care of your coffee. It will be worth 50 cents a pound if the war continues long. Tell your Mother I often think of her and hope to see her soon again. My love to Uncle Reece & Marion. Tell Marion to go ahead and do the best he can. I am glad to hear the Negroes doing well. Kiss the babies for me. May God bless you all is my prayer. Your husband,

H. A. Wallace

We had prayer last night and sung the hymn that begins, "Am I a soldier of the cross, a follower of the Lamb"[150].

---

[150] "Am I a Soldier of the Cross?" by Isaac Watts and composed by Thomas A. Arne (1724).

Sullivans Island
Sunday, one o'clock
May the 12th, '61

My dear Achsah,
I have taken my pen again to write to you, having no doubt but you are, like myself, glad at all times to get a letter from them nearest your heart. I am pretty well today. I was not well on yesterday; had the bowel affection. I did not do any duty on yesterday at all but got up pretty well this morning and am doing very well today. I went out this morning on duty to inspect the arms. We don't have any duty to do today but inspect the arms in the morning and clean out our houses and haul off all of everything that is dropped around the house. We have that to do every day. We have a dress parade at five this evening. Achsah you asked me about some stamps you lost. I got them out of the letter when I opened it. I thought you had sent them to me. There is so much confusion when I begin to write I always forget something. I never have tried on my new uniform yet. Glenn and Thompson put theirs right on but Campbell & me have just let ours lie in the trunk. I will tell you how it fits when I try it on before I close this. We have got new caps with a palmetto tree on the front. We have to get a 5 on one side of it, R on the other for 5th Regiment. They will cost us about three dollars & a half. We have to get badges made for the shoulders of our coats. They will cost us $4.00. So you see our tab is heavy, but once we get uniformed I suppose we will not have to be at so much expense. Achsah our boys are better today. Brother John is pretty well. Davisson Simril is better too. Billy Johnson[151] is pretty sick. I tell you, this bowel complaint misses very few, and when they get bad they pass nothing but blood & water. But it is remarkable that there has not been a death in the regiment since we have been together, now one month tomorrow, nor a accident. Achsah we have prayer by Mr.

---

[151] Private William Glenn Johnston (2/1840-7/3/1863), son of David and Mary (Glenn) Johnston, died of disease near Petersburg, Va. while serving with the Catawba Company.

Witherspoon every night. He prays for our absent wives and families. You know we can heartily join him. I was at preaching today. Durant[152], that used to be the Presiding Elder at Concord[153], is the Chaplain for our regiment. He gave us a very feeling discourse. I tell you, as hard as I am, when he turned the discourse to our absent families it makes me feel at once. He preached from the 33 chapt. of Isaiah, the second clause of the 20 verse. He gave us a splendid sermon. He told us when he got through he did not want us to look on him as a Methodist preacher but to look on him as a Minister of Jesus Christ. He did not come here to preach up doctrine, he came as the humble servant of all & wanted to go around all and pray with them at their quarters. And if anyone wanted him to send for him, if it was midnight. He preaches at three o'clock this evening. Mr. Landrom[154], a Baptist preacher, preaches tomorrow night at seven o'clock. Well Achsah, I got up this morning, washed up, and put on one of the fine shirts you sent me and a clean pair of drawers. It made me feel good to get on a white shirt that you had done up. I will send home one of my coarse shirts by Mr. Simril if he can carry it, and a knit shirt I bought when I first come down. It was then cold. It is so hot now I don't need it, and so many clothes are in my way. I will then have two coarse shirts, one striped one, and two fine ones. Achsah I got the handkerchief you sent me. I think it very pretty and will highly prize it, but might have done without it. I will send the poke you sent my provision in by Mr. Simril. I will send you one of the loaves of bread in it. Each man is allowed one a day but he gets plenty of rice. I have not eat none of it since your provisions come, but we are about up again enough to do us tomorrow. We have plenty of butter to do us this week. If we could only get biscuit like you sent & plenty of butter we will make out

---

[152] Rev. H. H. Durant

[153] Concord Methodist Church, located in the Clay Hill neighborhood on the Catawba River, had a very large and active congregation. It was also a popular Methodist camp meeting site.

[154] Rev. John Gill Landrum (10/22/1810-1/19/1882), of Spartanburg District, S. C., was a distinguished and well-known Carolina backcountry preacher.

very well. Our water is very warm, I tell you. About like your water after it stands a half of a day in the sun, only it don't taste as well. I bought one mess of sour milk. I allow to get it every chance. There is some of the best cows on this island I ever seen. There is lots of meadow on the lower end of the island, enough to pasture thousands of cows. Achsah if it was not for the wind blowing we could not live here, the sun would be so hot. Achsah we may get into a fight any time here. There was a United States vessel lying out in full view of us all day yesterday. They say there is three more of them today. I suppose they are there just to blockade our port[155]. They won't let no vessels come in to Charleston. They may come up and give us a fight. If they do we will have to do the best we can for them. I reckon they will quit talking about sending us to Virginia now when the Yankees are in sight. We can stand in our piazza and see the vessels plain. Achsah, tell Cousin Nelly's[156] people all howdy for me, & Mr. Cook & Cousin Polly[157], [and] any of the neighbors that think worthwhile to ask for me. Mrs. Wood get Mr. Choat[158] to write to Boyden[159] and see if that business can't be settled up in the last of this

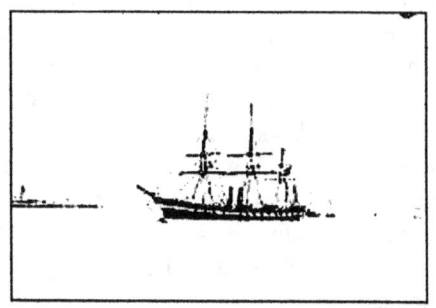

U.S.S. Niagara

---

[155] The *U.S.S. Niagara* led a blockading squadron that began patrolling the waters off the entrance to Charleston Harbor on May 10, 1861. E.B. Long, 73.

[156] Eleanor Gibson

[157] Reference here is to Dempsey (5/5/1805-12/8/1880) and Mary "Polly" (Gibson) Cook (10/8/1808-7/13/1872). Polly was the child of Matilda Wood's sister, Nancy "Sarah Ann" (Mayhew) Gibson and her husband, Ruebin.

[158] Mr. Augustine D. Choate

[159] Mr. Boyden, an attorney from Charlotte, N. C., was executor of the estate of Matilda Wood's sister, Jane (Mayhew) McCay.

month[160]. I have no doubt if Boyden will settle up, but Mr. Cook and Choat can settle your part too. If there is any chance to get the money don't let it slip. There is no telling how things may turn up in time, for these are gloomy looking times indeed. But we ought to put our trust in God and not murmer. You don't know how much good it would do me to get home to see you all, though I don't allow myself to fret. I will write to Marion tomorrow. Tell Uncle Reece howdy. Tell him I reckon he has quit catching Red Horse now. Tell Andy his watch runs very well. I will send his chain back in the poke as I don't need it. Tell the Negroes all howdy and to do the best they can.

[Harvey A. Wallace]

---

[160] Matilda Wood was owed money from the settlement of the estate of her sister, Jane (Mayhew) McCay of Rowan County, N. C. The estate consisted of a large plantation along with the personal effects of Jane and her deceased husband, James McCay. Apparently, the settlement issue had been an ongoing affair since the probation of Jane's will in 1857.

Sullivans Island
May the 12, 1861

To D. M. Wood
Well Marion, I received your kind letter you sent by Mr. Wright. I was glad to hear you were getting on well with the crop. You don't know how I would like to see a crop growing now. I don't see neither wheat, corn, cotton, nor precious little but white sand, only when I go down on the lower end of the island. I have not been there only the time Peter was down. I hope your corn and cotton has come up well before this time and growing some now. Yesterday was very hot here in the fore part of the day. The wind did not blow as much as common. Marion try to get your corn on the bottom land thinned evenly according to the ground. Thin out the poor land pretty thin. Work the crop often & don't let it get dirty at all if you can help it. Marion, from what Achsah wrote me, Miles is entirely above himself. I want you to make him do your way and not tell you he does things as I told him. If he won't do without timber, let him have it. When you write again tell me how Mary & Martin are coming on and what word you get from Nancy Ward[161] and from Rooker[162]. Marion the times look warlike indeed from the news. We get papers every day from Charleston. I hear since I began to write that they are fighting in Virginia[163], so if it is the case, no telling where it will end. The Yankee vessels are lying out here watching us. They may come up and drive us out of our houses any time, but if they attempt to land we will be on them sure. Our boys are all anxious for a fight. Take men away from home and keep them out, they would rather fight as not. They get hardened. I would say there is 200 hundred of the men in our regiment not able for duty. They do say nearly half of the men on Morris Island are sick. It is said to be [a] great deal sicklier than this island. They have no

---

[161] Nancy (Wood) Ward (12/25/1826-8/15/1916) was Marion's sister. Nancy was married to Martin Ward.
[162] Unidentified
[163] This report was evidently a rumor since no major land engagement took place in Virginia until the relatively minor battle at Big Bethel on June 10, 1861. E.B. Long, 84.

houses over there; have to stay in tents on the sand. You don't know how filthy so many men makes everything; so close together we can hardly have any place to go to stool. So many a running makes the necessary houses stink so you can hardly sit in them at all when they are cleaned out every day. Write to me soon. Tell me how you get on. I will write to Achsah again before Mr. Wright and Simril leave in the morning. Yours truly,

H. A. Wallace

Sullivans Island
Sunday evening
12th of May, '61

This is for yourself Achsah.

Achsah,
As I have nothing else to do I still continue to scribble to you. I wrote a letter this morning for J. Timberlick [Timberlake] to D. T. Partlowe[164] and have promised to write one for P. Anderson[165] this evening, but I had rather write to you while I have anything to write. If I write too much nonsense you can just say so to me in a letter and I will not bother you with so much of it. The mail has come since I began to write. I was a little disappointed in getting no letter from you. I got one from D. T. Partlowe in answer to one I had written him. He said you were all well. Achsah I have a very good bed now. The men all have beds. I have three blankets now. I put one under my head. There is a bedstead in the room we stay in. Uncle Arthur, Sam Campbell, & Grier lie on it on a mattress Sam hooked. There is 16 of us in the room. We are just as close as we can lie over the floor. I lie between Col. Bone [Bowen] and George Patrick. I generally get up first and roll up our bed; not our, but my bed. Achsah, I carry you and Matty in my side vest pocket. I am mightly pleased with the likenesses but I trust I will get to see you both before a great while face to face. It will cost me lots of money but I intend if I am spared to go home to see you soon as ever I can get off decently. Achsah I hate to bother you writing so much but do write as often as you can. I always told you that you were dear to me but I did not know myself half how dear you were until I was separated from you. I often think of the evening I left home. How

---

[164] David Theodore Partlow (7/4/1828-6/6/1897), son of David and Mary (Barnett) Partlow, served in The Lacy Guards (Co.-K, 17th S. C. Infantry) as a private.

[165] Private Joseph Pendle Anderson (c.1825-?), son of William and Mary V. Anderson, was discharged in June, 1861 and later enlisted in Co.-H, 6th S. C. Infantry.

unconcerned I tried to appear to keep you from fretting, when my heart was then aching. And of the hot tears you shed on my cheeks the last night I ever was in the bed with you the night before I left home. Achsah I try to take the best care of myself I can for your sake. I want you to do the same with your self on my account. Be as cheerful as you can and don't fret none you can help. I never go to wash but I think about what you always tell me about washing my ears. The doctors say we ought to be very cleanly and wash often. I have been in the ocean twice to wash. There is hundreds of the men in every day. I am afraid to go far out as there is sharks and things that sometimes catch men. Achsah there has been over a hundred men in bathing and hollering today. The men don't care for nothing; just run about here naked on the beach, sometimes wrestling. You do not know how much wickedness there is in camp; so much swearing & blackguarding; all kinds of wickedness. I read my Bible every day some 3 or 4 chapters. Achsah you know I feel at a loss here. I feel like I was alone in religious matters. Not a Baptist in our company but me[166]. No one to talk to about religious matters like I could with one of my own church, but I have been treated well by all. I have never a word with any man in the company out of the way yet. Achsah don't show this to anyone. Kiss our sweet children for your husband.

H. A. Wallace

---

[166] The Scots-Irish settlers of York District were staunch Presbyterians. They established their meeting houses to serve as focal points of the early communities. By 1850 about 46 percent of county residents claimed membership in the Presbyterian Church. The remainder was divided between the Baptists and Methodists. Most of the churches of the District counted slaves among their membership and church attendance was encouraged or demanded by many plantation owners. Arnold Shankman, et al. *York County South Carolina: Its People and Its Heritage* (Rock Hill, S.C.: Rock Hill Area Chamber of Commerce, 1983), 36.

So. Ca.
May the 12th, 1861

Dear Harvey,
[I] Seat myself to drop you a few lines this evening in answer to yours I received yesterday. I was glad to hear of you being well but I fear you will [be] very sickly when the weather gets hot. You say the companies are leaving there. I think you will be healthier when they get thinned out, but I hope you will not have to stay there the summer through. I hope that God will provide better for us. He is able to stop the wicked in their threatening and madness if we ask Him in the right manner, although we have a gloomy prospect now. God has promised to answer the prayers of the righteous, and of so many praying I hope there is some good ones. We were at Concord at preaching today. Mr. Roper[167] preached. He preached a great sermon; prayed for our nation and country; for the men that were gone and their families in great earnest. He begged the people to meet together some place every week and pray for the revival of religion and for the men that were gone and their families at home. He preached from the 1st Corinthians, 6th chapter, 19-20 verse. Harvey I am truly sorry you are thinking about going to Virginia and asking my advice. You know what I have said. I do not want you to go, but you know best. I think the married men ought to stay at home and take care of their families, for if the North conquer in Virginia they will come here. We will need protection by someone. You must act to your own judgment as I am not able to advise you. If anything should happen [to] you there and I had advised you either way, I should always reflect on myself. I do not think there is any women in the neighborhood willing for you men to go. We hear of some houses being burnt in Washington. Harvy when you get this you must write to me what you allow to do. If you go, I want you to come by home so as to take a final farewell with me and the dear little children. I do not want you to get excited, nor to be hired with money. Our crops looks very bad except wheat. It looks very well so far. Our mogul is mixed badly with May wheat. I do not know how we will manage it. The May wheat is all headed; will do

---

[167] Rev. Jonathan M. Roper (c.1799-?) of Yorkville

to cut in a few weeks. The corn is bad; cannot get a stand on it.
They keep replanting. The first that come up look tolerable well.
The cotton is bad. There is not half stand. They are talking about
planting it in corn. I wish it was so that you could see it [to] tell us
what to do. The sweet potatoes is coming up some in the beds and
patch. The patch began to come first. Uncle Reece watermelons is
coming up, and cucumber. The turnip looks fine. We thought there
was none hardly. They are plenty thick. They are as large nearly as a
goose egg. I wish you had some of them. We have more mustard
greens and turnip greens than we can eat. We have eat no onions.
They do not do much good. Bud and John[168] went in one day and
pulled up a good many of them. They are full of mischief, and so
lazy I do not know what to do. Bud is very fretful. He is wanting
some mashup[169] in the entry. Hariet[170] is getting him some. Willy
and Matty is there too. Matty hangs on to Frank all the time. She sits
in the big arm chair to her dinner. She eats mashup. The children all
eats clabber and sugar, and Mother and I do the same. Uncle
R[eece] eats sweet milk. Marion takes coffee all the time but we
shall not make it. I suppose you would think it takes smart of sugar
to do, but not much more than common, for the[y] has sugar in their
coffee anyway and it does not take much for Mother and me. I
would like to send you some more butter but fear the weather is too
warm. I will try it though when I get a chance. I suppose you could
not get none in the island. I am glad to hear of you getting milk.
Cousin P[eter] says you want cornbread. I think you might have
plenty of that. Mother say she is glad to hear of you faring so fine.
You fare much better than she expected. She had no idea of you
getting beds. Sorry to hear of the people not getting to see you, for
you are glad to see them. We got the shells you sent. Uncle
H[amilton] brought them and S.L.C.[Samuel L. Campbell's] here.
Sam sent some very curious ones. Mother say she allows to keep
hers for a milk skimmer. They are very pretty. The children would
soon break them if they had them to play with. Uncle H[amilton]

---

[168] John was a slave child.
[169] A mixture of cornbread and milk
[170] Achsah's cousin, Harriet Gibson

brought your epaulets. He went to Miss Hanner [Hannah] Mason's soon in the morning and stayed awhile. Her and them came and had dinner. Uncle H[amilton] says he will come back to see us every chance he has. The fruit is going to be very scarce. We have a few cherries, a very few apples, and not many peaches. I see a good many peaches in places. We will not have much to dry. There is no pears hardly. The Negroes are gone strawberry hunting. I think we will have plenty blackberries. If you had blackberry wine I think it would be good for your bowels. I suppose you have got the box Miss Mason and I sent you before this time and you know the provision apart. I sent you two letters by Wright. You can send what things you won't need by someone that is passing. Tell me whether to get Ed[171] a pair of shoes or not. You have not told me what to get. I do not want to buy much more than I can help. I have not got the children no hats for summer. I will try to make the old ones do a while yet. Well Harvey, I have scribble long enough. You will get tired of trying to read it. I am glad to hear you have prayer in your house at night but don't depend on that to do you. Pray for yourself and the rest of us to whom you say feels near and dear to you. You do the same to me. I will try to pray for you and myself and the family. You are never out of my mind. So farewell for a while. Write soon, I am always glad to hear from you. Mother and Uncle Reece sends their love to you. My love and best wishes to you.

A. Wallace

Upside down on bottom of page:
Harvy, I don't believe Marion cares anything for you.

---

[171] Edward (c.1845-?) was a slave given to Harvey by his father.

Sullivans Island
Monday morning
May the 13th, 1861

My dear Wife,
I write a few lines by Mr. Simril this morning again. I am well this morning. Have been out and drilled the company in the Manual of Arms[172]. The boys are all better. Brother John has got pretty well. Achsah I send by Mr. Simril one cotton shirt, one knit blue one, some shells, the poke you sent me, Andy's watch chain as I don't need it, & a loaf of our bread. We call it cannon wadding. So you can see for yourself that it is not as bad as some of them make it out. That loaf is a pretty fair sample. We get some a little better, some worse. I don't eat it when I can get any other. One of them is what a man gets for three meals in bread. He gets plenty of rice, but you know we can't cook rice so it is good. I did cook some that eat pretty well, but our cook don't cook rice well, though he does very well. Achsah I don't need the shirt I send home. I had just wore it one week. It never has been washed since I left home. I took it off yesterday morning. Achsah if I need any clothing I will let you know. I will try to send home one of my fine shirts by Capt. Glenn. He says he is going to start home Friday night so he can get there Saturday evening. Achsah you can tell how our washing is done by the knit shirt I send. This water won't wash half. Jim washed it. It feels like it was full of soap. I don't need it here. Achsah we got news here last evening that they had been fighting at Harpers Ferry

---

[172] The Manual of Arms was a section of rifle drill from Volume II, School of the Battalion, Hardee's Rifle & Light Infantry Tactics. It was a popular training manual used extensively by both armies during the Civil War. Lieutenant Wallace's copy of Hardee's, which he carried throughout the war, resides in the Wallace collection. Captain Wallace wrote inside the front cover, "Capt. H.A. Wallace's Book, Hardees Rifle & Light Infantry Tacticks. Purchased Jan. the 15th 1861 of Andrew Beard in Yorkville South Carolina. This writing done March the 4th 1863 at Camp Wright, 4 miles north of Pine Bluff Arkansas. McCullochs Brigade, Walkers Division, 2nd Army Corpse."   W. J. Hardee, *Hardee's Rifle & Light Infantry Tactics, Vol. II* (Philadelphia; J.B. Lippincott & Co., 1861).

in Virginia on yesterday and that our men whipped the Yankees[173]. We will get more news as soon as the boat comes over. I trust to God it is true. We are defending our homes, wives, and children, and our very existence, and if we be true to our God He will certainly give us the victory. I tell you, it is pretty hard to have to stand here and see the Yankee ships turning back our vessels. If we had any way to get at them we would move them sure. Achsah I will write every day or so. You must do so too. You can take the time to write to me, & if any of you gets sick be honest with me, as I intend to be with you. If I get sick you shall know it, and if any of you gets sick I want to know it too. Achsah I must close. May God bless you my beloved wife. Kiss the little ones. So fare you well.

H.A. Wallace

---

[173] Wallace's report proved false. The Federals abandoned Harpers Ferry on April 18, 1861. Confederate volunteers from Virginia were ordered there under the command of Colonel Thomas J. Jackson on May 1. E.B. Long, 61 & 68.

Mount Etney
Allisons Creek
May the 14th, 1861

To H. A. Wallis

Dear Son,
It is with pleasure I write you a few lines to let you know how we are getting along. I received your kind favor yesterday. We were sorry to hear you and Rufus[174] were not well but hope you are better. These leaves us all well. Your family were all well yesterday. I seen Wood at the office. The friends are generally well as far as I have heard of. There is a good deal of talking. There is grounds for it too. I expect that you may have some fighting to do shortly. They say they have blockaded Charleston. I suppose they will try to take the forts again. My opinion is they will work on South Carolina to tie her. They have the picket at any rate. It appears fighting must be done somewhere, and that pretty soon. You complain of my not writing. I acknowledge the receipt of three letters from you, but when I have written I thought I wrote family letters including you all, and allow you to see them. That is all the apology I will make. It is not because I don't respect you as the rest of the boys. I hope you will advise the boys. Tell them to be good boys and not be guilty of anything that will disgrace them. They are both young and needs experience. I put great confidence in you, Brother McKinzy, and Campbell. If you see anything with them, try to correct it. But I hope you will have no need. There is great complaints about a stand of cotton. It is slow coming; a good many planting over; some planting corn. I have got a good stand except on spots. It is still coming. Wood told me yesterday he thought he would have a stand. He was harrowing. We are at it too. I got a letter from Jo[175] last

---

[174] Harvey's brother, John R. H. Wallace
[175] Joseph Franklin Wallace (12/4/1831-3/14/1910) was the eighth child of James and Margaret (Barnett) Wallace. Joseph was the first of the Wallace family to move to Texas. He arrived in 1858 but returned to South Carolina in late 1861.

week. He was well. He had not seen none of them since Wm.[176] was married. He don't write as if there was any excitement much there; did not say anything about being volunteered. Some of the North Carolinians left Raleigh and came home. They say they have furloughs without dates. They had a fracas with their captain and Bill Baxter[177] shot him in the thigh. Jo Eakins[178] knocked the pistol down when in the act of firing or it would have killed him. They have him and Eakins in close quarters. He was to be tried yesterday and will be apt to be shot. These boys that came home, they say, will not tell anything about it. The captain is an Erwin[179]. I am very well pleased with my overseer. He works all the time and he makes the boys go it. And if they don't mind him, he brushes them. Jack has got it two or three times. Dave and Thad[180] are both pretty wily of him. Crops grows slow, but think they will grow now it has got warm. I think wheat is doing pretty well. I would be glad to neighbor with your people but as you are not here I don't know what to say about it. I will just have to do the best I can. I have been to your house 3 times since you left. I will go whenever I can make it suit. I think if I live and everything goes well I will pay you a visit. That is, if you remain where you are. And I think the harbor of

---

[176] William Marcellus Wallace (2/9/1827-7/27/1884), another son of James and Margaret (Barnett) Wallace, moved to Texas sometime between 1858 and 1860. He settled in Rusk County near Mount Enterprise. William and wife, Josephine G. (Ray), were married in February 1861.
[177] Unidentified
[178] Unidentified
[179] These soldiers were members of Co.-B (The Ranelsburg Riflemen), 13th N. C. Infantry. Co.-B was formed in April, 1861 at Ranelsburg, Mecklenburg County, just across the state line from York District. It consisted of men from both counties. The Captain was Albert A. Erwin. Captain Erwin eventually recovered from his wound but the fate of the men involved in the incident is not known. Their names do not appear on subsequent company muster rolls. Captain Erwin returned to his company and was wounded in the arm at Williamsburg, Va. on May 5, 1862. He resigned February 27, 1863 due to his wounds. *The Yorkville Enquirer*, May 28, 1861 and *The Quarterly*, Vol. III, No.-1, June 1991, 22-23.
[180] Jack (c.1849-?), Thaddeus (c.1847-?), and Dave were slaves on the James Wallace plantation. The overseer is unidentified.

Charleston needs close watching. I will close for this time. Tell Rufe to write. I know he can do it in a hurry. And may that God who is able to, protect you all and keep you from every evil. Look to Him for His aid and assistance. Put your trust in Him and it will be well with you all. Give my respects to A. A. McKinzie and Jo [McKenzie]. And now, goodbye.

Jas. Wallis

James and Margaret (Barnett) Wallace

Zeno, S. C.
May 14th, 1861

Bro. Wallace,
Your favor of 6th inst. has been duly received. I was glad to hear from you and the company; that you were all in better health and fine spirits. I was also rejoiced to hear that not one of the Catawbas have been in a guard house and hope there may never be any occasion for it. Your captain wrote to me that the company stands on the first page. May it ever do so and be an example for all others to follow. The men who first formed the Catawba Company were those who were ready to stand by their noble state and defend her rights and interests to the last extremity. Those who now compose the company are, many of them, the sons of those patriotic fathers, possessed of the same noble spirit of their ancestors. The Catawba Company will at all times and places win for itself a prominent place in the minds and estimation of their countrymen, so long as they conduct themselves as they have done since they have been called in defense of their state. I am glad to hear your company is not going to Virginia unless they are compelled or there is actual need. There will, no doubt, be 100 thousand men raised in the state of Virginia, [and] 30 thousand or more in North Carolina. Tennessee and all the southern states are sending troops there, so I think there will be more men there than can be of service. Virginia, it is true, is one of the Confederacy, but our own state is not out of danger yet. I am willing that Virginia should be protected by all means. I consider that our own state claims our assistance first. A man will naturally defend his own house first before he helps his friend. This is human nature, and it is justice to himself and family. There are many young men who have no charge at home. To such I have nothing to say in this matter. I leave the matter with them to decide as they see fit, but situated as you and many others are, I consider it your duty to remain where you are, satisfied your honor and reputation as a soldier and patriot will not, I consider, be the least impaired thereby. I am well aware that you officers have a great deal to attend to and the memorandum you keep will be very satisfactory to me and will supersede the necessity of writing for

the Enquirer as I suggested. My object in making this request was that the company might have a place with the others in the history of our country. I hope that I may be able to do justice in my sketches of the company's history when I get all the matters of interest connected with it. I am aware that I am incompetent to the task but I will do what I can. It may be some time yet before I complete the work as it will require a good deal of study, time, and writing and rewriting to get it in a proper form and arrangement. Much more so than letter writing, but if I shall live I intend to complete it. I have no doubt that you meet in the army men of all grades, from the refined, intelligent, and peaceable gentlemen down [to] the renegade outlaw, and perfectly reckless class of beings. It could not well be otherwise where there are such an immense quantity of men from every part of the country and from all grades of society. The civil and pious are often harassed by the wickedness and tumult of those regardless of self respect and without any regard for a Supreme Being. I have had some experience in this matter in college and academy. Yet amidst all these trials, there is a source of joy to the Christian. The Lord has promised to be with His followers in six troubles, and in the seventh will not forsake them in every condition, therefore, that we may be placed in. Though we may have fiery trials to pass through, we have the full assurance of the grace of God to sustain us. Though we may be tossed and driven to and fro on the rough sea of time and our bark often seems will be cast away, yet there is an anchor to the soul which is sure and steadfast. This is hope beyond the grave. The Captain of our salvation has gone before us, inviting us on to victory and glory. He is able to lead us through all dangers and tempest and land us on the shores of eternal bliss and happiness. Having therefore, Christ as our leader, the Holy Spirit to guide us, and the grace of God to sustain us, we may not fear what man can do unto us. Rely therefore upon the blessings of a crucified Redeemer. Put your trust in Him. Be reconciled to the dispensations of His providence and all things needful will be granted to you. May heaven's blessings attend you and the company. And if it is the Lord's will, I hope to welcome you all to your homes and families again, there to enjoy the liberty and peace that is due to all true lovers of our enlightened land and state. I am rejoiced to hear that you have prayer in your quarters and that the boys give every respect and attention. I trust they may be benefited thereby, and that they will all make a good improvement of the time thus spent and that they may return home soldiers of the cross of Christ. I hope the campaign may prove a blessing and a benefit to all. Many are the intercessions at a throne of grace in the behalf of those who have left their homes in defense of their country. This will be a great consolation to you and should be to all, that their friends and neighbors at home are deeply interested in their present and future welfare. I will close this part of my letter for the present to give you some items of news. The company formed at Erwin's Store, N.C.[181] have landed in Raleigh, N.C. Their destination is not yet known. Their uniforms will be sent to them in a few days. The cloth is a dark gray Rock Island. The officers have frock coats; 1 row of large palmetto buttons up before 3 buttons on each sleeve. The private's coat is cut something after the style of yours; skirt shorter. A beautiful flag said to be worth $50.00, was presented to the company on the day of their departure by the ladies. Miss Sarah Erwin, daughter of Randolph Erwin[182], presented the flag to the captain and made an appropriate address. The spirit of resistance is very high now in North Carolina. Mecklenburg Co[unty] appropriated 50 thousand dollars for the benefit of the volunteers and their families, besides large subscriptions by individuals. The county issued bonds after the same manner that our state did. These bonds are readily taken up at par as fast as they come out. I am rejoiced to hear that my native county has taken such an active part in the contest for liberty. The Gaston Guards left on last Monday. Have not heard from them since. John F. Glenn went with them. Gaston Co[unty] is not behind in her assistance to volunteers. Bonds to the amount of 15 thousand dollars have been issued.

[Remainder of letter missing][183]

---

[181] Co.-B, 13th N. C. Infantry
[182] Both are unidentified
[183] Although the autograph page is missing from this letter, it closely matches the writing of Harvey's friend, Zadoc Darby Smith (see letter of April 27, 1861), and can most likely be attributed to him.

Y. D.: S. C.
May the 15: '61

Dear Harvy,
I seat myself to drop you a few lines to let you know how we are getting along these troublesome times. We are all well at present. The friends are well so far as I know except old Mrs. N. A. Mason[184]. She is very poorly. Aunt Susan Brandon[185] was here yesterday. She says she is worse off than she has been for some time. Polly Dole[186] was here also. Harvey I have not much to write about but I feel like I must write something to you as I write three times a week and sometimes four; try to write all I think of; sometimes forget to write the particulars. I forget whether I told you I got your epaulets or not. I got them and your knife, your satin vest, and the little white shirt buttons. I did not put them in again, for I thought you had rather have the others. We got the shells. Well Harvey, the cotton is coming up better than I expected. We had two or three days very warm sunshine. We had a light shower last evening. The sun shines very pretty this morning but looks like we might have rain again soon. If it keeps warm the crops will soon grow off and look very pretty. The garden is beginning to look very well. The Irish potatoes does not make much show. I do not think they will be much account. Uncle Reece went to York yesterday with the mail for Sam Johnston[187]. Sam said he was not able to go. He went a fishing though. He has not been for the last few days. There was a Negro drowned in Catawba Creek last Monday. He belong to the widow Stow, White Stow's wife[188]. The Negroes seen him floating down at Wright's Ferry Sunday. Well, Mrs. Brandon

---

[184] Mrs. Nancy A. (Pegram) Mason (7/31/1796-9/20/1873), mother of Private George Washington Mason

[185] Mrs. Susannah Brandon (8/26/1793-10/14/1893) and husband, Edwin T. Brandon, were neighbors of the Wallaces. No record of a direct relationship between the two families could be located.

[186] Unidentified

[187] Mr. Samuel C. Johnson (12/11/1820-8/16/1893) was a farmer from Clay Hill.

[188] Unidentified

was saying yesterday that William Baxter had got drunk and fell out with their captain and shot him. Would have killed him but Joseph Eakins was standing by him and knocked down his pistol as he shot. He shot him through the thigh. They fell out about going to Virginia. The captain wanted to go and some of the men did not want to go. They put it to vote. Baxter said if they went he should shoot the captain first. Some of the men were arrested and some came home. I do not know what they came home for. Monday was his trial. They said they would shoot him. I never heard whether they shot him or not. I suppose you will hear more about it than I can tell you as I am a bad hand to tell news. I pity his poor wife. She is living at his father's. Harvey I think the men ought to be careful how they use pistol, but I hope there is no one so mean as Baxter. Well Harvey, Marion says we have a good stand of corn at the river. The last replant is very good. He was there today. The cotton is coming up fine. There is a very good stand on it now. Mrs. Boen [Bowen's] wagon came Monday and got corn. They never said a word to me about pay. They told Marion you told them to go to P[eter] McCallum. I do not know how they fix as I have never seen Peter. They got 10 bushel and says they must have more. I do not think we can spare more than 10 or 12 bushel at furtherest. Harvey, Uncle Reese went to Mr. Simril and got the things you sent to us: your knit shirt, the poke, and some of your filthy bread. We tried to eat some of it as you have to live on it. I do not think you will live on it long for I think it will kill you. I am not at all surprised at you all being sick after eating that bread and drinking wiggle tails. Mother says she would strain it before she would drink the nasty things. We got some shells. You do not know how glad the children was to get them. Uncle Reese made Willy a horn of the largest one of the conks; got Andy's chain. We got two letters from you at the same time. We were glad to get them. You say you sent a coarse shirt. I have not got it yet. I expect it is at Mr. Simril. Uncle R[eece] says they say there was one there that was not marked. Your knit shirt feels like it was all sticking together. I think you had it washed with turpentine soap. I suppose you do not dirty your clothes much as if you had to cook. Your sand is so clean and nice. Some of the boys says they are eating their peck of dirt there. I will try to send you some more bread soon. Mrs. H. Mason and I is going to send together I expect. I do not know whether we can send butter or not. It is so warm I think it would melt. I would be glad to hear of you getting clear of the bowel complaint but I suppose it is best so. You might have some other worse disease. Harvey I know I am poor. I think I have enough to make me poor. I tried to look as well as I could when I got my ambrotype taken to keep you in good spirits. They said you would be at home by the 1st of June. I was afraid you would not, and from the news we get now I think it uncertain when you will, or whether you ever [will] or not. I am afraid those vessels will whip you out if you attempt to fight them. I know it looks bad to see them driving back the southern vessel but it may not always be so. I hope the Lord will provide if we are on the right side. You speak of Mr. Witherspoon praying with and for you and your family. I thought Uncle Arthur would done that too but I hear no talk of that. I am glad to hear you have a preacher to preach for you, and of your reading the Bible; if the men will quit swearing and read the Bible more. Harvey you say you afraid you will tire me of writing. You never will do that as long as I have sense to read it. I am always glad to get your letter. Harvey you seem to think that I would not want you to know if I was sick. If I were to get bad sick you would soon know it. If you live there I feel you will have to fight the Yankees there, but some people says they will try very hard to scare you out. I would be glad it was nothing more than that. Harvey, Aunt Susan told me to give you and Uncle Arthur McKinzy her best wishes. Uncle tell[s] you howdy. Willy and Bud sends howdy. Willy can spell scab very well. He is improving in spelling fast, if I could get him to stick at it. Bud is learning his letters some. I must close. Mother joins me in prayers and wishes to you. So farewell. Write often.

Achsah Wallace

Mr. S[imril] has sent home your other shirt. The Negroes sends you howdy. Write soon.

Sullivans Island
Thursday evening
May the 15th, 1861

Ever dear Wife,
I take my pen this evening to write you a few lines. Well Achsah, I can thank God I am on my feet and able to be about through the encampment. I was pretty sick from Monday night until this morning. I lay a bed all day yesterday only when I had to be out. That was pretty often. My bowels worked me down pretty weak I tell you. I had a sick stomach too, but feel this evening like I would be able for duty in a day or two again. There is several of the com[pany] that have not been able to do any duty in a week, so if I get off with two or three days I fare pretty well to what some of the [illegible]. The company is out now drilling; some dozen or so of us in the house now. Achsah I have just done as I promised, to let you know if I was sick. I don't want you to be uneasy, for I feel well enough today, only weak. This bowel complaint weakens one very quick. I have a good appetite today. I got the letter you wrote Saturday Monday evening. I looked for one today but was disappointed. Capt. Glenn is going up. He will start Friday night & get home Saturday evening. I will try and send you a letter up by him. Achsah I told Mr. Wright to get me some checked cloth for you to make me a couple of shirts. If he got the cloth you need not bother about making the shirts as I allow to try to get a furlough as soon as Capt. Glenn gets back. It looks like a long trip for such a short time but I will go home to see you as soon as I can get off. Achsah, if you or any of the family was to get bad sick and you wanted me to come home, you must send me a certificate from the doctor that they were sick and dangerous. I just write this so if any of you was bad sick you would know how to send so I could get off. It is raining some this evening. I hope it will rain plenty. Our water is getting very bad again and the sun is very hot here these days. I tell you, it tries a fellow to muster in the heat of the day. We mostly have a good breeze. If it was not for the wind, we could not stand it at all. You say you don't want me to go to Virginia. Achsah I don't intend to go unless I am oblige to go. I don't believe, nor never have,

that they could take us unless we wanted to go. They have quit talking about taking us to Virginia. Report says now we will be moved to Summerville, 20 miles above Charleston. Our men would nearly all rather stay here as go up there in the swamps. It is on the railroad. Achsah I wrote to Thomas one evening this week. I am glad that Uncle Hamilton came to see you. I suppose you would get the things I sent by Mr. Simril, and the letters too. Achsah tell Marion to keep things a moving now and don't let the weeds and grass get a start in the crop. It is easier to keep them out before they get a hold than take them out after they get root. Achsah how does Willy come on spelling? And Aaron, does he get whips enough? Pretty little Matty, I have got her in my pocket. I hope she won't forget me before I get home. Tell your Mother it would have done me lots of good this morning to have had a bowl of her thickened milk as I did not eat anything at all on yesterday. But I took some coffee and biscuit. I have a few of the sweet cakes you sent me yet, and some of the butter. Achsah, do write often. Tell Uncle Reece howdy. May God bless you all is the prayer of your husband.

Harvey

May the 15th, 1861

Achsah,
I send this for yourself. I am sorry to hear that [illegible] does not think himself able to plow or hoe either, but get along the best you can. I trust, as you say, that won't last always. And I tell you now my dear wife, if God spares me to serve my time out and get home to you, I will not bind myself down from you again. I might be willing to serve my state when needed, but I won't volunteer to leave you twelve, nor six months either. Achsah I suppose the time appears long to you. It does to me, I do assure you. You say you had not time to fix up some of your hair for me. You hoped I would come home and see it. Well, I hope so too, and will come as soon as possible. If Capt. Glenn leaves Friday night I will try to get off the next Friday night so I can go with you to preaching at Sardis[189] if God is willing, as that will be the day for our Communion. If my memory serves me right, Uncle Arthur is going up with the Capt. Only two can go at a time. Achsah I will do my best to get off again that time, but if I can't don't be disappointed. You need not tell anyone about me writing I am a coming. I will write to you as soon as I find out. I think Jenkins will let me go if he can as I have his good will. Achsah, rest assured your & Matty's ambrotypes are a great satisfaction to me. Tell the Negroes all howdy. Achsah I will take my shirts home with me and get them done up. You told me to let you know about pants. When I come home you and me will fix that. I can do until I get home. May God bless you and enable us soon to meet is my prayer.

Harvey A. Wallace

Achsah this is for no ones eye but your own. Show it to no one. You say to me in one of your letters do not forget us so soon. Well Achsah, when I forget you my loved wife, I will have lost my reason. As I often have told you, you were dearer to me than life. You feel doubly so when separated from you. Achsah you are

---

[189] The Wallace's were members of the Sardis Baptist Church.

continually in my mind. I often dream of having you in my arms, but alas, I wake to find it a dream. So don't think of me forgetting you, or of me ever doing anything, by God's help, that would give you pain. It is a great pleasure to me to know that you pray for me and think often of me, but don't fret. I trust we will soon meet to spend the balance of our days here on earth as near in peace as sinful mortals can live. Achsah you say I can get a furlough and come home. I can't yet, but if I stay here a month or so longer I will. I will get one as soon as I can. Capt. Glenn will go home in two weeks. There has been no one got a furlough only them that had sick wives. Achsah, if there is any fighting in Virginia they will take us or try. Well, I have made up my mind if they take the company, to get off if possible and go home and stay with you. I think I can get off if they try that. Sam Campbell will do the same, but don't you let no one know this. I am not going to be taken so far from you if I can help it. Write often. Your letters give me so much pleasure. I got one from Z. D. Smith since I have been here. Kiss our loved ones for me & remember me to your Mother. So farewell my dear. Your affectionate husband,

H. A. Wallace

Thursday morning
May 16, '61

My dear Wife,

As I have a chance to put still a word in, I will do so. I am well this morning; feel like I could go out and drill, but will not drill today. I find it the best way here, for one only to work when they are fully able. The comp[any] appears in good spirits this morning. We have but one man at the hospital. He will come home this morning. Well Achsah you wanted to know if we had fire places. We have but one in our house. It is not in our room. We are going to move out of our house. We are too much crowded. The Moultrie House, a large hotel, has two hundred men in it. There is plenty of room for one hundred more. We are talking about going in it. There is over one hundred rooms in it and lots of fine furniture. Achsah you never seen furniture abused like it is here. I don't want to go in the Moultrie House much. There is such a crowd there and they have abused the house so. Why Achsah, the men have went in the rooms they don't live in and held themselves out in fine rooms with a fine pair of drawers, wash stand, and looking glass to every room. There was nothing in the house we are in but a few fine bedsteads and two or three fine tables. As I am writing, some of the boys have a fat piece of middling on a fine falling leaf table just scoring through, cutting it up. The boys raked around after we came here and hunted chairs in other houses. I give one of them ten cents for a fine cane bottom rocking chair. It is a splendid chair worth 6 or 8 dollars. We have three fine rocking chairs in our room. Achsah, tell Willy he just ought to be here a little while to hear them hollering right-left. Write soon, write often. This morning looks like rain again. So farewell my loved wife for the present. May God bless you.

H. A. Wallace

C[lay] Hill
May the 16th, 1861

Dear Harvey,
I take my pen to drop you a few lines as I have a chance to send you a few biscuit in your Mother['s] box. I send you four or five doz. in a poke, if they can put them in. I expect to send you some soon as I can get something to send the provision in. Your Father was here this morning. He said he would fetch me a box from York. I don't know whether it is worthwhile to try to send you any butter or not as it is so hot, but I will try, as you must be glad to get something from home. I would be glad you could get a mess of boiled dinner or milk and mush at home, but I fear you never will, as you will be sure to have to fight. Harvey I want you to save yourself for my sake and the children as you ask me to. The children talk about you a great deal. Bud still cries about you be gone so far and so long. He says he knows you would come home like a good boy if the mans would let you. Willy says he don't know how you can eat that mean old bread. He want me to send you lots of bread and not let you have none of their old bread. We hear there is a great deal of sickness on Morris Island, and some deaths. I fear you will be very sickly there. I would like you to come home if you get sick. Harvey I am glad and sorry too to hear you think so much of the ambrotypes. I [have] no doubt you will keep it. I think as much of yours. We all take a look at it once and a while and shed a few tears over them, and kiss them and put them by. You old one is much the best picture. I sent Martha mine and Sissy on oil cloth. I do not know whether she will ever get it or not as they are blockading the sea coasts. Harvey I do not spell my words right every time but I think you can understand them and that will do, for sometimes I am in a hurry. We are all well but the children, black and white. The white ones is playing about, but cross and ill the black is. Frank and Adline[190] is not well. They are all wormy. I must give them something. Harvey, the bull is got very bad to jump. Marion worked on him today. I wish you could sell him down there. He is in very good order. The hogs is

---

[190] A slave child

beginning to thrive. They look very well. The filly's eye, one of them, looks very good. The other is not much sore but is still blue. They does not work her any. Marion, when he works, he hoes. He say it hurts him to plow. They are plowing and hoeing the corn. They have harrowed and chopped the cotton. We have a very good stands of corn and cotton, and some weeds at the river. They will go there next week. Marion says he don't know whether to plow it out or throw four furrows and come home and work the cotton. We tell him to work the cotton and then he can go back and finish. Nothing more but my love.

A. Wallace

Written upside down on the first page:
Harvey I have 40 envelopes Uncle Rease got for me. This is some of my hair.

Sullivans Island
Friday morning
The 17th of May, 1861

My dear Wife,
I have taken my pen to answer your kind and heartsome letter of last Sabbath evening, which I received last evening. Achsah it cheers me up to get a long letter from you, particularly when it says all is well, even if it does not give a favorable account of the crop prospects. You said in your last you supposed I would be tired trying to read your letter. Achsah don't let that thought ever enter your head. I never get one of your letters that I do not read three or four times before I put it away. Achsah you speak of wanting to know about some things such as buying the boys hats, Edd shoes, & so on. Anything the boys need, get. Edd can do without shoes this summer. You asked me something about the corn. Mr. Henry got you done right if he was not willing to give his note with interest at one dollar per bushel. I don't want him to get the corn. Achsah, let no more go only what Col. Bone [Bowen] wants until I come home. I don't want to be scarce. My dear wife, I think you took me up wrong about going to Virginia. I think I always wrote to you that I would not go unless I was compelled to go. I never thought they could compel us to go, but I know now they can't. I always thought it my duty to my family not to leave So. Ca., but I did ask your advice about it, saying to you at the same time I would not go unless compelled. So give yourself no uneasiness about me going to Virginia. Achsah I have had the perfect trots since late last evening. My stomach has got very weak and we have nothing fit for a weak stomach to eat. It turns down on my bowels. I thought on yesterday evening I would go to drilling this morning, but I find I am not able to do it. Jenkins says I must not drill until I get stout. I think I will be stout as ever in a few days so you need not be uneasy. Well Achsah, we have had the greatest excitement in camp since five o'clock on last evening. The word come over from Charleston by W. C. Black[191] that the Governor had ordered us to be paid off today and sent home in two

---

[191] Unidentified

or three days to stay until we are called here to fight if the enemy come. The whole reg[iment] is on tiptoe to be off for home, but some of the officers are trying to get it fixed to keep us here, half of the reg[iment] at a time, but I don't think they will get it done. I think we will all be sent home some time next week unless the Yankees send an army around here, or we get word they are going to do it. I have the Col. promise this morning that me, G. W. Mason, & Col. Bone [Bowen] will get a furlough of a week against next Friday, so I will try to come whether we get off by that time or not. Achsah I just tell you, Mason is the greatest stake we have in the whole comp[any] sure. He has done lots for the comp[any]. Achsah I am truly glad that you put your trust in God for your protection and that you pray for me. For a soldier's life is a life of trials, but I do think a Christian soldier in camp has a great chance to do good by word and example. Tell Marion to keep everything a moving; not let the crop stand to get dirty. Work it often. Keep it perfectly clean. Achsah you know it would do me good to see wheat, corn, or cotton growing. We don't see scarcely a tree but the palmetto. I send you a palmetto limb by Capt. Glenn. I send you a little conk shell that was give to me. Achsah I have a beautiful walking stick. I will keep it until I come myself. I will send you a cannonball by Capt. Glenn, one that Anderson fired. My love to all of the family and neighbors. Write when you get this. I will write to you again and tell you when to send to York to meet me. May God bless you my dear wife. So farewell. May God bless and protect you, and enable us soon to meet is my prayer.

H. A. Wallace, 1st Lieut. of Com[pany] H

Sullivans Island
Sunday morning
6 o'clock
May the 19, 1861

My well beloved Wife,
I this Sabbath morning turn my thought to you and the pleasures of home. I can say to you this morning I have entirely got well. I feel very well this morning. The company is generally pretty well. There is no one that cannot go about now in the company, and fewer new cases of diarrhea. Well Achsah, I have got no letter from you since last Sunday evening. That is the time the last that I got from you was written. But I trust all is well, and I know you have the children to bother you when you want to write. I have no doubt you write to me as often as you can. Well, it does me lots of good to get one. I got one from Father Friday, and one from Z. D. Smith. Both very welcome visitors, but you know there is no letter comes to me can afford me the satisfaction one from you does. Achsah we have been in great excitement about going home. The Governor was about to send us home. President Davis has interfered and the order is countermanded so we will not get home. Col. Jenkins has treated us very bad in this. He kept it hid from us about the Gov. going to send us home and tried to get us to vote asking the Gov. to keep us here. We all believe that it is through his influence that we have to stay. I tell you my wife, some of the companies are down on him sure. The Spartanburg Rifles[192], it is said, have determined to go home next week. That is one of our rifle companies. They are going home to go to Virginia. There is some of the other companies that are ready for a most anything. If Jenkins don't come out and explain things and make them plain, the reg[iment] is not going to do no good. He has lost all the confidence of the men. He has showed them he had no confidence in them. I don't believe if Jenkins was to put it to vote

---

[192] The Spartan Rifles (Company-K, 5th S. C. Infantry) were organized in Spartanburg District, S. C. under the command of Captain Joseph Walker. Baldwin, 41&59.

today to go home or stay, and he would tell the men they were not needed and if they voted to go home they could go, they would vote for it. He has been trying to deceive us all the time, and the men would think he was trying to deceive them. Achsah you need not show this or say anything about what I write about Jenkins. It don't become me to write about him and I trust to be with you shortly and then I can tell you all about it. Mason, Col. Bone [Bowen], & me have the promise of getting off next Friday if these others get back in time, if we are not about moving some other place. Jenkins says we will be somewhere on the coast of our state but he don't think we will get to stay here. Achsah I will have to come to a close. My love to all; to your Mother and our dear little in particular. I trust you may spend a peaceable Sabbath today and sometimes think of your husband, who would like the best of all things spend it with you. You asked me if we got the York Enquirer. We do. Farewell my beloved wife. May God's choicest blessings rest on you all is the prayer of your husband.

H. A. Wallace

York D.
Sunday morning
May the 19, 1861

Dear Harvey,
I drop you a few lines this morning to inform you we are all well this morning, thank God, and hope these few lines may find you enjoying the same great blessing. We received your most welcome letter last evening. Was glad to get it as I had not got any since Tuesday. I was afraid you was sick, as you were. You said you had been unwell with your bowels in your last before this. Harvey it gives me great satisfaction for you to be candid in telling me whether you are sick or not as I would be uneasy if you were not to tell me. I will assure you, I will be the same with you. I do not want you to muster unless you are perfectly well, for your bowels are so easy deranged and it is so very hot there. I am sorry you have no good water as I think it is the greatest blessing we have on earth. Well Harvey, we allowed to went to preaching today but it is raining and we shant go. I thought we would stop and see Glen but Uncle Rease will go down for me and get the letter, for I am always glad to get one from you. We got a letter from Thomas and Martha yesterday evening. They are all well. They have been to Duncan's that week they wrote. They wrote April the 28. Duncan's people and William's were all well. They have good gardens. They have peas nearly fit for use, and lots of beans blooms and plenty of fruit. Their crops looks fine. He has plowed his upland corn and hoed it over; is boring his cotton and thinning it. He says he has ten acres of cotton to plant. They had got our letters the evening before they wrote, and your ambrotype. The children knew it and the tears ran down Jimmy's[193] cheeks when he saw it. William had got Fair's[194]. Thomas says there is exciting times there now. There is a call for three thousand men. He does not know how they are getting along; whether they will have to be drafted or not. He say it is a trying

---

[193] James McCallum, child of Duncan and Matilda Jane (Wood) McCallum
[194] Samuel Fair Campbell, child of Samuel L. and Rebecca (Wallace) Campbell

time and the North will have some hard fighting to do before they whip the South. I thought I would not send you the letter as you spoke of coming home so soon, which I hope you will. Who is coming with you? You must be sure to tell us whether you are coming or not, as I will know when to send for you. The corn looks very well; is beginning to grow, and cotton look just middling. Uncle D. Horsly[195] came down a Friday. He and wife went fishing but never caught nothing. Uncle D. is at Cousin Nelly's; will be here this evening. Harvey I do not know what sort of men you have to abuse a house that way. I think the head officers ought not to allow of that. I think you have a rough, dirty set of men. I think it would be a hard place for a Christian to live, right there where there is all kind of wickedness. As you say, there is none of your profession there. I thought there would be some from Rock Hill or Kings Mountain. I suppose you have to keep quiet. Well, it is as good plan as any; not have hard feelings and set good example, as you say, in camp.

[Remainder of letter missing]

---

[195] David Richard Horsley of Gastonia, N. C. was previously married to Matilda Wood's sister, Rachel (Mayhew) Horsley (1782-c.1856). His wife at the time of this letter is unidentified.

Sullivans Island
May the 20th, 1861

My beloved Wife,
I this evening commence the pleasant task of answering your kind and affectionate letter of the 15th, which came to hand last evening. I tell you, it was a treat. I had not got one from you only one this week that was written on the Sunday before. Achsah I am pretty well again. I have been mustering twice today. My bowels have been running off some today but I am quite well otherways. If I only was at home a few days to get something good to eat, I feel like I would be as stout as ever in a few days. The health of the company is getting better. Mason has not been well for several days. He is threaten[ed] with diarrhea. There is none of the company now but what is able to be up and about. But it takes men the longest time to get over this bowel disease that you ever seen. We have men that have not been able to muster in two weeks only a day or so at a time. I think it is the provisions as well as the water. About the time we begin to get strength, the bowels get wrong again. Your Mother says to strain the water. I tell you, when one is right dry they don't mind wiggle tails. I can just shut my eyes and go them sure. Achsah I have been out drilling the three o'clock drill since I wrote the other page. It is now four. At five we have officer's battalion drill one hour. We have moved our company today into new quarters. We now have two houses, one on each side of the street. We have only six in the room now. We have been too much crowded all the time. We have fine houses. The room us officers are in has a fireplace, a splendid sideboard, mahogany, a settee carpeted over the floor, two cupboards for our trunks, and we have a room below for to cook and eat in; fireplace in it. Mason's mess cooks there too. There is a large double table in the lower room to eat on. We won't have so many flies for a while. The house we came out of, the flies there was as thick as bees. They are very bad on this island. Anyhow, I think we will do better here. We were too thick to have health where we were before. I am glad to hear of the corn and cotton looking well. It would do my eyes good to see corn and cotton growing, and to see the trees. I reckon the leaves are full grown. We don't see nothing

here but sand, palmetto trees, and other shrubs. Achsah, I reckon Capt. Glenn, & Uncle Arthur, and Huddleston are enjoying the pleasures of home. Well, I hope to be with you in a week, if God is willing, a few days. Our camp appears pretty quiet today. The men have all found out there is no use to think about going home, as the Gov[ernor] says he never had any idea of sending us home; that it was all a mistake. I expect we will be moved from this island in the course of a week but have no idea where. They intend to let all the volunteers that want go to Virginia. I don't think there is many men in this reg[iment] that will go. Our company, won't none of them go. We will be kept in this state to defend this state. You need not fear about me going to Virginia. I never had any notion of going so far from you without I was oblige to. Now I know they won't make us go. Achsah it does me good to find you are so glad to read my letters. I know some of them are hard to read, for I have been writing in all kinds of places. I know it is hard for you to have to write so much, but if you knew how glad I was to get your letters, you would like to write. I enjoy myself better reading your letters and writing to you than anything I do. Achsah I suppose our men have been too hard on our Colonel. I don't want you to say anything about what I write about him as he is abused enough anyhow. He is powerfully hurt about them talking about him so. I think if the men don't get better satisfied, he will resign his commission. He has always treated me well and friendly. I am glad to hear of Willy learning to spell. Tell Bud to learn his letters. How is sweet little Matty doing? She looks so pretty on your new coat: low shoulders, short sleeves; so much lace around the body and sleeves; her beads, and her hair parted so nice. Kiss her for me. Learn her to say Pa. We are looking for a box, but if you have not sent before you get this you need not send until I get home. For when you send, I would like to be here. Butter looks prime that comes here from home. John Barry[196] got a box today with provisions and lots of butter. He gave

---

[196] 3rd Sergeant John Henderson Barry (8/10/1833-11/5/1915), son of William A. and Eliza (Watson) Barry, voted to go to Virginia with the regiment in June 1861. Barry served as Color Sergeant and 2nd Lieutenant of Co.-B after the 5th Regiment was re-organized in April 1862.

me a tin keeper full of butter. We all divide anything we get around. Tell your Mother, when I get home I hope she will be able to have some cherry pie. Tell Uncle Reece to try and raise some watermelons. I hope, if God spares me, to help to eat them. Tell Marion it would do him good to see us Catawba boys handling our guns now. Tell the Negroes all howdy. Tell Add I reckon he will raise some good watermelons for me. Tell Andy his watch keeps very good time, but if I was going home I would not expect to get $15.00 for it. Tell Cinth I want her to have good Irish potatoes so when I get home I can have one mess. Achsah I have been out drilling again. We take it one hour at a time. I feel quite well this evening. Saml. Campbell is complaining of his bowels this evening. Him and Mason has held up all the time, but their time to trot has come now. John is quite well again. Brother Sam is not well today. Robbison [Robertson] & Tommy[197] & John Cullender are all well. Tell Mrs. Cullender John looks well and is always ready for his duty. He has no trouble in getting along with anybody. Achsah write often. May God bless you all is the prayer of your affectionate husband.

Harvey A. Wallace

---

[197] Private Thomas J. Huddleston

May 20, [1861]

Achsah,
I will start you a letter every day until I know when I can get off if I get time. I don't know whether I will get off until the Capt. gets back or not. I allow to try to get off Friday night whether he comes or not. I will find out in time to send you word so you can send to York to meet me. I will quit tonight as [it] is getting dark.

Tuesday morning, the 21st

Well Achsah, I have spent another night on this island. I feel quite well this morning. [I] hear of no complaints in our house this morning except Mason. He is quite unwell, but I hope will improve like the rest in a day or so. S[amuel] Campbell is not complaining this morning. We have had two fine rains last night; will keep our cisterns filled up. May God bless you my dear wife.

H.A. Wallace

Sullivans Island
Wednesday evening
May the 22nd, 1861

My dear Wife,
I with pleasure have taken my pen to answer your kind and satisfactory letter of Sunday, which I got this evening. I was truly glad to hear of you all being as well as you were. I am quite well again, thank God. I have been very well since Sunday. I have been doing nearly all of the drilling myself, as Campbell & Thompson have both been unwell. Campbell is on guard duty today. Our company is in good spirits and pretty good health. Mason is still sick. He has been very sick but is considerably better this evening. I have no doubt will be up in a day or two. He was very bilious, but took some medicine that has worked him very well today. Achsah we have splendid quarters now. We have plenty of room, good chairs, tables, and everything. I think the men will have better health now. Pendle Anderson left for home this evening. He got a letter stating that his child was very bad. I went to the Col. and got him a furlough. I do hope his child may have got better. You did not say whether Capt. Glenn's wife[198] had been confined or not. Achsah I can't say to you whether I can get off or not this week. I hardly will get off before Monday or Tuesday. The Col. told me this evening he could not let more than one commissioned officer leave a comp[any] at once, but he would try and let me off if Glenn stayed long. I suppose we will hardly come this week. I won't go until Mason gets well enough to go. He says he thinks we will wait until Monday or Tuesday. I am going to try hard to get a furlough for ten days when I go. I feel very anxious to go. The time appears long since I have been thinking of going, but if I don't get off until next week, I will have the longer to stay then. Tell Willy and Aaron to be good boys. Their Pa will get home before long if it is God's will. Tell your Mother that I would have give nearly anything last week to had her to made me some sweet milk mush, but I could not get it. I was weak; had nothing I could eat. We got some Irish potatoes; last years crop. I roasted them three times a day. I can eat anything

---

[198] Mrs. E. L. Glenn (c.1839-?)

this week. John got his provisions last evening. I got the poke you sent. Sam Campbell got a jar of butter & a poke of biscuit. I tell you, we are living high now on biscuit and butter. Why Achsah, butter comes here as hard and firm as if it was winter. If you have not sent me no more provisions before you get this you need not send me any, for I want to be here when you send. We will live lots better here anyhow. We have a good place to cook; not in the sand where the wind was always blowing the sand in everything. Sam Campbell got a little flour. We had a big mess of fritters and molasses & butter this morning. The boys are all doing fine. They are in good spirits, and I have not much trouble no way with them. They are a little rude, but we might expect that. Give my love to Cousin Nelly's people and all enquiring friends. Tell the Negroes all howdy. I am sorry you are not going to write no more. I will think it a [illegible] time to be without a letter until [illegible].

H. A. Wallace

May the 23, [1861]
Sunrise

Dear Wife,
I this morning continue to write you a few lines before our mail leaves. It leaves every morning at eight. Well, the Col. was up to see Mason last night. He told me he would give me the Governor's orders this morning calling for eight thousand volunteers for Virginia. The Gov. is to review and inspect us today. I don't know whether they will try us today to see if we will volunteer to go or not, but we will be sure to have the trial today or tomorrow one. Achsah, if I was a single man I would be right off for Virginia, but as it is, I feel my duty is to stay in my own state where you and my little children are. So you need have no fears for me going. I have no doubt but some of our company will go. I had thought they would not, but when they hear of fighting, that is where they want to be. I feel quite well this morning. Mason is still unwell this morning but better than he was on yesterday morning. Achsah I had the pleasure of being home with you and the children in a dream last night but waked up to find it all imagination. This morning is quite cold here. In fact, a person can lie wrapped up in a blanket every night here. Achsah you need not show this letter to everyone, as I write things to you I am not at liberty to tell in camp. The camp is now parading. I must stop and go and drill. I will drop you a line more when I get through. Achsah, we will be called on in a few days to volunteer to go to Virginia. None of our company will go. Some of the companies in the reg[iment] may go. Our Col. is doing his best now to get the Governor to let him move us up to Ebenezer[199] and camp there this summer. If everything had have kept quiet for two or three weeks I think we would have got up there, but the telegraph brings news that they are fighting right away in Virginia today[200]. So there

---

[199] The Ebenezer community is located in eastern York District near Rock Hill.

[200] Virginia citizens voted to secede from the Union on this day, but no major military action occurred in the state. This reference may be to a reconnaissance by Federal troops under General Benjamin Butler from Fort Monroe toward Hampton, Va. E.B. Long, 77.

is no telling whether we will get to leave this place or not. They have oblige to keep some volunteers on this island. Our reg[iment] is all the vol[unteers] that is on this island. They are bringing in 30 or 40 Regulars every day or so. I can't have any idea these times what we may have to do in a day or two ahead. Achsah I give you a few more lines. Mason is considerably better this morning. He will be up by this evening or morning. The doctor says he might start home by tomorrow evening, but him and me want to go together. He says he won't leave me. I can't get off before Monday or Tuesday so I would not leave him either, & I think now we will leave here Monday or Tuesday night but I will write to you and let you know every day or so. I am very sorry you will not write this week. I will feel lost to get no letters from you. I hope Capt. Glenn will get back by Monday. If he don't, I will try to get off by Tuesday anyway. May God bless and protect you my dear wife is my prayer. Kiss the children for me. So farewell. I hope we may soon meet face. Tell Marion I hope to see a pretty crop, and clean. Achsah please send the within to Mrs. Mason.

H. A. Wallace

Clay Hill, S.C.
May 23, '61

Dear friend,
I take my pen in hand to acknowledge the receipt of your kind favor, which came to hand yesterday evening. It found us well and anxious to hear from you, a little more so than common, if possible. We had heard by Capt. Glenn that there was some probability of you all returning home. And on Tuesday evening, which is always our largest mails, we received no letters at all from Charleston and there was a great many conjectures with what the cause was. We was expecting to hear when you would be home but was disappointed and remained very anxious until yesterday evening, when our hopes was blasted by the news that there was no prospect of you getting off. I understand your Col. do not want you to be dismiss and turn out of employment without anything to eat. I think if we have a few more rains that we could find employment for you, and probably something to eat too. You state that you had not been well, which made me sorry & glad both. Sorry to hear of you being sick and glad to hear of you getting better. From what I hear, you generally get a receipt when you get well, (that is, do not have the second attack). I am in hopes you may get one. Very sorry to hear yesterday evening that G.M.[George Mason] was sick. I am in hopes I will hear this evening that he is better. You say you & him is talking of coming home as soon as Capt. Glenn returns. Rest assured, you will be received by us all as welcome visitors, and we will churn & kill a chicken if you come. I would much rather you could have come to stay, but will be glad to see you on a visit. I hear that there is some talk of not allowing your friends to visit you. If that should be the case it will be bad. I fear your Col. is not just what we might wish him to be. I am in hopes I may be mistaken. We have heard a good many lies on him which we do not believe, but we are beginning to censure him now. John Timberlake returned home [illegible] evening. John was very near done out when he arrived; is improving some but very slow; has no appetite. John has got his fill of a soldier's life. I called at your home this morning a little while. Found all well and in very good spirits. The neighbors is all well

and we are doing the best we can. We have singular weather. It has been almost cold enough for frost the two or three last mornings. We had beautiful rains and they have always come in good time, but after every rain it is cold and windy; has been very difficult to get good stands, but I do not hear much complaint now. Cotton has got up very well when the seed was good. My seed was not good. I ploughed up about 45 acres; planted about 15 over in cotton and the balance in corn. I did [illegible] plough up any on the place I got from you but have a bad stand. Corn is trying to grow some but it is too cold for cotton. Wheat crops is pretty fair but is with rust. It is [illegible]. It is gratifying to all the friends of the Catawbas to hear and be assured that they have gain such a noble reputation as to be considered the nicest, best behave comp[any] on the island. And it also is a pleasure to me to hear that nobody of the comp[any] had either been drunk or in the guard house since you have been in camp. Such good conduct speaks much for them. It shows that they did not volunteer for the frolics, but to defend their country. It shows that the comp[any] is composed of men who has respect for themselves, and such men can be relied on in any emergency. Such men will, (I am satisfied), never be seen to turn their back to an enemy while there is any strength in them to resist. I am in hopes that no one of the Catawbas may ever be put under guard or overcome by intoxication. Such a victory would be more honorable than the taking of Fort Sumter. Give my respects to all the boys, and if you should not get home as you expect write soon. I remain your friend.

T.L. Patton

Sullivans Island
Friday night
May the 24, 1861

My dear Wife,
I this night have taken my pen to write you a few lines to let you know how we are getting on. I am well and hearty this week, able for my duty all of the time. The health of the company is pretty good. Mason is still quite sick. He was considerably better, but he spent quite a sick day yesterday and last night. He was very bilious & taking medicine. He is better this evening. Calhoun Stewart[201] is quite sick today too. The rest of the company are all up. Achsah I trust to God these lines may find you all enjoying the same great blessing. Achsah we had a hard days work yesterday. We drilled one hour before breakfast; went out at nine; stayed out until half past ten; called out again at eleven without dinner; stayed on duty until three. The Governor and Adjutant General reviewed us and the Regulars together. There was from 2000 to 2500 men in a line on the beach. It [is] as level as the floor and as smooth too; two fine bands of music; the guns all new and bright; the men all in full uniform. You know it was a pretty sight. The Governor give us great praise. I had the honor of leading the Catawbas by in review. Achsah, we are called on now to volunteer our services to the Confederate States. They gave us lists to enroll our names. We have until Sunday at ten o'clock to report our companies. Eight of the companies have volunteered. Our company has not moved yet. A good many of our boys are anxious to volunteer. A good many say they will go whether the company go or not. Achsah I am placed in a tight place. The boys all want me to head the list. The Col. wants me to head it, but my duty to you and my little children will not let me. Nothing else keeps me from volunteering but my duty to you. The companies that volunteer will be sent home to fill up their ranks. I think they will start home by Monday or Tuesday. I don't know what they will do with us that don't volunteer. Some say one

---

[201] 3rd Corporal James Calhoun Stewart (c.1840-1879), son of James M. and Margaret (Rooker) Stewart

thing, some another. We can't tell until ordered. I suppose you will be looking for me home tomorrow evening but I could not get off. I have a hope of getting off Monday or Tuesday on furlough if this volunteering don't interfere. I don't want to leave until Mason gets able to go, so you must excuse me. I would like as well to be at home as you possibly can to see me at home. Achsah I hope Capt. Glenn will be back in a day or two and then I will stand a better chance to get off. I don't much fancy staying here all summer. Our company may go into it tomorrow if the men all go into it pretty generally. I may get home, though I can have no idea what they will do with us that don't go. I have got tired of the flies. They are as thick as bees where we eat. We are looking for Uncle Arthur & Huddleston back tomorrow. May God bless you my dear wife.

H. A. Wallace

May the 25
In the morning

Well Achsah, I send you a few lines this morning to let you know how we are. I feel very well this morning. I think Mason easier but sick yet. I hope now he will be able to go home by Monday night; that is, start. If he does, I will come with him if I can get off. Some of our boys are going around with a paper this morning to get vol[unteers] for Virginia. The boys pull at me lots but I can't go into it. You need not be uneasy. I have give you my word to not. I will not. Farewell my beloved wife. May God bless you is my prayer.

H.A. Wallace

Rusk County, Texas
May the 26, 1861

Dear brother,
I seat myself to drop you a few lines in answer to your kind favor of May the 5, which came to hand three days ago. We are always glad to hear from you, and particular at this time. We were sorry to hear of you being so unwell but hope you have got better before this time. Our family is all well except the little Negro, Dave. He has been unwell for a week but is still able to be about a part of the time. I think he will get along without a doctor. Harvy, the health of this neighborhood is good, but there is some sickness in other neighborhood. There is some cases of sickness in James A.[202] neighborhood. I heard from his family. He had a chill yesterday, and Margaret Ann[203] had been sick. They thought she had the fever. William[204] and family are well. I have not heard from Duncan's[205] for some time. They were well the last account. Brother Jo[206] was up last week at [Mount] Enterprise to attend a Masonic meeting. He did not come out to see us. Jo is a great curiosity. He has been at Enterprise twice since he left and never came to see none of us. He stayed two or three days each time. The last time he came on Thursday and left Enterprise the next morning and came back Saturday night. They say he went to see a young lady that had went to school at Enterprise by the name of Brown. Well Harvy, I see from what you write you don't fancy a soldier's life much. I know a encampment is a confining business and so much hard drilling very tiresome, but you boys have got your hands into it and you will have to bear with it. I think our cause is a just one and it is our duty to have our rights; have them at all hazard, let it cost what it may. Harvy I know it was a hard trial for you to part with Achsah and the children, but I am in hopes, if it is the Lord's will, you will be spared to get back to your family, and we may have peace and harmony in

---

[202] James Adams Wallace
[203] Margaret Ann Wallace, child of James A. and Margaret E. (Faris) Wallace
[204] William Marcellus Wallace
[205] Harvey's brother-in-law, Duncan A. McCallum
[206] Joseph Franklin Wallace

our land, and our rights. Harvy they can raise volunteers in Texas without much trouble. They have raised two fine companies in Henderson. One of them has been gone some time and the other holds themselves in readiness. I have no notion of volunteering yet. I am very anxious to make a crop this year if it is the Lord's will. I did not make anything last year hardly and it has cost us a great deal to live. The wheat crop is cut and very fine. It is generally thought that wheat won't bring more than twenty five cents per bushel out in western Texas. I don't think it will bring more than fifty cents per bushel here again. It is put out. People has had to feed a great deal of it to their horses, but oats will soon be ripe. They are fine, and barley and rye. My wheat is light; sowed late. The late wheat is all light but the early the finest I ever seen. The late seem like it would be good too but it just dried up and got ripe nearly as soon as the early. The corn and cotton is small here for the time of year. We have had so much rain, a part of our land has never been in good plow season this year; too wet all the time. There is a good deal of corn laid by. I shall gave you a history of my crop. I have not laid by any of my corn yet but expect to come this week. My upland corn is large enough to lay by. My bottoms have been overflowed three times since they were planted. Some places washed away. I have got them all bared off and replanted and have commenced to throw the dirt to them. They will make me a fine chance of corn if they get a little more rain and we don't have no more frosts. My early cotton has begun to grow. It is began to make squares. The last cotton I planted is pretty young cotton. I have not worked it yet. The people here plant cotton here pretty much when it suits them; plant some in March and April, and till June. They say the late one have had a busy time of it since we planted; have too much crop for our force. We work about sixty acres of crop. Aunt Oliva McCarter[207] says for you tell David[208] they are all well and she wants to hear from him. She says she wants you always to mention his name in

---
[207] Elizabeth O. (Patrick) McCarter and her husband, Elias, settled in the Minden community of Rusk County after leaving York District. Kinship ties with the Wallace family could not be determined.
[208] Private David A. McCarter (c. 1838-6/15/1861), son of Elias and Elizabeth O. McCarter, died of disease at Charlottesville, Va. while serving with the Catawba Company.

your letters so she can hear whether he is well or not. She is very anxious to hear. She has the reading of all the letters we get. When she gets one she sends it here and we get the reading of it. Martha got a letter from Achsah the same date of the last you wrote. She said they were all well. She sent her ambrotype and the baby's. It is a beautiful child. We think it favors our Achsah very much. Harvy I want you to tell John and Sam to be sure to write to me and give the news. I want to know how they like a soldier's life. Achsah said Rebecca stayed at night at Father's. She was afraid to stay at night; Fair[209] had the croup so bad. I got a letter from Father some time ago. He spoke like he had a notion of moving to this country to live and he wanted our advice about it. I wrote to him I thought he could do better here than he can do there. As for my own part, I would rather risk the chance here than back there. I like Texas a great deal better than South Carolina; that is, rather live here. Achsah says you have Marion Wood living with you. Harvy, we live a long way behind the times here. It is from ten to twelve days before we get the news from them old states. Harvy, from the way Achsah writes, she bears up with parting with you a great deal better than I thought she could. Be sure to write often and gave us the news. We are so anxious to hear from you all. Harvy we live fine this year; have plenty of everything to live upon; have a fine garden; have peas, and beans, and Irish potatoes; any amount of them; have had huckleberry tart every day for three weeks and there is plenty of them yet. There is a fine crop of fruit of all kinds here this year. I have a fine peach orchard and a good many apple trees. They are loaded with fruit. Our children grow fast and have good health. Hope[210] has fine health and grows fast. He stays in the field a heap and hoes all the time if he can get a hoe. Harvy I must close. May God bless you and protect you.

Thos. S. Wallace

---

[209] Samuel Fair Campbell was the child of Samuel and Rebecca (Wallace) Campbell

[210] Stanhope E. Wallace was the third child of Thomas Stanhope and Martha C. (Wood) Wallace.

Sullivans Island
May the 26, 1861

My dear Wife,
I this Sabbath day do drop you a few lines to let you know how we fare in this unfriendly world. I am well. Thank God for His mercies. I trust to God you are all enjoying a like blessing. Achsah I am sorry to inform you that our esteemed friend, Mason, is seriously bad[211]. I fear for him. He is getting low and no turn for the better. Achsah I would be so glad his wife[212] was here. I feel for her. I trust she will get word this evening & come as soon as possible, as we send a telegram today to Adams & McCorkles to her. Achsah we have been deceived he was getting better. I have been uneasy the last two days. When I wrote on yesterday, I thought him better. [illegible] told me what to write. I hope his wife will be here by Tuesday. Mr. Wright came down this morning. He told me he seen Uncle Reece Thursday; that you were all well. The balance of the company are well except Calhoun Stewart is sick, but not serious.

[Remainder of letter missing]

---

[211] 6th Corporal George Washington Mason died at Columbia, S. C. on May 30, 1861 while enroute back to York District. The Yorkville Enquirer reported that his remains arrived at the depot and were escorted through Yorkville by a detachment of the Catawba Light Infantry, the Kings Mountain Cadets, and the Jasper Light Infantry. *Yorkville Enquirer*, June 6, 1861.

[212] Nancy Hannah (Stowe) Mason

At home
Evening
May the 28th, 1861

Well Samuell[213], I drop you a few lines. I landed safe home before sunset last evening. Found all well and glad to see me. Saw the neighbors at Clay Hill; anxious to hear from the volunteers, Father amongst them. He said all was well. Achsah and me are going there tomorrow. The volunteers landed at York this evening[214]. They had a big supper ready there for them. Crops are small but stands good. Wheat looks well. May wheat will be to cut next week. People are generally well. Samuell, I want you to attend to my interest in camp if you are organized before I come. I will be there by Monday morning, or that is my calculature now. Tell the boys to keep up in good spirits. I will stick to them. Tell James Stewart I have seen his Father and Mother. They are well. Do the best you can. Let us have our rights or try. My best respects to all the boys. Tell them it is a great pleasure to me to have the old woman by my side and the little fellows at my knee. My love. So farewell.

H. A. Wallace
1st Lieut. of the Reserve of Comp[any] H on Sullivans Island

---

[213] 2nd Lieutenant Samuel Campbell

[214] About three-fourths (900) of the volunteers of the 5th S. C. Infantry voted to convert their state enlistments to enlistments in the Confederate Provisional Army. They were given five days furlough and then mustered into service at Orangeburg, S. C. on June 4, 1861. The regiment left by train for Virginia the following day. Those who voted not to go to Virginia were kept on Sullivans Island in reserve status until the middle of June, when they were disbanded and discharged by Governor Pickens. *The Yorkville Enquirer*, June 13, 1861 and Baldwin, 45-46.

Sullivans Island
June the 4th, 1861

My dear Wife,
I drop you a few lines. I landed safe on my island home half past seven this morning, having good luck coming down. I landed at Charleston at ten o'clock last night; took the omnibus[215]; went to the Pavilion Hotel; went to bed; got up this morning feeling refreshed. I found the company all well. John Divinny[216] has got able to be up. He has been bad. The doctors that attended him visited him four times a day. The company thinks the world of them. They were so kind and attentive to him. There is several cases of typhoid fever amongst the Regulars. One of them is buried today. He died with typhoid fever. The boys all appeared rejoiced to see me. They are just fishing and knocking about; don't parade but once a day; have not been throwed into companies yet. The Governor has told them that he would have us organized against Wednesday, so I can't tell you what we have to do yet. They have drawn their provision from the Regulars. I have not the least idea of what they will do with us. I seen Brother Sam at Orangeburg; just spoke to him as I passed. Capt. Glenn goes up there to see them tonight and to come back with Sam, Bob Choat[217], & Chesly Wood[218]. I can see one [of] Abraham's vessels very plainly today. The boys are making sport of her. Augustice says he is going to get a boat this evening and take

---

[215] A long, four-wheeled carriage with seats running lengthwise used to convey passengers short distances.
[216] Private John McFarland Divinney (12/15/1847-12/21/1910), son of Aaron and Rachel Divinney, was the company fifer.
[217] Private Robert Walker Choate (c.1838-5/21/1864), son of Augustine and Dorcas (Garrison) Choate, enlisted as a private in Company-B, 13th N. C. Infantry after being discharged in June 1861. He died at home of wounds received at an unlisted place or date.
[218] Private Chesley G. Wood (c.1838-6/30/1862) decided to volunteer for Virginia. He was wounded severely in the head on June 30, 1862 during the Battle of Frayser's Farm and died later that day. No direct relationship to the Wallaces could be established.

the Yankees out some ice to put in their water, so you may guess they don't bother us bad. It is very hot here today. I tell you, this water tastes bad after being at home, but I will soon get used to it. Sam Campbell and John Barnes met me at the wharf this morning. Samuel is going up home as soon as we know what they are going to do with us, probably by Friday. Achsah it cost me $4.62 as railroad fare, 50 cents for omnibus to the hotel, 50 cents for the bed, 25 cents to get my trunk to the boat; $5.87 cts. Mr. East[219] come down from Orangeburg with me to Charleston last night. Achsah don't fret yourself about me. I intend to take as good care of myself as I can. We must trust to God for protection. I will go back and see you again if I am spared as soon as I can. You know it injures one for to fret. Besides, it is wrong, for we ought to submit cheerfully to whatever circumstances we are placed in. So cheer up. Don't fret and hurt yourself. If I get home, I want to see you looking stout and hearty. I felt sad all day yesterday to think how lonesome you would be. I brought my trunk of provisions through with me. I tell you, the boys was glad to get it as they were sorter scarce. I will write to you in a day or two again. Tell Willy and Bud to be good boys. I will come home again if it is God's will. There is no talk of paying us any money as yet. Tell Uncle Reece I did not think he would have went off without telling me goodbye. J. V. Choat is writing at the same table with me. Achsah don't forget to put your trust in God, for we know He does all things for good of them that love Him and keep His commandments. So farewell my beloved wife for the present. Your affectionate husband,

Harvey

---

[219] Corporal William W. East (c.1836-?) of Co.-I, 5th S. C. Infantry was editor of the Yorkville Enquirer Newspaper.

Sullivans Island
June the 4th, 1861

Achsah we have got flour the last draw or two. When the reg[iment] left, the men were about to get nothing to eat. When Capt. Glenn got back, he went to Charleston and went to the Governor and got something for them to eat. We have been getting from the city regular since. Achsah I have no doubt we will be moved off this island in a few days. I am anxious to get off. There is so much dirt and filth here, and the typhoid fever has got a start amongst the Regulars. The doctors here say if the island is not cleaned up the men will all have it. Achsah do not be uneasy nor fret yourself about me. I will try to take good care of myself. You know when I feel that one as near & dear to me as you are to me is so anxious about me, that I will try to take care of myself so I may get home again to enjoy the very great pleasure of being with you. Tell Willy and Aaron their Pa wants them to be good boys and he will come to see them again if spared. Kiss Matty for me. It looks this morning like rain. It has not rained here since before I went home. I hope you have had some rain. Tell Pa Brother Sam is quite well but powerfully sunburnt. The men that went to Orangeburg are all sunburnt. They had to stay in an old field up there. We have fine air here yet, though it is hot in the morning. Tell Mrs. Cullender John is well and hearty. Tell Cousin Dempsy [that] Robbesson [Robertson][220] is well. We are all spoiling with laziness. The first day I come back, I was not out of the house three times. Achsah, write to me. Direct your letters to Lieut. H. A. Wallace - Charleston - Sullivans Island. If we leave here I will have them sent on where we are sent. So farewell. May God bless & protect you all is my prayer. Your affectionate husband,

Harvey

Achsah I don't care about you showing this. I have a very bad pen to write with.

---

[220] Dempsey Cook and son, Private James Robertson Cook

Sullivans Island
June the 5th, 1861

My dear Wife,
I have taken my pen to write you a few lines to let you know how we are employing ourselves on our island home. Well Achsah, in the first place, we are all up except young Adkins[221]. He is quite sick. I think taking fever. I am very well myself but perfectly lost. We have no organization yet. Every man does as he pleases; have no muster; only turn out once a day at dress parade. Capt. Sarter[222], our commander, don't know anything. He appointed a man by the name of Thomas for Adjutant that has not got common sense. When we do go out on dress parade, them goes that wants; them that don't, stays. We just go out for to have a laugh and we get it. Capt. Glenn left Monday evening and went up to Orangeburg to meet the volunteers and to bring back Sam, Bob Choat, & Chesly Wood. He was to have come back this morning but none of them have come. We hear this morning that Jenkins' Reg[iment] has started for Virginia today. Sam Campbell has gone to the city today, and some four or five others of our men. They can get over pretty much as they please now. The Regulars guard the gates at the wharf. Achsah we are just living here in the dirt and flies. It looks like the flies would eat us up. While I am writing, I have some of the boys washing out Adkin's room; moved him in another room. The doctors say if we stay here we will all be sick, [as] there is so much filth about this house. There is two young doctors attends to our sick. They are the kindest men I ever knew. They come to see Divinny four times a day while he was sick. They got him up right off. If Capt. Sarter had any sense, he might have kept up some kind of order, but as it is, we are doing nothing. We draw provisions from the city. I tell you, our fare goes pretty rough with me after living at

---

[221] Private S. Randolph Adkins
[222] Captain Jacob W. Sartor of Union District, S. C. was captain of Co.- D (The Tyger Volunteers), 5th S. C. Infantry. After choosing not to go to Virginia, Sartor was placed in charge of the reserve troops on Sullivans Island.

home a week, but I have to take it as it comes. Capt. Sarter told us last evening the Governor would tell us today what he was going to do with us, so I will not close this letter until morning probably. I can then give you more satisfaction. The Yankee ship is in full view of me where I am sitting writing. I am writing upstairs in the piazza. There is a large piazza all around down below & upstairs; two in this house. There is a long ways over one hundred rooms in this house[223]. Achsah I don't think we will have to stay here long on this island, but think we will be moved somewhere else if they get us organized. We won't serve under Sarter. He is very conceity about being in command. I have got this mornings paper from the city; nothing new from Virginia. I expect the officers of us will draw our pay. I believe all of the other officers have got their pay, only our company. We will get it as soon as Capt. Glenn comes back. Officers can draw theirs every month. There is nothing said about paying the soldiers as yet. I do hope we will get something done in a day or two. I don't like to be lying here doing nothing. Another of the Regulars died this morning with typhoid fever.

[Wallace did not close this letter but finished it the next day.]

---

[223] The Moultrie House Hotel in Moultrieville

Sunrise
June the 6th

Dear Wife,
I this morning write you a few lines more. We are all well this morning. We started Adkins home last night. Frank Boyd[224] went with him. Frank got word that some of his Negroes was sick. Achsah, Capt. Glenn and the boys come over on the 5 o'clock boat last evening. They seen the companies mustered in the service. The reg[iment] took the cars at two o'clock for Virginia. Our boys all come back in good spirits. Achsah we have no orders what we will do yet. General Gist[225] told Capt. Glenn yesterday we would be moved off this island in a few days somewhere up the country. We are no better organized yet; not doing any good here. Capt. Glenn & me are going over to the city today to get our pay and see if we can't have some understanding of what we are going to do. If we stay in the service we are oblige to have new officers at our head I have no doubt, but if we have to elect a major we will elect Capt. Glenn. The men all want him. Some men are leaving every day for home. The most of them say if they don't do something in a few days they will go home. Campbell, James A. Glenn, and William Moore are going to start home Friday night. So goodbye my loving wife.

H. A. Wallace

---

[224] Private Benjamin Franklin Boyd (5/12/1816-5/18/1895), son of Thomas and Elizabeth Boyd

[225] Brigadier General States Rights Gist (1831-1864), a lawyer from Union District, S. C., served as adjutant and inspector general of the state after secession. He was promoted to brigadier general in 1859 while serving with the South Carolina Militia. Gist served as a brigade commander after appointment to brigadier general in the Confederate Army on March 20, 1862. He was sent to North Carolina, then Mississippi, after which he was transferred to the Army of Tennessee. General Gist fought commendably at Chickamauga, Chattanooga, and Atlanta and was killed while leading his men at Franklin, Tennessee. Warner, 106-107.

Manassas Junction, [Virginia]
June the 20, 1861

Dear Brother,
I assume the pleasant task this pleasant morning of dropping you a few lines to let you know how we are getting along. This leaves all well with some few exceptions, but there is no one very bad sick. The worst of it is we have the measles in camp at present. The doctors take every care not to let them spread. As for myself, my health is remarkably good. This is quite a healthy country; water good but not very handy. We left Richmond on Tuesday the 18; landed at this place on the 19. We are encamped two miles from Manassas Junction on the road between there and Alexandria. It is now about twenty miles to where the enemy are camped. There is two or three regiments between us and Alexandria. Col. Gregg[226] & some other I don't know, but I think they are all from S. C. Gregg's boys fired on a car load of Yankees the other day with a heavy piece of cannon and knocked the engine off the track. The Yankees jumped out of the cars, fired one round, and then took to their heels. Gregg's boys killed seven of them, took nearly all of their arms, and besides, captured fifteen thousand barrels of flour. Gregg loss was nothing[227]. The Yankees are bad to make overshots it seems. There is scouting parties all over this country. I tell you, a Yankee fares badly about here now. They have several prisoners in Richmond, Virginia. They are very low down looking fellows. Richmond is a fine place, much ahead of Charleston. I saw General Washington's

---

[226] Colonel Maxcy Gregg (1814 -1862) of Columbia, S. C. commanded the 1st S.C. Infantry (a state unit enlisted for six-months service). Gregg, a Mexican War veteran, was a lawyer and leading supporter of the States Rights principle. Colonel Gregg was promoted to brigadier general on December 14, 1861 and led an infantry brigade in the Army of Northern Virginia. He died of wounds received during the Battle of Fredericksburg. Warner, 119-120.

[227] This action occurred near Vienna, Va. on June 17, 1861. Gregg's Regiment, along with Kemper's Artillery Battery, ambushed a train loaded with Ohio troops enroute to repair and guard the Loudoun and Hampshire Railroad, about fifteen miles from Alexandria. E.B. Long, 86.

monument in the State House yard; is certainly a great curiosity. I suppose you have heard of it. We drill the battalion drill almost all time now. We are getting pretty good at that. Our officers do remarkably well. Bone [Bowen] is a good Captain in the battalion drill. The chat is here now that we will march on and take Alexandria in a few days, but I do not think so. It is my notion that everything will lie quiet until the 4 of July, but I cannot say. One thing, I saw Gen. Beauregard yesterday riding around looking at the troops. They say he has been in Alexandria in disguise a few days ago. I suppose it is true. He speaks of going to the City of Washington as an egg trader but I cannot vouch for the truth of that. This is a hilly, broken country; water good but not very handy. We have to carry it a half mile, but that is better than none. I was truly very glad to hear of you boys coming home from the island but sorry to hear of Guss and James Stuart[228] being sick. But I am in hopes that they are better by time. I will come to a close at present. Nothing more at present, but your Brother,

Ruff

When you write to, direct your letters to Richmond, Virginia, in the care of J.N. Lewis. Lewis is the man that kept the jewelry store in Yorkville. He is now clerk in the post office in Richmond. Capt. Bone [Bowen] made arrangements with him to forward our letters to wherever we should be taken. I have received a letter from T. S. Wallace directed to you, which I will enclose in with this one. I took the privilege of opening it, which I suppose you would not object to. There is one thing certain. I am in good spirits and if I have to fight I will do the best I can. I am not afraid of the Yankees much without they do better than they have [been] doing. Give my love to all the friends and receive a portion yourself and family. Nothing more but your friend and brother,

Ruff Wallace

---

[228] Privates William Augustus McCallum and James A. Stewart

Written upside down at the bottom of the last page:

Be sure to write to me and give me the news of the country in general.

Second Lieutenant Samuel L. "Blind Sam" Campbell
Catawba Light Infantry
Photographed soon after his near fatal wound at South Mountain, Maryland

Clay Hill
York Dist., S. C.
Tuesday Night
Oct. 15th, 1861

Well Harvey, according to promise I seat myself to write you a few lines. This leaves us all well but your Father. He is miserably confined to the house from cold. Your Father received your letter last night that you wrote while you were near Greenville C.[ourt] H.[ouse][229]. It had been 7 days on the road. We were very glad to hear of your welfare & that you had got along so finely. The eve that I came from York where I left you, I received 2 letters for you; one from Thomas & the other from Robt. Choat. Robt. praised you pretty highly & bid you goodbye. Thomas said nothing about a way bill in his letter that I got that eve. Since then your Father has got one from him & he said in that one that there was but two men in that country that had way bills of the right kind & they were James A. Wallace & Duncan McCallum & that they were both gone to Shreveport, but as soon as they came back he would get one & send it to Mississippi & you should get it as you passed through. I also got one letter from D. A. McCallum last week for you. He said they were all well but himself. He had just got up out of a spell of bilious fever. It was a light attack. There is nothing of note occurred in this neighborhood since you left. Your Father got your log chain at Dempsy Cook's. I have your saddle here at my house. Your Father talks of taking it. I was at the old place Saturday after you left & moved the corn out of the little crib into the larger one & nailed it up. T.M. Whitaker[230] has not came after his stack of fodder yet. Mr. Brandon[231] got 25 lbs. bacon side. Add was there in the eve & got

---

[229] This letter was sent while the Wallaces were enroute to Texas.

[230] T. Morrison Whitaker (12/25/1822-c.1879) of Yorkville raised and trained racehorses. It was said that he owned "some of the finest and swiftest horses to be found in the state." Whitaker was known to care for his horses as if they were his children. *Yorkville Enquirer*, Feb. 3,1879.

[231] Edwin T. Brandon

his piece. There was a small piece left, 7 lbs. He wanted it & I let him have it. And next came the old ham. I sold it today to a lady from Rock Hill that had got lost & came by here on the hunt of bacon. It weighed 10 1/2 lbs. I sold to her for $1.50 cts., as long as her son & husband were gone to the wars. So that ends that chapter, but there is still more if I could think of it at the right time. Yes, Mr. Wright sold both them swords at $20 but did not get the cash. He sold them to good men & holds himself responsible for the cash. Col. McCorkle got one & Dr. somebody the other (I forgot his name). Again, Billy B.'s wife[232] got her pot but she says she got no oven. And I am told that one of Sam Johnston's lids was taken that morn that you started & I think the lid & oven went together. I should say here where I think it went but I had better keep my mouth shut. Billy and old Mrs. Whiteside[233] have both been bad off since you left. Mrs. W. is not much, if any, better yet. I would not be surprised she would not get up again. She is plumb deaf & crazy also. David G. Wallace[234] is scratching on slowly at his cotton, & the talk is that Mr. Cook is to move there this week (don't know though). George Turner[235] left me when you did & I am now sowing mogul wheat in my old field. You may tell Leonard[236] that I find Kit to be a great mule to plough. She got crippled a little

---

[232] Unidentified

[233] Both are unidentified

[234] David G. Wallace (9/11/1793-6/21/1878) and wife Ann owned a plantation in the New Center community. Direct kinship with Harvey and his family could not be established.

[235] George R. Turner (4/25/1834-3/14/1914), son of William Turner of the Zeno community, is listed as a day laborer in the 1860 census.

[236] Leonard Thomas Mason Wood (7/17/1844-1/19/1918) was the son of David Johnston and Elizabeth (Bailey) Wood, and nephew of Harvey and Achsah Wallace. Leonard moved to Texas with the Wallace family and later enlisted in Wallace's Co.-H, 19th Texas Infantry as a private. After the war, Wood returned to York District where he was active in the York County Confederate Veterans Survivor's Association.

on the pole in the stable but has got well again. I have got 2 more hogs yesterday. Sam Johnston had a sow and 2 shoats (wild) stayed out about the ore bank; told me if I would catch the sow for him, I might have the shoats. I had been baiting her a week & was going to build a pen to her out there when her & the shoats came home to the house & I put them in the barn lot & sent for him to send for her. I put the shoats in a pen at the house. They will weigh about 60 lbs. apiece (pretty good haul). Saml. C. Johnston says that you were a little too quick for J. L. Watson[237] in the hog trade. Sam was to get one hundred lbs. worth of the 2nd size at 7 cents gross when John got them. That would have done well on John W.'s side. Harvy, I engaged to take 20 bushels of potatoes to York next Monday after you started & went down and dug two thirds of the patch & got only 10 bushel & about 3 bushels of little ones. Sold 10 bushels at 50 cents a bush.; makes $5.00 & my work gone. That's what went with my speculation; began at the lower side of the hill that time. I do not think of anything else at this time. It has just struck 9 o'clock & I got to be in bed. I have to air my shirt (tail) very early these morning. It has not frosted any here since you left but has rained a good deal. Rebecca sends her love to all. Yours as ever,

S. L. Campbell
Sam

If you do not write before, you must be certain to write a long epistle when you get to Miss[issippi]. I don't think you will be in much danger of the Yankees there. We hear here yesterday that the blockade is knocked into a cocked hat at [New] Orleans.
Sam

---

[237] John L. Watson

Mount Etney
November the 13, 1861

Dear Son,
I embrace the present opportunity to write you a few lines to let you know how we are. And I will, in the first place, say that through a kind providence we are all well, hoping these lines may find you and family enjoying. I received a letter from you from Jefferson, Alabama. I have been looking for either myself or Campbell to get a letter from Cooksville but none has come as yet; may be too soon. I concluded to write to you to Texas if you should get through. If you don't, some of the boys will get it. I get letters from Rufus regular, generally once a week. We got one on Monday; everything quiet. He has good health. Another battle looked for, but long looked for. Several boys started better than a week ago; the 2 Simrel boys[238], J. Stewert[239], Jo Wallis[240], and Wm. Watson[241]. We have had great excitement in our neighborhood. One of the brutalest murders ever perpetrated in our country. Sarah Anderson[242], last Monday morning was a week ago, left her grandfather's to go to Lathem's[243] to pick cotton and not more than a hundred and fifty yards from Panels[244] was murdered and the body was not found 'til Wednesday

---

[238] Samuel Davidson Simril and Franklin M. Simril (1/15/1846-5/20/1864), sons of Hugh and Nancy (Partlow) Simril, joined Co.-H, 18th S. C. Infantry as privates. Franklin was killed in action during the Battle of Clay's Farm, Va.

[239] James A. Stewart

[240] Joseph Franklin Wallace (c.1839-11/24/62), son of Harvey's Cousin, George F. Wallace and wife Ellen, served in Co.-H, 5th S. C. Infantry. (Note- this Joseph F. Wallace is not to be confused with Harvey's younger brother, Joseph F. Wallace, who was in Texas at this time).

[241] Private William D. Watson (c.1842-6/4/1862), the son of William and Elizabeth (Currence) Watson, was a member of Co.-H, 5th S. C. Infantry. Watson died of wounds suffered on May 31, 1862, during the Battle of Seven Pines.

[242] Sarah E. Anderson (5/2/1846-11/6/1861), daughter of William Anderson, lived with her grandparents, William (Billy) and Mary V. Anderson in the Clay Hill community on Beaver Dam Creek.

[243] John W. (c.1824-?) and Elizabeth (c.1824-?) Latham were Sarah Anderson's aunt and uncle.

[244] Unidentified

evening lying in the road; her throat cut; four cuts on one side and two on the other; the knife clear through her swallow; both of the big veins and windpipe cut. The neighborhood was gathered and inquest held. In searching and tracing, a suspicion took place on Mack[245]. He was taken to jail, brought to Clay Hill, and tried. It consumed two days. The proof was sufficient to convict him. He [will] be hanged the 29 of this month[246]. The Anderson family done everything they could to clear him. There was all sort of swearing, both white and black. They are done. They took Mack back to jail and on Monday morning he made a full confession of the whole deed. He had made an attempt at Panels last spring when Panels and Panels' wife was away to go to bed to her. She got away from him. He met her on the road that morning and violated her person and then murdered her for to keep her from telling.

November 14th
I just read your letter to Campbell from Cooksville. We were glad to hear from you all and your getting along so well, but sorry to hear Mrs. Woods not being well, but I hope she is better. If you can get through without getting into his hands all will be well, but I am sorry to say to you the Yankees have got their feet on South Carolina soil[247]. But it is nothing but what I looked for. I am surprised to think they were not better prepared for them. The Governor has called for more volunteers. If they don't volunteer there will be a draft. I think they will turn out. Sam[248] is ready and

---

[245] Mack Wood, the son of Addison (Add) Wood, was sold to William Anderson when the Wallace family moved to Texas in the fall of 1861. Addison was either sold or given to Harvey's father.
[246] Mack was hanged November 29, 1861 at the site where the crime was committed. *Yorkville Enquirer*, Nov. 14, 1861 & Nov. 27, 1931.
[247] On November 7, 1861, Federal naval forces quickly overran Confederate defenders at Forts Walker and Beauregard, which protected Port Royal, South Carolina. Landing parties soon captured Port Royal and Hilton Head Island, both of which later served as supply depots and bases of operations for Union blockading squadrons, and for coastal attacks against the thinly manned Carolina defenses. E. B. Long, 135-136.
[248] Harvey's youngest brother, Samuel Watson Wallace

will go any time. If there is not something done in the neighborhood, he says he will go to York. Wilson[249] is going to try to raise a company for 4 months. He says he will go on Monday to see about it. We are getting along pretty well with our work. We are done sowing wheat, all but a piece of cotton ground. I want to get the cotton off it. Add does pretty well considering his trouble. I have been sorry for him. When I told him Mack had confessed, he said he would not fret no more about him. I have not had a letter from none of the boys since you left. I am anxious to hear from Jo[250] whether he is in the army or not. Mrs. Watson[251] got a letter from him some time ago. She told me he talked something of coming home. If he don't come home, I suppose I will be left without 'ere a one, as I have no doubt but Sam will go to the army, and it is unknowing whether either of them ever will get back. Rufus has good health and keeps in good spirits. I expect enjoys himself as well as he can at any rate. He has the first time to complain yet. He never misses being ready for his duty. We have had fine weather for the last ten or twelve days. We are very busy at our cotton. It got ahead of us when seeding. It will take us some time to get up, but if the weather keeps good we will get along. I think our cotton will turn out pretty well. I think we have 11 or betwixt that and 12 out and probably two open; maybe not so much. We have a good deal to open yet. Our cotton is not killed with the frost yet. I don't know what people is to do for money unless we get a market for our cotton; everything so high. We have all quit coffee; take rye and wheat. It does fine. I like it just as well as coffee. I have sowed a patch. We are worst off about salt. It has been selling in York at 12 ½ the sack. It is said to have gone up to 15. I will be obliged to have some by hog killing time be it what it will. It is an article of necessity people have obliged to have. I don't know where you will be able to read this letter. I am so nervous I can scarcely hold the pen. I have been

---

[249] Captain William Blackburn Wilson (4/5/1827-3/3/1894) raised the Carolina Rifles in York District. This unit became Co.-F, 17th S. C. Infantry.
[250] Harvey's brother, Joseph Franklin Wallace
[251] Unidentified

worse since I have been sick. I believe I am pretty nigh through with news but will try to say something that you can read. Things goes on pretty much as they did before you left. The Yankees getting Port Royal makes considerable excitement. Report says they got two thousand of our Negroes; a pretty good grab. I believe their object is to plunder and destroy property. I have no doubt but they will try [to] get to Charleston. It is said General Lee has offered five thousand troops to South Carolina. I don't think they ever can get an army through the states. I think their object is the costs. I will now close this badly composed letter, and bad written. You must excuse it. Give my love to the boys and families. Tell them to write to me when they feel like it and I will do the best I can. If you should see Jo tell him to come home, as we are very lonely and will be more so when Sam leaves, which I have no doubt he will do. 'Tis pretty trying to raise as many sons as I have and not one of them to speak to when I am getting old and pretty near wore out. You will write when you get to Texas. Write the particulars how they are getting along, as I suppose some of them is not disposed to write to me. And now in conclusion, may God bless you all is the prayer of your Father.

Jas. Wallis

To H. A. Wallis,
There is one thing I forgot to ask you. When you allowed Add to keep a pistol? They broke his box open and found a pistol and ammunition in it. The Squire[252] asked me if I claimed it. I told him no. He said you [allowed] he keep it and never hindered him. Please to let me know.

---

[252] Sheriff

1862

A Soldier's Life Is A Hard One

".... a soldier's life is a very hard one and we are beginning to find it out."

Captain Harvey Wallace to his wife
October 5, 1862

Clay Hill
York Dist., S.C.
January 1st, 1862

H. A. Wallace

Dear Sir,
After my compliments and best wishes joined with that of family to yourself and family, I would say that we are all in the enjoyment of good health. We moved over to the old place about six weeks after you left. David G. Wallace got fourteen thousand pounds of seed cotton. I have seen Mr. Boyden since you, Mr. A. D. Choat[253] and I met over to court at Charlotte to see him. The intelligence that he gave us in regard to our affairs was more satisfactory than any we have got yet and the amount due Uncle Reese would be forthcoming with the balance. From what Mr. Boyden said, there will be no collection made of any consequence until after the stay law is removed. The amount will draw interest. Also, Aunt Matilda will have to send a new power of attorney. There is nothing wrong with the one that I have, only it is made to Harvey and they will not pay the money to anyone else. You will have to send one made to whoever you want the money paid to. If you should need the one that I have to have one drawn by, let me know and I will send you this one. My new gin performs finely; as well as I can wish. And I am getting along very well upon the whole. We have a great deal of excitement here about the war. Oats Howe[254] and Tommie Youngblood[255] left today in Capt. Glenn's Company[256].

---

[253] Augustine D. Choat

[254] Private Richard Oates Howe (1/28/1840-12/3/1914), son of David and Jane (Horsley) Howe, was Achsah's first cousin. Private Howe served in Co.-H, 18th S. C. Infantry and surrendered with his regiment at Appomattox on April 9, 1865.

[255] Private Thomas W. Youngblood (c.1839-7/22/1862), son of Henry and Eliza (Faris) Youngblood, served with Harvey in Co.-H, 5th S. C. Infantry and later joined Co.-H, 18th S. C. Infantry. Private Youngblood died of disease at Charleston, S. C.

[256] Captain Robert Henry Glenn, former Captain of the Catawba Light Infantry (Co.-H, 5th S. C. Infantry), organized another company in late 1861 that carried the same name. This company was mustered into the 18th S. C. Infantry as Company-

Robison [Robertson][257] has joined a cavalry company; Jones[258] near Rock Hill as Captain and Major Berry[259] as 1st Lieut. They will leave in a short time. We have no young men left in the country now at all. Leroy Quinn[260], Robt. Patrick[261], and William Glenn[262] have all been sent home dead from Virginia, making in all, seven members of that company that have died. Our legislature here passed a stay law stopping the collections of all debts. The Misses Gibson are all well and getting along very well. J. L. Watson has left the store too. Sam Johnston is to take charge of the post office. We have sent on a petition to have Sam appointed Post Master. He and Elias McElhaney[263] speak of keeping some groceries at the forks of the road. Hilliard[264] is gone to the war. He is in Capt. Meacham's Company[265], the same one that your Brother Sam is in.

H. Many of those who served in the original Catawba Company but declined to go to Virginia joined this company

[257] James Robertson Cook

[258] Captain Robin A. P. Cadwallader Jones (c.1827-6/9/1863) was Captain of Co.-H, 1st S. C. Cavalry. Captain Jones was killed while leading a cavalry charge at Brandy Station, Va.

[259] 1st Lieutenant James Hanna Barry (c.1819-4/14/1888), son of John and Violet (Moore) Barry, was promoted from 1st Lieutenant to Captain of Co.-H, 1st S. C. Cavalry. He later served as major of the regiment.

[260] Private Leroy D. Quinn (5/1/1836-11/26/1861), son of Walter and Elizabeth (Denham) Quinn, died of disease in Virginia while serving with Co.-H, 5th S. C. Infantry.

[261] Robert Vaughn Patrick

[262] 5th Corporal William R. Glenn (7/19/1832-12/26/1861), son of William and Eliza (Boyd) Glenn, died of disease at Culpeper, Va. while serving with Co.- H, 5th S. C. Infantry.

[263] Elias McElhaney (c.1804 -?) and wife Lucinda were neighbors of Mr. Simril. McElhaney worked as a farm manager or overseer.

[264] Private Hilliard J. Felts (c.1835-10/24/1862), son of William Sr. and Sarah Felts, was Dempsey Cook's son-in-law. Felts served in Co.-E, 17th S. C. Infantry and was captured September 14, 1862 during the Battle of South Mountain, Md. He was released one month later suffering from typhoid fever. Private Felts died of typhoid at Winder Hospital in Richmond, Va.

[265] Dr. Thomas Boyd Meacham (1/3/1836-10/25/1908) organized Co.-E (The Indian Land Tigers), 17th S. C. Infantry in York District in late 1861 or early 1862.

[illegible] and child are with us. Write to me soon. My family joins me in sending you and family and Aunt Matilda our love and respects. Very truly,

Dempsey Cook

Dempsey Cook

Meacham also performed extra duty as surgeon when needed. Captain Meacham resigned when the regiment was reorganized in April 1862.

Crowders Creek
York District
January the 22nd, 1862

Dear Cousin Achsah,
I take this opportunity of writing these few lines to you to let you know we are all well at present, thanks be to God for His mercies to us all. Hoping these few lines will find you and all enquiring friends in the same way. Dear Achsah, I received your letter the fourteenth of December, which gave us much pleasure to hear of you all being in good health after your long journey. They are all well generally in this neighborhood as can be expected. Times is hard and money scarce; everything at double & treble price. The most all the young men is gone to the army. J. R. Cook and Oats Howe, Sam'l Faris[266], and many other is all gone down to Charleston to drive the Yankees back home again or die in the attempt. There is a good deal of sickness prevailing among the volunteers. Thos. Youngblood is lying sick at the camp. He had the measles and got over them, and got sick again. Dear Achsah, we recd. a letter yesterday from Sister Dorcas Wilson[267] from Arkansas stating they were well. Two of the boys is gone to the army and J. J.[268] is living at home with her. Nancy, his wife, has got a son and calls him Jefferson Davis. We had some very cold weather last week; cold sleet falling two days and cleared off again. J. F. Glenn and his brother, Wm., died out in Virginia. Winchester Pegram[269] of Dallas[270] got killed by the fall of a tree. We have not much to write at this time but we are all busy a pining. We picked cotton for D. G. Wallis[271] until he was done, and the to the wheel factory. Yarn is one dollar & 50 cts. per bale. We

---

[266] Private Samuel Thomas Faris (2/20/1842-1/22/1916), son of Miles and Sarah G. (Faris) Faris, served in Co.-H, 18th S. C. Infantry.
[267] Unidentified
[268] Unidentified
[269] Unidentified
[270] Dallas was the county seat of Gaston County, N. C.
[271] David G. Wallace

all send our best respects to you one and all without distinction. We want you [to] write often. We will be glad to hear from one [and] all without exception. The writer sends his best respects to all.

L. C.[272]

Enclosed with the above letter was this note:
I am glad to hear you are all satisfied in your move, most specially Aunt & Uncle. Give my best respects to Martha & to Jane, & to all enquiring friends. We are very lonesome. We are off in a little corner to ourselves. There is very little stirring. We can't see Uncle Reese. Mahala[273] says she thinks mighty long of going to your house. She had been at Dempsy Cook's, but it don't look like your house. She don't see you there. She says she wants to see [illegible] worse than any. Hilyard Felts is in the army and Miram[274] is at her father's. They got a letter from Robberson [Robertson] the other day. He said Hilyard had the measles. The day is cold. I must come to a close. Nothing more, only remains yours affectionate until death.

Eleanor Gibson[275]

---

[272] Unidentified
[273] Mahala Gibson
[274] Miriam (Cook) Felts (c.1835-1916), daughter of Dempsey and Mary (Gibson) Cook, was married to Private Hilliard J. Felts.
[275] "Nelly" Gibson

South Carolina
Mount Etney
January the 22, 1862

Well Harvy, it is with pleasure I avail myself of the opportunity of dropping you a few lines. These leaves us all in good health but myself. I never have been right well since you left. I was confined to the house and bed part of the time for weeks and am not stout yet, but am improving slow. We were glad to hear of your safe landing in Texas. Jo[276] landed on Christmas evening. We were glad to see him once more at the old domain, although he did not stay long with us. They sent for him to go to York. He has been there going on three weeks posting their books and drawing off accounts. I don't know how long he may remain there, McCorkles[277] being in the army. The men in our district is pretty well gone to the losts. There's not a young man left but I. Hulender[278] and Andy Stewart[279], and he sent a substitute. Your brother Sam is in Meacham's Company[280] and Campbell[281] is First Lieutenant in Glenn's Company. The companies are stationed in two hundred yards of each other so they see each other every day. They are at Camp Lee in sight of the city[282]. There is lots of vessels and Yankees about there. There seem to have any disposition to come out. They say there is a solid column of men from Charleston to Savanna. Sam writes occasionally. His health has been good ever since he left home. He likes the officers fine. We got a letter from Rufus last night. His

---

[276] Harvey's brother, Joseph Franklin Wallace
[277] Captain William H. McCorkle
[278] Unidentified
[279] John Andrew Martin Luther Stewart (4/22/1843-5/19/1928), son of Joseph B. and Eliza (Tate) Stewart, eventually enlisted in Co.-B, 5th S. C. Infantry as 3rd Corporal. He was later promoted to 2nd Corporal and was present at the surrender at Appomattox.
[280] Company-E, 17th S. C. Infantry
[281] 1st. Lieutenant Samuel L. Campbell of Co.-H, 18th S. C. Infantry
[282] Charleston, S. C.

health is good and has been. There is a great deal of sickness and a great many deaths. John F. Glenn, and William Glenn, and Leroy Quinn, and Robert Patrick have all been sent home and buried at Bethel. There has been seven or eight deaths in the Catawbas, but so it is all armies. There is a heap of sickness on the coasts. They have measles and mumps both. Rebecca got a letter from you last night directed to Sam. She opened it and read it, and will send it to him. As for the paper, we will tend to it and send it. Times is tight here; everything high. Corn 60 cts., flour from 3 ½ to 4 and three fourths, sugar 16 ct., pork 12 ½ , coffee none, salt from 25 to 30 dollars a sack and scarce at that, beef 60 ct., butter 25 to 30 cts. We don't pretend to get coffee. Rich and poor use rye, potatoes, wheat, and corn meal. Coffee is worth 65 ct. in Charleston and the government takes it all at that for the soldiers. I want you to tell Jas. A.[283] that Bill Barnett[284] is making a considerable talk about the money he left for him to collect for him. He says he has written frequently and he don't answer his letters. He ought to give him some satisfaction about it. If he has collected it and used it, tell him to let the man know and try and pay it or he will not do right. We are getting along about as usual. Rebecca and the children is with us. She is looking for Sam home this week if he can get off. They are passing very often. I was sorry for Add, the difficulty about his son, but he is doing very well and appears to be satisfied. I never said anything to him about what you wrote to me at any rate. At any rate, he lost his pistol. I dislike very much his being so much among them, but if there is any more difficulty with them Andersons he will either have to quit them or me. He wanted me to try to get his wife but there is no chance for that. There has been a good many deaths through the country, although there has not been no bad sickness. Alexander Bigger[285] has moved back to his own place and is doing about as usual. Barnett has left him and I suppose he will tend to his own place. I sent two bales of cotton to Charlotte. I got eight and a half

---

[283] Harvey's brother, James Adams Wallace
[284] William Barnett was Harvey's cousin.
[285] Alexander M. Bigger (c.1818-?), son of Matthew and Erixeny (Barnett) Bigger, was Harvey's first cousin.

for it. I made 13 bags and 3 for Rufus. Our cotton done very well. We hauled our cotton to Franklin's Gin. If I could sell it for a good price it would help me very much. As soon as you get fixed and time to look round, you write and give me a full history of Texas. You had better look out in Texas, for old Abe talks of colonizing Texas to put the Negroes on when they are set free. Adison sends his old Mistress, Harvy, and Miss Achsah howdy. To all of you howdy, and to tell you all he is thankful to you for leaving him at a good home, and to say to you all he's perfectly satisfied. He says Miles is satisfied and pleased with his home[286]. Please answer this, and may the Lord bless you all. Please let any of the boys see this letter.

Jas. Wallis

---

[286] Miles was sold or possibly traded to Mr. Hugh Simril.

South Carolina
York Dist.
Feb. 7th, 1862

Mr. Harvey A. Wallace

Dear Friend,
On the 5th of this month I received your letter of the 12th Jan. We were sorry to hear of Achsah's sickness. We thought from traveling she would get clear of her chills and weakness. We are glad to hear that the rest are well and that you have landed safe. Mr. Cook told me that you had made the trip quicker than any man had made it from South Carolina yet, and that you had no bad luck on the way, and that Aunt Matilda, after traveling all day became very tired, but after getting a good nights rest was able to travel again. Your lines found us all well except myself. I have not been well since that night that I had a chill at your house before you went away. I took jaundice and turned as yellow as a pumpkin, but I am able to travel about and attend to my business. I believe the friends are generally well. Mr. Cook's family had scarlet fever but are well. Capt. Campbell[287] had a child sick last week. We have not heard from it this week. Harvey, I am glad to hear that you have got a place with good houses and plenty of land to work, and that you have good range for your stock. You have got to a fresh country where you can get land and make plenty. I hope you may all be well pleased with your move. You say you feel rather lost for the want of news. This will be the case for a while at first, but [you] will soon become used to it. I have been listening to hear of Uncle Rezin's sending word that he will be back about next fall, but we may be disappointed about that. You will all of you feel lost at first a while until you get used to the people and the customs of the place. There is a great change in Carolina since you left here. The men mostly have gone to the army and have left the old men, women, and children to shift for themselves, though there are some married men and some single men in our neighborhood that calculates on others fighting for their

---

[287] Unidentified, but may refer to Lieutenant Samuel L. Campbell.

liberties. Capt. Glenn[288] and Colonel Elison [Allison][289], and a great many of our young men have gone to the southern seashore. My son James[290] is at Charleston, John's Island, under Capt. Meacham; Meen's Regiment, 17th Reg. Robison [Robertson] Cook, Thomas Youngblood, and Oats Howe is in Capt. Glenn's Company, Gadbury's Reg. I do not know the number of that regiment. Your Brother[291] and James are both in the same mess. Harvey, you did not give the value of your plantation in Carolina. Mr. Cook has found a mill seat on your place and has built a mill on it on the branch between him and Stewart. There is a fall on the branch where he has built a hominy mill by firing a spout that empties into a tray on the end of a pole, and a nestle in the other end that this tray, when it is filled with water, empties itself. The other end falls into the mortar, the middle of the pole working and pivot. It works to a fraction. Mr. Cook has sowed your cotton patch on the road in wheat, and that barn piece and his old plantation all in wheat; him and the neighbor's. I think he made 15 bales cotton this year. You said you would like to hear from the boy, Miles, that you let Simril have. At first, I understand he was not satisfied and had nothing to say for a while, but now he seems to be satisfied and has become lively. I am glad to hear that you are pleased with the boy, Laston [Lawson][292]. He was born and raised within a half mile of me and I always found him to be a first rate boy. Tell him howdy for me. I believe his Mother and friends as well. Mr. Wallace, Mr Cook, and myself went to Charlotte on Monday of court week. We supposed Boyden would be there. We got there about twelve o'clock. We went to Carr's

---

[288] Captain Robert Henry Glenn commanded Co.-H, 18th S. C. Infantry, under the leadership of Colonel James M. Gadberry at the time of this letter.
[289] William Barry Allison (1/28/1816-11/13/1896) served as 1st Lieutenant of Co.-H, 18th S. C. Infantry. He was promoted to Major and Lieutenant Colonel of the 18th Infantry in 1862 and surrendered with his regiment at Appomattox.
[290] Corporal James Van Buren Choate
[291] Private Samuel Watson Wallace
[292] Lawson Simril (c.1835-?) was a slave born in South Carolina as stated in the 1880 Rusk County, Texas census. Lawson married Caroline of the Wallace plantation after the war and the couple farmed and raised eight children.

Public Hotel expecting to find him at dinner but he had went to bed to rest himself. He said he had the headache. They told me where he was and we took Frank Simril[293] of Steel Creek with us to witness our contract with Boyden. You know the little obligation between himself and us was worth not much, if anything. We found him in a fine humor. We wanted to know before Simril whether he considered himself bound in that contract, naming over the contract himself in the presence of Frank Simril. We asked him if Uncle Rezin's [Reece] part of the estate could be collected or not. He gave us not much satisfaction about that. I think it is doubtful. We wanted to know if he had collected anything. He said he had not collected one dollar. He said he could not do it on the account of the stay law. He said it was in the hand of the Sheriff, or at least a part of it. We wanted to know whether or not the security property ought not to be more secure, lest he might squander it before the stay law should be taken off or not. He said there was no danger. The security was perfectly good for the debt. He said his Ford's Plantation was worth twenty thousand dollars, and his other property was very good; that he could not squander it so easily. Harvey, the times are against us. You cannot collect a debt now by law. We seem to be unfortunate, but we must wait. Perhaps we may yet see a better day, though we may be disappointed. Boyden said he was glad we had met him in Charlotte. Mr. Cook told him that you handed him your power of attorney. He said that did not authorize him (Cook) to collect your part of the estate. You will have to send him another power of attorney authorizing him to collect your part. You know from experience how it ought to be got up. Harvey, you wished to know where Robert[294] was. They are at Smithfield, Virginia; Rugged Island, 13th Regiment N. C. Vol., Company B. I received yesterday from them. They are well and hearty. They have never been sick since they had the measles. I wrote to them yesterday. I sent your friendship to them. We are looking for William[295] back on furlough for one week. I take the Tri-Weekly Mercury this year and the

---

[293] Unidentified
[294] Private Robert Walker Choat
[295] Private William Choat (12/16/1825-11/17/1913), son of Augustine D. and Dorcas (Garrison) Choat, was a member of Co.-E, 17th S. C. Infantry.

Catawba Journal; one from Charlotte and one from Charleston. I take an interest in the times and I am anxious to get the news. Aunt, you and Achsah wanted to know who preached at Sardis. There has been only one days preaching there since you left. Mr. Logan[296] preached once. Our churches seem to be vacated. I think generally this is case for the present. I understand the minister's fees in the army has been shortened and a great many of them have left; a wonderful time of coldness. What we shall come to is hard to tell. Tell Thomas and Martha we have looked for a letter but have received none yet. Aunt, Nancy sends word to you and Achsah and Uncle Rezin that she is fat and saucy, stepping about with Achsah's bonnet on. She sends her best respects to you all, to Thomas, to Duncan McCallum. Adieu,

A.D. Choat
Nancy Choat

---

[296] John Randolph Logan (1811-1884), son of John B. and Lois (Rainey) Logan, served as a lay Baptist Minister and clerk of the Broad River Baptist Association. John was a surveyor by trade and served as a state legislator during the war. His son, Lieutenant David Jackson Logan of Co.-F, 17th S. C. Infantry, became quite notable for his wartime articles sent to the Yorkville Enquirer under the name of "Our Correspondent." Samuel N. Thomas Jr. and Jason Silverman, *A Rising Star of Promise: The Civil War Odyssey of David Jackson Logan, 17th South Carolina Volunteers, 1861-1864.* (Campbell, Ca.: Savas Publishing Company, 1998).

York Dist., So.Ca.
April 13, 1862

Dear Cousin,
It is with much pleasure that I take my pen in hand to let you know how we all are. Emily[297] is sick today with the cold and a pain in her leg. I have been sick for a week with the cold and sore throat but I am nearly well. The rest is all well except colds. Times is hard and money is scarce. Groceries are scarce and high. Mr. Johnson[298] put up a grocery at Clay Hill and is selling molasses at $1.50 per gallon and sugar at 22 cents per pound. He has nothing else that I know of. There is a heap of sickness and deaths about here now and has been for a few weeks back. Two of Mr. Mitchell's sons[299] died in one week. One died in the army after a spell of measles. The other brought him home and buried him and he took sick, but was not bad. The Dr. gave him some phisic[300] and told the family not to give him anything 'til he came back, but they gave him a dose of oil that was poison to the other and killed him. Mr. Zed Smith's wife[301] is dead. Mr. Wm. Moore's wife[302] is dead, and Wm. Barnett's baby[303] is dead and was buried at Concord yesterday evening. John, I have heard that your Sister, Sarah Ann[304], was dead. She died of typhoid fever. John, it seems to me that the war will never end. There is none of the soldiers returned home yet but there is some still going

---

[297] Emily Black (c.1850-?) was the daughter of John D. and Eliza Black of the Clay Hill Community.
[298] Samuel C. Johnson
[299] Privates William R. (c.1839-1862) and James Thomas Mitchell (c.1844-1862), sons of Dawson N. and Nancy (Carothers) Mitchell, served in Co.-E, 17th S. C. Infantry. William died of disease at Johns Island, S. C.
[300] Phisic was an oil-based medication used as a laxative or purgative for the bowels.
[301] Martha Jane (Glenn) Smith (c.1829-1862), wife of Zadoc Darby Smith
[302] Mary H. Moore (12/1828- 3/1862)
[303] Reference here is to an unidentified child of Harvey's cousin, William Barnett, and wife Sally.
[304] Unidentified

off. I wish they would make peace and come home. I would like to see some of the boys very well. We have a school house not far from Clay Hill, and a very nice teacher and a large school. J. J. & G. A.[305] is going to school. Billy Boyd[306] is the teacher. There has been a heap of the soldiers home sick but they are all gone back. I will name some of them: T. R. Starns[307], J. R. Cook, James Tate, Tom Youngblood, Hil Felts, Oats Howe, and others too tedious to name. I want you to write as soon as you get this. Excuse bad writing and spelling if you please. So no more.

From T. M. Black[308] to J. J. Devinny[309]
Farewell

Envelope inscription:
Mr. J. J. Devinny
Minden P. O., Rusk Co., Texas
From: Clay Hill, S. C., April 12
Paid 10 cents

---

[305] Both are unidentified.
[306] William Boyd (c.1826-?).
[307] Thomas R. Starnes (c.1843-?), son of Joseph and Feriba Starnes, served as a private in Co.-E, 17th S. C. Infantry.
[308] Turentine Black (c.1846-?), daughter of John D. and Eliza Black
[309] John J. Devinny (c.1840-?) served as a private and fifer with Co.-H, 5th S. C. Infantry. He declined to volunteer for Virginia in 1861 and moved to Rusk County, Texas after discharge.

April 13, 1862

Dear Aunt,
I now settle myself to write you a few lines to inform you that we are all well at present, hoping these lines may find you all enjoying the same blessing. Robinson [Robertson] has had a long spell of pneumonia. He had the measles and came home by 7 weeks. He volunteered to go in the horse company for 12 months but they went for the war and he would not go. He went to Glenn's Company. I said we were all well but Jethro[310] is not well. He has something like the cold. Darby[311] has got a pretty bad burn. He set down on the hot lid. We have had more sickness since we have had in 12 months. We are all been sick. Jethro arm [is] so sore he has done nothing for 2 months. He carries it in a swing all the time. Hilliard has had the measles and came home and then he took the mumps. He stayed two months. Thomas Youngblood came home and stayed 5 weeks. He started back two weeks ago, and Robby [Robertson] started back last Wednesday. Nelly's[312] people is all well as common. Rees Horsley[313] was here today. He said they were all well. Mr. Cullinder[314] is not well. He is sick with the cold. Fair Campbell[315] is very bad sick. I don't know what is the matter with him. And for the rest of the neighbors, I believe is well. Zedick [Zadoc] Smith's wife is dead. She died with 3 days sickness. She left a little babe 4 weeks old. William Moore's wife is dead. She was a spinning at 10 o'clock and was a corpse at 2 o'clock. William Mitchell was in Captain Meachem's Company from Rock Hill. He has died and his brother, Thomas, came home with him and took the sore throat and died too. There was not a week's difference between them. Sally Barnett's

---

[310] Jethro G. Cook (c.1845- 6/25/1864), son of Dempsey and Mary (Gibson) Cook, enlisted in Co.-E, 17th S. C. Infantry and was killed in action at Petersburg, Va.

[311] Unidentified

[312] Eleanor Gibson

[313] Unidentified

[314] Lawrence Cullender (c.1790-?) was a neighbor and father of private William J. Cullender.

[315] Samuel Fair Campbell, son of Harvey's sister, Margaret Rebecca and husband Samuel L. Campbell, died from his illness May 1, 1862.

little baby died last Friday night. It was sick 3 weeks. Do you want your book sent by mail or by some person? Your loom is here yet. It don't look like any person is a going to get it. I must come to a close for this time. So nothing more at this time but remaining your affectionate friend. So write soon and fail not. I want you to write and let me know whether you seen Aunt Betsey[316] or not.
Mary Cook to Matilda Wood

Achsah,
I would like to see you and spend a few hours with you. You said you wanted like to hear from Chris Glenn[317]. She is a living with her three little children. Jim Glenn[318] administered on the estate so he had sale about three weeks ago. Her Negro boy went for 11 hundred dollars. She rented out all of her land. They gave her almost all of her house furnity. Give my respects to Uncle Reece and all the family. Write as soon as you get this.
Mary Cook to Achsah Wallace

Aunt Matilda,
I take up my pen to inform you that we are as well at this time as we have been in nine weeks, although we are not well at present. Jethro has had chill and fever for the last four days. We have had a great deal of sickness in that time. Jethro has not done any work in the last seven weeks with swelling in his arm. My family has every one had a spell except myself. There has been so much rain in the later part of the winter and spring that we cannot get plowing done. I planted about fourteen acres of corn week before last and that is nearly all I have got ready. Corn is selling at one dollar per bushel, flour five dollars per hundred, bacon thirty cents per pound, fodder one dollar and fifty cents per hundred pounds. I have sold seven bales of my cotton at eight cents. I have eight bales yet in the barn. Harvey, respected friend, I received your letter of the 9th of January

---

[316] Unidentified
[317] Christine (Wood) Glenn (1/3/1829-7/29/1872) was the widow of Private John F. Glenn and older sister of Marion Wood. John and Christine Glenn had three children: Sarah (age-8), William (age-3), and Nancy (age-7 months).
[318] James A. Glenn, brother of Private John F. Glenn.

with pleasure. The friends are well so far as I know. The power of attorney had better be sent on as Boyden said it might be that he would get part of the money during the present year. Write to me soon. Tell Martha and Thomas [Wallace] and Jane and Duncan [McCallum] that I wish them well and wants them to write to me.

Dempsy Cook

Murvaul P. O.[319]
April 17th, 1862

Mr. Wallace,
Sir, The citizens in this part of the beat[320] on Saturday last made some arrangements in relation to seeing into the condition of and providing for the families of our soldiers that are in the war. They appointed Prof. Buckner[321], Capt. McReammon[322], & myself from this part of the beat and request that your part of the beat appoint the same number, and that the committee meet at my house on the 26th day of April and make the necessary preparation for the discharge of their duty. They decline acting under the Henderson appointment as it involves unnecessary trouble and expense. I was to have visited your company today but have been sick and am unable to ride. This matter should be attended to promptly enforce it claims, and have the appointments made today or as soon as possible so they can meet in committee at the time named above. Yours,

A. H. Watkins[323]

---

[319] The little farming community of Murvaul, now known as Brachfield, was situated on Murvaul Creek about three miles north of Minden and nearly the same distance south of Pine Hill in southeastern Rusk County. It was settled in the late 1850's.

[320] In 1860, Rusk County was divided into fourteen precincts, or beats, for census enumeration purposes. Beat number six was located in the southeastern part of the county and consisted of the communities of Pine Hill in the northern section and Minden in the southern.

[321] John S. Buckner (1806-1870) and wife Mariah (?-1874) settled at Pine Hill in the 1840's after moving from Georgia.

[322] Unidentified

[323] Archibald H. Watkins (1812-1881) of the Pine Hill Community served as the first Chief Justice of Rusk County from 1843 to 1844. The Chief Justice office was the same as the present-day office of County Judge.

South Carolina
York District
May 1, 1862

Dear Cousin,
I take the present opportunity of writing a few lines to you in answer to your kind letter dated February 13. Those lines leaves us all well, thank God for the precious blessing, and I hope these lines may find you all enjoying the same great blessing. Achsah I hant no thing of much importance to write only the times is hard and troublesome. You wanted to know what Mahala[324] done for coffee. Well, it is bad. We make use of wheat and rye. It is bad to do without coffee, but it is worse to do without salt. I don't reckon there could be as much as a bushel of salt got at any price. They say they carry it from York in papers like we used to get soda. I don't know it to be so I heard it, but I know it is bad enough to make the best of it. Some people is almost crazy about cloth. I don't fret much about cloth. We can [illegible] the back. Bacon is selling at 30 cent per pound and everything else in proportion. We have had a very wet winter and spring. We have got very little plowing done. Trisvan[325] has been bad off with his eyes. He went to the doctor and got cupped and blistered[326]. They are better. We have tried to hire a boy to help him but we could not get nary one. Mahala has gone to plowing. I don't think she can stand plowing if we had planting done. I don't know whether we can work a crop or not. There is a call for all the men & boys from 18 to 35. Trisvan is a weak steaks, but if he goes I don't know how we will tend a crop. We have done it when we were young & it was tough then. I don't think we can stand it now, the Lord knows. You said you wanted to know whether John F. Glenn was dead or not. He is dead. Cristana is a living by herself, her and her children. Jane Smith is dead. James Boyd[327] is dead. Franca

---

[324] Mahala Gibson
[325] Tresvan Cook
[326] Cupping was a medical procedure in which a small incision was made in the skin and blood drawn from it with a glass, cup shaped vacuum device. Blisters formed at the site if the process was done without making an incision.
[327] James D. Boyd (c.1831-1862), of the Zeno Community.

Patrick[328] was burnt up in her house. It was thought by some that she was murdered. Uncle David Horsly family was all well the last I heard from them. I have not seen none of them since you left except Robertus[329]. I have seen him. We are very lonesome; scarcely ever see anybody. I feel like an old tree looks standing with all the limbs off. Achsah, you have no idea how lonesome we feel. If I could only see you all I would not feel quite so lonesome. Give my love to your Mother. Tell her I think of her often if I can't see her. Give my love to Uncle Reason. Tell him I think about him often. Give my love to Thomas, Martha [Wallace], & Duncan & Jane [McCallum], & James A. & Elisa[330]. Mahala & Harriet [Gibson] sends their best respects to you all. Trisvan sends his best respects to you all. He says he would like to go and see them pretty girls but he will have to wait 'til the times is better. Harriet & Mahala was at old Mr. Anderson's[331] a Sunday. The old people is very poorly. They saw Addison. He [illegible] as glad as a cousin. He likes to talk about you all. You must excuse my bad spelling & writing. I must come to a close for the present. Write soon.

Eleanor Gibson to Achsah Wallace

---

[328] Frances Patrick (c.1796-1862) lived alone in the Zeno community.
[329] Robertus Horsley, son of David and Rachel (Mayhew) Horsley.
[330] James Adams and Margaret Elizabeth (Farris) Wallace
[331] Mr. William Anderson

Near Rondo, Arkansas[332]
Saturday evening
Sept. 6th, 1862

Dear Wife,
This being Saturday evening, I feel like writing you a few lines just for your own eye. Achsah I am getting along as well, and as well satisfied, as I expect to do while I am cut off from your society. I have every hope now that my health may be good, but Achsah, when I think about you and our children, I can't but long for the time that I will get back to you, and more particularly, of a Saturday evening and Sunday evenings when I think of the happy hours we spent together. Yet I hope we will be spared to meet and spend many days together again. Achsah, when we are together we do not know how much we are blessed. Do not think that I can forget you. You are in my mind through the day and often through the night. When I wake you are the first one I think of. I often look at your and Matty's likeness. I would not part with them for anything. Don't forget to send me a bracelet of your hair. Be sure to write to me as often as you can. You know it gives me as great a satisfaction as anything I get. Tell Willy to be a good boy and try to learn. Tell Bud to learn his letters, and that I say for him to mind you. Tell Matty her Papa will come to see her & Ma again. Tell your Mother not to forget me. I think of her often. Tell Leonard to be a good boy. Tell the Negroes to do the best they can. May God bless you. What a pleasure to be with you. So farewell. Your husband,

Harvey A. Wallace

Achsah we are all doing pretty well cooking. If we could just have some soda, we can make good biscuits. Dr. Rettig[333] brought us

---

[332] The town of Rondo was established in 1835 on the National Post Road (Trammel's Trace), near present day Texarkana, Texas. William D. Leet, *Texarkana: A Pictorial History* (Texarkana: Texarkana Historical Museum, 1982), 20-21.

[333] Dr. Conrad Rettig (1809-?), son of Frederic Rettig, practiced medicine in the Mount Enterprise community. Dr. Rettig and his wife, Lucie, immigrated to the United States from Heidelburg, Germany in 1834.

some soda. We have had good bread ever since. I wish you could have as plenty of flour as we have.

Addressed: Mrs. Achsah Wallace
At home
For your own eye alone.

**William Marcellus Wallace
Served as 2nd Lieutenant in
Company-H, 19th Texas
Infantry**

Sept. the 7th, 1862

My dear Achsah,
I send you a few lines for your own eye alone. How often do I think of the many hot tears you shed lying on my arm while thinking of our separation. And Achsah, while I was sick it would have done me so much good to have seen your face; that face of all others that gives life any joy to me. You know I thought about how hard I was when I could not shed tears with you, but alas Achsah, we are separated for a time. I hope not long, for I do feel like the Lord will bring us together again. I feel more like trusting to His will than I ever did in my life. I hope you do too. Let us look to Him in all of our trials and troubles. Achsah don't forget to pray for me. When I try to pray I always remember you and our little ones, lying on my blankets at night while there is some a singing, some laughing, some a swearing. Dear me, the swearing and cursing I do hear daily, but so it is. Achsah, William[334] is writing on one side of the table, John Brooks[335] on another. Duncan[336] is lying asleep under the arbor we are writing under. I never sleep in daylight and then I can sleep at night. Ach, continue to learn our children to say their little prayers, and take good care of them. Send Willy to school all you can. I would like for Bud to learn his letters. Kiss Matty for me. Achsah send me word how your health is and what your situation. Be candid with me as I have been with you. I have wrote to you all the time how I was as near as I knew. So may God bless and preserve you my dear wife. You do not know how dear you are to me. Your husband,

Harvey A. Wallace

---

[334] Harvey's brother, Private William M. Wallace
[335] 3rd Lieutenant John Reece King Brooks (11/16/1831-8/25/1916) was the son of William III and Martha (Wilson) Brooks. Lieutenant Brooks farmed and worked as a civil engineer after the war.
[336] Harvey's brother-in-law, 1st Lieutenant Duncan A. McCallum

Camp Josephine McDermott
Rondo, Arkansas
Sept. the 16, 1862

My dear Wife,
I send you a few lines by Capt. Jones[337] who leaves here in the morning for home. I am well at this time and have been since I last wrote to you, with the exception of an attack of bowel complaint. I was unwell Saturday & Sunday but able for duty. I wish I could say so for the company. Achsah we have buried five men from the 10th to the 15th in my company. I wrote to you before of some of the deaths. I will write again. John Koonce[338] died on Wednesday, Abner Stanly[339] on Thursday, Jasper Edge[340] on Friday, R.H. Gowens[341] on Sunday, & Tommy Easly[342] on Sunday. We now have one very bad case, Archie Barry[343]. He is very low indeed with pneumonia. These other men all died with measles. They nearly all had flux[344] with the measles. We don't have much trouble with measles when there is no flux or fever with them. William Burns[345] has been pretty bad but is now getting well. The whole company is sick nearly, but none of them dangerous. Achsah we only have from

---

[337] Thomas Jones (c.1808-?), a farmer from the Mt. Enterprise community, had two sons, James and Thomas P. Jones, serving in Wallace's Company. Evidently, he visited camp often and carried what mail and supplies that he could for the company.

[338] Private John Alexander Koonce (3/29/1832-9/10/1862), son of Daniel Sr. and Mary Koonce

[339] Private Abner Stanley (c.1833-9/11/1862)

[340] Private Jasper Edge (c.1838-9/12/1862)

[341] Private Robert H. Gowens (c.1828-9/14/1862)

[342] Private Thomas F. Easley (c.1838-9/15/1862), son of John and Nancy Easley.

[343] Private Archibald Barry (c.1834-9/16/1862) served with his twin brother, Andrew. Private Barry died later in the day after this letter was sent.

[344] Flux was generally used to describe diarrhea or loose bowels, also called the "bowel complaint" elsewhere in Wallace's writings. It was also used for the symptoms of dysentery, which included the passing of water or blood in the form of diarrhea.

[345] Private William S. H. (Billy) Burns (c.1844 -9/28/1863)

2 to 12 men to go out on duty. The balance of the men are sick or nursing the sick. We have not more than twenty men that are well in the company, waggoners and all. Brother William is sick at this time. He is threatened with bilious fever. He is one mile from here at a Mr. Dillard's[346]. He went out there last evening. I have just come home from there. I took dinner today. He is up and I have no doubt he will be in camps in a day or two. Dr. Becton[347] says he will break it up without him having fever. Lawson[348] is down with measles. He took down Saturday. The measles come out on him Monday morning. He is doing well. He is lying in the tent. I am taking good care of him. If the weather keeps good, I hope he will be up in a few days. If he is well enough when Mr. Hays[349] comes back I will send him home a while. Achsah I am getting scarce of paper. I hope you will not get out of paper. Get some from somewhere. I will have paper, if I can find any, to write to you. So farewell for the present. Duncan and John Ray[350] are well. Rhodes[351] is unwell. Brooks is in the country sick.

H. A. Wallace

---

[346] Unidentified

[347] Dr. Edward P. Becton (c.1834-?), son of Rev. J. M. and Emeline Becton, originally enlisted in Co.-I, 19th Texas Infantry. He was later promoted to Surgeon of the 22nd (Hubbard's) Texas Infantry. In February of 1863, Dr. Becton was again transferred within Walker's Division to serve as Surgeon of the 16th (Fitzhugh's) Texas Dismounted Cavalry.

[348] Harvey's slave, Lawson, accompanied him as a servant and cook.

[349] William C. Hays (c.1816-?) and wife Mary (Wilson) had four sons serving in Co.-H at the time of this letter: Cunningham, Benjamin, William Henry, and Daniel. William told his sons when they enlisted in 1862, "Now I don't want any heroes. I just want you home for the spring plowing." Rusk County Historical Commission, eds. *Rusk County History.* (Dallas: Taylor Publishing Co., 1982), 230.

[350] 2nd Sergeant John R. Ray (c.1832-11/14/1862), son of William D. and Eleanor (Templeton) Ray, was a brother of Harvey's sister-in-law, Josephine (Ray) Wallace.

[351] Private James Olen Rhodes (c.1829-4/30/1864), son of Nathaniel and Elizabeth (Thompson) Rhodes

Another note on the same sheet:
There is a sight of sickness in the reg[iment], but more in my company than any of the rest. There has not been more than five deaths in all of the other companies since we came here, beside mine. We have been very unfortunate since we came here, but I hope a better time is coming for us. The men that have measles don't get able for duty. We have so few men, what is well are on duty every other day and night. Capt. Jones has been here several days with his boys[352]. He found them both down with measles.

H. A. Wallace

Envelope Cover:
From Capt. H.A. Wallace
Com. Comp. {H} of 19th Reg.
of Texas Vol. Inft.
Through the politeness of Capt. Jones

To

Mrs. Achsah Wallace
At Home
Minden Po. Off.
Rusk County, Texas

---

[352] Privates James M. (c.1843-6/27/1864) and Thomas P. Jones (c.1840-11/24/1862) were sons of Thomas and Ellen Jones.

Rondo, Arkansas
Tuesday evening
Sept. 16th, 1862

My Dear Wife,
I send you a few lines for your own eye. Achsah I am busy all of the time from day until 8 or 9 o'clock at night. We have so much sickness. I have so much to attend to, and now we have our own cooking to do. Duncan & John have the most of the cooking to do, but I feel best when I am busy. I don't think so much about you and our children when I am kept busy. Achsah I have no idea how long we will be here. The Col[353]. now says we will be here until we get our tents, which will be two or three weeks yet. He give orders on last Friday for each company to saw boards and put up shelters to keep dry until we get our tents. The most of the companies are now got their shelters up. We have got 5 or six hundred boards made, but the most of the men are sick and we have had a man to bury nearly every day so we are behind. Achsah I would like very much to see you indeed, but the Lord only knows when it will be. If you could have come to have seen me I would have been glad, but I know you have no chance to come unless I get sick. Then I would like for you to come at all events if you could. I expect I could have got a

---

[353] Colonel Richard Waterhouse Jr. (1832-1876), a merchant from San Augustine, Texas and a Mexican War veteran, organized the 19th Texas Infantry at Jefferson in the spring of 1862. He was appointed Colonel of the regiment on May 13, 1862. Waterhouse proved a capable officer and was commended by Gen. Henry E. McCulloch for his leadership of the regiment in action at Millikens Bend, Louisiana on June 7, 1863. During the Red River Campaign in early 1864, Waterhouse again showed his ability to lead troops in action, and, as a result, was promoted to the rank of brigadier general on May 12, 1864, replacing Brigadier General William R. Scurry who was killed at Jenkins Ferry, Arkansas. President Davis, however, did not officially sign the appointment until March 17, 1865. General Waterhouse served as commander of the 3rd Brigade of Walker's Division until the end of the war. He engaged in land speculation in East Texas after the war, residing in San Augustine and Jefferson. Waterhouse died of pneumonia during a business trip after a fall down the stairs of a local hotel in Austin. Warner, 326-327.

Colonel Richard Waterhouse, Jr.
19th Texas Infantry

furlough to go home from here but the men could not, and I could not leave them here and so many of them sick unless I knew you or some of our sweet children were sick, then I would come sure. Our Colonel is very kind to me and does most anything I ask him for me & the men. I want to keep on the good side of him so I can get favors. Achsah I have got but one letter from you since I left home. I write often, but I know you like to hear from me, and you cannot tell how much good it does me to get a letter from you. I know I am hard, but I can't read your letters without shedding tears. I spend many an hour thinking about you on my bed. It would be a great pleasure to sleep with you on my arm one night, but so it is. I am as well satisfied as I could be to be away from you. To be sure, we are in the hands of bad officers, but I can do a lot for my men and that does me good. If any of my men ever have thought hard of me I don't know it. Achsah, you can't tell how hardened men get. Just to give you an idea, last night Tommy Easley was lying in the tent a corpse. Not more than fifty yards off in another company, the fiddle was a playing and the men a dancing a reel[354]. Even in our own company they don't mind it. Bury the poor men without shedding a tear, and their poor wives and children at home. We have buried all of our men at a burying ground[355]. I have written to all of the men's wives that have died. Achsah I never had filled up my bed until Lawson took the measles. I had it filled up with straw. I gave him my blue blanket and I lie beside him every night. I will give him every attention I can, and if the weather keeps good he will be up in a few days. He has not eat one bite since he took sick. Dr. Becton is our doctor now, and between you and me, I think we done fine to get the exchange. Don't say a word, Rettig is a great

---

[354] Private D. D. Page of Co.-C was one of the 19th Texas Infantry's prized fiddlers. Years later he remembered that the boys liked to hear the tunes, "The Virginia Reel", "Arkansas Traveler", "Billy In The Low Ground", "Money Musk", "Packenham's March", and "Have You Any Good Things". These were all lively dance tunes normally played at parties, dances, or holiday gatherings. *Confederate Veteran*; Vol.-33, No.-7; July, 1924.

[355] These soldiers rest in the Old Rondo, Arkansas Cemetery. A historical marker listing the names of those known to have been buried there marks the site. Eighty-five soldiers from various Texas regiments that camped nearby were interred at this cemetery in a plot donated by the town's citizens.

friend of mine. May the Lord bless [and] protect you. Remember me in your prayers. I try to remember you in my night and morning petitions.

Write soon, write often my sweet wife.

H. A. Wallace

<u>Addressed to:</u>
Mrs. Achsah Wallace
At home
For your own eye

Arkansas
In camps 4 miles north of Washington
Oct. the 5th, 1862

Dear and affectionate Wife,
I this Sabbath evening turn my thoughts to my privilege of writing to you, as I cannot be with you to talk face to face. Achsah, we arose at 4 o'clock this morning and were on the march before sunrise. We marched to music in regular order until we passed through Washington. It is a considerable town. I marched at the head of the company today. All the men that could walk had to get in ranks to come through town to make a show. The ladies waved their handkerchiefs some & the men waved their hats. As we got to the far end of town there was some Texan soldiers that had been left there to take care of the sick by the regiments ahead of us. They raised the shout for Texas. The whole reg[iment] took it up. They made a perfect roar of it. We came on 4 miles to this place to camp; got here about 11 o'clock. We got our tents sent and everything fixed up, & eat a bite of cold dinner, beef and biscuit; rested a while and carried up wood; a good long ways to carry it. There is a splendid spring here; very cold water, just enough for us to drink. We get cooking water out of the branch. I feel pretty well today. I tell you, I have lots to do, and the truth is Achsah, a soldier's life is a very hard one and we are beginning to find it out. I have had to eat what I would not think about at home and work when I was tired enough to lie down, but I am improving now and if I can get stout I will stand it better. I wish we had someone to do our cooking, but Achsah I cannot get my consent to bring Lawson back. I know he might die at home, but a man in camps stands ten chances to die to one he does at home if he never sees a battle. My own chances for escaping would be better than Lawson from sickness. I still have $90 dollars, and if I get sick I will try to have myself cared for. I know if I am not spared to come home to you, it will be bad enough if Lawson is there. Achsah you have no idea how much I think about you. I often dream of you at night. I have been looking at you and Matty today. I wish I could see Willy & Aaron too. It is some satisfaction to see your picture. Achsah, I read my Bible often and try to pray to God regular. I want you to read the Ninety Third

Psalm. There is a lot of consolation in it. Some few of the men are study and try to read their Bibles. The most of them are wicked and wild. Even in my company there is lots of them that play cards on Sunday. I have seen some of my men at it today. Achsah I have no doubt you would get a long letter from me today [illegible] Mrs. Riley[356]. I have no doubt but I write so much to you that it tires you to read my letters. Don't think so about me. It gives me more pleasure to read your letters than any pleasure I have. I want you to write me all about your health every time. Let me know what you have to eat. Don't want for anything you can get. Let me know how the potatoes are doing. I have eat one little one that Tommy Riley[357] gave me. We cannot buy anything from the people here to eat. Just have to eat such as we have along. Achsah, William is getting better. He walked all the way today except one mile. Billy Burns is along. He is lots of trouble. The measles made him very weak. He mends up a few days and then eats until he is nearly dead for a day or two. Smith[358], his brother-in-law, has lots of trouble with him. If he don't get better he will be sure to kill himself. Don't say anything to his people about what I write in this. James Easley[359] is bad with pneumonia and still in camps. We have several very weak men along. We haul them. Achsah, direct your next letters to Little Rock. I will be anxious to hear from you there. We will stay here until Tuesday morning when we will leave for Little Rock. It is about 120 miles from here to Little Rock. As weak as the men are, it will take us 15 or twenty days travel. Why, we have lots of men who give out in walking one or two miles. You will pass them all of the time sitting on the side of the road. Besides, they haul about 100 all of the time. Achsah show this letter to no one. I just write it to you. I

---

[356] Mrs. Anna Riley (c.1841-?), wife of Private Thomas J. Riley.
[357] Private Thomas J. Riley (c.1835-5/30/1864)
[358] Unidentified
[359] Private James O. Easley (c.1828-10/19/1862) was the son of John and Nancy Easley.

hope to get home to see you sometime between this and spring. So take care of yourself for me and don't allow yourself to fret. Trouble is bad enough when it comes without us troubling ourselves too soon. My love to your Mother. Tell Uncle Reece I want some of his tobacco. I don't know what I will do when I get out. I got a lot of envelopes today. I will send you some. May God bless & protect you & family is the prayer of your husband.

H. A. Wallace

Camp Nelson[360]
Prairie County, Arkansas
Oct. the 26, 1862

My dear & affectionate Wife,
I this morning write you a few lines to let you know how we are getting on. I am quite well and hearty since I last wrote to you. We left our camps at Little Rock Wednesday morning at daylight; marched into town and commenced crossing the Arkansas River. We crossed in a steamboat. The men got over by eleven o'clock. They commenced on the wagons. It took 'till midnight to get the wagons all over the river. Our company wagons got over about nine o'clock at night. We all camped on the bank of the river; nothing to eat only what we carried in our haversacks, beef and blue flour made up with water. I met with Jim Talbert[361]. He was stationed over there to guard a cannon. He told me all about the Carolinians[362] about this place. William, Duncan, and me took supper with Jim, Logan Douglass[363], and William Fewel[364]. Old Jimmy's son drove in there about night on their way to the salt works. They had left home that morning and had good biscuit & fresh pone & barbecued beef. I

---

[360] The beginning of the harsh Arkansas winter of 1862-63 found the Texas and Arkansas troops assigned to Generals Henry E. McCulloch and Allison Nelson encamped northeast of Little Rock near the village of Austin. The camp was named in honor of General Nelson, who died of pneumonia October 7, 1862. Sickness soon set in and epidemics of typhoid fever, measles, pneumonia, dysentery, and other diseases common to crowded winter camps claimed hundreds of lives. Every regiment at Camp Nelson suffered to the point that most became unfit for service as fighting units. The 19th Texas arrived at Camp Nelson in mid-October with men already weakened from previous bouts with disease. The results were swift and devastating.
[361] Unidentified- The Talbert family was kin through marriage to Achsah and the Mayhew family of York District.
[362] A large number of York District residents moved to Arkansas during the 1850's in search of better farmland.
[363] James Logan Douglass (c.1807-1863) from York District was distant kin to Achsah.
[364] Unidentified

tell you, it was a treat to us about ten o'clock at night. We took up the march next morning at eight o'clock; traveled twelve miles [and] camped. Duncan and me heard it was four miles to Jim Neely's[365]. We started about one hour before sunset. We traveled ten miles before we got to his house about eight o'clock at night. We passed Martin West's[366] and several other Carolinians without knowing it. We got a fine supper & breakfast. The first butter & milk or hog meat I had eat for some time. Neely lives four miles from here. The Cooks[367] live about 6, Douglass about eight. In fact, the South Carolinians all live from 2 to 10 miles of here. William Nichols[368] lives within two miles of here. Miles Barns[369] the same distance. Nichols was in here yesterday. He took out all of our dirty clothes to have them washed. I sent three shirts, a table cloth, drawers, & so on. I will go to see the old Carolinians as soon as I can get out of camps if we stay here long enough. The people here have made very good crops but they have nothing to spare to eat. The army has eat them all out. Our living here is pretty hard, but I reckon it is fair. The men draw about two meals a day and do without the other. They don't get only about what will make two meals. They grumble considerably. We have improved in health since we left Rondo. We have one case of sickness now in our company that is a very bad one, James Parker[370]. He took the chills after we left Little Rock. He has had several. I think he will die. There is a bad chance here to take care of the sick [since] it is so cold now. It commenced snowing here early yesterday morning and snowed fast until eleven o'clock. It then blew off cold. There is snow lying all around now. It is quite cold today indeed; plenty of ice this morning. The axes are going all around. While I write there is two or three games of town ball[371] going on, some playing cards, the drums a beating to mount

---

[365] Unidentified
[366] Unidentified
[367] John Cook (c.1800-?) and wife Ann were from York District.
[368] Unidentified
[369] Unidentified
[370] Private James Parker (c.1825-2/28/1863)
[371] Town ball was a favorite pastime for soldiers of both sides during the Civil War. It dated to colonial times in America and is considered a forerunner to modern

guard, and yet it is Sunday. About half of my company have got passes from the Col. and gone to see the other Texas regiments around here. They are camped all around from 2 to 4 miles. I cannot tell how many; some twenty or twenty-five Texas regiments. The Arkansas troops are all gone up north of this. I do not know how many there is of them. We have a very good camp ground in a grove of large oak timber. We have cut nearly all of the timber down already. We have our water to carry a half of a mile, but it is fine when we get it. The spring affords water a plenty for ten thousand men. This country is about the best I have seen in Arkansas. The people are very sickly here; a lot of deaths. Your husband,

H. A. Wallace

---

baseball. Town ball was played with a bat and ball. Players used posts, trees, or rocks as bases.

Camp Nelson
Prairie County, Arkansas
Nov. the 3rd, 1862

My beloved Wife,
I this morning take my pen to write you a few lines. Well Achsah, in the first place, I am well and hearty, thank God for the blessing of health, and my prayer is that you and our children & the rest of the family are enjoying a like blessing. William is not very well, but able for duty. He is on guard today. Duncan has been complaining for some days but is better. Brooks is unwell too. Rhodes is complaining of his back. John Ray & me are the only ones not complaining in our mess. The health of the men is generally improving some. They get well very slow. Our diet is not fit for men who have been sick; poor beef and bread. It keeps the men's bowels running off all the time. We all have diarrhea. We drawed a half a pound of bacon to the man on yesterday for the first we have drawed since before we left Rondo. The beef we get now is very poor. We will now get a half of a pound of bacon to the man every seven days. That will help. The other reg[iments] that have been here are drawing potatoes and turnips & pumpkins. I suppose we will get some shortly. The men got one little mess last week. We have plenty of bread and meat. In my mess we buy about twenty five pounds of flour a week, a gallon of molasses & sugar, and what beef we can eat. I bought a small middling of bacon from Miles Barnes last week weighing 13 pounds; gave 40 cents a pound; glad to get it at that. As for butter, milk, or any kind of vegetables, we don't get them. Achsah some soldiers will give the last cent of money and any price to get something fresh to eat. I have not come to that yet. A soldier dearly earns his money and I do hate to see them fooled out of it. James Parker is some better but is low yet with typhoid fever; just lying here in a tent. You know it is a bad chance for a man with fever on the ground in cold weather. We have several other men who are up and down but none much sick as yet. I heard from the men we left at Rondo. They will be in here this week. Billy Burns has got pretty well, as has George Burns[372]. The

---

[372] Private Charles George Burns (c.1845-8/22/1899)

men you know are generally well. Joe Akins[373] is sick. He has roseolio[374]. There was one man died in Capt. Furguson's comp[any][375] this morning who only had been sick one day. One of Capt. Loving's[376] Lieutenants & men will die today, so they say. In fact, there is some bad cases of sickness in the regiment at this time. There is a sight of sickness in the Texas regiments that have been here some time. They are dying every day; not more than from two to three hundred men able for duty to the regiments. John Brooks was in Randal's Brigade[377] Saturday evening some two hours. He said they hauled off ten or eleven men to bury while he was there. The weather has been beautiful since the day after we got here; clear & cool; some frost every night. William and me took our bed ticks Friday evening and went into a corn field and pulled crab grass and filled them. We have been lying comfortable since. Achsah, John Cook come into camp to see us last Saturday evening. He looks well; says his people are well. He wants us all to go to see him if we stay here any length of time. I am going to try to get out to see them all. He lives 4 miles from here. Darky Wilson[378] lives eight or ten. He says she has seen lots of trouble here. John James[379] died in the

---

[373] Private Joseph F. Akins (c.1832-11/1862)

[374] Roseola is the medical term for a skin condition marked by maculae or red spots of varying sizes on the skin. It may also be used to describe any rose colored rash. *Tabors Cyclopedic Medical Dictionary, Ed.-18*, (Philadelphia: F.A. Davis Co., 1997), 1696.

[375] Co.-G, 19th Texas Infantry, under the leadership of Captain L. M. Ferguson

[376] Captain William C. Loving of Co.-B, 19th Texas Infantry

[377] Colonel Horace Randal (1833-1864) of the 28th Texas Cavalry (Dismounted) commanded the 2nd Brigade of McCulloch's (later Walker's) Division. This brigade consisted of the 11th and 14th Texas Infantry Regiments and the 28th Texas Dismounted Cavalry. Also attached to the brigade were Gould's Infantry Battalion, under Major Robert S. Gould, and Daniel's Battery of light artillery.

[378] Dorcas Wilson

[379] Unidentified

army last fall. Her two youngest sons[380] were taken prisoners at Island [Number] Ten and she has never heard from them since. John's three youngest sons[381] are in the army. Randolph[382], Green[383], & William[384], and Mary's man William[385] & me went out to Bill Nichol's Tuesday night to get our clothes. Sally was so glad to see us. They have all suffered lots with sickness except Sally herself. The children don't look like the same family. Bill has had a hard spell of fever. The old man is about the same. Blankenship & his wife[386] live in Little Rock. I did not see them. Sally is the worst dissatisfied woman you ever seen. She says she is determined to go back to York when the war closes. Bill made a good crop of corn. They appear to live pretty well. They have no cows or hogs. Sally charged us 15 cents a garment for washing & ironing. She washed our clothes clean for the first time they have been since Lawson left us. Achsah, this army has orders to be ready to march at a moments warning. We have no guns yet but expect to get them in a few days. The report here is that Hindman[387] is retreating before the Yankees from the northern part of the state. If so, we may have some lively times this month yet, though we don't know one hour what we have to do next. There is lots of reports afloat in camps about peace, but I put no faith in camp rumors unless I know how they start. I have no

---

[380] Robert and William Wilson served in Co.-A, 11th Arkansas Infantry. This regiment was part of the garrison defending Island Number-10 in the Mississippi River near New Madrid, Missouri. Confederate forces on the island surrendered on April 8, 1862 and were exchanged soon after.
[381] Private Elijah G., and 2nd Lieutenant William L. Cook served in Co.-K, 28th/36th Arkansas Infantry. John R. Cook's service could not be verified.
[382] Unidentified
[383] Unidentified
[384] Private William Wallace
[385] Unidentified
[386] Unidentified
[387] Major General Thomas C. Hindman (1828-1868), an Arkansas congressman, was instrumental in the Arkansas push for secession. Hindman was in command of the Trans-Mississippi Department at the time of this letter. Warner, 137-138.

doubt you know more about what is going on than I do, so Achsah you need not expect me to write much news. I will write more before I close this. May God bless you my wife. Your affectionate and distant husband,

H. A. Wallace

Show this to no one Achsah.
Camp Nelson
Tuesday morning
Nov. the 4th, 1862

Dear Achsah,
I this morning write you a few more lines. I am very well this morning. The health of the company is about as it was. We still have beautiful weather, clear and white frosts at night. Achsah, William and me are going out to John Cook's tonight. We will stay until Thursday and see all of them we can. Achsah I would like to write a long letter but have not time this morning. I have not been out of our reg[iment] since I have been here, only the night William and me went to Nichol's. The balance of the camp have all been around amongst the other regiments, but you know I don't know but few Texans outside of our own regiment. Jim Welch[388] and Lee Moore[389] have sent for me to come to see them but I have not had time as yet. Welch is well. William and Ray have been to see them twice. Welch wants you to let me know how his people are as he has not heard from them in a long time. Lee Moore is sick they say. I drill my company altogether myself so far. The Lieuts. have not been well. Duncan is well enough now. Achsah, John Ray and J. O. Rhodes received letters last night. Rhodes had heard a Sunday of the death of his little daughter[390]. We hear tales from Texas of the abolitionists cutting up in some places. It makes us feel bad here 325 miles from home, but if ever they do rise, Texans are going home to take care of their families. I hope the reports we hear are not true. There is considerable excitement among the soldiers about a law that exempts tradesmen and men that have twenty Negroes, horses, & so on[391]. We heard last night that the President had

---

[388] 2nd Lieutenant James W. Welch of Minden served in Co.-B, 11th Texas Infantry.
[389] Unidentified
[390] Elizabeth Rhodes (10/1859-1862), daughter of Private James Olen and Nancy (Whitfield) Rhodes.
[391] On October 11, 1862, the Confederate Congress passed an act to amend the draft exemption law. This controversial act soon became known as the "Twenty

ordered out all men from thirty five to forty. Tell Thomas[392] not to volunteer, but to stay at home. He can get off by attending to our Negroes and his own. And I don't see how you would all get along without him, and we must have some men at home. Achsah we have fife & drums, brass bands, & bugles play nearly all the time. While I write, the Flying Artillery[393] is rattling by a drilling. Three regiments drill on the same field with us over in a brigade[394] two miles from here. The guns have been rattling, practicing I suppose, the last fifteen minutes, so there is always noise and confusion until one don't hear it. I can pass along as if everything was quiet. Achsah tell Thomas I would have written to him if I had have got time. I wrote to Brother James on Sunday. You asked me to send you a lock of my hair. I will put one in this. My hair is short yet. I have had it cut at Rondo, but if I live until it gets longer I can send you another. I have the bracelet you sent me. It was too large for my arm. I wore it a while. I then put it in my pocketbook. I wish you would send me another and make it smaller. Send me one of Matty's curls. Achsah you have no idea how I long to see you and our little children, your Mother, and all. I think of you by day and night. When we lie down on our hard beds I always turn my thoughts to you and the happy time we have spent together, and think will ever be so again. Then I can't but pray the Lord to spare our lives to meet. When I wake up [I] call your name instead of one of the boy's. I cannot give you no idea of the pleasure it would give me to see you, but Achsah I owe duty to my country and company so I

Negro Law" as it exempted those who owned twenty or more slaves and those of certain occupations deemed necessary to the war effort. To many impoverished southerners, the war was quickly becoming a "rich man's war but a poor man's fight."

[392] Thomas Wallace

[393] Flying Artillery was a name given to light artillery units during the Mexican war. These units consisted of small, light, highly mobile cannon usually grouped into a battery of three or four guns. Walker's Division made extremely effective use of these units to support its infantry operations.

[394] The 19th Texas Infantry was assigned to the 3rd Brigade of the recently formed Texas Infantry Division under Brigadier General Henry McCulloch. The 3rd Brigade was commanded at this time by Colonel George Flournoy of the 16th Texas Infantry and consisted of the 16th, 17th, and 19th Texas Infantries and the 16th Texas Dismounted Cavalry, along with Edgar's Battery of light artillery.

must not complain. Do write to me as often as you can. You have written me such long and satisfactory letters. It does me lots of good. I can't give you no idea when we may leave here. They are making every effort to get us guns. The men that have arms are holding themselves ready to march at a moments notice. Achsah, Andrew Berry[395] will get a furlough in a few days if McCullough[396] will sign it, to go home until January to get his family a home as he is weakly. We expect to draw pay in a few days. If we do, I will have some money to send you. I will send you two or three hundred dollars by him if I get my pay. All I will have to pay for [is] a sword, but if they pay me all, I will have nearly six hundred dollars. I suppose Jerry Deason[397] has give you all of the news and is on his way with our clothes. We need them. Write often. I will do the same. Tell the Negroes howdy for me. My love to your Mother, Thomas & Martha. Tell her if I ever get back I am coming over to get something good to eat. May God's blessings rest on you my dear wife, and may He preserve you and our little ones until we meet to live happy together in this world again is the prayer of your affectionate husband.
H. A. Wallace

Brigadier General Henry E. McCulloch

---

[395] Private Andrew L. Barry (c.1834-11/25/1862), twin brother of Private Archibald Barry.

[396] Brigadier General Henry E. McCulloch (1816-1895), a veteran of the Texas Rangers during the Mexican War and a Texas legislator, was assigned the task of organizing the various Texas units at Camp Nelson into a division consisting of four brigades with four regiments of infantry and a battery of light artillery per brigade. McCulloch commanded the division until relieved by Brigadier General John G. Walker in January 1863, after which he took command of the 3rd Brigade of the division. The unit soon became known as Walker's Texas Division and held the distinction of being the largest Confederate Army organization composed of troops from a single state. Warner, 201.

[397] 4th Sergeant Jeremiah Deason (1829-2/14/1863) was the son of Joseph and Jelico (Cates) Deason.

Camp Nelson
Prairie County, Arkansas
Nov. the 10th, 1862

My beloved Wife,
I this morning have taken my pen to write you a few lines to inform you how we are getting along in camp. I am in moderately good health. I have been able for duty every day since I came here. The health of the company is only moderately good. The whole army is suffering with colds; the worst of coughs. We have but one bad case at this time in the company. William Whitfield[398] is down with typhoid fever; will be a very bad case. Marion Grimes[399] has typhoid fever too. There is several other men not well. There is lots of cases of fever in our regiment. We lost three men in our regiment this morning, and some 1 or 2 more that will die today from pneumonia and typhoid fever. Achsah they are burying soldiers all the time here. There is so much sickness in the different regiments. I hope the health will improve. Well Achsah, William and me got permission to leave camp last Tuesday evening and stay until Thursday. Jim Wood[400] came in that day so I got Dr. Becton's horse. Jim had two. William and me went home with him and stayed all night. It is ten miles to his house. Jim has a good place and plenty of everything. He is doing fine here. He don't owe a cent; has plenty of money; a fine stock of hogs. He will kill between 3 and 4 thousand pounds of pork this year. Jim was very kind. So was his wife. She is the same Rachel yet. They have four children, two boys and two girls; the boy 3 weeks old. We went to Bob's[401] next morning. He lives a mile from Jim's. He has a good place; a good new house and a good stock, and 7 children. Mary Douglas[402] lives with him. Manerva[403] has been dead some 2 months. Bob was at Douglases[404]

---

[398] Private William B. Whitfield (c.1831-12/12/1862), son of Bryan and Emily (Bailey) Whitfield.
[399] Private Marion H. Grimes (c.1831-?).
[400] James A. (c.1827-?) and Rachel (Hall) Wood from York District, S. C.
[401] Unidentified
[402] Unidentified
[403] Unidentified

We went there to dinner. Douglases 2 oldest boys are in Kentucky. His next boy has been lying for a month low with typhoid fever. They treated us very kind. Sarah is lean, but the same old Sarah. Douglas has made money every year since being here. After dinner, we went to Jesy Wilson's[405]. They are well fixed. Old Jesy has [a] splendid house. Elias[406] and his children are there. His wife died this fall. Old Aunt Peggy[407] was very kind. We went to see Darky Wilson. She lives in sight. She just has three daughters at home, the oldest about grown. Darky looks younger than I expected to see her. She is poor. John James died this fall in the army here. Robert and William were both taken prisoners at Island [Number] Ten. She has not heard from them since. She was so kind; told us to come back to see her and she would give us some butter. She lives 8 miles from camp. We came to John Cook's that night. He is four miles from camp. Cousin Anny looks pretty old. They have Mary[408] with them. She has a baby about ten months old. John Cook has a house full of corn. He has a good stock of cattle. He says he can do as well here as he wants to. He takes his ease and lives well. We had a good supper and breakfast there. We went to Andrew Gingles[409] for dinner. His wife was gone to Jim Neely's. Neely's wife is about to die. Andy treated us very kind. We came to the camp that evening both a little sick. A change of diet did not agree with us. We eat a little too strong. Gingles has a trunk I want. It is as large again as mine and very strong. He has lost the key. I think I will send over and swap for it as mine is entirely too small. Duncan is gone out to Gingles today. Duncan has a bad cold and has done no duty in a week. Hays[410] is unwell and does no duty. Brooks is sick the most of

---

[404] Unidentified
[405] Jesse (c.1797-?) and Margaret Wilson from York District, S. C.
[406] Elias C. Wilson (c.1826-?), son of Jesse and Margaret Wilson
[407] Mrs. Margaret Wilson
[408] Mary E. Cook (c.1845-?), daughter of John and Ann Cook
[409] Andrew J. (c.1824-?) and Eliza Gingles were from York District, S. C. Andrew is listed as a merchant in the 1850 York District census.
[410] 2nd Lieutenant Cunningham S. Hays (c.1834-?), son of William and Mary (Wilson) Hays.

the time but still helps all he can. He is in command today. William is able for duty but still has a bad cough. John Ray keeps stout. Rhodes is complaining most of the time of his back. Achsah we have got arms for the most of our men who are well. Each company has drawn 30 good muskets that was taken at [illegible]. All of this army now is pretty well armed, and they are getting guns every day. We are expecting every day to move from here. Our orders are to be ready at a moments warning. We don't know where. We think to reinforce Hindman. He is said to be falling back before 35,000 Yankees in the northern part of the state. I think a part of this army will be kept here to keep the army at Helena back. The rest of us go to help Hindman. The weather is clear and cold; a fine time on us so far. Achsah I have not heard from you since the 16th of Oct., nearly one month. I am very anxious to hear. Do write often. Your husband until death, and may God bless and protect you all is my prayer.

H. A. Wallace

Tuesday morning
[November] the 11, [1862]

My Beloved Wife,
I this morning write you a few more lines. Alas Achsah, the news I have is sad indeed. Duncan, poor fellow, is no more. He died last night at Capt. Gingles. He rode out there on yesterday morning to see them. He had been complaining for a week or so but was as hearty as any of us. The Col. gave him leave to go out. He told me when he left he would probably stay at John Cook's last night. This morning Cook came in to tell us he was dead. He said Gingles said he took something like [illegible] before he got to his house and was deranged when he got there and died last night; none of us with him. I sent his best clothes out by John Cook. None of us can get out until we get permission from McCulloch. The company will go out and I will have him buried decently. Poor Jane, poor thing, I do pity her & the children. I had no idea I would send such news as this when I wrote my letter last evening, but so it is. The Lord knows best, but it does seem hard to us. I will leave Duncan's things at Gingles. Achsah, William got a letter last night. I got none. Us Captains were all relieve[d] this morning. They are very tight on us here indeed. Our Col. is as kind as he can be and does all he can for us. There is no telling here how long a man is to live. They die so sudden. Remember me in your prayers my dear wife. I have not despaired, but the Lord has seen fit to put a heavy affliction on us and my company. We have had more deaths than are a company in the regiment so far. I suppose it is for our good, if we could see it so. I will write to Jane if spared. I have not time to write more now. May God bless, protect, and preserve you all from harm is the prayer of your husband.

H. A. Wallace

Camp Nelson, Arkansas
Nov. the 15th, 1862

Dear and beloved Wife,
I this morning, with a sad heart, write you a few lines. Achsah, death has claimed its share in our happy little mess. This week John Ray, poor fellow, now lies cold in death in my tent beside me. He died last evening at dusk; was taken the evening before at four o'clock with a chill. He died with congestion of the whole system, the same disease that killed Duncan[411]. I wrote to you in my last about Duncan's death. For fear you may not have got it I will write it again. Duncan had been unwell for several days. He went to the Col. Monday morning and asked leave to go out to Gingles. He got a beast and started at nine o'clock. He was hearty enough to eat breakfast just like the rest of us; had been able for some duty. He said to me when he started he had a notion to stay that night with John Cook. I told him it would be alright. He said he wanted to hear Gingles talk that day. It is four miles to Gingles. He got there at eleven, very bad off and deranged. Some told them he had a very bad spell on the road. He went to bed. They thought him better in the evening. He told Gingles he wanted to go to camp but he got suddenly worse about dark and told Gingles he was a going to die. Gingles said he suffered powerfully, perfectly deranged; kept him busy to keep him in bed until just before he died, when he died easy. He never spoke anything that they could understand. He died just before six in the morning. John Cook came in next morning at eight. I sent his clothes out by him. It was twelve o'clock before any of us could get out. I took a wagon and 2 men to make a coffin; 4 to dig a grave: William, John Ray, Andy Barry. We got out there between two and three. We had to get plank at John Cook's to make the coffin. Bill Barron[412] came there that morning. He wanted him taken to where his Amelia was buried, and two of old Mr. Anderson's

---

[411] Lieutenant McCallum and Sergeant Ray died of a disease that the medical officers usually diagnosed as "brain fever." The symptoms were that of an inflammation or infection of the brain or meninges, most often caused by encephalitis or meningitis.
[412] Bill and Amelia Barron from York District, S. C.

daughters[413]. It was ten miles from Gingles. I got Barron to go on and have the grave dug. I then sent the men all back to camp, except William, John Ray, Andrew Barry, John Giles[414], & Billy Bates[415] stayed to make the coffin. Giles had a chill. Bates and Ray made the coffin. William and Barry went home with Cook. Ray and me set up all night with the corpse; put on his coat in the morning. We started at sunrise; took a two horse wagon. John drove the wagon. William and Barry rode in the wagon with him. We got him buried by 12. We went by Jim Wood's. He went with us as we buried him at Bethel Church. William [and] me came to Jim Wood's for dinner. Ray, Barry, & Gingles went to Bill Barron's. He is married again. We got back to camp against dusk. John Ray went on guard duty next morning at eight. He came in at 12 to dinner; eat a hearty dinner. He would not have to go back until six. At three o'clock when the drum beat for battalion drill, I was cleaning my pistol; had it to pieces. John told me he would put it together and put it away. I went out; stayed 2 hours. When I came in John was in bed; said he had a chill. He kept cold; appeared bad off about dusk. William got Becton to come to see him. He give him some medicine. John did not rest much through the night. We were not uneasy; thought he had a common chill. He got worse in the morning. The doctor came to see him. He called in several others. John appeared better before twelve; told me he thought he was better but he was deranged, only when you spoke to him. About twelve he grew worse. It took four men to hold him in bed. He was the worst deranged man I ever seen. He never knew anything more; just grew weaker and died about dusk, perfectly easy; has as pretty a smile on his countenance as you ever seen; just looks like he was asleep. Oh Achsah, you do not know how I feel. Poor Duncan first, now John, not four days between them; cut down so suddenly, and our little mess most broke up. John felt like a brother to me, but the Lord's will be done. Achsah these may be the last lines I ever write to you. The men are dying here rapidly every day, about twelve a day in our brigade.

---

[413] Unidentified
[414] Private John Giles (c.1829-?)
[415] Private William J. Bates (8/1829-3/3/1906)

There is 4 brigades. We lose about 50 a week. From 2 to about 12 hundred out of this army die a month at the present rate. Col. Allen's Reg[iment][416] has a disease just broke out yesterday. They had all of the doctors together last night. The doctors did not decide what it is. The men's tongues swell up until they can't keep them in their mouths. Allen is losing lots of men. He is in our brigade. I am in good health and do not despair, for I feel I am in the hands of my God who will spare me or cut me down as it seems best to Him. Therefore, I pass amongst all kinds of sickness every day. I have four very sick men in camp: Whitfield, Robertson[417], Giles, Grimes; none of them dangerous at present. They have camp fever. We have sent nine to Little Rock to the hospital this week[418]. These other four were not able to go. They are taking all the sick that are able to be moved to Little Rock to the hospital. Achsah I never craved to go into battle, but I would rather risk the battlefield as the diseases we have here now. I have no idea how long we will stay here. I am anxious to move if it was only ten miles. I think we would have better health. Achsah I got your letter and Thomases night before last. It came in 11 days. It done me lots of good to hear of you being in better health and of little Matty getting better, and that the rest were well except Bud's burn, and getting along well. Tell Thomas I am glad he wrote to me. He give me lots of satisfaction about the crop. And to manage about sowing the wheat just as if it was his own. If spared I will write to him as soon as I get time. Tell him to write again. I write to you nearly all the idle time I have. Achsah, old Holmes[419] & McCulloch are very hard on us indeed; on the captains in particular. We have no blank forms of no kind. We have

---

[416] The 17th Texas Infantry, under Colonel R. T. P. Allen, was attached to the 3rd Brigade of the division.
[417] Private E. T. Robertson (c.1832-?)
[418] Privates J. E. Anderson, Newton A. Golden, Sion Holly, J. T. Hudman, and James Parker were sent to St. Johns Hospital in Little Rock on Nov. 10, 1862. 4th Corporal W. D. Harris and Privates John T. Ghentry and James D. Raburn went to St. Johns two days later.
[419] Lieutenant General Theophilus H. Holmes (1804-1880), an old-line U.S. Army officer and Mexican War veteran from North Carolina, had recently replaced Major General Thomas Hindman in command of the Trans-Mississippi Department. General Holmes was renowned for being a strict disciplinarian. Warner, 141

so much sickness, we have to make out forms of some kind every day. They take no excuse when we are not drilling. We are always busy. Achsah, Brooks & me has got G. L. Stoveall[420] to cook for us. We have no time to cook now in daylight. I needed Lawson but would much rather you had have kept him at home, as we could hire George Stovall to cook and we could shift some way to get washing done. I like to be busy all the time to keep my mind employed, but I have a plenty to do now. Achsah, John Brooks is as good a fellow as ever lived in camps; always ready to do anything you want done. I do not know how I could get along without him. He has a very bad cough ever since we were at Rondo. He is not stout at all. Achsah, the men who are at home sick had better stay there until they get able for duty, for sick men are best off at home. This army is miserably fed. That is one thing that causes so much sickness; sometimes 3 or 4 days without a bite of meat unless they buy it. A good many of the mess have bought hogs; give 20 cents a pound for thin pork. Some of us sent out a wagon 10 or 12 miles. It got in last night. We bought at 12 ½ cents per pound. I got 90 pounds; the first pork I have got. May God bless you my dear wife.

H. A. Wallace

---

[420] Private George L. Stoveall (c.1835-?)

Camp Bayou Meto[421]
Saturday
Nov. the 29th, 1862

My Dear Wife,
I this day write you a few lines again as it is wash day and I have a little more time than usual. Achsah we are still at the same camp where I wrote from on Tuesday. I am well and have been since I last wrote. Thank God for one of the greatest of temporal blessings, and my prayer is these lines may find you and the rest of the family enjoying a like blessing. Brother William is well. He is out today working on the road from our company. They have men from all the companies out ahead. I don't know what for. Probably to enable them to haul corn and fodder. Some say it is to move on. John Brooks is very unwell; has been since we come here; just able to be up. About half of the men here belonging to the company are sick; none of them dangerous. I expect we will send Tom Hunt[422] and Henderson Reinhart[423] back to the hospital at Little Rock. The talk in camp this morning is that we will move tomorrow two miles to get a dryer camp ground. Achsah this is the disagreeablest wet country I ever saw. The ground is perfectly level, and wet and swampy. I don't see how we will do when it sets in wet. Every day looks like it would rain. We will be in a perfect swamp. We are on the edge of a large prairie, not a stick of timber on it. I don't think we will remain here but a few days now, but have no idea where we will go. I don't want to stay here, nor I don't like the idea of going on down the river. People who know say the country is a perfect swamp below this. Achsah I have no news from the Yankees. We

---

[421] On November 24, 1862, McCulloch's Division moved to a location on Bayou Meto, east of Little Rock. The move was intended to bring relief from the crippling epidemics that were ravaging the soldiers at Camp Nelson. J. P. Blessington, *The Campaigns of Walker's Texas Division* (Austin, Tx.: State House Press, 1994), 61.
[422] Private Thomas J. Hunt Jr. (c.1835-10/5/1888), son of Thomas and Lucy Hunt
[423] Private James P. Henderson Reinhart (c.1840-12/7/1862), son of Martin F. and Mary Reinhart.

get no news now at all, but I have no doubt but we will meet them this winter when Arkansas River gets up. If the Yankee gunboats come up we will be in a bad box, as all of our provision have to come across the river. If they should get possession of Arkansas River, I can't see how we could get out. We get no news from the other side of the Mississippi here. Achsah, Andrew Barry & Joe Akins have both died at Camp Nelson since we left, so I hear. Joe was very sick when we left with pneumonia. Andrew allowed to come along until that morning but felt unwell and said he would stay. Now I hear he is dead. That makes 19 men I have lost; nearly one out of five. I trust the Lord will give us better health than we have had, but the way men are exposed and have to live in this most sickly country, we can't but expect to lose lots more men this winter. John Connally[424] has got a discharge & will start home in a day or two. I got a paper of needles at Austin, which I will either send in this letter or by him. I also bought a spool of coats thread for you, which I will send. I gave fifty cents for the needles & the same for the thread. Deason has not come yet. Some of the men are needing their clothes bad. It is cold weather here and they have to be out on guard so much. Some have no coats, only linsey overshirts. I have all of my woolen clothes on and do very well. Jim Acrey[425] is down with pneumonia in an old house. He had nothing but two blankets so I sent him my bed. I had a man riding all yesterday trying to get a house for him. I failed. I have one out today again. I got a good wagon load of hay yesterday; enough for all my company, so we will do fine until it rains. But one or two more companies got any. Achsah, I want you to buy a cow or two if you need milk. I can't give you much advice how to do. My love to your Mother and all enquiring friends. I must stop as I have to get dinner today. Rhodes is on guard; Stoveall gone to another reg[iment] today. May God bless you my dear wife and children.

Harvey A. Wallace

---

[424] Private John W. Connally (c.1835-?)
[425] Private James Acrey (c.1829-9/25/1899), son of Abner and Martha (Jackson) Acrey

My dear Wife I this morning write ⎰ Shreveport Louisianna
you a few more lines. I am ⎱ Wednesday morning May 20th 1863
tolerable well thank the Giver
of all Good, for the Blessing of health and my pray is that
you and the rest of our Family are Enjoying a like Blessing
Hensah I am getting along very well in our new Quarters
Tommy, Riley, Tommy, Huitt, Timmy, Guthrie & me are staying in
a large upstairs Room in Town it is over a Carriage Factory
we have fine Blankets amongst us there is a plenty of Chairs
Tables a desk, & Wash Stand & Bolt. we Borrowed a Skillet and
pan to Cook in Borrowed a water Bucket from James Wright
my tin and one other is all the Tableware we have We
draw their Rations I Bought 20 pound of Flour for $1.50
and one pound of Butter for $1.50 they have a nice ham
they brought from home that we fry the Cook down in
the street Wright saves us all the Chips and Chunks in
his shop that is the way we get wood so we can live
verry well and, not be at to much Expense I paid over
$45.00 Board before I came here besides other Expenses Mrs
Ward now has Three & a half Dollars a day for Board in
town. here it is Four & a half. I have not much news
Report says this morning the Federals have Evacuated
Alexandria and that our Pickets have the place Col
Randals brother has got in Town from Walkers Division
he says they will get to Grants Core to night if their order
were not Changed he has been sent by Gen Walker for us & the
men who belong to him so we Expect to get off the
Exgaine or in the Morning to meet him we will be
agreed on a boat I will find out before I close this and
let you know where we go if I can learn

1863
Hard Fighting

"I look for nothing else......, if the war goes on but our division to have lots of hard fighting this year."

*Captain Harvey Wallace to his wife,
June 12, 1863*

February the 2nd, 1863

Dear Husband,
I write you a few lines this morning to inform you how we are getting along the hard, trouble times. We are all well at present. The friends are well so far as I know. Martha[426] is getting along as well as could be expected. I sent you a letter Thursday; told you all about her. I don't know whether you will get it or not; will tell you again. She took sick Sunday night. Her child was not born until Tuesday night. She had two very bad spasms; came nigh dying. They had Doc March[427]. The child was born dead; the largest boy I ever seen. It was a terrible sight to me. I expect you would not think it so as you have seen so many dying. I was up there from Monday morning until Thursday morning. I came home a few minutes Wednesday. I tell you, I was wore out. I thought of you so much, although it kept us all busy. I thought, what if you [were] sick and as bad as she, and not half the attention that we were giving her. For I know it would be the case if you were sick. Martha did not send for Josaphine[428] as it was such bad weather and so cold. Jo sent up Green[429] yesterday to know if I had heard from you lately. She had not heard since the 26th of Dec. I got one from you dated the 3rd of Jan., one month tomorrow. The friends and neighbors are all anxious to hear from you all. Mr. Ray['s] people is well. Thos. is going after her this week if nothing happens. Leonard took Jane home yesterday. Blackstock[430] told him George Rhodes[431] seen Wm. Wallace on his

---

[426] Achsah's sister, Martha (Wood) Wallace
[427] Dr. S. W. March (c.1825-?) practiced medicine at Mount Enterprise.
[428] Josephine (Ray) Wallace, wife of Harvey's brother, William
[429] Green Wallace (c.1845-?), a slave of the William Wallace family, was born in Georgia according to the 1870 Rusk County, Texas census.
[430] Daniel K. Blackstock (10/16/1819-5/11/1891), son of Richard and Cassandra (Wright) Blackstock, enlisted in Co.-F, Border's Texas Cavalry on August 5, 1863.
[431] George W. Rhodes (c.1833-?) served earlier in Wallace's Company as a private. Rhodes was discharged when Private Daniel Dulin enlisted as his substitute.

road home. He stayed at Flanagan[432] all night. I hope it is so. We will hear all the news and I will get a letter from you. I am going to send this by Mr. Draper[433]; wish I had something to send. You would be glad I had some coffee or rye. It is so far and he is a stranger, or I would send you some rye. I hope though, if Wm. has come by the time he goes back, you will get to come home or [I] will get the chance to send you something. Joe[434] got a letter from Adline[435]. They were well. Your Father is not stout; has a bad cough. S. L. C.[436] had got home. Him and Rebecca has gone home. She says they are very lonesome. S. W. Wallace has gone back to camps. Father went to see him & stayed two days with him in camps. Brother Jo was well and stout. They both are in one regiment. S. L. C. was shot on Sunday and lay until Tuesday before he was found. He had been robbed of his watch, his buttons cut off his coat, and 60 or 70 dollars; the bottoms of his pockets cut off. He knew nothing for three weeks; could not see. He lay five weeks in the hospital. He was taken to a private house in Maryland. They treated him very kind. They were strong secessions but was afraid to let it be known. They gave him a good suit of clothes; sent Rebecca and child some presents. He can see some now;

---

[432] The Flanagan Community was located in Rusk County near present day Tatum

[433] James Madison Draper Sr. (c.1806-?) of the Pine Hill community was discharged on medical certificate in December 1862 from Co.-I, 18th Tx. Infantry. His sons, James M. Jr. (Co.-I, 18th Tx. Infantry) and Marion W. (Co.-I, 19th Tx. Infantry & Co.-D, 14th Tx. Cavalry) were stationed near Wallace's company.

[434] Josephine (Ray) Wallace

[435] Harvey's youngest sister, Martha Adeline Wallace (1/7/1836-3/28/1927), was the tenth child of James and Margaret (Barnett) Wallace.

[436] 1st Lieutenant Samuel Leroy Campbell

An aged Samuel L. "Blind Sam" Campbell displays his whittling skill

can see his hand[437].Franklin Wallace['s] [son] Joe[438] is dead. Larken Robison[439] is dead. Archie Barron['s] son Sam[440] is dead. Sam Youngblood[441] is dead. Mary[442] is gone back to her Father's. The people are well of the smallpox. She says Jimmy Stewart is a sight he is so pock marked. Tell Mr. Welch[443] I seen his people yesterday at Thos. They are well. The children grows fast; is pretty. She got a letter week before last and answered it. Well Harvey, you would like to know what we are doing by this time. We started four plows this morning breaking up the balance of the Hays land. Sam[444] is helping me to garden; Cinth spinning. Caroline and Candis is scalding and scouring. Willy & W. Peter[445] is at school; Mother at Thos. Matty has eat her dinner and is lying on a pallet by the fire sleeping. Bud and John[446] has the pup down at the branch playing. They will finish breaking up nearly today; will commence on the stock land and then get ready to plant. They say we will have about

---

[437] Harvey's brother-in-law, Sam Campbell, never completely regained his sight following his wound in action at South Mountain, Maryland. He returned home to become a local legend affectionately known as "Blind Sam". Sam moved to the growing York District town of Clover and found employment pumping water at the railroad watering tank. Blind Sam was an exceptional conversationalist and kept up with all the news. He became known throughout the area for his whittling skill, his works showing the marks of fine craftsmanship.

[438] Private Joseph Franklin Wallace (c.1838-11/24/1862), son of Harvey's cousin, George Franklin Wallace, was a member of the Catawba Light Infantry. Private Wallace died of pneumonia at Winder Hospital, Richmond, Va.

[439] Private Larkin B. Robinson (c.1831-1863) of Co.-D, 6th S. C. Infantry, was the son of John W. and Mary (Clark) Robinson. Private Robinson died of disease at home in York District.

[440] Private Samuel Watson Barron (1/10/1840-12/23/1862), son of Archibald and Margaret (Watson) Barron, served in Co.-E, 17th S. C. Infantry. Private Barron was killed in action at Goldsboro, N. C.

[441] Private Samuel C. Youngblood of Co.-B, 13th N. C. Infantry

[442] Unidentified, but probably wife of Private Samuel Youngblood.

[443] Private Joseph Alexander Hamilton Welch (4/1844-10/9/1928), son of John and Larissa (McKnight) Welch

[444] Sam was a slave on the Wood plantation in South Carolina who moved to Texas with the Wallace family in 1861.

[445] W. Peter is unidentified.

[446] A slave child

one hundred and thirty acres to work this year. We want to send down and help Jane to roll logs as soon as Thos. can leave home. He is going to take Mc.[447] and me two hands. She has a few logs they cannot put up. There is no one down there to help her and her Negroes are like all others, won't work unless they have someone to see to it. They are getting so saucy she can scarcely put up with them. She says she will hire them if they don't do better. She believes Jackson[448] puts mischief in them. She frets [a] great deal. I am sorry for her. She hopes you will be spared to get home. We all are looking forward to that with great anxiety, too much for it to be so. We are so unworthy, but still live in hopes. I am like what Aunt Oliva said about Bredner[449]. If she could only get him with breath in his body she would be thankful he came home; just alive and that was all. He has not seen a well day since, but in hopes he will get well someday. He is mending. I would be thankful to get you home alive if you could not help yourself no way. We hear of another big battle in Virginia. We whipped them badly. You have heard of it before this. The old men is getting in fine spirits. They think this year will close the war. I would be glad to think so. I fear not, though we know not what is to be. William Zuber[450] went and joined a company Saturday; was going to be sworn in today. Calven Lacy[451] is going over the river. They say Billy[452] is not going out the state. George Birdwell[453] starts tomorrow. We see men passing today; don't know where they are going. I have heard nothing from

---

[447] Jane McCallum

[448] Unidentified

[449] Private Joseph Bredner McCarter (c.1835-8/22/1864) of Minden was the son of Elias and Elizabeth Olivia McCarter. Joseph initially served in Co.-E, 10th/3rd Tx. Cavalry and joined Co.-H, 19th Texas Infantry in September 1863.

[450] William Zuber (c.1846-?), son of W. M. and Mariah (Brooks) Zuber

[451] Calvin Lacy (c.1845-?), son of Andrew and Margaret (Aiken) Lacy of Pine Hill, enlisted in Co.-C, 15th / 32nd Texas Cavalry as a private.

[452] William Lacy (c.1828-?)

[453] George Birdwell (c.1825-?) of Pine Hill enlisted in Co.-G, 10th Texas Cavalry as a private.

George Brown[454] lately. James Hays[455] said he had made a contract with the government to make shoes and harness. J. D. Akins[456] is still at home; don't know when he will go as his company is broke up. I think old Aunt Nancy[457] has been highly favored. She got a letter that Davis[458] is stout and hearty, and so was Cogwell[459]. We heard that reg[iment] was all killed and wounded to a hundred men but don't believe it. There is some men breaks open all the letters at the Mount to hear the news. I tell you, I would not like them to break open mine. Harvey we have had bad luck with pigs sure. The blue sow slunk[460] her pigs yesterday, so the two old sows have slunk their pigs. We have the two now with pig, Willy's and the Morris sow. Jane gave Mother a sow. Her pigs died. I am going to try to get some lambs if I can from Minor Clinton[461]. He came and paid Leonard 70 dollars, no interest. I lost all the trunk keys last week; could not find them to get his note. I lost them Friday morning. He came in the evening. I lost them about the house. I was no further than the smokehouse and garden. We have looked everywhere but cannot find them. There is so much meanness carried on, they might have been picked up. I have not paid any debts yet, nor won't until I get the keys, if soon. I have got every cent of money you sent; the three dollars, ear rings, and everything you have, unless you have

---

[454] George W. Brown (c.1826-4/5/1878) was a saddler from Minden. He enlisted in Co.-D, 34th Tx. Cavalry in March 1862 but was subsequently discharged.

[455] James William Hays (c.1829-?), a farmer from Minden.

[456] Private John Durham Akins (6/1843-?), son of John and Nancy (Wallace) Akins, originally enlisted in Wallace's company but was transferred to the 1st (Lane's) Partisan Rangers on Sept. 24, 1862. Akins later served in Co.-B, 19th Tx. Cavalry.

[457] Nancy T. (Wallace) Akins (c.1802-?), mother of John and William Akins, may have been direct kin to Harvey.

[458] Private William Davis Akins (c.1834-?), son of John and Nancy (Wallace) Akins, served in Co.-C, 15th (aka 32nd) Tx. Cavalry.

[459] Unidentified

[460] Weaned

[461] Peter Minor Clinton (1800-1888) was the son of Peter and Mary (Barnett) Clinton of York District S. C. Minor Clinton and several other York District families immigrated together to Rusk County in 1853.

sent something lately. You say you are sorry you have nothing to send. You need not trouble yourself so much to try to get something where there is nothing to get; have to pay so high for everything. Keep enough to buy anything you can eat or make you comfortable there in that mean place. We heard you were coming to Arkadelphia. If it is so, I hope you will get something better to eat than what you have been getting. I do not often sit down to eat a meal's vittles but what I think of what you have to eat. I wish you had as good as we have, although we have seen the time we would thought it rough. We have plenty meat, and bread, and molasses, and good health to eat it. Thank God for it. I must quit. Farewell, and my prayers is that He may bless you in the same way.

A. Wallace

Camp Mills, Arkansas
Saturday evening
February the 7th, 1863

Achsah show this to no one.
I am now out of stamps. You will have to pay postage.

My dear and loving Wife,
I this evening write you a few lines in answer to your kind and loving letter of Jan. the 15th. This evening it gives me great pleasure to hear from you, but I am sorry to hear of Willy cutting his foot and of your not being stout, but I feel thankful it is no worse my dear wife. I am sorry you think you are always unfortunate, as I feel that we should both thank the Lord for His mercies to us thus far and humbly pray Him to continue them to us. Why, you have been blessed with moderate health, and our family too since I have been away. And the good Lord has blessed me with health and strength to undergo hardships and exposure more than I ever thought I could endure, while many of my fellow soldiers stouter than me have been cut down by disease & death, and thousands more who are lying in hospitals suffering. So cheer up. I think the Lord has blessed us thus far. Why not trust Him for the future my dear wife. I am in quite good health at this time. Brother's health is improving slowly. The health of my company is improving some. I have 56 men here; 26 of them report sick; all able to be up. Achsah the truth is, about half of them are well enough to do duty, but they have got so lazy lying about the convalescent camp they don't take exercise enough to get well. They report sick to try to get sick furloughs; don't do no duty, nor don't intend to. There is still lots of sickness in the reg[iment]. My company is the strongest now. Capt. Allen's company[462] has only been reporting 6 well men this week. Achsah we are still encamped on the same ground; have been two weeks now on the same ground. We have had very cold weather here indeed; as cold

---

[462] Co.-C, 19th Texas Infantry under the command of Captain Augustus C. Allen of Jefferson, Tx.

as I ever experienced anywhere. We had a snow on Tuesday and Tuesday night from four to 6 inches deep. There is a plenty of it on the ground now. We have had to cut and carry our wood. The ground is so swampy a wagon can't haul wood. I pitch in and cut more wood than any man in our two messes. Achsah I take lots of exercise, more than most any of my men. I think that is one reason why my health is good. For while men are lying up like we are now, men, lots of them, get so lazy. They just eat and lie down, and then they put us on a hard march they get sick. We were five days and nights while down below on the river without tents; the snow from 6 to 8 inches deep and it very cold and raining a part of the time. We had nothing but one blanket to the man, so we fared well this time having all of our clothing and tents too. I sleep between William and Brooks. I never suffer with cold since you sent me the big linsey quilt. I hardly ever lie down at night but I think of you when I pull up my big quilt. It is so warm. It shows to me you knew better what I needed than I did. Well, after eating a hearty supper of hard corn dodger, some pork, and sassafras tea, I will finish my letter by candlelight as Col. Ochiltree[463] starts home to Jefferson in the morning. I want to send it by him. Achsah I am writing this letter for your own eye alone. I have taken good care of my clothes. I have not burnt my pants any yet. The men have nearly all burnt their pants legs and lots of them burnt their coats. I change my clothes every week and get them washed. I, nearly every time I strip, warm a pot of water, take it in my tent, and wash my whole body clean. I always think about you cautioning me about washing my neck and try to keep it clean. I tell you, if a man don't keep clean he will get full of body lice. Some of my company have had lots of them. They soon get clear of them by cleaning up. I have kept clear of body lice and head lice too so far. Achsah, our fare is pretty hard yet.

Colonel William B. Ochiltree

---

[463] Colonel William B. Ochiltree (1811-1867) of the 18th Texas Infantry

We get very poor beef, coarse corn meal, and a little sugar. We have drawed some pork this week. I have enough to do my mess a month now. We eat lye hominy when we can get corn. I have lived two days at a time on hominy without bread. In fact, I would rather eat it as our bread. I have eat lots of parched corn. We have some rye now. We use it a while. We can't make it good like you can. And then we try sassafras tea a while. I don't like to use too much of the tea, but like it the best. I hope we may always get as good as we do now, and as much. Achsah I hope now this unnatural war will cease this spring or summer. From what little news I get, I am in great hopes that by the first of April the fighting will be over. All the accounts we get from the northwestern states, they will not fight much longer. If they fail at Vicksburg and don't get the advantage of us too much somewhere else, they will compel Lincoln to make peace next summer or spring I think. I think the Feds will take this river when they get through at Vicksburg. We can't hinder them. I got a letter from Cousin Peter McCallum this week dated the 25th of December. He stated the friends were all well and that Samuel Campbell had got home and was in good health and spirits, though nearly blind. He spoke of times being very hard there. Achsah, you speak of paying out all of your money. You ought to try to keep some kind of account of what you lay out if you can. I would like very much to be there now to finish settling up for you, and to advise with your Mother about collecting what is coming from Aunt Jinny's estate. If I was her I would not hurry, as she can't get the money now no how. I wrote to you in my last what to do about paying the Hayses' & blacksmith bill. I hope I may get home to settle with them. Achsah don't fret about Clinton's talking about me. You know I never told him an untruth about the old mare, so I have a clear conscience about the matter. My sweet wife, I don't want you to fret about me. I will take all the care of myself I can on your account and our sweet little children, and your good and kind old Mother. She has been a mother to me. Tell poor Jane I often think of her in her lonely condition, and she may rest assured, if the Lord spares me, I will try to be a friend to her. Cousin Peter says to me he would be much better satisfied if I was at home. How could I be anything but a friend to her. Poor Duncan felt like a brother to me indeed. He laid his life down for our common country. My dear

Achsah, a week ago when I tried to get a furlough I did not sleep much for two or three nights. I thought then I would get a furlough, and the thoughts of meeting my sweet wife and clasping her to my bosom drove sleep away, but I was disappointed. I don't allow myself to fret about it. It is no use for a man to fret here. If he does, he is most sure to get sick. I am in good spirits yet. I have got on the good side of the Col. I now allow to wait a week or two and try for a seven days furlough. The Col. told me to do that; says he will help me to get it. He says for me to go home on that. They shant hurt me if I do if he can help it. I have done lots more duty than are a captain he has. I have stayed all the time with my company. Some of the others have been half of their time in town sick, or one place or another. So if I can get seven days I will come home, if I don't stay more than one week. They will be apt to cut me out of my wages while gone but that is nothing to getting to see you. I have been pricing horses. I will have to pay at least two hundred dollars to get a horse to carry me home. Horses are selling from two [to] six hundred dollars here. I don't want you to sell Nance yet I believe. Achsah, continue to write to me. If I find I can get a furlough I will write to you. Don't build no calculation on my coming until you know I am coming, for we may have to move any day. We get one mail a week from Little Rock. I write to you every mail. Oh what a pleasure to get your letters so loving. For Achsah, you [are] the first woman I ever knew what it was to love, and you have been such a kind and loving wife to me. Oh what a pleasure it would be to me to hug you up to my bosom these cold nights. Poor little Matty did not get her ear rings. Old Golden[464] was to mail the letter at Rake Pocket[465]. I did not like him much but men who knew him said he was honest. He lives in Shelby County. I will learn from his son where his post office is. Do take care of yourself my sweet wife.

---

[464] Mr. Ruben Golden was the father of Private Newton A. Golden of Wallace's company.
[465] The town of Pine Hill, located about six miles north of Minden, was settled in 1844. It was also known as Rake Pocket because of the local hotel's notoriety for "raking a traveler's pocket clean".

Don't let anything trouble you [that] you can help, nor don't lift anything to hurt yourself, for this world would be sad to me if you were gone. Tell Willy and Bud I want them to be good boys. I will come home to see them too. Try and have some eggs for me. Tell Matty to wear her pretty coats. So farewell my sweet wife. May the good Lord bless and protect you all and enable us soon to meet on earth to be happy together is the prayer of your husband.

Harvey A. Wallace to his wife, Achsah Wallace

Camp Mills, Arkansas
Sabbath noon
Feb. the 22nd, 1863

Achsah this is for your own eye alone.

My dear Wife,
I write you a few lines for your own eye alone as I have a chance to send this by Mr. Draper, and I know you are, like myself, glad to get long letters. And I have no doubt but anything I write to you is interesting to you, though it would be so to no one else. I get a good many letters from one and another but if I get none from you, I feel like I was lost. I always read yours first. If I am eating, I must know what is in your letters before I go any further. I would have got none this week if Mr. Draper had not have come, as our mail rider did not get in last evening. The waters are too high between here and Little Rock. Achsah, the reason we write on Sunday always is we start a man every Monday morning to Little Rock. He comes in Saturday evening so we wait to see if he brings us letters before we write. My dear wife, I am glad to hear that the Negroes are doing better. I hope they will continue to do so. I am glad, too, that you don't intend to let them fret you as they have done, and that you feel more comfort in serving the Lord. My dear Achsah, you give me some good advice in your last, to try and keep good company and give my men good advice. Achsay, I have to associate more or less with all kinds of men, and am sorry to say the large majority of them are wicked, swearing men, though some few noble exceptions. I never have allowed myself to use any vain words. In fact, I am perfectly disgusted hearing others do so. I have more sturdy men than any other one company in our regiment; sorry to say, some very vain ones, and some who play cards on Sunday as fast as any other day. I don't show any countenance to card playing at all. I always try to give my men good advice, but Achsah, there is so many men who want to be discharged. They pretend to be sick; won't do anything. I have to just put them on duty, then they are mad. But I allow to try to do my duty and leave the result to my maker. I don't feel like it is my duty to try to have men discharged who are as stout as I am only because they want to get home and get clear of duty. My dear wife,

you ask me to love you and our little children and to pray for you. Oh Achsah, do you suppose I could forget you or our little dears while I have my right mind and reason about me; my loving wife who has lay on my arm and shed hot tears on my face so often while thinking of our separation. Oh no, never. You are my last thoughts at night on my bed before going to sleep. My thoughts turn to you first thing in the night when I awake and the first thing in the morning. You ask me to pray for you. Achsah I know I live farther from my maker than I ought by far, but I always pray the Lord to spare you and protect you from all harm and enable you to live as you ought, and to give you comfort & consolation in your lonely condition. I trust I will not forget to pray for myself and you, and our little dears. I feel that I am unworthy to approach the Lord in prayer, but still I feel consolation in trying to pray to Him and feel sad and bad if I neglect it, so [I] do continue to pray. Remember me in your prayers, for I am surrounded by wickedness. Where men are alone and none of the sacred influences of women to constrain them, they become perfectly reckless. Here there is thousands of us men sometimes never see a woman in weeks. Achsah I have not spoke to a dozen of women in Arkansas I don't suppose. My hopes, my prayers are that the Lord will spare me to return to you and our little dears, and that I may find you all alive and well. In all of my hardships, that cheers me on to duty. So let us trust the Lord and try to do our duty and serve Him faithful. He has certainly dealt kindly with us thus far. Why not trust Him for the future? Achsah I send you a silver ring for yourself and one for Matty. They were made here in camp by a soldier out of a dime. I got three, one for myself to remember you. I know you will wear it for my sake if it is not fine. I have tried to get my name cut on it but could get no one to do it. I gave fifty cents in silver for the one I send you, one dollar and fifty for Matty's, and two for mine in Confederate. That was the way they sold, four bits in silver or two dollars in Confederate. Tell Willie and Bud I have not forgot them. If I live to come home I will bring them something. Achsah I have not been well this week. I have had diarrhea two weeks now; some days pretty bad off, others not so bad. I have been on duty all the time. I have no doubt if I would lie up like some of them I would be worse off. I have been very careful about what I eat, but everything I eat just run off like water. Friday night was so clear. I took a portion of blue mass & opium, but it came on rain by midnight. I had to be out in the rain then. It rained all the fore part of the day yesterday. I had to go two or three hundred yards when my pills worked through, the mud shoe mouth deep. But I have felt very well since twelve yesterday when my pills quit operating and now hope I will keep clear of it. Half of the regiment is in the same fix, only some a great deal worse. Achsah I must tell you what I had for breakfast this morning. We had biscuit, butter, fried meat, & coffee. I have still kept some of the coffee you sent me. I parched some when I had the bowel complaint. I still have a little. We have some rye too, enough to do us some time. I got leave from the Col. Thursday morning and give Sergt. Riley[466] my horse. He went out 18 miles into the country. He bought 5 pounds of butter at $1.00 cts. per pound, 10 dozen of eggs at 50 cts. a dozen, 10 chickens at 50 cents each. He brought me three little gut sausages and two cooked potatoes. He got back at dark Friday night. He engaged me 100 pounds of flour at 25 cents per pound and 200 hundred for the camp. We are to get it next Thursday. We have been eating mean, coarse corn meal. I think that makes our bowels worse. The Col. told me to go to the surgeon and get an order to [illegible] on the commissary for flour as I was unwell, so I got an order for myself & Brooks as he had diarrhea. They sent us 15 pounds at ten cents a pound. An officer can get in, if sick, on an order from the surgeon; no other way. Riley brought in two shoulders of pork; gave 25 cents per pound. When men bring it to camp they have 50 cents a pound. We have drawed pork enough the last week. We have plenty to do us two weeks now and they are getting more. Our Col. does all he can to have pork for his men. Achsah, Riley was offered $225.00 cash for my horse. If I had have been with him I would have sold him and risked buying again, though they are very high. I gave $160.00 for him and twenty five for the saddle. He is about a good $100.00 horse but I don't know whether I could get as good a one now for two hundred or not. I want to get a good stout pony for him that rides well if I live to go home and can. I don't want to be without him now as I can send out and get things. Someone is on him every day. I have never rode him

---

[466] Sergeant Thomas J. Riley

but once yet. I have nothing to do but draw corn and fodder. The Col. finds feed for him so he is no expense to me about feeding, & the bran the men sift out of their meal would feed him. There is wagon loads of corn wasted every day. The most of men just throw the corn down on the ground to their horses and waste it. They don't have to pay for it. Achsah, [illegible] has been like myself; had the diarrhea this week. Achsah I don't want you to say a word about it but he is just to wait on. He done fine last fall, then he got sick and quit doing. He let on to be sick until they put him on duty. He had got fat. He will eat as hearty as any of us and go and lie down or sit down and hold his head; hardly ever helps to get a stick of wood unless I just order him. He eat as hearty as any of us this morning and stretched himself down. I told him to get up and take exercise. That was what he needed. Yesterday he sit and held his head. We cut and split wood and carried it 200 yards through the mud. I carried all the time, as bad off as he was. When dinner came, he was ready. He is stingy too, but don't say anything about it. He hardly ever does anything. If he was in a lazy mess he would be like some of the rest, never able for duty. Jo Rhodes is not doing any duty yet; looks fat; eat hearty too. Tell Willy and Bud I done my best to get a furlough but failed. I hope the time will come soon when I can get one. If the news we hear from the northwest is true, I hope the war will close this summer, & that the time will soon come when we can get a furlough. Oh Achsah, it would be such a pleasure to be at home with you. I have dreamed of you nearly every night this week. I hope nothing is wrong, and pray how soon the time may come when I can clasp my own lovely wife to my bosom and be permitted to remain with her and enjoy the comforts of a happy home. Then I will consider that all my suffering and hardships were for my good. Tell your Mother I hope to see her [and] to take good care of herself. Tell Jane [McCallum] to be of good cheer; try to take things as easy as she can. I trust she will be able to get along, and if spared to come home, will try to treat her as I would a sister. Achsah continue to direct your letters to Little Rock. I will put a piece of paper in to show you how to back them. I get them regular now. May the Lord bless & protect you my dear wife is my prayer. So farewell for the present my sweet wife.

From Capt. H. A. Wallace to his wife, Achsah Wallace.

Clay Hill, So. Ca.
Apr. the 19th, 1863

Sister Achsah,
I will attempt to answer yours of the 5th of Feb., which did not come to hand until a few days ago. Father received a letter from you written since mine was; also, one from Thomas dated the 8th of Mar[ch]. We got letters this last week from William & Harvey. We were glad to hear from them I assure you. William's dated the 8th of Mar[ch], Harvey the 6th. We are all well & getting along very well. The health of neighborhood is good. There was some cases of typhoid fever some three or four weeks ago. All have got well except Cousin Adaline Wallace[467]. She is no more. She died the 27th of March. She took Joe's death very hard, poor woman. She was but four months behind him. Uncle Jo Wallace's[468] health has not been good this winter at times. They think he will not live any time and in a few days he will be able to be up. He takes sick fainting spells. He is very poor; looks badly. We have had no late letter from Jo[469]. The last account he was well. Their brigade is on Blackwater River near Suffolk, Va. That is Jenkins' Brigade. The 5th Regt. is in his brigade. Uncle McKenzie[470] [is] out there at this time. They got a letter from him a few days ago. He stated they were expecting a fight every day. He would not leave until it was over. Aunt Eliza Barnett's son Joe[471] is dead. He died the 6th of this month with sickness. I expect pneumonia. I do not know the name of the hospital he died at. Joe's health has generally been good with the exception of pains. He was

---
[467] Mrs. Ellen Adaline Wallace was the wife of Harvey's cousin, George F. Wallace. The couple's son, Joseph Franklin Wallace had recently died while serving in Virginia with the 5th S. C. Infantry.
[468] Joseph Wallace (c.1776-1864), brother of Harvey's father.
[469] Harvey's brother, Joseph Franklin Wallace, was serving in Co.-G, 5th S. C. Infantry at this time.
[470] Arthur A. McKenzie
[471] Private Joseph Josiah Barnett (c.1825-4/6/1863), son of James and Eliza (Currence) Barnett, was a member of Co.-B, 5th S. C. Infantry. Private Barnett died of pneumonia at Jerusalem, Va.

afflicted with pains this last winter, poor fellow. He had been in service two years and endured many hardships, and has never been at home since the 5th Regt. went to Virginia. We had two letters from Sam[472] last week. He was quite well and has been ever since he got over the fever. They are near Wilmington, N. Ca. When Sam wrote they were under marching orders to go to Charleston. We heard since [that] the orders were countermanded. Sam was at home on furlough this winter. He came home the 25th of Feb. and left the 29th of Jan. He was detailed and sent after recruits. Father wrote to some of you while Sam was at home. I wrote a part of the letter to Martha. I know from the way Thomas write they had not got it. Lt. Campbell's[473] family was well the first of the week. They were spending the week with Mrs. Campbell. There has been little or no improvement on Sam's eye for some time. Some days it is very much inflamed and then again it looks better. He can't see to do any good. Anything moving before him or by him he can tell there is something there moving but can't tell what it is. He goes about home there to garden, stables, and all about. He carries a stick and feels before him. He can walk and go any place when there is anyone with him. He lays his hand on their shoulder and walks beside them. That's the way he goes without he goes too far to walk. He can't ride horseback. It is remarked by many persons what great patience Sam has. He says it will do no good to set to grieve. He must exercise all the patience he can and hope for the better. Rebecca is stout and hearty, and as fleshy as ever. Lizzie[474] grows fast; looks stout, but is subject to brashes. She is a great talker. You can tell Bud Lizzie suck tits yet. She is very often talking about Mother weaning her but she will beg for a little drop. The Uncles and Aunts are all well as far as I know. Aunt Minerva[475] has had no child since you

---

[472] Harvey's brother, Samuel Wallace, of Co.-E, 17th S. C. Infantry
[473] Samuel L. Campbell
[474] Unidentified
[475] Martha Minerva (Stowe) Barnett (12/12/1824-3/19/1911), wife of William Amzi Barnett

left. Aunt Jane[476] has a fine son nearly a year old she calls Joseph Arthur. Aunt Catharine[477] makes her home at Uncle Arthur's. Aunt Martha[478] is no better. I suppose you have heard ere this time Bob Jackson[479] was dead. Emily[480] has one child. She and her Mother live with Mary[481]. John[482] is in the army. Also, Margaret's husband, Uncle Harvey's oldest son John[483], is in the army. I saw Newton Wood[484] at S.L.C.['s] last week. He was on furlough from the army in Va. He and Dave had been up to see Caroline[485]. As him and Sam had seen each other in Va., he called to see Sam. He looked well. He expected to start back next morning. Mother and Father are gone to church today. I am at home by myself except the Negroes. I would say to Mrs. Wood, the reed she gave me make [the] nicest cloth I ever seen for home made. I wove myself a dress with it. I will send you a piece. I am weaving a web of check now to make shirts for Jo and Tom[486]. They make the dresses very long now, trailing the ground behind. Home made dresses generally made plain bodied; pleat on the waist with box pleat, and worn with capes. Hats are all the style for married ladies, and all turned down all round called Dixies. Some have home made on, others alter old ones; none to be bought. There is nothing to be bought here now. Can't get anything

---

[476] Jane Meek (Adams) Barnett (9/3/1818-2/14/1902), wife of Alexander Hamilton Barnett
[477] Mary Catharine (Barnett) Grier (2/26/1816-8/1/1892), wife of Thomas H. Grier
[478] Martha Patrick (Barnett) Currence (5/14/1808-2/1888), wife of John N. Currence
[479] Robert P. Jackson (c.1827- c.1863) was a carpenter from Yorkville.
[480] Unidentified
[481] Unidentified
[482] Private John McClain Jackson (1/21/1829-11/21/1901), brother of Robert P. Jackson, served in Co.-H, 18th S. C. Infantry.
[483] Margaret, Uncle Harvey, and John are unidentified.
[484] Newton L. Wood (5/30/1831-1/4/1885), son of Joseph and Elizabeth (Johnston) Wood, was Achsah's first cousin.
[485] Dave and Caroline are unidentified.
[486] Jo and Tom are unidentified.

to put on the dead. Such as they have by them has to be put on them. If we could get cards[487] we could make our clothing and it do very well. I live in hope we will have better times before long. If this war was at an end, we could do without many comforts we were accustomed to before it began. We are doing without many now.

Apr. the 20th [488]
S.L. Campbell to Harvey,
Samuel says he not being fit to attend to any business for himself or anyone. He proposed putting Harvey's business into Mr. Zadok Smith's hands, thinking Mr. Smith the most suitable hand he could get, and knowing he and Harvey were particular friends &c. Mr. Smith was very willing to take the business; has had the papers for some time. Samuel says there was several hundred dollars paid when Mr. Smith took the business. The Robinson money is paid not long since. Robinson[489], poor fellow, is dead. He died this winter in the army.

A line for Negroes:
Adison is well. He mailed a letter to Miney[490] not long since. Letty[491] sends howdy to all her boys. She wants them to be good boys. Tell Ed his folks is well. Tell Candis Sally can weave some; I think would do very well if there was no one but her to do the

---

[487] Cotton cards were used to stretch cotton fibers in preparation for spinning and weaving. They were wooden blocks fitted with handles and covered with short, metal spikes. Card manufacturing almost ceased in the south when factories were converted to manufacture weapons and military equipment.

[488] This letter is a continuation of the previous one dated April 19. The writer adds a section here for Sam Campbell and a section for the slaves on Harvey's Father's plantation.

[489] Unidentified

[490] Unidentified

[491] Letty was a beloved house servant on the James Wallace plantation. She practically raised all the Wallace children and they regarded her as they would a grandmother. According to family tradition, Letty asked to move to Texas with Harvey and his family. Estate records show that she stayed on the James Wallace plantation until James' death in 1863. Samuel (Blind Sam) Campbell bought Letty as a house servant at the Wallace plantation estate sale in early 1864. No other record could be located concerning her disposition after that time.

Letty

weaving. The Negroes all send howdy to all of the Colored friends in Texas. I believe I stop this scribble. Excuse bad writing and spelling. Give my love to all the children. Mother sends her love to you all. Write soon, for we are glad to get a letter from Texas any time. So no more at present.

Add[492]

---

[492] Harvey's sister, Martha Adeline Wallace, took care of her aging parents while her brothers were in the army.

Shreveport, Louisiana[493]
Wednesday morning
May the 20th, 1863

My dear Wife,
I this morning write you a few more lines. I am pretty well, thank the giver of all good for the blessing of health. And my prayer is that you and the rest of our family are enjoying a like blessing. Achsah I am getting along very well in our new quarters. Tommy Riley, Tommy Hull[494], Tommy Guthrie[495], and me are staying in a large upstair room in town. It is over a carriage factory. We have five blankets amongst us. There is a plenty of chairs, tables, a desk, & wash stand & bowl. We borrowed a skillet and pan to cook in; borrowed a water bucket from James Wright[496]. My tin and one other is all the tableware we have. They draw their rations. I bought 20 pound of flour for $5.00 and one pound of butter for $1.50. They have a nice ham they brought from home that we fry. We cook down in the street. Wright saves us all the chips and chunks in his shop. That is the way we get wood. So we can live very well and not be at too much expense. I paid over $45.00 board before I came here, besides other expenses. Mrs. Ward[497] now has three & a half dollars a day for board. In town here it is four & a half. I have not much news. Report says this morning the Federals have evacuated Alexandria and that our pickets have the place. Col. Randal's brother[498] has got in town from Walker's Division. He says they will get to Grand Ecore tonight if their orders were not changed. He has

---

[493] Captain Wallace and others of his company were in Shreveport awaiting transportation back to their command while returning from leave.
[494] Private Thomas Jefferson Hull (c.1846-?), son of James and Sarah Hull
[495] Private Thomas C. Guthrie (c.1842-4/12/1899), son of Nelson and Panina Guthrie
[496] Unidentified- may have been the owner of the carriage factory.
[497] Unidentified
[498] Lieutenant John Leonard Randal Jr. (1838-1919), served as Ordnance Officer on the staff of the 2nd Brigade under his brother, Colonel Horace Randal.

been sent by Gen. Walker[499] for us officers and men who belong to him, so we expect to get off this evening or in the morning to meet them. We will go down on a boat. I will find out before I close this and let you know where we go if I can learn. Achsah, one prisoner made his escape from the guard last night. He had been put in for shooting a Marine soldier. It is thought the soldier will die. When I was on duty Friday night we had him up for shooting at soldiers. We turned him out. He is a young man living here. He made out he wanted to go to the privy. The officer of the guard sent two guards with him. Some of his friends had taken a plank off the back of the privy. He got through and run. The guard shot at him but missed him. They had a horse ready. He got away. The old man I wrote to you in my last about arresting as a spy, there was an order brought to the guard house last night at eleven o'clock for him. The Adjutant brought it; said they were going to send him to Little Rock. He took him off. I have no doubt they hanged him as his papers all went to prove him to be a spy. They did it secretly to keep the Feds from retaliating. At least that is the opinion of everyone. I tell you, men's lives are not safe here now unless he can give an account of himself. The account we now have from the Virginia fight is we took ten thousand prisoners and lots of arms and ammunition; give them a complete whipping. We also have news that the Feds have arrested & imprisoned Vallandingham[500], and that there was

---

[499] Major General John George Walker (1822-1893) of Cole County, Missouri, served as an officer in the U. S. Army during the Mexican War. He resigned his commission in 1861 to enter Confederate service as a Major of cavalry. Walker subsequently served as Lieutenant Colonel of the 8th (Terry's) Texas Cavalry and later as Brigadier and Major General in the Army of Northern Virginia. After the Maryland Campaign, General Walker took command of the Texas Infantry Division that would bear his name for the remainder of the war. Walker was a soldier's general who took care of his troops and his men held him in high esteem in return. He was wounded leading the division at Pleasant Hill, La. and relieved General Richard Taylor in command of the District of West Louisiana in 1864. At the close of the war, General Walker was in charge of a cavalry division in Texas. Warner, 319-320.

[500] Wallace refers to the arrest of former Ohio Congressman Clement L. Vallandigham on May 5, 1863. Vallandigham was the leader of the Peace Democrats, otherwise known as "Copperheads". He was arrested by Federal authorities on charges of expressing treasonable sympathies after declaring that the

great excitement in Ohio amongst his friends and that likely they would fight some about it. Indeed, the news is rather cheering.

Major General John George Walker

---

war was an attempt to destroy slavery in order to establish a Republican dictatorship. E. B. Long, 349.

Thursday morning
May the 21st, 1863

My dear Wife,
I write you a few more lines. This morning I am quite well. Can't tell when we go down the river; just have to wait until Gen. Smith[501] says go. Our command is gone to Grand Ecore. Achsah, Tom Guthrie has just been pretending. He went to the surgeon yesterday for a furlough. He just told me there was nothing the matter with him. The cough was all put on, so we just plagued Tom and when he coughed we coughed too. So he has quit and got lively. He has been pretending sure, like some others at home. We received the sad news last evening of Stonewall Jackson's death, which is a great loss to our cause. I will send this by Parson Hyter[502] as he is here. I learned on yesterday all of our trunks was left at Monticello, Arkansas. I never expect to see mine if left. It is said this morning we go down the river today. If so, I will let you know where to write as soon as possible. I am so anxious to get to my company. Let me know if you have rain, how the crop looks, and how you get on with the potato patch. Tell Thomas to write to me. He can tell me about the crops. I will close. May the Lord bless you all is the prayer of your husband. So farewell for the present my loving wife.

General Edmund Kirby Smith

---

[501] General Edmund Kirby Smith (1824-1893), a Mexican War veteran and West Point graduate from St. Augustine, Florida, was in command of the Trans-Mississippi Department. Smith had earlier served in Virginia under General Joseph E. Johnston, and as commander of the Department of East Tennessee. General Smith held the distinction of being the last Confederate general in the field, surrendering his department on May 26, 1865. Warner, 279-280.

[502] Unidentified

To Mrs. Achsah Wallace from her husband, H. A. Wallace

Note written upside down at top of letter:

Achsah I don't know whether you can read some of my scribbling or not. I have a bad pen. Don't let yourself get out of paper. I will send you money as soon as I get to the command and draw, and have an opportunity. Make out the best you can until then. I have done the best I could thus far but have done nothing but spend this trip. I still have sixty dollars in Confederate and fifteen in gold.

Camp Tensas, Louisiana
June 12, 1863

My dear Wife,
I this morning write you a few lines as I have the time, and I cannot spend an hour more pleasant than writing to my much loved wife. I am well this morning. My bowels are better. I feel thankful for as good health as I have. My prayers are that you my dear wife, our little ones, and the rest of our family are enjoying a like blessing. I received a letter on Sunday by Singletary[503] [that] you wrote the 23 of May. I was truly glad to hear of you all being well, as I had not heard from you since Len Riley[504] came. Oh, if I could only hear from you once a week and know you were all well, the consolation it would afford me in leading the hard life of a soldier, but now I will not hear once a month. Still, I must not complain. The health of my company is good. All the men are up and a stirring this morning; some complaining some; [illegible] chance of diarrhea; considerable colds and coughs since we have been lying without tents. Dr. Mathews[505] came by our camps on yesterday. He told me he seen Brother William in Shreveport a week ago ready to start home. He had got the furlough I sent him. I am glad to hear it as I was very uneasy about him. I have no doubt you have seen him before this time. Dan Hariss[506] of my company was going with him home. I trust his health will improve so he can get back when his furlough is out as I miss his company so much. It has cleared off more pleasant; not so hot. We are still guarding this bridge. All of us very anxious to be with our regiment as we have so much duty to do here and think our commander, Major Redwood[507], shows partiality between our company and Smith's[508]. We get a plenty to eat; meal, beef, &

---

[503] Private Robert Singletary (c.1833-?), son of Nancy Singletary
[504] Unidentified
[505] Assistant Surgeon Y. A. Matthews of the 19th Texas Infantry
[506] 4th Corporal W. D. Harris (c.1828-?)
[507] Major William H. Redwood of the 16th Texas Infantry was in charge of the guard detail.
[508] Company-I, 17th Texas Infantry, under the command of Captain John Smith

fresh pork; kill it in the woods here. But you know hogs killed off the range, if they are in good order are not fit to eat. We can't save pork or beef here more than one day. I sent this morning to try to get a piece of bacon and some milk and butter. Sent four miles to a man who lives up the river who is very kind; has given my pickets two nice hams & some molasses & milk. There is lots of honey in this country. As our army came up Bayou Mason, at some farms which were deserted, our men got buckets full; just knocked the heads out of the hives and took the honey. There is lots of bee trees in these swamps too but the nasty meal we get is good with nothing. But thank the Lord we have enough of it so far. Our brigade is still at Richmond; so is General Hawes'[509]. Col. Tappan's Brigade[510] from Arkansas will be there tomorrow or next day. Col. Randal's Brigade[511] is gone to Monroe. I have no idea how long we will remain in these swamps. I hope not long, as it is bound to be unhealthy. We have all kinds of reports the number the enemy lost. It is said they acknowledge a loss of 2000 killed, wounded, drowned, and missing[512]. The cannon commenced roaring at Vicksburg just before night last evening. They kept up a continual roar until 7 or 8 o'clock this morning. Some of the citizens here think the fight is going on on Yazoo River in the rear of Vicksburg. We have got pretty well used to the roar of cannon the last two weeks, but it is a little hard to get used to when one is near enough for them to be fired at himself. My dear wife, I look for nothing else, as I often told while at home, if the war goes on but our

---

[509] The 1st Brigade of Walker's Division under Brigadier General James M. Hawes
[510] Tappan's Arkansas Brigade was led by Brigadier General James C. Tappan (1825-1906), a lawyer and legislator from Helena, Arkansas.
[511] The 2nd Brigade of Walker's Division under Colonel Horace Randal
[512] In an effort to disrupt General U. S. Grant's supply line and relieve pressure on Vicksburg, McCulloch's 3rd Brigade attacked the Federal garrison at Milliken's Bend, La. on June 7, 1863. The Federal post on the Mississippi River was defended by Black troops of the African Brigade. This casualty report refers to that action, which Company-H missed while on guard assignment. Colonel Waterhouse reported 2 killed, 11 wounded, and 6 missing in action in his casualty report for the 19th Texas Infantry. Total losses for the 3rd Brigade were 44 killed, 130 wounded, and 10 missing. The Federals reported losses of 118 killed, 310 wounded, and numerous missing. Winters, 201-203; O. R., series-1, vol.-24, part-2, 451-453.

division to have lots of hard fighting this year. Our brigade has done all of the fighting thus far. McCulloch is fond of it and fears nothing so we will catch our share of it. Well, it is right we should. That is what we started for. My dear, have you ever paid the $12.50 that was going to William Whitfield's wife, or the $2.50 that was going to Mrs. Hawkins[513]? You speak of letting wheat go for leather. Do what you think best as you all will need shoes. Keep plenty of wheat. If I am spared to come home, I do not think I shall ever like corn bread. I hope Mrs. Rhodes will not take the thresher away until you thresh our wheat. I can't see what they want with it. Let me know all about how you are getting along; all about the crop. Let me know if Acy Parker's wife[514] got the corn; if Bartly[515] got his. I think you did right to make the cattle drivers pay damages. You did not say what you made Zuber[516] pay for fodder, nor what them conscripts allowed you. It grieves me for them to come taking corn & fodder from soldier's wives, but so it is. My love to Thomas, Martha, & family. Tell them I have had no chance to have any rings made yet. My love to Brother James, Eliza, & family; to Jane and her children. Tell her I will pay Doherty[517] as soon as I draw. Tell the Negroes all howdy for me. I want them to do the best they can. My love to your Mother. Remember me to our children. Write as often as you can, and you have my whole and undivided love. May the Lord protect and preserve you all is the prayer of your husband. So farewell my loving wife for the present.

To Mrs. A. Wallace from her husband, H. A. Wallace.

I would like, if Brother gets able to return, to have a pair of summer pants as my jeans are so hot in this hot country.

---

[513] Mrs. Sarah O. Hawkins (c.1821-?), wife of Private Columbus C. Hawkins.
[514] Mrs. Susan M. A. (Bates) Parker (c.1832-?), wife of Private Asa Parker
[515] Mr. Bartley Wallace (1813-?) was a neighbor. Kinship to Harvey and Achsah could not be determined.
[516] Mr. William M. Zuber (1814-?) of Minden
[517] Unidentified

In camps near Trenton, La.
Friday evening
July the 17th, '63

My beloved Wife,
I this evening again write you a few lines, although I wrote to you on yesterday and mailed it this morning. But I find no letters go through by mail, as I have written to you twice a week nearly every week since leaving Alexandria. I have a chance to send this right home by Mr. Long[518]. We are camped 4 miles above Monroe on Washita. I left the place where I have been sick and got to camps by 12 o'clock, tired enough. I there found a letter from you dated the 7th of July. Also, one from Brother James dated the 5th. Oh how glad to get them and hear all was well at home but the sad news of Father's death, and the distress you have suffered from false reports about me being killed. I do not know how such reports start. We never had any fight at Tensas Bridge but two false alarms at night. I know it distressed you so much. It makes my heart ache to think of it, but thank the Lord He has spared me thus far, and I trust will spare me to meet you again on earth. Though I have been quite sick, I am now getting well again. I have written you all about my sickness but will write again as you do not get the letters I send by mail. I kept up very well in the swamps for about one month. I was taken sick the last Sunday in June near Lake Providence; taken with fever. I had been unwell [page torn] or more, but we expected a fight and I wanted [page torn] my co[mpany], so I kept up. I lay on my blanket from 12 o'clock [page torn] in the woods until Monday morning. We expected an [page torn]. The doctor put me and 7 others in the ambulance. [page torn] amongst them and told the ambulance driver to take [page torn] back and leave us. [A page or portion is missing here] through the hot plantations, me taking calomel[519]. A wagon came along as the ambulance left us so we got on it and got to Delhi

---

[518] W. D. and Nancy Long's sons, G. W. & J. E. Long, served in Co.-I, 19th Texas Infantry. The Long family resided in the Pine Hill Community.

[519] Calomel was a tasteless, heavy, white substance made from mercury and used as a purgative.

by sunset. Asa[520] got me into a house there. We stayed with a Methodist preacher by the name of Upton[521]. He was crowded. I had to lie in the piazza on my blanket, very sick. My medicine operated severely. I thought I was taking flux I passed so much blood. Asa got our assistant surgeon to come to see me. He come back in the evening; brought another doctor with him. I was salivated[522]. They put me through another course of medicine, calomel again. Dr. Mathews said I had to have it to keep me out of typhoid, so I was very weak. I stayed there until Saturday evening. Asa nursed me so kindly. They then put us on the cars and sent us to Monroe. Parson Upton charged us 25 dollars for five days. We got to Monroe after night. I had got hungry. We could get in nowhere. We just went in the piazza. I got a little cornbread and bacon to eat. We spread our blankets down and lay until morning. Then I met Hays and got your letter. We then went up the river opposite Trenton; found our wagons we had left at Alexandria with our bedding & trunks. I found my clothing & bedding all right. Asa got a mule and crossed the river and went to hunt us a house. I stayed there and wrote you a long letter. Asa got back by night. We stayed all night with the Acrys[523] with the wagons. I got plenty of cake once we crossed the river. At sunrise, came out four miles on the Nachitoches Road to a Widow Graham's[524]. She had [page torn] daughters and some Negroes. She had moved out off Tensas River [page torn] Feds. She was very kind to us but had nothing to eat but [page torn] bacon, molasses, and some vegetables; no milk or butter at all. She charged us one dollar & a half a day. We found Lieut. Barksdale[525] [page torn] back. We all stayed there until this morning, and as

---

[520] Private Asa J. Parker (2/22/1829-4/7/1887)
[521] Unidentified
[522] Salivating was a purgative medical procedure designed to cleanse the body's systems. It consisted of causing excessive salivation by the application of mercury to oral tissues.
[523] Privates Cosby D. (c.1828-?) and James Acrey were on detached duty as regimental teamsters.
[524] Unidentified
[525] 2nd Lieutenant William E. Barksdale (1/6/1829-12/24/1887)

our [page torn] had come out from Delhi [page torn] Wednesday evening, so we come to camps this morning. If the [page torn] stays here a few days I will be able to march with it. If it moves, I will go along some way. I think we will go back on Red River soon as they are moving everything belonging to the government off, and the people are all moving for Texas since the fall of Vicksburg. The health of the co[mpany] is getting better again. There is 49 of us here, [illegible] at the convalescent camp. The balance in the hospital at Monroe; none much sick. You wish to know how we lived in the swamps, how many was in my mess & so on. We lived bad indeed. Sometimes did not get half enough, and not time to cook it; nothing to cook in. We got spoil meal a part of the time. We had to drink bayou water with a perfect green scum on it. They lost nearly all of our cooking utensils in the retreat from Richmond. Brooks, Stoveall, Singletary, Riley, the two Hulls, and me messed together. Barksdale's mess and my mess had one small skillet, and one little stove pot to boil our beef in was all we had to cook in, but if we only could have got water fit to drink we could have done. You ask if I have my ring yet. I have them both; have wore them every day. It is not injured any yet. You speak of having fine watermelons. I seen three little ones in Monroe at $2.50 apiece. Oh how I would like to help you to eat them. I have eat a few green peaches, and a few roasting ears is all the fruit I have got. They do not allow a soldier to go in a orchard or field to get anything. I never wanted flour bread as bad in my life as I do now. I feel like it would cure my bowels. I am wore out on cornbread and beef, but I hope we will get some soon. We have seen hard times in the swamps and suffered marches by day and night, but the good Lord has preserved me thus far, and preserved my sweet wife and children. Let us trust Him for the future and pray for His protecting care. You say you want my advice about buying the Moriss lands. I had hoped to get home to buy land, but if you get it reasonable, and Thos. & William think it will suit, it will be best to buy it so you will have a home. We will soon pay the price of a place in rent. If I can collect what the gov[ernment] owes me, I could now send you five hundred dollars, & you could sell Dock or Nance for four hundred more. And what we have coming to us in Carolina, we could pay for some. So if Brothers think it will suit, buy it in my name. And if the terms are not too hard, don't mind going in debt some. I think as they are going to tax cotton so high, it would be best to sell it and put it in land. You could weigh Haltom's[526] out. If there was anything to bale it with it would be well to have it ginned to get the seed. So I am anxious for you to get the place. I had hoped to be there to move but now I see no prospect of the war closing for years. It might be possible I can get a furlough against winter if I live. So, if Brothers think the place will suit us, get someone of them to attend to it and do not miss it. Do not think that I do not write. I write often. I never wanted to see you as bad in my life. I would write to my Mother but don't think it could now go. I will answer Brother James' kind letter soon. I have written to Brothers Thomas and William. Tell William I have got the pants Singletary brought. They just fit me; are too small for him. As I need them, he better get another pair and sell me these as I am wearing them. The army is in low spirits since Vicksburg was sold. The Feds bought it; did not take it by fighting. I hope Brothers James and Thomas will not be drafted. My love to all the friends, to Mother & Leonard. Tell the children howdy. Tell them I hope to get home to see them sometime. Give the Negroes howdy. Tell them I am glad they are doing well. My love to yourself. Pray for me. May the Lord in mercy bless & protect you all is the prayer of your husband. So farewell for this time my sweet wife.

To Achsah Wallace from her husband, H. A. Wallace.

Franklin Hays[527], Matt[528], George Burns, Billy Burns, J. D. Smith[529], T. Guthrie, the Parkers are all well. Sergt. Hull[530] is sick at the convalescent camp.

---

[526] Unidentified

[527] 3rd Sergeant Benjamin Franklin Hays (4/29/1836-4/12/1907), son of William and Mary (Wilson) Hays

[528] 2nd Corporal Daniel Matterson (Matt) Hays (c.1837-10/21/1893), son of William and Mary (Wilson) Hays

[529] Private Jerome Decatur Smith (5/1830-12/20/1913)

[530] 1st Sergeant John L. Hull (c.1843-?) was the son of James and Sarah Hull of Mount Enterprise.

In camps four miles north of Vernon, Louisiana
July the 23rd, 1863

My beloved Wife,
I this evening with pleasure have taken my pen to perform the pleasing task of writing to you. My health is slowly improving since I wrote last Friday. My prayer is the good Lord is blessing you all with health. On last Saturday morning our regimental surgeon received orders to send all the men who could not keep up with the regiment to the convalescent camp, as the convalescents would start Sunday morning and travel five or six miles a day. As me and Lieut. Barksdale had just come in the day before and were not able to march far, he sent us with the rest. I got him to give us a recommendation to the chief surgeon to let us travel along as we could and put up at houses. The Capt. in command of the convalescents told us his orders was positive to allow no man to [page torn] in houses but to keep all the men together. I soon seen he was an overbearing big head so I went to General Walker. He give us permission at once, so Barksdale and me started Saturday evening; went four miles and put up. So we have just traveled along as we were able before. The sick some days travel five miles, one ten before anyone would let us stay. Some of the people are very kind; others won't take us in atall. We are both weak; sometimes have to rest every half of a mile. We are pretty well matched for strength and both worked just alike. Our victuals sour on our stomach, swell us up, and then our bowels run off. We are both improving some now. The convalescents started Sunday morning; McCulloch's Brigade on Monday. Barksdale and me stayed with the regiment yesterday & last night at Vernon. They are now furloughing nearly all of the sick officers. Barksdale sent up a petition for one. The brigade started at day this morning for Grand Ecore. Barksdale went on with them as the Col. told him he knew he would get his furlough by this evening. He was to ride today. I knew I could not keep up so I stopped at Vernon. The convalescents took another road and went four miles north of Vernon, so I went out one mile and a half towards the road they were on; got my breakfast and

dinner. I came on to the camp this evening and I am now writing in camps. I will stay with the boys tonight. I will then knock along and get ahead of them and put up at night. I expect to be very lonesome but I will be apt to fall in with someone traveling loose. I know I will improve faster to put up where I can get something to suit me to eat. My great danger is in eating too much. I have got some very good peaches the last three days and two little messes of watermelons, but I try to be careful. They are now feeding the convalescents very well; give them a plenty. They give the sickest of them flour; give them all plenty of molasses, sugar, and bacon. We are on the Shreveport Road. The talk is we are going to Campti. I don't know where yet. The convalescent are the men who are able to travel a little. They leave the sick at the hospital. There is 12 of my company along, all doing well. Sergt. Hull is along. I was uneasy about him but he is improving fast now. Tommy Hull is with the company, fat and stout. John Brooks keeps quite stout; looks better than I ever seen him. We left Corp. Turner[531], George Stoveall, John Mabrey[532] sick at Monroe, all improving. Amos Peurifoy[533] and Doherty[534] are both there too. They got themselves detailed as [page torn] keep out of hard marching and fighting. We have no reliable war news. One day we hear Lee is carrying everything before him, the next he has been badly whipped; the same way about Johnson's Army. One day we hear the Feds have Alexandria, the next there is no Feds in Red River, so I don't put no confidence in reports. One thing I know, our army is all moving for Red River and leaving this country. The settlers are nearly all fixing to move to Texas with their Negroes and just leave their crops and stock, so Texas will be crowded sure. In your last you asked my advice about buying the Moriss land. I wrote to you in the letter I

---

[531] 1st Corporal Rice Ross Turner (c.1831-11/22/1905), son of Samuel Turner, also served as 2nd Lieutenant of Co.-B, 11th Texas Infantry. Turner afterward served for a short time in Co.-C, 32nd Texas Cavalry before re-enlisting with or transferring to Wallace's Company.

[532] Private John F. Mabry (c.1842-?) was the son of Joseph and Hester Mabry. Private Mabry served earlier in Co.-B, 11th Texas Infantry.

[533] Private Amos J. Peurifoy (c.1833-?)

[534] Private R. J. Doherty (c.1830-?)

sent by Long to buy it if possible if Brothers thought it would do. I still think it would be best to buy it if possible. Don't be afraid to risk some. Get a home. Lieut. Corby[535] of Co. C in our regiment died suddenly at the hospital in Monroe Sunday. He had been sent there a few days before with bilious fever; thought he was getting well. Five minutes before he died he was laughing and talking; said he would get well. I want to be careful and try to improve my health. If it does not improve and I live until Brother and Barksdale get back, I will have to quit the service a while to try to improve it. Two of our Capt. have resigned and gone home. I don't know when or where I will mail this. I may write more before sending. My love to all, to Mother and our sweet little ones and yourself. May God bless and save you all is the prayer of your husband. So farewell my dear wife for this time.

To Mrs. A. Wallace from her husband, H. A. Wallace

Written upside down at the top:
I often think of you all while trudging along through the deep sand. I have plenty of clothes along in my knapsack. My trunk is gone on with the regiment. I have not wore out my checked shirts or overshirts either as I did not take them in the swamps, but took my strongest clothing there. I have my best clothes with me now. Kiss Matty for me.

---

[535] 1st Lieutenant Thomas J. Corbey died July 15, 1863.

In camp
Sept. the 4th, 1863

Capt. Wallace

Dear Sir,
I seat myself to drop you a few lines to let you know how we are getting along in camp and what little news I can gather, which is not much. The health of the company is in better health than usual in past. The regiment is in good health throughout. [illegible] is not well yet. [illegible] the boys is a [illegible] sick list. [illegible] Camp Texas by A. J. Parker. [illegible] now writing from the [illegible] will explain. Last Sunday [illegible] to march immediately. We started about 1 o'clock in the direction of Alexandria and continued until we arrive[d] at Alexandria about 11 o'clock that night and camped on this side of the river and one mile above town. There we lay in the hot sun until Tuesday evening and then took up the march for this place, which is about 22 miles west of Alexandria in the pine

Major General Richard Taylor

timber; a high place and good water, and enough for the Confederacy. As to the war news, I am not certain that I have any, although the chat in camps is that Gen. Taylor[536] has been badly whipped and is falling back; that Sibley's Brigade has been entirely lost. The rumor is believed by many and none dispute it right out. I

---

[536] Major General Richard Taylor (1826-1879), son of President Zachary Taylor, commanded the District of West Louisiana under General Edmund Kirby Smith. General Taylor served with his father in the Mexican War and afterward as a Louisiana legislator and sugar planter. He was a capable military leader and astute tactician. Taylor was enormously popular with his troops, as well as the citizens of Louisiana who supported the southern cause.

can write no good news from this division, (more than the good health of the soldiers), for there is more dissatisfaction in camps than I ever saw. Last night is one to be remembered. About dark, the men commenced the war hoops and firing signal guns all over the division. I was at church at the time. The Parson was requested to close the service and send the men to their camp. [illegible] the first gun [illegible] got together [illegible] firing [illegible]. The men loaded their guns [illegible]. They all collected together at [illegible] and they marched off in good order for Texas[537]. The number of men that is gone is variously estimated at from 500 to 1500. It is also said that they took 2 pieces of artillery and spiked the remainder. This I do not believe, and would not believe any had I not seen them go off. The regiment was called out in line. Company H turned out to a man, all present and ready for action. But we was on the line at least 20 minutes before any other company, and half of the men present in the regiment refused to come at all, and consequently, the guard house is full today. We remained in line for 1 hour. Co. H was then ordered to load their guns well and go out as picket. Our company was highly complimented for their promptness and soldier like bearing, both by Col. Waterhouse and Capt. Crawford[538]. There was but 7 men that went from this regiment, all from Co. E. I am still in hopes that not so many has gone as reported. We have marching orders and I think will leave tonight. And report says to Harrisonburg but the officers is afraid [illegible]. There has been a revival of religion in camps and is all going on both in this brigade and Gen. Haws'[539]. I saw 6 men baptized by

---

[537] Lieutenant Brooks describes a mass desertion of troops from various regiments of the division. These soldiers deserted in protest of a refusal to grant furloughs by the division commanders. Many returned to their regiments afterward and were not counted as deserters.

[538] Captain William L. Crawford (1/22/1839-2/17/1920) of Co.-A was later promoted to Major and Lieutenant Colonel of the 19th Texas Infantry.

[539] Reverend Martin V. Smith started this wave of revival that swept the division from September to November 1863. Reverend Smith was a Baptist Missionary to Walker's Division and the former Captain of Co.-D, 28th Texas Dismounted Cavalry. Smith reportedly baptized more than 139 converts during this time, including 23 in one day in late November. Johansson, "Peculiar Honor: A History of the 28th Texas Cavalry (Dismounted), Walker's Texas Division, 1862-1865." 144-146.

immersion last Tuesday on the falls of Red River. It is quite an interesting meeting, but the division is cut up now and I think religion will go down. Capt., I am sorry to have to inform you that I have been forced to report some of Co. H as absent without leave. But I was called up to account for all the men and was compelled to report 2 officers and 8 privates absent without leave. I will name them and request you to notify them to come to camps by the 30th of this month as nothing will be done to those that report by that time. I have also furnished their names to [illegible]: Lieut. Wallace, Lieut. Barksdale, J. T. Arnold[540], R. G. W. Turner[541], J. M. Reid[542], P. J. Harris[543], W. D. Harris, W. H .H. Hays[544], J. A. H. Welch[545], T. W. Strickland[546]. I would advise them to bring with them certificates from their physicians, and still better, where they can get them, from a surgeon of the Confederacy Service. And, those that are detailed must send a certificate specifying the detail with date of detail. Gen. Haws' Brigade started off in the direction of Alexandria this evening. We follow immediately. It is now about 5 o'clock p. m. So no more, but remember your friend. Write soon.

J. R. K. Brooks
To Capt. Wallace

---

[540] Private John Thomas Arnold (7/1/1833-11/5/1889)
[541] Private Romulus G. W. Turner (7/12/1837-1/11/1910)
[542] Private John M. Reid (c.1831-?)
[543] Private Peter J. Harris (c.1841-?)
[544] Private William Henry Harrison Hays (7/1840-1/28/1906), son of William C. and Mary (Wilson) Hays
[545] Private Joseph A. H. Welch
[546] Private Thomas W. Strickland (c.1834-2/27/1865)

Camp Bayou Boeuf, La.
Nov. the 6th, 1863

My dear Achsah,
I this Friday evening write you a few lines as our mail goes out in the morning. I am in as good health as I could expect; able for duty and business. My bowels [are] somewhat deranged but I think will be all right in a day or two. William's health is about like when Leonard left. He is in very bad health indeed. I trust you and the rest of our family are enjoying the blessing of health. The health of the company is very good. We are still lying at the camps Leonard left us; very filthy, dirty camps. The whole army camped along the Bayou Boeuf; the water filthy. We have had lots of rain this week; a plenty of mud; no talk of moving any way. Two regiments of our division, Robert's & Ochiltree's old regiment, and Green's Cavalry, attacked the Federals 12 miles below Opelousas on Carrion Crow Bayou Monday as they were retreating towards New Orleans[547]. The report we have up here is that we took 12 hundred prisoners. We have not heard the enemy's loss in killed but hear that Hill's Regiment, formerly Ochiltree's, lost 30 killed on the field and sixty or seventy wounded. Col. Robert's Regiment only one man killed. There was 100 men sent from our regiment on yesterday, it a pouring down rain, to Washington to bring up 500 prisoners. Capt. Northrop's Company[548] was sent. 10 men from mine went; enough from the other companies to make out the hundred men, all under the command of Capt. Northrop. I suppose they will be along tomorrow with the prisoners. The general opinion here is we will go no further down as there is no provisions below this to feed our army. The Federals are said to be gone back to New Orleans, as they

---

[547] On November 3, 1863, the 11th (Robert's), 18th (Ochiltree's), and 15th Texas Infantry Regiments, with General Thomas Green's Cavalry Division, attacked the Federal encampment of Brigadier General Stephen Burbridge on Bayou Bourbeau (Carrion Crow) near Grand Coteau, La. The Confederates routed the surprised Federals in a sharp engagement and took 562 prisoners, along with a large amount of supplies. John D Winters. *The Civil War In Louisiana*. (Baton Rouge: Louisiana State University Press, 1963), 298-299.

[548] Co.-E, 19th Texas Infantry under Captain A. R. K. Northrop

say they can't invade this country until the waters get up as there is no provisions left below this and they can't haul enough for a large army. So I think we will eat out this country and fall back to provisions if not called somewhere else. That is my opinion. It is not worth much. We have a report here of a fight in Virginia between Lee & Meade in which Lee gained a victory. We have nothing reliable from Bragg's Army. The men here are in good spirits and full of life; would now make a big fight. We get plenty of beef, meal, potatoes, sugar & molasses, and flour or bacon. Our mess has lots of butter yet. It has been so hot it is about to spoil. So we are living fine yet. The soldiers make free with anything on these farms. They all just use what sugar cane they can eat. It is said to be very healthy. There is thousands of acres of it here just going to loss as the owners are gone. This is the richest country I have ever seen. On Monday we were called out to witness the execution of a soldier in Randal's Brigade. He was shot at 12 o'clock. He had deserted and attempted to go to the Feds. There is several more who attempted to go over to the Feds who will be shot. Three of Capt. Crawford's men of our regiment were caught going to the Feds. It is a melancholy sight to see a fellow soldier march out behind his coffin and be shot to death by his own men, but such is war. I now think someone of the company will get off home in a few days on furlough. If they do, I will write again. They have not paid us yet but we are looking for it every day. If they pay, I will send you some money home. The Federal prisoners are said to be passing the road. I will go out to see them. Write to me. I feel anxious to hear from home indeed. Tell Matty I just wish she could have a plenty of sugar cane. Tell Willy he must raise some if Leonard takes home some. Tell Bud to take good care of Jim and Amanda[549] and learn his letters. We have had some royal messes of white pudding. Give my love to your Mother, Martha and the children, and to all enquiring friends, and receive a portion for yourself and our loved ones. And may God in mercy

---

[549] Unidentified

bless you all is the prayer of your husband. So farewell for this time my dear wife.

To Mrs. Achsah Wallace from her husband, H. A. Wallace.

On picket near Miss. River
Monday evening
Nov. 16th, 1863

My dear Achsah,
I write you a few lines this evening for your own eye alone. Achsah we have had some pretty hard times since I came to camps. It goes pretty hard with me, the exposure, but I have stood it much better than I expected to. I have had two severe spells with my bowels but have got about right again. I have been able all the time for duty. Our fare is cornbread, beef, & potatoes now; not much to cook in; live like hogs. You know after me living so well at home where you were so anxious to have everything good for me it is hard, but if I can have health I don't mind the fare; and my maker only spares me sound to return to my loved wife and children, I feel I should ever be thankful to Him. I still have the most of my flour. We use it careful. We have William's side of bacon and part of our butter. It is all back with the train. We never draw a dust of flour or a pound of bacon or pork. I make out on as little beef as possible. William & me had a mess of milk and mush yesterday. I have suffered some from jaw ache. When we get so cold at night we can't lie, we get up and make a fire. Our bed clothes are as wet these mornings from dew and frost as if we had been in a shower. I have no clothes with me except what I have on: overshirt, coat, and pants. We have been one week from our train; may be a month longer from it. My dear, I received the note last evening you sent by the stranger. I was glad to get it, though I had got the letters Deason and Wolverton[550] brought. I was sorry to hear of you and Bud being sick. Oh how I would have like to have been with you. You speak of me getting tired of your complaints. Not so my dear. I expect you to write me all the trials, troubles, and sufferings you have. I will do the same with you. If we can't write our whole hearts to each other, who can we go to? I dreamed so much about Bud, about his being sick, before I got to camps, and about you. I feel that I left you in a delicate situation and

---

[550] Greenville Wolverton of Mount Enterprise had three sons serving in the 11th Texas Infantry at this time (see note-557).

am anxious to hear from you all the time[551]. I want you to write me just how you are. I can sympathize with you my dear if I can't be with you. Oh Achsah, when I look back at the happy hours I spent with you while at home, and how kind and loving you were to my every whim or want, and how kind our little dears and your Mother was to me, I feel that I am unworthy. Such kindness, and how hardened I was to scarcely ever shed a tear. I feel, as you say, I did not live while at home as I ought, but my prayer is the Lord will forgive us. I heard an excellent sermon last evening from Parson Hay[s][552]. His text was from First Corinthians: 16th Chapter and 22nd verse, when he compared our love for our Savior to our love for our wives and children. And in conclusion, warned us of that final separation that would be between husbands and wives and loved children, as many of us were bound to never see them in this world, [and] unless we loved and served our Savior, never in the world to come. It made the tears roll from my eyes. So let us pray the Lord continually my dear to spare us to meet on earth if not in Heaven, where parting comes no more. I could write as much more but have no more paper out here. I will try to write every week while spared able. You do the same. My love to your Mother and all of the friends. Tell the Negroes howdy; to do their best. So farewell my dear for this time. May God in mercy bless and protect you from all harm and enable you to undergo all the trials and troubles you may have is the prayer of your unworthy husband.

To Mrs. Achsah Wallace from her husband, Harvey A. Wallace

<u>Written upside down at the top:</u>
Let me hear from Brothers and their families when you write. Tell Sam[553] to put me up some good tobacco; some 12 or 15 pounds of his best. If I live I may need it this summer.

---

[551] Achsah was pregnant with the couple's fifth child, Harvey Jr., at this time.
[552] Private William Henry Harrison Hays of Wallace's Company was also a Baptist minister. Reverend Hays pastored churches in Rusk County for many years after the war.
[553] Sam was a slave (see note-444)

In camp on Bayou Fordoche, La.
December the 6th, 1863

My dear Achsah,
I this beautiful Sabbath morning feel like I could not spend a little time more profitable than writing to loved ones at home, though it may be several days before I have an opportunity of sending this by mail. Yet it does my heart good to write to you my dear Achsah, for I know if you receive it you will appreciate anything I write and be rejoiced to hear from me. I am in good health, thank the Lord. My prayer is you and our family are enjoying a like blessing. Brother William's health is considerably improved since I come to camps, yet he is considerably bothered with his bowels & stomach yet. The health of the company is good. All the men are up; two or three complaining some little. In fact, our army is in as good health as we could ever expect an army; no sick men in the regiment. Achsah I will give you a history of our moves since I last wrote. I then stated we would go on picket; that was, our regiment. On Monday evening we packed our haversacks with poor beef and cornbread; carried a blanket to the man; left our old camps at one o'clock Monday evening. We got to the river [at] half past three. My company was ordered up the river to relieve a company at the mouth of Red River, one mile above where the regiment stopped. We loaded our guns and started up the levy. It was not more than waist high part of the way; three gunboats lying at the mouth of Red River in full view. I tell you, we stooped low to keep hid. We knew if the Feds seen us they would send some shell at us. Major Crawford went up with us. We stopped at a house by the levy where the levy was as high as our heads. The other company left. Major Crawford told me to keep the men concealed and if any steamboat or transport passed, not to fire until our artillery opened. It was two miles below us. After it opened, to fire into every one passed that come near enough, and to watch the gunboats and transports and report to the Col. if they started down. I put one man up on a stable loft that stood near the

The U.S.S. *Carondelet* in the Mississippi River

levy. There was a split in the weatherboard so we could see every move the Feds made. I put two on the levy to to look through some cuckle burs to watch them. Our artillery went out about sunset. Directly, a transport started down; a gunboat with it. I sent the Col. word. She kept close to the other bank of the river. We had two companies a mile or two below, Northrop's & Allen's[554]. She came in two or three hundred yards of them. They popped away at her with their rifles. The gunboat opened on them with grape and canister shot and shells. The boat up where we were opened with shell; threw them past us down the river at the lower companies. Our boys, after firing, run and hid behind the levy. About dark they quit shelling. It was very cold indeed. We were allowed no fire for fear they would see the smoke and open fire on us. We kept a few coals to warm our feet. The most of the men crawled in the houses and rolled up in their blankets. We had to keep six on post at different points on the river bank to watch the enemy. We relieved them every two hours there. We kept quiet and shook with cold. The ground froze like a rock; the enemy in camps right across the river, their gunboats lying there. They had big fires. They looked so warm. We could hear them talk, laugh, & cough, and even hear them spit. I lay down about two hours but was too cold to sleep. At daylight Major Crawford came up; told us a courier had brought orders for us to move from there at seven, or sunrise, and meet the balance of the army at Williamsport, five miles from where we were down south, as the whole army would move on another expedition. We left at sunrise; got to Williamport [and] waited there for our brigade. It came up. We traveled between twenty & twenty five miles; got to camps tired and hungry. We traveled 10 [page torn] through the cane brake and swamp. That was as far [page torn]; had our cooking to do after night. We camped on the ground General Green had the fight on about the time I left home[555]. It was at a

---

[554] Companies E and C of the 19th Texas Infantry
[555] Captain Wallace describes the Battle of Sterling's Plantation, fought on September 29, 1863 between General Thomas Green's Cavalry Division and a Federal advance detachment under Colonel J. B. Leake. The Federals lost 16 killed, 45 wounded, and 462 prisoners as opposed to the Confederates 26 killed and 85 wounded. Winters, 296-297.

sugar farm; a large brick sugar manufactory, dwelling house, and Negro quarter. The Feds fought in the houses until drove out. They then got behind a levy about breast high and a plank fence. The houses were all riddle with bullets, so was the plank fence. There was dead horses lying every direction. After Green ran them off and took 400 prisoners, their main army came up. It was only six miles off at Morganza so he had to leave his men unburied. The Feds had just piled our dead, some 25 or 40, in a ditch and covered them over with dirt. Some of my company went to see. They said one man's foot was sticking out, another's chin. Our men covered them over. We kept on south at sunrise Thursday; traveled 20 miles down Bayou Fordoche; came to another large bayou four miles from West Baton Rouge Parish, about opposite Baton Rouge. There we camped. Gen. Walker called a council of his generals next morning to decide whether to attack Plaquemine, a town on the Miss. River that Taylor had ordered him to take. The town was 20 miles from us. Walker had learned it was strongly fortified; forty pieces of heavy cannon; lots of gunboats; only one way for us to get there, so the enemy could rake us for miles with his cannon and gunboats. They had 20,000 men, us 8 or 10 thousand. They decided not to attack as we would lose too many men to take it and then could not hold it. So we lay there until Saturday morning. We then moved back here some 20 miles to Green's battleground. We are 8 or 10 miles from Morgan's Ferry on Atchafalaya River. Our pontoon bridge and wagon train is there. We are living better down here; have had three days ration of pork and plenty of potatoes. There is lots of hogs on these big farms; the greatest potato country I ever seen. In fact, it is the richest country I ever seen. I have not seen a foot of poor land since I left the piney woods above Alexandria. [page torn] fine manufacturing, sugar & molasses, and [page torn] selling it to the Yankees. They are kind to our soldiers but don't [page torn] to sell anything for our money. We sometimes get some of the best molasses I ever seen; pure syrup. Our officers keep guards at every house as the men would help themselves. We never get any pure syrup in the country like they have here. There is a large fatigue party out today cutting a road; some say to Morgan's

Ferry so we can get out of here when it rains, but I don't know when we will go out of here. We now have a good army down here in good health and spirits. We have some 10 thousand men here. Green has some 5 or six thousand with him, so we have enough of men to guard Eastern Texas against thirty thousand Feds, though we have bad news from Bragg's Army. We hear that Bragg was defeated at Chattanooga and had to retreat, and that Lee has been whipped. There is men crossing the Miss. River every day or two from the other side so we hear frequently. There is four or five of my men as good as barefooted. Two of them entirely barefooted, yet they have to keep up. Our bedding and clothes that was left in Arkansas last spring has been brought to Morgan's Ferry on Atchafalaya. We sent one man from each company to get them sorted out, each company's to themself. T. J. Riley went from my company.

Monday evening, the 8th
Sergt. Riley returned from seeing about the clothing and bedding; says what little of it came is rotten. Our mess chest is over at the river. James Welch was to see us last evening. He is fat and stout. Bredner[556] is well. The Wolverton boys[557] are well. One of them was here today. We have one of the regiments from our brigade is on the Miss. River with five pieces of cannon planted, ready for to fire in the transports; a gunboat waiting to open on our men. I expect we will have to picket on the river while we stay in here. We will stay until the Atchafalaya gets up or the Feds come out and fight us one. Brooks tried to get a furlough but has failed thus far. It is nearly impossible for anyone to get a furlough at this time. Tell Sam to take care of the stock and get the fencing done. I think you are right not to pick cotton at one dollar per hundred. It won't pay. Tell the Negroes all howdy. Give my love to Uncle Reece. Tell him if he can spare it to send me four or five pounds more tobacco as what he give me is the best in camps. My love to Martha, Jane, Eliza, and

---

[556] Private Joseph Bredner McCarter
[557] Sergeant William T., Private Elijah H., and Private Thornton B. Wolverton of Co.-E, 11th Texas Infantry were sons of Greenville and Parmelia (Guinn) Wolverton of Mount Enterprise.

the children. My love to your Mother. I have wore the seat all out of my yellow pants. William patched it for me yesterday. We go as dirty as Negroes. The army is full of lice. We have none yet but haul our bedding all together. May God's blessings attend you my dear wife. So farewell for this time. Do take care of yourself. That sore throat is dangerous.

From H. A. Wallace to his wife, A. Wallace, at home; that sweet word, home.

<u>Written upside down on top of the first page:</u>
This Monday the 8th is clear and cold. Let me know where Brothers James and Thomas are[558]. I did not write by this mail to Mother for want of time. We are under strict discipline now. The boys will kill hogs and steal potatoes. In fact, there is men in the army just to steal.

---

[558] James A. Wallace was serving as Captain of Co.-G, 2nd Regiment Texas State Troops at this time. The regiment was organized in August 1863 for six months service as a home guard unit. Shortly after organizing, it was ordered to Houston to help prepare coastal defenses. The unit worked on coastal and river defenses in southeast Texas until January 1864, when it was mustered into regular army service at Galveston under Colonel Ashbel Smith. Apparently, Thomas Wallace was also a member of Co.-G but no record of this could be located.

Rampart Street New Orleans La
June the 2nd 1864

My Dear Wife
            as Col. Blair one
of our fellow Prisoners has been
Exchanged and leaves us to day I
send a few lines to inform
you of my welfare I am quite
well for which I fell thankfull
to God the giver of all good my
Prayrs are that you and our family may be Enjoying a like
Blessing Lieuts. Brooks & Barksdale
are well in fact the officers in
this prison some 80 are in good
health and faceing as well as
we could Expect for Prisners
I have sad news to write in
Regard to my men my fellow
Soldier T.J. Riley Died in the St

1864

Prisoners Of Us All

---

*Captain Wallace's journal entry
March 14, 1864*

Fort Derussy, La.[559]
Wednesday night
Feb. 10th, '64

My dear Achsah,
I this night write you a few lines to let you know how I am getting along in this world of trouble. I am well and healthy, for which I feel thankful. My prayer is you and our family are enjoying a like blessing, although I must confess, I have been somewhat uneasy the last week since I received yours of the 22nd of Jan. stating Willy was so unwell. But I hope he has got well. Brother is only moderately well; able for duty but suffering from his bowels & stomach. I don't think he will ever get stout in the service. The company is in good health; some three or four cases of chills but none serious. Well Achsah I know you wish to know how we like our new post. We have lots of duty to do here, both men and officers. Steamboats come down every two or three days from Alexandria with corn & provisions. I am on a board with two other officers. We have to inspect the corn and provisions and make our reports to see if they hold out or are damaged. So we are two or three days of each week at that. It is called a board of survey. We are living better here. I can buy as much flour as I want at twenty cents per pound; a plenty of sugar & molasses. The boat that came today brought several barrels of lard. I will get some of that. They now issue pickled beef. It is much better than the poor green beef. I think we are bettered about living here but our water is not good; just seeps our little well 8 or ten feet deep. I fear this place will be sickly by spring. Red River is rising down here; backwater from the Miss. River. They are pushing the work on the fort as fast as possible but I fear will not get it completed in time. Oh how I pity these poor Negroes here. They work them from daybreak until dark; about half feed them. They

---

[559] Fort DeRussy was located on the Red River below Alexandria, La. near Marksville. It guarded against attack by water from the Mississippi via Red River. One company from each regiment of Walker's Division was assigned to man the post and help rebuild the fortifications, as the Federals had destroyed them the year before. Co.- H was detached from the 19th Texas Infantry for this duty on January 30, 1864.

look so bad. I never would let them have one of mine to treat this way. I would feed them in the woods first. I have no idea how long we will remain here. Gen. Walker says he won't let us stay any longer than he can help as he dislikes very much to fort his men up, but he has to obey old Taylor. I have no idea we can hold the fort any length of time against gunboats. The general impression is, when the Feds come they will take us prisoners. If they get us all they will have to be smart. We will do the best we can for them. Our whole army loves Gen. Walker. He is the best general on this side of the Miss. sure; treats his men best. We are looking every day for Brooks. I made sure he would get here today; not come yet. We are counting high on good living when he comes. Achsah, if Brother Thomas is dissatisfied, if he gets off he can certainly come on here. I would be better satisfied if he was here with William and me so we could all mess together and assist each other. He need have no fears about getting in the company if he will come. William Conner[560] has got a recruit and got sixty days furlough[561]. He will carry this. He starts in the morning for home.

Your Harvey

---

[560] Private William B. Conner (c.1833-?) was the son of Nelson and Elizabeth Conner of Panola County.
[561] Private Conner's furlough was an incentive for the soldiers to find new recruits as replacements for those lost through the previous years. It is estimated that Co.-H had only 35-40 men left who were fit for duty by this time, and many of those were sick. Most of the regiments and companies of Walker's Division were in the same shape, with no recruits to be found unless they were conscripted by force.

Fort Derussy, La.
Saturday evening
Feb the 24th, '64

My dear Achsah,
As I have a chance of sending a few lines direct to Marshall by a soldier and I was so unwell when Brother left, I know you will be anxious to hear I have improved some every day since he left and hope will be alright soon, though I am very weak. The least walk completely overcomes me. I took quinine at first; am now getting over the effects of it. The janders [jaundice] makes one feel so badly; no appetite to eat anything, and it is near two weeks since I have been sick; more or less fever every day. I am using eggnog; will begin on dogwood and cherry bitters in a day or two. Tommy Riley is gone to Marksville today to get me some rum. I am taking nothing else. The company are all doing well except Jesse Arledge[562]. He is low with pneumonia; a doubtful case. The boys are all in camps now, getting along very well at present. I have no war news of interest at all; everything quiet at present; Red River falling. They just completed our raft[563] below the fort this week. It is undermining; will soon be all gone. This is certain news. Trade and speculation [is] going on as usual. We have plenty of everything necessary to eat at present; no want. William will be apt to see you before you get this. He can give you more news of how we are getting along in camps. I hope I will be stout soon again. I am not doing any duty now, just taking care of myself. I nearly finished making out my muster rolls before the company got in yesterday. Tommy Riley is as kind to me as any brother can be. He has got back; got me a quart of rum; paid $15.00 dollars for it. Write soon and as often as you can. I will write every opportunity. I reckon Joe would be surprised when Will[564] got home, and rejoiced too. Well

---

[562] Private Jesse Arledge (c.1833-1/12/1865)
[563] The raft was a river obstruction made of heavy logs and chain located downstream from the fort. It was designed to slow or stop the progress of Federal gunboats during a riverine attack against the installation.
[564] Lieutenant William Wallace

my time will roll around soon I hope, when I will be permitted to enjoy the pleasures of home for a short time at least. So farewell for the present my dear wife. May God in mercy bless you is the prayer of your husband,

H.A. Wallace

My love to Mother & the children. I only had a few minutes to write this as the boat leaves.

Rampart Street
New Orleans, La.
June the 2nd, 1864

My dear Wife,
As Col. Blair[565], one of our fellow prisoners, has been exchanged and leaves us today, I send a few lines to inform you of my welfare. I am quite well, for which I feel thankful to God, the giver of all good. My prayers are that you and our family may be enjoying a like blessing. Lieutenants Brooks and Barksdale are well. In fact, the officers in this prison, some 80, are in good health and faring as well as we could expect for prisoners. I have sad news to write in regard to my men. My fellow soldier, T. J. Riley, died in the St. Louis Hospital Monday the 30 of May of pneumonia. I received a note from him dated the 27th stating he was getting better. I received it the 29. Franklin Hays wrote me on yesterday from the hospital. He was with him when he died. P. W. S. Stone[566] died at the same hospital Sunday the 29th. He had been down with pneumonia but recovered and took smallpox. Hays was sent there from a sore arm. Mat Jones[567] was there; had diarrhea but was getting well. Old man Billingsley[568] was improving, Hays wrote. They are the only ones I know anything of as I have not heard from the remainder of the company in two weeks. They were all well then, and getting well all here in prison. Them two are the first and only deaths in the company. Our wounded men had got well. We have all had high hopes of an exchange this week but now have great doubts as our generals appear to only be making exchange for some few favorite officers. Still, I hope we may soon be exchanged so that I can return to my family. My respects to my friends. My love to Mother and our little dears. I will close this short, unsatisfactory scroll. May God in

---

[565] Lieutenant Colonel James Douglas Blair of the 2nd Louisiana Cavalry.
[566] Private Peter Wynn Stovall Stone (c.1842-5/29/1864)
[567] Private James M. Jones
[568] Private T. P. Billingsley (c.1812-6/9/1864)

mercy bless and protect you is the prayer of your ever loving husband.

H. A. Wallace

P.S.: Say to Mrs. Riley I will get all the particulars I can from her husband's sickness, and if I live to get back, will give her what satisfaction I can. There is a Confederate burial ground[569] here. Each soldier's grave is marked with his name, company, & regiment & state. It is nicely kept up by the ladies.

H. A. Wallace

---

[569] This burial ground is reported to have been in a section of the Cypress Grove Cemetery Number 2. The cemetery is now located beneath Canal Boulevard, adjacent to the present Greenwood Cemetery. A separate section of the cemetery was used for burial of Union soldiers, whose graves were moved to the Chalmette National Cemetery in the 1920's. The Confederate graves and those of civilians were destroyed or paved over as the city expanded. Some of these graves have been recently discovered through construction activity.

My Dear Wife & Kids   (Piedmont Springs Grimes County Texas
Morning with you   April the 11th 186[5]
a few lines to inform

you how we are getting along we had a pleasant march
after leaving the Trinity except some rain and deep black
sticky mud the last day or two before coming to this Camp.
the morning John Morris left us with the letter I sent you
we came on through Huntsville that day it is a consider-
-able town we passed through Prairies principally since
crossing the Trinity River very Rich Lands a Rich Country
indeed thinly settled we came through Anderson the
county seat of this county it is in the Middle of a Prairie
the Land as black as a coal earth and perfectly sticky
the rain a pelting down on us we could not form a very
favorable opinion of it we came to this camp Sunday
morning the 9th the whole division is here we were told
yesterday we would stay here possibly one month. this
morning we have orders to leave in the morning for
Fairfield 40 miles southeast of here these springs are
very strong with sulphur nearly as strong as Blount Springs
Alabama very finely fixed up a great many people attend
them in the Summer season I was in hopes we would remain
here some time as we are tired travelling but we need
expect no rest from Magruder the water in this prairie country
is bad and scarce Timber scarce people can make lots
and raise stock without any trouble but I don't think I would
like to live here I would rather live where I made less and
be out of the mud and have other conveniences
but as it is I am bound to live where they send me at present

1865

Homeward Bound

"[I] feel as anxious to go home as if I had been out twelve months."

Captain Harvey Wallace to his wife
May 3, 1865.

Piedmont Springs[570]
Grimes County, Texas
April the 11th, 1865

My dear Wife,
I this morning write you a few lines to inform you how we are getting along. We had a pleasant march after leaving the Trinity except some rain and deep, black, sticky mud the last day or two before coming to this camp the morning John Meabra [Mabry] left us with the letter I sent you. We came on through Huntsville that day. It is a considerable town. We passed through prairies, principally, since crossing the Trinity River; very rich lands; a rich country indeed; thinly settled. We came through Anderson, the county seat of this county. It is in the middle of a prairie; the land as black as a coal hearth and perfectly sticky; the rain a pelting down on us so we could not form a very favorable opinion of it. We came to this camp Sunday morning the 9th. The whole division is here. We were told yesterday we would stay here possibly one month. This morning we have orders to leave in the morning for Hempstead, 40 miles southeast of here. These springs are very strong with sulphur; nearly as strong as Blunt Springs, Alabama; very finely fixed up. A great many people attend them in the summer season. I was in hopes we would remain here some time as we are tired traveling, but we need expect no rest from Magruder[571]. The water in this prairie country

Major General John
Bankhead "Prince John"
Magruder

---

[570] Piedmont Springs was a popular resort and health spa located near the town of Anderson. It boasted three sulfur springs, numerous bathhouses, and a large four-story hotel with 100 rooms. Walker's Division camped at the springs for about a week to rest and allow the sick to recuperate.

[571] Major General John Bankhead Magruder (1807-1871), a West Point graduate and decorated Mexican War veteran from Port Royal, Virginia, was in charge of

is bad and scarce; timber scarce. People can make lots and raise stock without any trouble but I don't think I would like to live here. I would rather live where I made less and be out of the mud, and have other conveniences. But as it is, I am bound to live where they send me at present. I am in good health except my right eye has been sore two days. It is getting well. I have not rode one step since Lawson left me. Leonard is quite well. The company all in good health except D. M. Hays still has rheumatism, but he is no worse as yet. Robert Ray[572] is with us; came in last evening. He is quite well. Their regiment is camped 15 miles from us. I don't think they will be dismounted at all. I am looking for Lieut. Brooks in as his time was out last night. Then I expect a letter. I have not heard a word from home only what D. M. Hays brought. We have fixed up here expecting to stay; are camped in a very pretty place but soldiers need make no calculations. I suppose you have heard of Col. Baylor killing Major General Wharton[573]. I expect he killed a good man and General. If he only had have killed one or two, I know he would have done good service to his country. We had a report in camps

---

the District of Texas, New Mexico, and Arizona at this time. Magruder, known as "Prince John" by his associates, was considered a born soldier who would fight all day and dance all night.

[572] Private Robert T. Ray (c.1846-?), son of William and Eleanor (Templeton) Ray, served in Co.-B, Morgan's Texas Cavalry Battalion, Parson's Cavalry Brigade. Private Ray was a brother of Sergeant John R. Ray of Wallace's Company.

[573] On April 6, 1865, Colonel George W. Baylor of the 2nd Texas Cavalry shot Major General John A. Wharton to death at General Magruder's headquarters at the Fannin Hotel in Houston. The pair was arguing over the coming reorganization of the Trans-Mississippi Department when Wharton slapped Baylor's face and called him a liar. Baylor pulled his pistol and shot the unarmed Wharton. In 1868, George Baylor was acquitted of murder in the case, but years later he would lament that the event had been a lifelong sorrow for him.

yesterday that Magruder was killed but the report is contradicted. We get no war news at all; get reports one day, have them contradicted the next. I don't think they allow us to get any news. We hear the Missouri Cavalry are coming on after us coming south too, and that one division of the infantry is coming too. We cannot imagine what they want with so many men down here. Well, it has rained some every day since Friday; cloudy, dark, damp weather; is raining now while I write, a wetting rain. Leonard is washing as our clothes are dirty. What a bad time to do anything on the farm. I cannot give you any directions about the crop. Try to get them to push ahead and work when they can. Our rations are corn meal and bacon as yet; half a pound of bacon a day; light for men who have nothing but meal. Bread & meat three times a day is tiresome, but no chance for anything else. I will close. Give my respects to my friends and acquaintances. My love to Mother. Tell her I would like to take dinner with her today. I think I could do justice by almost anything. My love to the children. Tell Matty I am having her a ring made today; will send it the first good chance. I will close for the present by signing myself your husband,

H. A. Wallace

Camp Groce
Near Hempstead, Texas
May the 3rd, 1865

My dear Wife,
I this Wednesday evening write to you again, though I wrote to you yesterday morning. But as I will have a chance of sending this by a man who is going to ride and go close by home I will write again, as I know you are always glad to hear from me. I am well and have been moderately well since leaving home. I have had cold two or three times. My company are in good health. D. M. Hays is badly crippled up with pains. I have not been able to get him off. Old Magruder would rather see a sick man dead than furlough him. The weather has become very [illegible] now and no rain for several days; appears to have settled. Crops will certainly grow fast now. As for news, I wrote all I knew yesterday morning in the letter I sent you. I can but say we get no news, only reports, as they allow no news published at all. But from every appearance, our officers are fixing everything for fighting as fast as possible; having belts, cartridge boxes, and everything else mended as fast as possible; drilling us heavy nearly every day; having war meetings at every town, and big war speeches. I cannot tell what the consequence will be. Our men are very much dissatisfied indeed; have lost all hopes of success and are tired being the slave & fools of such men as Magruder, Smith, Forney[574], & co[mpany], who are faring sumptuously while we are undergoing hardships and living like brutes; miserable poor rations, them scarce at that. To see the citizens down here living like lords, and plenty of specie[575]; buy

---

[574] Major General John H. Forney (1829-1902), a West Point graduate from Lincolnton, N. C., resigned his U. S. Army commission to serve as Colonel of the 10th Alabama Infantry in 1861. He saw action in Virginia under General E. Kirby Smith and was in charge of a division at Vicksburg when the city fell in July 1863. Forney took command of Walker's Division in June 1864 after General Walker was promoted to replace General Richard Taylor. General Forney was a strict military disciplinarian who was never popular with his unbridled Texas charges. Warner, 90-91.

[575] Coinage or coined money

anything they want. A soldier can see anything him or his family needs in the stores but can buy nothing. Even if he happens to have a little Confederate money he cannot buy anything with it. But few of them have any. Yet these men who will sell nothing to a soldier for Confederate money say we must fight on while there is a man to fight. I think it poor encouragement to a soldier to stay here and suffer when he gets no pay; can do nothing for his family. And if what we hear is true, they are pressing and robbing our families of what they have at home too. [illegible] cotton trade now in Houston. There is lots of [illegible] clothing, hats, and shoes, yet they will not let us have anything. Only some old red shoes for barefooted men is everything we have got yet. I am nearly as good as bareheaded but cannot get a government hat. Our quartermaster says there is plenty there but they won't let him have one. The cotton trade is a perfect stealing business of old Smith & Magruder. That is the reason Magruder was sent here. Walker would not steal enough to please Smith. I see Walker nearly every day. He is in command of all the cavalry. His headquarters are within a mile of our camp. There is no telling what is to be the consequences with this army. They are in a bad state. If anything should turn up to start them, it is hard to tell where it would stop. I don't believe under present circumstances they would fight any at all, but there is no accounting for soldiers. They might deceive me. Reports say the Yankees are landing a large force at Velasco but I don't believe it or we would be on the move to meet them. We have news that they have taken Brownsville on the Rio Grande River and have a large force there. I suppose that is so. One thing I think is pretty certain, they will soon give us a plenty to do soon, and when they do come, they will come in overpowering force. I cannot see that our fighting can do any good now more than insure the destruction of what little they have not rolled us of, even if we are so fortunate as to have our lives spared. Achsah, tell Sam I want him to push ahead. Now is the time to work to make a crop; not wait until it is in the grass to begin. The harvest, if you have any, will soon be on too. They ought to use every industry all the time. Try to have the stock, horses, hogs, sheep, and cows all taken good care of. Let me know how the colts grow. Achsah, from what I hear I have no doubt they will come to press corn and meat from you for the government. Don't let them know anything about the corn in the kitchen. Let them have none no way unless they take it by force, as it is just a rolling business anyway and you need it all. If any soldier's family are needing corn and cannot get, let them have it without any regard to money or price. Let me know if Price Brooks[576] has taken all the fodder or paid for it. The money is now worthless. Achsah we had a fine sermon preached last night from the 14th Chapter and 32nd verse of Proverbs; a good sermon at three o'clock in the evening. While I write they are beginning to preach. They have good attention and I hope good is doing; just preach under a tree, the men sitting around on the ground. I look for Thomas up to see me in a few days as they are giving passes and he can get one to come up. He can come up in a day or two. I have not left camps since coming from home but a few hours one day to hunt, and then I got a poor dinner; the only meal I have eat out of camps. We live like hogs; our bread half raw sometimes; sometimes burnt up; never get any meat for to eat. We have not seen flour in a month. Hunger makes a man eat anything. Our water is bad. We carry our wood near half a mile; our water 5 or 6 hundred yards. And we get almost too lazy to cook drilling in the hot sun. Give my love to Mother. Tell her I hope I will get home again to get something good to eat. Tell Willy I hope he is a good boy to work. Tell Bud I am glad he can hoe. I hope Matty has got well. I want to know how she likes her ring. My sweet boy[577] I reckon will soon walk. Kiss him for me. Sam Hunt[578] of Capt. Pegues[579] Company carries this. I will send you a half string of buttons by him. I gave 25 in specie for them. They are not good. I have $140.00 in Confederate yet. I am going to send down to Houston tomorrow by our preacher for paper, and if he can buy it with it, I will try to get

---

[576] Unidentified
[577] Wallace refers to his infant son, Harvey Alexander Wallace Jr. (6/14/1864-8/7/1865).
[578] Corporal James Samuel Hunt (c.1840-?), son of Joseph J. Hunt of Henderson, served in Co. I, 19th Texas Infantry.
[579] Captain James A. Pegues (c.1838-?), son of O. H. Pegues, served as 1st Lieutenant and later Captain of Co.-I, 19th Texas Infantry.

my boy some aprons. Send me a letter by Hunt when he comes back. Write as often as you can. Keep in good spirits as possible. I know it does no good to complain and I do too much of it. I would like very much indeed to see you all. [I] feel as anxious to go home as if I had been out twelve months. May the God of mercy bless and take care of you and our family is the prayer of your husband.

To Mrs. Achsah Wallace from her husband, H. A. Wallace

Prison Diary

Capt. H. A. Wallace's Memorandum Book

New Orleans, La.

April the 4th, 1864

Presented by Miss Emma Loverett of New Orleans, April 4th,

1864[580]

1 Peter, 1 Chap. – 11

---

[580] Emma Loverett made a tremendous sacrifice when she volunteered this pocket sized merchants ledger book. The Union blockade rendered paper of any kind unavailable. That which could be found sold for exorbitant prices. Southerners resorted to using any material at their disposal to write on, including wallpaper from parlors of lavish homes. No positive identification of Emma Loverett could be made, although an Emma Leverich, age 15, is listed in the New Orleans census records. This could possibly be the young lady that donated this diary book.
Bell Irvin Wiley. *The Life Of Johnny Reb- The Common Soldier Of The Confederacy*. (Baton Rouge: Louisiana State University Press, 1978), 196; Winters, 125-137.

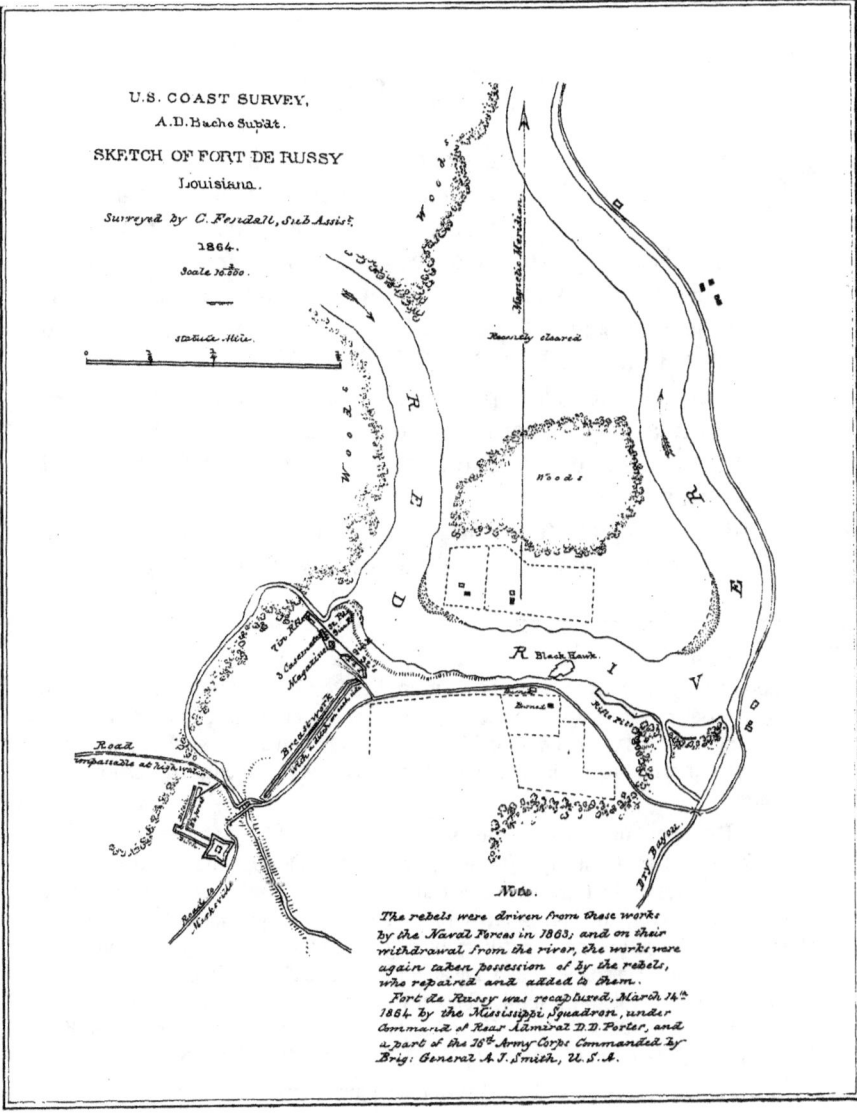

Memorandum kept by
Capt. H. A. Wallace from the
13th of April [March][581] during his imprisonment

April [March]

<u>13th</u>: Marched into Fort DeRussy at 9 o'clock at night.

<u>14th</u>: Fort surrounded & attac[ked] half past two this evening. The enemy charged the fort with 6000 men at four; was repulsed; repulsed in a second attack; carried the fort at sunset at the point of the bayonet, our men fighting until the enemy mounted the fort all around.[582] Our loss, two killed & 8 wounded. J. M. Nall[583] & J. A. Bane[584] of my company severely wounded; prisoners of us all; placed in the inner fort; a heavy guard placed around us. Lay down on the ground on our blankets [and] passed a cold, unpleasant night.

<u>15th</u>: At nine o'clock, the officers of us, separated from our men, marched under a guard to the river; placed aboard the

---

[581] Captain Wallace was confused about the entry for the month. His memorandum book was presented to him in April on the day before he was to be released from prison. He began recording events sometime near the 18th of April after being returned to prison, as evidenced by the fact that he switched his entries from past to present tense on that date. By mistake, Wallace entered April instead of March.

[582] The Battle of Fort DeRussy was the opening fight of Major General Nathaniel P. Banks' Red River Campaign. It was imperative that DeRussy be in Federal hands to ensure control of the lower Red River for the fleet of Admiral David Porter. Two brigades of infantry, numbering about 4000 men under Major General J. A. Mower, stormed the fort following an artillery barrage lasting one and one-half hours. No match for the little garrison of 275 Texan and Louisianan defenders, the fort fell at sunset to the Federals with minimal losses to both sides. *O.R . Series-I, Vol-34, Part-I,* 304-305, 492-493, and 597-601; William Byrd, "The Capture of Fort DeRussy, La.," *The Land We Love,* 6, No.-3, January, 1869, 184-187.

[583] Private John M. Nall (c.1833-?) suffered a gunshot wound to the right shoulder.

[584] Private James A. Bane (c.1832-?) was wounded in the foot.

steamer Clara Bell, the flag boat of Gen. Smith[585]. Got a good dinner at 2 p. m., the first they had given us to eat; treated us kindly on the boat.

16th: Moved to the Gun Boat No.13[586] where we were placed under a strict guard. Our men, all aboard on the lower deck, passed a cold, disagreeable night.

17th: The boat anchored at Battenrouge [Baton Rouge] at 9 a. m. in the morning. Our men were landed and marched off under a heavy guard to the penitentiary. The officers of us landed and marched under a heavy guard to the jail; placed in an upper story in two rooms, closely guarded. Our rations: salt beef and bakers bread for dinner, tea & bread for supper, coffee & bread for breakfast.

18th: Marched from prison at 7 at night to the steamer John Warner; went aboard [and] found our men there. Boat steamed off for New Orleans at nine, arrived at New Orleans the morning of the 19th at 8.

19th: Landed and marched under a guard to No. 21 on Rampart Street. Found 27 Rebel officers there in prison. Amongst them Capt. Allen[587] of my reg[iment], who furnished us a good breakfast; a very acceptable present. Left our men aboard the boat.

---

[585] Brigadier General Andrew J. Smith (1815-1897) was commander-in-chief of the Union forces that captured Fort DeRussy. His total command consisted of 21 regiments of infantry and 3 batteries of artillery detached from the Sixteenth and Seventeenth Army Corps. Winters, 327; O.R. Series-I, Vol-34, Part-I, 304.

[586] The U.S.S. Fort Hindman (Gunboat Number-13), was a 286-ton, side-wheel, tinclad gunboat built in 1862 as a civilian steamer. Captain Wallace's fellow prisoner, Sergeant John C. Porter of Co.-H, 18th Texas Infantry, remembered that the Captain of the Fort Hindman ignored a signal gun as the boat passed the batteries at Port Hudson while enroute to Baton Rouge. The batteries fired three more times at the boat, the third shot cutting away one of the posts supporting the hurricane deck only a few feet away from where Sergeant Porter was standing. James H. Davis. *Texans In Gray: A Regimental History of the Eighteenth Texas Infantry, Walker's Texas Division, in the Civil War* (Tulsa: Heritage Oak Press, 1999), 75.

[587] Captain Augustus C. Allen (1835-1914) of Jefferson, Tx. commanded Co.-C, 19th Texas Infantry. Following exchange, Captain Allen was promoted to Major and remained with the regiment through the remainder of the war.

The *U.S.S. Fort Hindman* (Gunboat #13) carried the Fort DeRussy prisoners to Baton Rouge

**Major Augustus C. Allen
19th Texas Infantry**

20th: Looked around the prison. The prison [is] a large, three story building; two rooms on the lower floor and kitchen; upper stories 12 rooms; small yard; no room for exercise; cistern in the yard, also [a] privy. Guard consisted of three soldiers; two sergts., one for the commissary, & one corporal. Our fare: pickled beef & salt pork, bread, coffee, some rice, potatoes or dry beans prepared miserably by dirty Negroes.

Sunday, 20th: A quiet day.
21st: Damp, dreary, & cold.
22nd: Quite cool. Each officer received a bedstead.
23rd: 7 mattresses furnished by Mrs. Shute[588].
24th: Wet, disagreeable day. Received a shirt.
25th: 20 officers of the 2nd La. Cavalry & 9 of Edgar's Battery brought in to our prison[589]; now 82 officers in prison.
26th: Three more officers brought in.
27th: Sabbath; all well. Nothing new.
28th: All up.
29th: All well.
30th: Today vaccinated[590].

---

[588] Unidentified

[589] The night of March 21, 1864 found the weary troops of the 2nd Louisiana Cavalry and Captain William Edgar's Texas artillery battery encamped on Henderson's Hill, 25 miles north of Alexandria, La. They had skirmished and fallen back before Union cavalry all day. Now they were encamped in a strong position facing a division of infantry and artillery under Union General J. A. Mower, ready for an attack. A cold "blue norther" roared in that evening. Wind howled through the pine tops above the camps. Rain, hail, and sleet beat off exposed men and beast alike as the miserable troops huddled around their campfires. Even the lonely pickets guarding the camp gathered at their fires. After all, who would make an attack on a night like this? How surprised they must have been when they suddenly found themselves surrounded by Yankee infantry! The 35th Iowa and 33rd Missouri regiments were pushed around and behind the Rebel camp in the storm, capturing the pickets without a shot. They proceeded to the main camp, fixed bayonets, and charged. Almost the entire Confederate command was captured with no loss of life. Only a few escaped into the darkness of the night. The Federals reported 261 men captured, along with all four cannon of Edgar's Battery. *O.R. Series-I, Vol.-34, Part-I*, 314 and 326-327; Richard Taylor. *Destruction And Reconstruction: Personal Experiences Of The Late War.* (New York: Bantam Books, 1992), 157; Winters, 330.

31st: All well.

April

March[591] [April] lst: Today drew 10 day rations; hired a cook outside of the prison.
2nd: Lieut. Brooks taken sick.
Sunday 3rd: A fine dinner given to all the officers by the ladies. Received notice to have our clothes all ready by the morning of the 5th to move to be exchanged.[592]
Monday 4th: All excitement about the exchange. Quite a number of ladies visited the prison; the pavement crowded around the door all day with others wanting in. Signed a parole after dark to not attempt to escape while on our way up to be exchanged, nor to take up arms until exchanged, and we were to be allowed all of the privilege of passengers.
5th: All up and stirring early. Baggage all placed on a hack. Roll called and formed on pavement at 7 a. m. Marched to the boat [*Polar Star*] at foot of Canal Street, the ladies

---

[590] Smallpox was very prevalent during the war among civilian and military populations alike. Prisoners were particularly susceptible to epidemics of the dreaded disease. Smallpox vaccine had been developed over sixty years earlier in England but very few were vaccinated in the U. S. by this time. Confederate medical authorities ordered vaccination of troops early in the war but the supply of vaccine was soon overcome by demand and many Rebel soldiers were never vaccinated. Captain Wallace and his fellow prisoners were vaccinated in response to a local epidemic of smallpox in progress within the city and among the enlisted prisoners in other prisons nearby. Robert E. Denny. *Civil War Prisons & Escapes: A Day-by-Day Chronicle.* (New York: Sterling Publishing Co. Inc., 1993), 12.; H.H Cunningham. *Doctors In Gray: The Confederate Medical Service.* (Baton Rouge, Louisiana: State University Press, 1958). 195-199.

[591] Wallace has again recorded the wrong date.

[592] Prisoner exchange was practiced liberally during the war, particularly with high-ranking officers. The exchange was to be man-for-man and rank-for-rank. During the last years of the war, the Federals stopped the exchange program in order to further deplete the South of much needed manpower. However, Federal authorities in the Trans-Mississippi region ignored the order and exchanges still occurred through the end of the war.

marching along with us and crowds following to the boat. All aboard. The ladies cheered us by waving their handkerchiefs as the boat steamed down the river, the officers cheering for the ladies of New Orleans & the Confederacy. Steamed down the river 2 miles. Our soldiers were brought aboard. Crowds of ladies gathered on the wharf. Our men cheered as they came aboard. Boat steamed off up the river at 11 a. m., the officers and men cheering for Jeff Davis [and] the Confederacy, the ladies waving their handkerchiefs.

<u>6th</u>: Passed Battenrogue [Baton Rouge] at day. Passed Port Hudson at 12 a. m.; reported to a Gulf steamer at the mouth of Red River at sunset; steamed up Red River at dark; anchored at the mouth of Black River until morning.

<u>7th</u>: Passed Fort DeRussy at 9 this morning; arrived at Alexandria at 5 p. m. Lieut. Barksdale taken sick.

<u>8th</u>: Steamed up Red River for Grantico [Grand Ecore] at day; landed at Grantico at night.

<u>9th</u>: Moved on up Red River. Lay over in rear of the fleet at night.

<u>Sunday 10th</u>: Steamed up in rear of the fleet. Passed gin houses burnt, houses burnt. The enemy anchoring at every farm, killing all the stock not fit for use [and] carrying off all provision, fowls, and everything of value. About sunset met some of the fleet coming down the river. Said, "look out for yourselves, the Rebs are a coming"[593]! Turned our boat; run down the river. Lay over until morning.

---

[593] The Confederates were closely pursuing the retreating Federal army after soundly whipping it at Mansfield, La. on April 8, and putting it to flight at Pleasant Hill the next day. Walker's Division and the 19th Texas Infantry were heavily engaged in both actions. Admiral David Porter's fleet, which Wallace's boat was following, steamed up the Red River with gunboats and reserve troops to support General Banks' Federal force. When it was learned that Bank's army was retreating, the fleet turned back to Alexandria in confusion. The boats were repeatedly attacked by Confederates on both sides of the river with much loss of life, particularly aboard the relatively unprotected transports. In order to block the fleet's progress upriver, the Confederates sank the steamer *New Falls City* across the river channel at Loggy Bayou. The lead gunboat crew of Porter's fleet found a large sign inviting the Yankees to "A Grand Ball in Shreveport" attached to the exposed smokestacks of the wreck.

11th: Steamed down the river under the white flag. Met the steamer Benefit, which had been fired into by our men; considerably damaged; her captain killed. Met the steamer Red Cheirs [Chief] going up. It had been fired into. Our boat run aground; turned across the river, the bow on one bank, the stern on the other. Two Rebel officers came on the bank of the river with a flag of truce [and] consulted with Major Bradley[594], the Federal commander. The Federals threw overboard tobacco, cheese, & so on. While the boat was aground, heard the news of the fights at Mansfield & Pleasant Hill. Got the boat off; went on down the river. At 11 the boat was again stopped by our men[595]. Three officers came aboard under a flag of truce; let us pass on. I would say here I think the Rebel officers ought to have released us prisoners and sunk the boat as the enemy had men aboard taking up as reinforcements.[596] Anchored at Grantico [Grand Ecore] at dark; two gunboats lying in the river; Bank's army encamped around Grantico.

12th: Banks' men moving in different directions. Three transports came up the river with reinforcements for Banks. At

---

[594] Unidentified

[595] During one of these stops the Polar Star was halted under the guns of the 4th Louisiana Artillery Battery, which was posted on the east side of the river at Berdelon's Point. The battery commander, Captain Thomas K. Fauntleroy, allowed the boat to continue without releasing the prisoners after meeting with the Federal and Confederate ranking officers aboard. Captain Edward T. King and Steve Mayeux, ed. *E.T. King Papers*. (Lafayette, La.: Dupre Library, USL N.P., 1910), 19-20. and *O.R. Series-I, Vol.- 34/1, No.-105 Report of Gen. St. John R. Liddell of operations Jan. 26- May 22, 1864*.

[596] No official reason could be found in existing records for this disastrous event, which led to the re-internment and subsequent death of many of the prisoners. Most likely, the ranking Confederate officers refused to break their promise not to escape while being transported to the place of exchange (see diary entry for April 4, 1864). Sergeant John C. Porter recalled that the Federal officers aboard had promised to exchange the prisoners "at some point below" after turning back toward Alexandria. Porter states, "When they had decoyed us to Alexandria, within their lines, they became bold and told us they were taking us back to New Orleans." James H. Davis. *Texans In Gray*, 79.

midnight, moved down the river two miles; anchored alongside of a gunboat. Federals, having built a pontoon bridge across the river, crossed their [wagon] train over it; was passing out to the country and back all day hauling in corn.

<u>13th</u>: Remained all day in the river.

<u>14th</u>: Drs. Ectors [Estarge], Thompson, & [Gibbs] were took ashore to be released[597]. Our boat moved down the river at two in the evening; anchored at the falls until morning.

<u>15th</u>: Landed & marched around the falls to Alexandria. Again went aboard. Mrs. Josephine McDermott came aboard and gave Capt. Allen and me all the news she had. Steamed down the river at 9 p. m.; entered Miss. River at midnight.

<u>16th</u>: Anchored at BattenRouge [Baton Rouge] one half hour. At 9 p. m., anchored in the river opposite Canal Street, New Orleans at dark.

<u>Sunday 17th</u>: Landed at 10 a. m.; marched to Rampart No. 21. Found the officers we left still there, and 6 new recruits.

<u>18th</u>: Nothing new.

<u>19th</u>: Quite unwell from derangement of stomach & bowels.

---

[597] Doctors T. C. Thompson of Edgar's Texas Battery, R. T. Gibbs of the 2nd La. Cavalry, and Joseph L. Estarge of the Confederate General Staff were released under an agreement stating that medical personnel of either side were not to be held captive. Doctor H. Griffin of the 14th Texas Cavalry was left aboard the boat to care for the sick. Doctor Gibbs carried with him a secret dispatch to General Richard Taylor from fellow prisoner, Captain David F. Boyd. Captain Boyd was attached to General Taylor's staff before his capture in February 1864. Knowing Taylor would need accurate intelligence, Captain Boyd took careful note of Union troop strengths and movements, along with river conditions as the steamboat made its way up Red River. He recorded his observations on the inside margin of a New York Herald newspaper, which Doctor Gibbs carried off the boat when he was released. This message eventually made its way to General Taylor's headquarters in Shreveport, too late to be of any use.   O.R. Series II, Vol.7, No.6, R.T. Gibbs to Maj. Gen. R. Taylor; Germaine Reed. *David French Boyd: Founder of Louisiana State University.* (Baton Rouge: LSU Press, 1977), 48-49.

20th: Still unwell. Lieut. Barksdale getting well. Lieut. Upshar [Upshaw][598] of our brigade was brought in today a prisoner.
21st: Nothing new.
22nd: Received a vest from Mrs. Shute.
23rd: Nothing new.
24th: A quiet day.
25th: Nothing of interest.
26th: All well.
27th: Rumors of a fight between Price and Steel.[599]
29th: Capt. Baker, Lieut. Jackson, and Lieut. Mclaster [McLester][600] brought in to our prison today.
30th: All well.

---

[598] Lieutenant R. L. Upshaw served as Adjutant on the staff of the 16th Texas Infantry.

[599] The reports were probably of the Battle of Mark's Mills, Arkansas, fought on April 25, 1864 between Confederate forces under General Sterling Price and Union under Major General Frederick Steele.

[600] Captain B. A. Baker of Co.-B, 19th Texas Infantry was captured at Pleasant Hill, La.; Lieutenant H. McLester served in Co.-F, 17th Texas Infantry; Lieutenant Jackson is unidentified.

May

May 1st: A quiet Sabbath.
2nd: Damp day.
3rd: Cold
4th: Nothing of interest.
5th. "   "   "
6th. "   "   "
7th. "   "   "
8th: Sabbath; all well.
9th: All quiet.
10th: Rained at night.
11th & 12th: Reports of a fightings in Virginia on May the 5th & 7th in which the Federals claiming victories.[601]
13th: All well.
14th: Reports still uncertain from Virginia.
15th: Sabbath; all well.
16th: Nothing new.
17th: Various rumors from the battles in Virginia.
18th: Weather hot.
19th: Nothing positive from Virginia.
20th: All well.
21st: Gen. Banks[602] back in New Orleans, his army at Simmesport.

---

[601] These reports were on the Battle of the Wilderness, where Lee's outnumbered Army of Northern Virginia met Grant in fierce combat on May 5 and 6, 1864. Lee suffered many irreplaceable casualties at the Wilderness. Among them, a talented young general named Micah Jenkins. Captain Wallace's former Colonel and mentor from South Carolina was killed by friendly fire while scouting the battle lines with General James Longstreet.

[602] General Edward R. S. Canby (1817-1873) replaced General Nathaniel P. Banks (1816-1894) on May 18, 1864. Canby took command at Simmesport, where the Federal Army lay licking its wounds after the failed Red River Campaign. Banks, stripped of his military command, was placed in charge of civil affairs for the Department of the Gulf. He returned to New Orleans on the 21st of May defeated and hated by many, carrying squarely on his shoulders the blame for the failure of the Red River Campaign. Banks never held another military command. Winters, 378 and 388-389.

22ⁿᵈ: Sabbath; very hot.
23ʳᵈ: Nothing of interest.
24ᵗʰ: All well.
25ᵗʰ.   "   "
26ᵗʰ.   "   "
27ᵗʰ.   "   "
28ᵗʰ.   "   "
29ᵗʰ: P. W. S. Stone died [at] half past four in the afternoon in the St. Louis hospital of smallpox. Received a note from T. J. Riley stating he was in the St. Louis hospital with pneumonia, improving, dated 27ᵗʰ; also stating B. F. Hayes & J. M. Jones was there.
30ᵗʰ: T. J. Riley died in the afternoon.
31ˢᵗ: Nothing new.

June

June 1ˢᵗ: All well.
2ⁿᵈ: Col. Blair exchanged.
June 3ʳᵈ: Rumors of an early exchange. Port Hudson prisoners[603] sent off to be paroled.
June 4ᵗʰ: Very wet day.
June 5ᵗʰ: Sabbath
6ᵗʰ: Heavy rains.
7ᵗʰ: Reports of a Confederate victory in Virg. & Georgia.[604]
8ᵗʰ: Still showers of rain.
9ᵗʰ: Ordered to hold ourselves ready to start at a moments warning to be exchanged.
June 10ᵗʰ: Lieuts. Ball, Burbank, Wood, & Fogerty[605] taken to the Parish Prison at 4 in the morning for breaking their parole.

---

[603] Some of Captain Wallace's fellow prisoners were captured on July 9, 1863 when the Confederate stronghold on the Mississippi River at Port Hudson, La. surrendered to the Federals.

[604] General Lee's last great victory came May 31 to June 3, 1864 at Cold Harbor, Va. The battle was so costly to the Union that General Grant would later declare that it was the only attack he ever regretted making.

11th : Heard of T. P. Billingsley's death on the 9th at the St. Louis Hospital.

12th: Sabbath; heavy shower of rain in the forenoon. J. L. Hull sent to the barracks[606] with smallpox on Friday, the 4th of June.

13th Monday: Suffering from muscular rheumatism.

14th: All well.

15th: Nothing new.

16th: J. M. Jones sent to the barracks with smallpox.

17th: B. F. Hayes sent to barracks with smallpox.

18th: Rumors of a speedy exchange.

19th: Sabbath; three months today since we first landed here as prisoners.

20th: I was this day attacked with palpitation of the heart; visited by Dr. Moss[607] late in the evening; relieved somewhat by 12 at night.

21st: Able to be up a little.

22nd: Still improving; heavy showers of rain.

23rd: This day heard from Leonard[608] & the other boys at the hospital, all improving.

24th: Felt much better today.

25th: Spent quite a restless night being quite unwell; feeling better this morning.

26th: Still unwell.

---

[605] 2nd Lieutenant George J. Ball of Co.-E, 22nd Texas Infantry, 1st Lieutenant M. Fogarty and 2nd Lieutenant F. G. Burbank of Co.-H, Consolidated Louisiana Crescent Regiment were captured at Fort DeRussy. 3rd Lieutenant Charles A. Wood served in Co.-C, Consolidated Louisiana Crescent Regiment.

[606] The New Orleans Barracks, now known as the Jackson Barracks, was a brick, citadel style U. S. Army installation located on the Mississippi River. The Barracks dated to 1835 and was in continuous use since that time to house troops. After Federal occupation of New Orleans, the Barracks was converted into a general hospital. It was apparently being used as a quarantine hospital at this time. Powell A. Casey, *Encyclopedia Of Forts, Posts, Named Camps And Other Military Installations In Louisiana, 1700- 1981*. (Baton Rouge: Claitor's Publishing Division, 1983), 84- 92.

[607] Unidentified

[608] Harvey's nephew, Private Leonard Wood

27th: Quite unwell today; great difficulty in breathing; now at sunset, much better. I am under many obligations to Lieut. John Brooks for his kind attention to me since I have been sick. He spares no pains to try to make me as comfortable as possible.

28th: Looking every day to be exchanged; rested better today until about 10 at night.

29th: Passed a very restless night; quite unwell all day. Today heard that Leonard and Tommy Hull had got well and gone back to the cotton press[609]; Gray Conner[610] at St. Louis Hospital dangerously sick.

30th: I arose this morning feeling much better; kept up all day.

July 1864

July the 1st: Still improving this morning. Brooks received a note from J. L. Hull stating J. M. Jones had died at the barracks the 26th or 27th; that B. F. Hayes was getting well.

2nd: My health still improving slowly. Our prospects for a speedy exchange very bad.

July 3rd: A quiet Sabbath morning; my health improving; nothing new of interest.

4th: A very warm day. The day celebrated by the Federals. 6 batterys of light and 2 of heavy artillery passed in review on Canal Street.

July 5th: Nothing of interest; my health improving.

---

[609] The enlisted prisoners from Fort DeRussy were confined at the Picayune Cotton Press Number-4 (The Lower Cotton Press Quarters), located between St. Ferdinand and Montegut streets in New Orleans, near the levee. This location was one of several cotton presses in the area used to house prisoners. Sergeant John Porter describes the Picayune Press as, "A square, containing two acres, enclosed by a brick wall, fourteen feet high, with a large gate on the east and west sides. The other two sides were shedded, about 30 feet deep, draining the water inside, which was carried off by gutters." James Davis, *Texans In Gray*, 77 & 132.

[610] Private Pleasonton G. Conner (c.1841-7/2/1864) was the son of Nelson and Elizabeth Conner of Panola County, Texas.

6th: Very warm morning with refreshing showers. Received news we would be sent up the river for exchange in the morning.

7th: This day heard P. G. Conner died at St. Louis Hospital the 2nd; A. J. Parker very sick at hospital.

8th: Nothing of interest; rumors that we may leave any hour for exchange.

9th: All well. Nothing new.

10th: A quiet Sabbath day. Asa Parker sent back to the prison from the hospital on yesterday.

July 11th: A pleasant day. Good air a stirring. Nothing new.

12th: Nothing of interest.

13th: Morning warm; a shower of rain at 1 p. m. 2 prisoners escaped from the [cotton] press by going out with the guard[611]. Still affected with muscular rheumatism, it being all through my system.

14th: Nothing of interest still; quite unwell; prisoners 4 months today.

15th: Feeling much better today.

16th: Still improving. Heard from Thompson[612] today; still at the hospital.

17th: Sabbath; quite a warm day; nothing of interest.

18th: Still & warm; feeling improved in health.

19th: A warm morning; showers in the forenoon; all up and stirring on Rampart.

20th: My health improving; various rumors of exchange.

21st: At 9 in the morning came in to sign for exchange. Left the prison at three; marched to the boat at the foot of Canal

---

[611] One of these prisoners may have been Private Houston West of Wallace's Company. Private West escaped from prison in New Orleans on an unlisted date and eventually made his way back home. He returned to duty and served through the remainder of the war. Sergeant John Porter remembered that, "Some tried to make their escape in various ways, some by bribery, some by picking through the wall, one by blacking himself, hoping to pass as one of the Negro cooks, still another made a wooden gun, sewed up an oilcloth case, and intended to pass out as a guard, but all failed." James Davis, *Texans In Gray*, 81; *Compiled Service Records of Confederate Soldiers From The State of Texas: 19th Texas Infantry*. (Microfilm, Washington D.C.: National Archives).

[612] Private John R. Thompson (c.1846-?)

Street. Went aboard the Nebraska; steamed down the river [and] landed; took our men aboard. 26 of Co[mpany] H came aboard; B. F. Hayes left at the hospital[613]. Steamed up the river at half past five in the evening.

22nd: Passed Battenrouge [Baton Rouge] at six in the morning, Port Hudson at 9. Landed at Red River Landing & exchanged at two[614].

23rd: Steamed up Red River at 10 a.m.

24th: Landed at Alexandria at 4 p. m.; camped on the river.

25th: All furloughed; went aboard the steamer Indian No. 2; left Alexandria at 5 p. m.

26th: Passed Grauntico [Grand Ecore] at 6 p. m.; tied up and stayed all night 9 miles above.

27th: Left at daylight; boat landed at Dickson Landing at dark. Brooks, myself, & 8 of our company walked to Bayou Pierre.

28th: Passed through Mansfield; stayed all night with Mr. Small[615].

29th: Started at day; took dinner with Tillis Waltom[616]. He sent his wagon with us; stayed two miles east of Carthage with Mr. Walker[617].

30th: Started at day; got home at four in the evening.

---

[613] See footnote 637

[614] On this date, 82 officers and 956 enlisted men were exchanged for an equal number of Federal prisoners at Red River Landing. Most of these soldiers were captured in the recent Red River Campaign. *O. R.,* series-2, vol.-7, serial-120, 483.

[615] Unidentified

[616] Unidentified

[617] Unidentified

Page 1

Memorandum whilst the Capt the 5th Waltase from the 13th of April during his imprisonment attached in to fort — Sunday at 9 oclock at night the fort bombardment & attacked half hour two. This evening the enemy charged the fort with 600 men at down we repulsed them in a ½ hour & killed a thousand at the point of the bayonet our men fighting until the enemy's amunition ... the fort all alone and our Log pillars & ... riddled. J A Noble it

J A Bain of my Company severely wounded Belongs us all, placed in the enemy fort a heavy guard placed around us laid down on the ground on our blankets highest in order my team as night 13 at nine oclock the officers of us to be carried ten men mar... under a guard to the River stayed a board the Lenard Clan Ball the Old 9 Boat of Gunboats got a good dinner at 2 P.M. the ... They had given in the East ... in humility on the Boat removed to the ... boat ... ... in ...

JOURNALS

The Different Camps of Comp. H of the 19th Reg. of Texas Inft. From the Time They Took Up the Line of March From Home

[As recorded in Captain Wallace's Company Ledger Book]

Left home July the 28th, 1862. Joined our reg[iment] at Jefferson on the evening of the 31st. Regimental flag[618] presented to the reg[iment] on the 6th of Aug. by Miss Josaphene McDermott. The First Battalion left the same evening for Little Rock, Arkansas. The Second Battalion left Camp Waterhouse at Jefferson Tuesday the 19th for Little Rock, Comp[any] H leading the way. Camped the first night at a branch 13 miles from Jefferson. Camped the night of the 20th three miles north of Linden in Davis Co[unty]. Camped the night of the 21st three miles north of Douglassville at a well. The 22nd moved three miles to a lake on the north bank of Sulphur River. Remained there until the morning of the 24th. Took up the line of march. Camped in Bowie County, Texas at Randal's. Camped the night of the 26th at Camp Moore in Bowie Co[unty]. Remained there until the morning of the 29th. Took up the march. Encamped 2 miles from Rondo, Arkansas at Camp Josaphene McDermott. Remained there until the 2nd of Oct., the reg[iment] generally having measles [and] diarrhea. Comp. H had one man to die at Camp Waterhouse and six at Rondo. Took up the march from Rondo the 2nd of Oct., Comp. H leaving 25 men at the hospital sick and as nurses and

---

[618] The regimental battle flag of the 19th Texas Infantry was captured during a charge at Pleasant Hill, La. after the color bearer fell severely wounded. Lieutenant Henry Fairbanks of Co.-E, 30th Maine Infantry recalled that the captured flag had "Texans Can Never Be Slaves" inscribed upon it. Captain Wallace does not mention a company flag in any of his surviving manuscripts. It is possible that one never existed since material to make it was scarce in the south by the time Wallace's Company formed at Minden.
Henry Fairbanks, "The Red River Expedition of 1864"; *Military Order of the Loyal Legion of the United States- Maine, Vol- I* (Wilmington, N.C.: Broadfoot Publishing Co., 1992), 186; Henry C. Joiner. "Requesting information on the battle flag of the 19th Tx. Infantry". *Confederate Veteran Magazine* 13, no. 11 (November, 1905).

seven in Rusk Co[unty], Tex. are sick. Four men sent home discharged. Strength of comp. on the march, seventy rank and file. Camped at Swan Lake on Red River. Camped the night of the 3rd in Hempstead County, [Arkansas] at the artesian wells. Camped 2 miles south of Washington at Camp Taylor on the night of the 4th. Moved on the 5th to Camp Vanderbilt, three miles north of Washington. Remained there until the morning of the 7th, Comp. H leaving J. O. Easley in the hospital with pneumonia with G. L. Stovall as nurse. Camped the night of the 7th on the south bank of Little Missouri. Camped the night of the 8th at Gum Springs. Camped the night of the 9th at Camp Roseman, 5 miles south of Arkadelphia. Remained there until the morning of the 11th. Camped the night of the 11th at Camp Caddo on Caddo River. Remained there until the morning of the 13th. W. R. Grimes[619] of Comp. H died in Arkadelphia on the 12th of pneumonia. Camped the night of the 13th at Smith's Creek. Camped the night of the 14th at Rockport. Camped the night of the 15th on the north bank of Saline River, 2 miles south of Benton. Camped the night of the 16th thirteen miles south of Little Rock on a creek. [Company] H took up camps on the evening of the 19th half a mile south of Little Rock near the hospital. Sergeant Deason detailed and started to Rusk County for clothing the 20th at noon. The reg[iment] remained encamped at Little Rock until Wednesday the 22nd of Oct. Took up the march Oct. the 22nd at day; all day crossing Arkansas River. Camped on the north bank that night. We took up the line of march Thursday morning the 23rd at 8. March[ed] 13 miles. Encamped north of a bayou. Took up the march on the 24th at sunrise. Joined our brigade at Camp Nelson at 2 p. m. It commence snowing the morning of the 25th at 7 and snowed until eleven; very cold nights. Commenced drilling in company drills Monday the 27th four hour each day, Company H having 40 men able for duty, 19 on the sick list, & 32 behind sick. Seventeen of the sick left at Rondo came in at Camp Nelson the 7th of Nov., 6 came in the 9th of Nov. Lieut. McCallum died Nov. the 11th. Sergeant J. R. Ray died the 14th of Nov. We took up the march from Camp Nelson Sunday morning the 23rd of Nov. Marched 7 miles. Had 47 men on the march. Left 26 at Camp Nelson, 12 in Little

---

[619] Private W. R. Grimes (c.1830-10/12/1862)

Rock sick, 11 in Rusk County. T. P. Jones[620] died suddenly the morning of the 24th of congestion. Took up the march the morning of the 24th. Marched 8 miles. Camped on the edge of Long Prairie. Took up the march the morning of the 25th. Marched 6 miles. Camped on Bayou Metre [Meto]. Stayed there until the next Monday morning, (30th), then took up the march. Marched 6 miles down Bayou Metre [Meto]. There encamped, being the 1st day of Dec. Our clothing came that night, brought by J. A. Wallace & Mr. Hudman[621]. Received orders the 10th to take up the march for Vicksburg. Took up the march Friday morning the 12th of December. Marched 4 miles. Camped in Long Prairie in a skirt of timber. Took up the march Saturday the 13th. Marched 18 miles. Camped at the toll bridge on Bayou Metre [Meto], 12 miles from Little Rock. Took up the march Sunday morning the 14th. Marched 8 miles. Camped on a bayou 4 miles from Little Rock. Came on rain that evening; rained all night. Overflowed our encampment; a perfect flood of water. Took up the march at day Monday the 15th. Moved on & encamped 2 miles below Little Rock on the north bank of Arkansas River. C. C. Hawkins[622] died at Camp Nelson the 16th of Dec. Remained encamped there until Saturday the 27th. Took up the march. Crossed Arkansas River. Camped near St. Johns Hospital. Took up the march to Pine Bluff. Went 4 miles down the river; camped. Remained there until Tuesday evening the 30th. Struck tents. Moved back near St. Johns Hospital. Camped there. Took up the march Wednesday the 31st under orders to join Hindman at Fort Smith. Crossed Arkansas River. Marched 4 miles up the river. Camped in the mountains. Still encamped there the 2nd of January, 1863. Received orders Saturday, Jan. the 3rd, to move at day Sunday the 4th for Pine Bluff. Took up the march at day. Crossed Arkansas River. Took the Pine Bluff Road. Marched four miles; encamped. Took up the line of march the 5th at day. Marched 15 miles. Camped on Long Lake. Moved on the 6th 15 miles. Took up the march Wednesday the 7th. Marched 10 miles; encamped.

---

[620] Private Thomas P. Jones
[621] Mr. Francis Hudman (c.1820-?) and wife, Elizabeth, of Panola County, Texas were parents of Private James T. Hudman.
[622] Private Columbus C. Hawkins (c.1833-12/16/1862)

Moved on Thursday the 8th. Encamped 5 miles west of Pine Bluff. On Friday evening, the brigade was drawn up in line and 2 men of Col. Flournoy's Reg[iment][623] was publicly drummed out of the army by General McCulloch for hog stealing. Saturday evening the 10th received orders to march at day for Arkansas Post on a forced march as the fight had began[624], to reinforce the garrison there. Took up the line of march at daybreak. Marched twenty miles down the river. Encamped on the bank of the river. Took up the march Monday the 12th at day. Marched 15 miles. Heard of the surrender of Arkansas Post. Encamped in Kimbro Bend of the Arkansas River in Desha County, 7 miles below Richland. Had rain all day Wednesday. Snow commenced falling at night; snowed all night. Had orders to be ready to march at day. Rose at four, the snow six inches deep and still a falling. Got part of our baggage in the wagons. Received orders to remain there that day. Friday morning the 16th received orders to send off our baggage and wagon; each man to keep one blanket, each mess a skillet or frying pan and axe. Sent off everything, tents and all. Snowed considerably that day. Lay down at night by our fires; a cold, comfortless night[625]. Saturday morning the 17th Feds said to be advancing. 40 men detailed from each reg[iment] to build a breast work. Still very cold; another night in the snow without tents. Sunday morning the 18th 40 men more from each reg[iment] to work on the breast work. Our scouts came in at ten in the morning. Reported the Feds had left; gone down the Arkansas River. The working party was called in after having built a breast work of logs from the levy to the swamp

---

[623] The 16th Texas Infantry under Colonel George M. Flournoy

[624] The Federal assault on Fort Hindman on the Arkansas River near Arkansas Post began on January 9, 1863. Three brigades of Walker's Division were immediately dispatched to reinforce the garrison and started on a forced march the next day. On the evening of January 11, Brigadier General Thomas J. Churchill surrendered Arkansas Post after being shelled by Union gunboats for two days and assaulted by overwhelming numbers of the enemy. Walker's three brigades did not arrive in time to be of any assistance to the defenders. The Fourth Brigade of Walker's Division under Colonel James Deshler was sent earlier to reinforce Arkansas Post and participated in the action. The entire brigade was captured at the surrender.

[625] This camp was fondly known as "Camp Freeze Out" by the soldiers of Walker's Division. Blessington, 70.

and improved the levy for rifle firing under the direction of Col. Allen. Sunday night at dark received orders to march at day in the direction of Pine Bluff, but one wagon to the reg[iment]. Marched Monday the 19th at sunrise, it having been raining from dark and still raining; each man having his blanket, gun, & accoutrements, and fifty rounds of cartridge to carry. The roads from shoe mouth to knee deep in mud and water; some snow still on the ground; the ground still frozen underneath in places. Marched 15 miles. Camped where we camped as we went down. Had considerable rain; wet that night. Tents up and on the march by sunrise, some men without breakfast and nothing prepared for dinner. Marched 16 miles. Camped one mile above Pine Bluff on the Little Rock Road. Passed over the worst roads I ever seen. Myself and Brother William were the first to get to camps from my co[mpany]. Major Taylor[626] and myself laid off the camp. Brother and me got a fire made. The company began to come in one at a time. Our tents and clothing come in. Got our tents up before dark. The co[mpany] all got in that night except nine who were unable to make the march. The men all got in Wednesday the 21st. Thursday morning the 22nd Lieut. Barksdale, Brother, & me took our dirty clothing to town to get washing done. Stayed all day. Got our ambrotypes taken. Friday morning the 23rd moved our camps four miles up the Little Rock Road to our present Camp Mills. Saturday, Col. Shepherd[627] of Flournoy's Reg[iment], Capt. Brown[628] of Randal's, and myself of Waterhouse's were detailed as a board of survey by Gen. Walker to examine into and report on the condition of the quartermaster stores in Pine Bluff. We met at ten, got through at 3 o'clock that evening. The boat come down from Little Rock. Brought 100 men for our reg[iment] from the convalescent camp, thirteen of them for my

---

[626] Major Enos Ward Taylor (c.1840-?) of Jefferson, Tx. was later promoted to Lieutenant Colonel and afterward to Colonel of the 19th Texas Infantry.
[627] James E. Shepard served as Lieutenant Colonel and later as Colonel of the 16th Texas Infantry.
[628] Captain Phil Brown of Harrison County, Tx. commanded Co.-F, 28th Texas Dismounted Cavalry.

company. Sunday morning the 25th still raining. Jerry Parker[629] of Taylor's Reg[iment] left our company for home with large mail for us and carried our ambrotypes. W. A. Kuykendall[630] died Feb. the 7th at Pine Bluff Hospital. Sergt. Deason died at a private house near Camp Mills of pneumonia Feb. the 14th. Corp. Cook[631] died at Pine Bluff Hospital of pneumonia Feb. the 17th. A portion of the reg[iment] moved to Camp Wright, 4 miles above Pine Bluff on Arkansas River, Sunday the 22nd of Feb. Company H moved on Monday and Tuesday the 23rd & 24th. Daniel Dulin[632] was discharged the 22nd of Feb. Jesse Arledge received a twenty days furlough the same day. P. G. Conner received fifty days furlough the 27th of Feb.; started home the 28th. The reg[iment] still camped at Camp Wright this the 6th of March. Two men belonging to Halderman's Battery to be publicly shot tomorrow for desertion. Regiment moved from Camp Wright for Monroe, Louisiana April the 24th, 1863. Arrived at Monroe May the [date missing]. Left for Alexandria May the [date missing]. Arrived at Alexandria May the 27th. Left on the expedition up the Miss. the evening of the 29th. Took steamboats on Little River the evening of the 29th, Waterhouse's & Fitzhugh's[633] Regiments aboard the steamer Louis Deor. Landed at sunset the 30th on Tensas River. Moved from camps at two the morning of the 31st. Attacked the gunboat at

---

[629] Jeremiah Parker (c.1839-?), son of Robert F. and Pertima (Simmons) Parker of Minden, served in Co.-B, 11th Texas Infantry.

[630] Private William Asher Kuykendall (7/30/1841-1/26/1863), son of Middleton and Marian (Branch) Kukyendall

[631] Corporal James E. Cook (c.1834-2/17/1863)

[632] Private Daniel Dulin (1823-1/8/1887), son of James and Frances (Durham) Dulin, was serving as a substitute for George W. Rhodes.

[633] The 19th Texas Infantry and 16th Texas Dismounted Cavalry Regiments

Perkin's Landing[634] at eleven a. m. of the same day; under fire 2 hours. Returned to camps on Tensas the same evening having marched 30 miles that day. Moved through the swamps to Bayou Mason the 2nd of June. Built a bridge across Tensas. Co[mpany] H and Smith's Co[mpany] of Allen's Reg[iment] left under Col. Redwood to guard the bridge. The Division moved on to Richmond the 6th of June. Gen. McCulloch's Brigade attacked Milliken's Bend Sunday morning at day. Carried the breast work at the point of the bayonet. Had to evacuate it at ten from the gunboats. Lost 181 men killed and wounded. The enemy loss, 500 killed and 60 prisoners. The Division was attacked the 15th of June at Richmond by a superior Federal force. Fell back to Tensas River that evening with slight loss. Fell back to Delhi the 16th [and] 17th. Moved in the direction of Lake Providence the 22nd. Returned to Delhi the 29th. Moved again for Lake Providence the 5th of July. Returned to Delhi the 7th. Returned to Monroe the 16th. Camped above Trenton at Dripping Springs until the morning of the 20th. Moved for Campta [Campti] on Red River. Arrived there the 1st of Aug. Went to Nachitoches. Left there for Alexandria the 4th of Aug. Camped at Camp Green the 5th. Remained there until the morning of the 10th. Crossed Red River. Moved to Camp Texas. Remained there until the [date missing] Sept. I received a furlough for 50 days on

---

[634] In order to relieve some of the pressure on Vicksburg, Walker's Division was instructed to disrupt the Federal supply and communication lines on the Louisiana side of the Mississippi, and if possible, send reinforcements across. On May 31, 1863 the division struck a surprise blow at Perkin's Landing, a Federal supply depot located about fifteen miles downriver from Vicksburg near New Carthage. A small infantry detachment, along with the gunboat *U.S.S. Carondelet* and several transports in support guarded the camp. After the Confederates drove the garrison troops onto their transports, Edgar's Artillery Battery and the 19th Texas Infantry were pushed out ahead into an open field near the river. They dueled with the gunboat and transports for nearly two hours before driving them away. The soldiers of the 19th Texas Infantry experienced their baptism of fire and won praise from General McCulloch for withstanding the withering fire from the heavy guns of the *Carondelet* in their exposed position. McCulloch reported 1 killed, 2 wounded, and 2 missing from his command and 11 Federals killed and several wounded in the action. Edwin Bearss, *The Campaign for Vicksburg*. 3 vols. (Dayton, OH: Morningside House, Inc., 1991), 1172.; J. P. Blessington, 89-92.

The 19th Texas Infantry withstood heavy fire from the *U.S.S. Carondelet* at Perkins Landing

surgeon's certificate. Left camps the 10th of Aug. Landed at home Aug. the 15th. Had my time extended 30 days. Left home Oct. the 19th. Found the reg[iment] camped 8 miles below Chinaville [Cheneyville] on Bayou Boeff [Beouf] Oct. 29th. Remained there until Nov. the 3. Moved 8 miles up the bayou. Took up the march the 4th for Simsport. Crossed the Atchafalaya River the 9th. Moved over near the Miss. River the 12th. Camped on Bayou Letsworth. Picketed on the Miss. River. Had a fight with the gunboats the 22nd. The 29th had another brush with the gunboats. 30th took up the march for Plagimine [Plaquemine]. The 2 of Dec. camped on Bayou Grostake [Grosse Tete]. The 5th marched back. Camped 9 miles from Morgan's Ferry on Atchafalaya. The 9th, crossed that ferry. The 13th moved for Simsport; 14th camped above Simsport. The 24th of Dec. crossed at Simsport. The 25th crossed back and camped above Yellow Bayou. January the 1st moved 2 miles up Bayou DeGlaze. Camped in a Negro quarter. Worked on the fortifications on Yellow Bayou. Jan. the 27th Comp. H ordered to Fort DeRussy. Left on the 28th. Arrived at the fort the 30th. The fort was attacked and carried the 14th of March by the Federal Army under General Smith after 4 hours fighting. J. M. Nall & J. A. Bane of Co. H both severely wounded, 36 of Co. H taken prisoner. We were carried down Red River in a gunboat the evening of the 16th. Landed at Baton Rouge the 17th. Left there the night of the 18th. Landed in New Orleans the morning of the 19th and put in prison. April the 5th put aboard the Polar Star. Took up Red River for exchange. April the 8th the Battle of Mansfield was fought, the 9th the Battle of Pleasant Hill. The 29th the Battle of Jenkins Ferry on Saline River in Ark. was fought[635], in

---

[635] After the battles of Mansfield and Pleasant Hill, Walker's weary Division turned north for Arkansas again. A Federal army under General Frederick Steele threatened Shreveport and Walker's Division was under way on a fast march to meet it. Steele soon decided to retreat back to Little Rock and was crossing his army over the Saline River at Jenkin's Ferry when Walker's Greyhounds caught up with him on April 30. The ensuing battle, fought in a heavy rain in a river bottom swamp with knee-deep mud and water, quickly became fierce and deadly. The division, along with General Sterling Price's Arkansas and Missouri Infantry, charged the fortified Yankees and took heavy casualties in the confusion that followed. The 19th Texas Infantry was closely engaged on the division's right flank, where the Federals tried desperately to break the Confederate line of battle. Casualties among Walker's Division included Third Brigade commander Brigadier

which J. O. Rhodes of Co. H was killed and G. W. Osburn[636] wounded. April the 10th we prisoners were turned back down Red River from near the mouth of Loggy Bayou and carried back to New Orleans and again imprisoned. P. W. Stone died in St. Louis Hospital the 29th of May, Serg. T. J. Riley the 30th of May, T. P. Billingsley June the 9th, J. M. Jones June the 27th, P. G. Conner July the 2nd. July the 21st all put aboard the steamer Nebraska for exchange except B. F. Hays, who was left behind in the smallpox hospital[637]. We were exchanged the evening of the 22nd at the mouth of Red River. Landed at Alexandria the 25th. The 26th all furloughed home. I got home Aug. the 1st. Left home for camps Sept. the 19th. Got to Camden, Ark. the 28th, where we are still waiting transportation to our command this Oct. the 2nd; our command being at Monticello, Ark. Joined our command 12 miles west of Camden the 6th. Camped 4 miles from Camden the 6th. Moved the 14th. Crossed Washita. Camped at the pontoon bridge. Capt. John Guine[638] publicly shot the 15th. Commenced our march the morning of the 14th of Nov. for Springhill to go into winter quarters. Camped the 18th near Springhill. Received orders to move to Minden, La. Took up our march for Minden the morning of the 22nd. Camped near Minden the

Brigadier General William Scurry

General William Scurry and First Brigade commander Brigadier General Horace Randal. After several hours of fighting the Confederates withdrew, allowing the Federals to continue their retreat to Little Rock. Soldiers of Walker's Division harbored animosity toward General Edmund Kirby Smith for many years afterward for ordering what they considered a senseless attack against an enemy already in retreat.

[636] Private George W. Osburn (c.1829-?)

[637] Sergeant Benjamin F. Hays recovered from his illness and was exchanged October 29, 1864.

[638] Captain John Guynes (c.1814-10/16/1864) of Co.-F, 22nd Texas Infantry was accused of encouraging his men to desert when it was rumored that the Division would be ordered across the Mississippi to support the eastern armies. J. P. Blessington, 279-280.

27th. Thursday the 1st of Dec. moved to our present camp 10 miles southwest of Minden, where we are now building winter quarters. Dec. the 5th W. J. Bates left the company today on detached service[639]. Dec. the 12th finished our cabins and moved into them. I received a leave of absence for thirty days beginning Dec. 24th. Arrived at home the 25th. Left for camps Jan. 21st, 1865. Arrived there 23rd. T. J. Clark[640] died at Camp Magruder Jan. the 12th, 1865. Jesse Arledge died at his home in Rusk County, Texas Jan. the 12th, 1865 of consumption. We marched from our winter quarters near Minden, La. the morning of the 26th of Jan. 1865 for Shreveport, with orders for to go to Houston, Texas. Crossed Red River & camped near Shreveport the 28th. Still encamped near Shreveport Feb. the 9th. T.

Brigadier General Wilburn H. King

W. Strickland died at Shreveport Hospital Feb. the 27th, 1865. Moved in the direction of Nachitoches March the 2nd. Passed through Keachi and Mansfield. Camped 12 miles south of Mansfield March the 11th. The morning of the 12th took up the march for Texas by way of Logansport, the 1st and Second Brigades under Brig. Gen. Waterhouse, the 3rd & 4th under Brig. Gen. King[641] by the way of Grand Bluff. The 1st and 2nd Brigades crossed Sabine the 14th; passed through Mount Enterprise the 18th. Camped near Crockett the 24th. Gen. Forney came up the 25th. The 2nd and 3rd

---

[639] Private Bates was detached to the Ordinance Department, most likely at Shreveport.
[640] Private T. J. Clark (c.1847-1/12/1865)
[641] Brigadier General Wilburn H. King (1839-1910) of Cullodenville, Georgia served previously as Major and Colonel of the 18th Texas Infantry. After being severely wounded at Mansfield, La. King was promoted to Brigadier General and placed in brigade command.

Brigades came up the 27th. Waterhouse's Brigade dismounted Wellse's & Demorse's Regiments of Cavalry[642] Sunday the 25th.

---

[642] The 29th Texas Cavalry under Colonel Charles DeMorse and Well's Texas Cavalry Battalion under Lieutenant Colonel John W. Wells were attached to the brigade in February 1865.

Writings of
Captain Harvey A. Wallace, C. S. A.
The 19th Texas Volunteer Infantry, Company H

[Captain Wallace's Personal Journal]

H. A. Wallace enlisted in the Confederate States Service May the 4th, 1862 at Jefferson, Texas. Organized a company at Minden, Rusk County, Texas May the 10th, 1862. Took up the line of march for Jefferson the 28th of July, [the] company 113 strong. Arrived at Jefferson the 31st of July. Returned home the 13th of August. Returned to camps the 17th of August. Took up the march for Little Rock, Ark. the 19th. Stopped at Rondo, Ark. the 29th. The company there had measles; 7 died. Broke up camps there on the 2nd of Oct. Moved for Little Rock. Arrived there the 17th. Crossed Ark. River the 21st. Moved for Camp Nelson. Landed there the 23. Remained there until the 23 of November. Broke up camps. Marched down on Bayou Metre [Meto]. Camped on Bayou Meto the 26th of November. Remained there until the 12th of Dec. Left camps with orders for Vicksburg. Camped on Ark. River on the north bank, one mile below Little Rock. Remained there until the 26. Crossed the river. Camped the 28th 5 miles south of Little Rock on the south side of the river. Received orders the 30th to march for Fort Smith. Encamped the 31st four miles north of Little Rock on the north side of the river. Remained there until the 4th of January. There Gen. Walker took command of the division. Marched for Pine Bluff Sunday the 4th. Took up camps there the 8th on Bayou Bartholomew. Received orders the 10th to move for Arkansas Post as the fight was going on. Marched at day the 11th. Went 20 miles. Started the 12th at day. Marched 15 miles. Received news of the fall of the post. Encamped at the 3 levies. There fortified and remained in the snow ten inches deep without tents until the 18th. Marched back up the river for Pine Bluff, the mud knee deep. Camped at Pine Bluff the night of the 19th. Marched 4 miles the 22. Camped at Camp Mills. Remained there until the 22 of February. Moved back on Ark. River 4 miles above Pine Bluff. The command then remained there until the 20th of April, when they moved for Campta [Campti], Louisiana. I received a furlough the 14th of March for fifty days. Landed home the 21st. Started for command the 27th. Was stopped in Shreveport. Remained there until the 20th of May. Took a boat down Red River. Joined my co[mpany] at Campta [Campti] the 23rd. Took a boat the 27 for Alexandria. Landed the morning of the 28th at Alexandria. Took up the line of march that evening at 5 p. m. for Little River. Took a steamboat on Little River at 2 p. m. the 29th. Landed 15 miles from Perkin's Landing on Tensas River at sunset the 30th. Took up the march at two o'clock in the morning of the 31st for Perkin's Landing. Had a fight with the gunboats by ten o'clock. Returned to the camps we left in the morning that night. Crossed the Tensas the 1st of June. The 3rd marched for Bayou Mason. Camped on Bayou Mason that night. Took up the march the next morning up the bayou. Struck across for Tensas the 5th. Camped on Tensas that night. My co[mpany] and Capt. Smith's was detailed to guard the bridge over Tensas that evening and took post at the bridge that night. The rest of the division moved for Richmond at day the 6th. Attacked Milliken's Bend at day the 7th. Fell back to Richmond. Remained there until the morning of the 15th, when being attacked, they retreated back across Tensas. My co[mpany] & Capt. Smith was relieved at the bridge at dark by Tappan's Brigade of Arkansas troops and joined our regiments that night. We continued the retreat the 16th. Camped on Bayou Mason. The 17th we marched 2 miles north of Delhi. Camped on Bayou Mason. Remained there until the morning of the 22. We then marched for Goodrich Landing on the Miss. River. Camped the 23rd on Tensas River. Remained there until the 26. Marched back to Bayou Mason. Started for Lake Providence at 5 in the evening the 27th. Camped at 11 o'clock at night on Bayou Mason. Moved on next morning 3 miles. Again camped. There I took the fever the 28th. Was sent back to Delhi the 29th. Remained at Parson Upton's until the evening of the 4th of [illegible]. Took the cars with a crowd of sick for Monroe. Went to a private house, the widow Jackson's, 7 miles from Monroe; Lieut. Barksdale and A. J. Parker being with me sick. The command came back the 30th to our old camps. Started the 8th of July for Lake Providence. Received the news of the fall of Vicksburg the 9th. Returned to their old camps the 11th. Remained there until the 15th, when they took the cars. Came to

Monroe the 15th. They camped 4 miles above Trenton. I went to the command the 17. Left there the 18th with the other sick for Campta [Campti]. Landed at Campti. Joined the command at Alexandria the 6th of August, very sick. Received a sick furlough. Started home the 10th. Landed home the 15th. Started to my command Oct. the 19th. Found the command the 28th of Oct. on Bayou Boeff [Beouf], 8 miles south of Chinaville [Cheneyville]. Started for Simsport Nov. 8th. Crossed the Atchalafaya [Atchafalaya] River the 11th. Picketed on the Miss. River. Fought the gunboats the 22nd and 29th. Started to Plackamine [Plaquemine] the 30th. Camped on Bayou Grostake [Grosse Tete] a few days. Cross Atchalafaya [Atchafalaya] at Morgan's Ferry the night of Dec. the 9th. Camped at our old camp above Simsport the 12th. Recrossed Atchalafaya [Atchafalaya] the 23 of Dec. on a pontoon bridge. Lost a wagon and baggage in the river. Was taken prisoner the 14 of March. Landed in New Orleans the 17th, '64; put in prison the 20 of March. Was exchanged the 25 of July, '64. Started to command Sept. the 19th, '64. Met the command October the 6th. Left Camden, Ark. Nov. the 12th. Landed at Minden, La. Dec. the 5th. Received a furlough Dec. the 23rd. Got home the 25th on 30 days pass. Left home Jan. the 16th. Got to the command the 18. Came to Shreveport. Stayed one month. Received a seven days pass. Got home the 19. Started back the 25. Found myself water bound. Came home and started back January the 30.

Moves of the 19th Texas Vol. Inft. from Jan., 1865

[A continuation of Capt. Wallace's Personal Journal]

Marched from winter quarters near Minden, La. Jan. the 26th. Camped near Shreveport the 28. Remained near Shreveport until March the 6th. Moved to Keachi distant 26 miles, thence to Mansfield distant 20 miles, thence to the sawmill on the Pleasant Hill road, 12 miles. Took up the march the 12th of March for Texas. Marched to Logansport on Sabine River distant 35 miles, thence to Mt. Enterprise in Rusk County, distant 44. Passed through The Mount the 18, thence to Rusk in Cherokee County distant 40 miles, thence to Canon's Bridge on the Neches River distant 32 miles, thence through a portion of Anderson County into Houston County to Crockett, distant 40 miles, where we camped the 26; where we remained until April the 1st. We moved for Huntsville, Walker County, distant 45 miles, thence to Piedmont Springs in Grimes County, distant 45 miles. Camped at the springs April the 9th. Piedmont Springs [is] situated 8 miles west of Anderson in Grimes County; a fine boarding house; several beautiful springs very strong with sulpher; bathing accom[odations]. Commenced our march for Hempstead in Washington County April the 14th. Camped near Hempstead the 17th; distance traveled 43 miles. Passed through some fine lands in Grimes County. Gen. Lee evacuated Richmond April 5. Surrendered his army the 9th day of April to Gen. Grant. April 29th Col. Carter[643] made a speech to our division. May 2nd a day of rest; a sermon at night by Rev. [illegible] from the 14th Chapt. & 32nd verse of Proverbs.

---

[643] Colonel George Washington Carter (c.1828-1901) of the 21st Texas Cavalry was an outspoken Virginia born Methodist Minister and educator. Carter had been actively seeking a brigade command position since having partial command of Parson's Cavalry Brigade during 1863-64.

Moves of the 12th Texas ...
from Jan 1845"

Marched from Winter Quarters near
Minden La Jan the 25th Camped
near Shreveport the 28th. Remained
near Shreveport until March the 5th
Moved to Kechi distant 26 miles
thence to Mansfield distant 22 miles
thence to the sawmill on the Fort
Jessup road 12 miles. Took up the
march the 12 of March for Texas
Marched to Logansport on Sabine
River distant 30 miles Thence
to Mt. Enterprise in Rusk County
distant 44 passed through there the
18th thence to Rusk in Cherokee
County distant 40 miles.

Epilogue

The breaking rays of a beautiful Virginia sunrise caught the bone weary, starving soldiers of the Catawba Light Infantry preparing to die. They peered down the road at Yankee troops gathered in overwhelming numbers. The Fifth South Carolina Infantry was acting as part of the rear guard of General Robert E. Lee's ragged Army of Northern Virginia as it retreated west from Petersburg. The Fifth South Carolina fought hard and fell back behind the army until now, as far as could be told, it blocked the road two miles from a little village called Appomattox Courthouse. The day was Palm Sunday, April 9, 1865, but the men took no notice as they hurriedly began to throw up dirt earthworks across the road. They could already hear the deep, rhythmic boom of artillery at work in the distance and knew the end was near. Their army was almost completely surrounded by the Federals.

Colonel Asbury Coward wondered how long his battered Fifth South Carolina could stand against the assault that he knew must come. Shortly after noon, the Colonel took his field glasses to study the wide space that separated his men from the sea of blue clad foe to his front. Suddenly, Coward saw a mounted rider carrying a white flag gallop between the lines. Could it be so? Was his weary mind playing tricks? Colonel Coward could not believe what he was seeing. It was a white flag[644]! Soon the guns fell strangely silent all along the lines. An hour later, the soldiers saw their commander appear on the road. General Lee was mounted straight in the saddle of his warhorse, Traveler, dressed in his finest uniform. The men of the brigade gave the general a cheer as he slowly rode by. Several hours later the general returned with his head bent, hat in his hand, and tears in his eyes. The men surged around him, trying to get as close as they could to their beloved commander. General Lee began to speak, softly and emotionally. "I have done for you all that it was in my power to do. You have done all your duty. Leave the result to God. Go to your homes and resume your occupations. Obey the laws and become as good citizens as you were soldiers". The old general bid his men goodbye then turned and rode off, never looking back, and the war was over.

---

[644] Bond and Coward, 177.

Before the surrender ceremonies the soldiers of the Fifth South Carolina cut up their war torn regimental battle flag[645] so that each man could take a small piece home with him. After paroles were issued, the remnants of each company stacked their arms and marched out into the dusty road that led south and home.

A Commander Without an Army

News of General Lee's surrender at Appomattox did not reach Texas until April 20. It was the final blow to morale for citizens and soldiers alike. They were depressed, despondent, and sick of war. Confederate leaders and others in Texas remained defiant and vowed to continue the fight, but by the middle of May they finally accepted the inevitable. The Confederate forces in Texas were already starting to disintegrate by wholesale desertion. The soldiers, fed up with years of deprivation, starvation, poor leadership, and no pay, simply walked out of camp alone or sometimes in groups the size of squads or companies. The formal dissolution of the army in Texas started May 19 and by May 30, all Confederate military units were disbanded. When Trans-Mississippi Department commander General Edmund Kirby Smith arrived in Houston, he found that he had no troops to command. In his final address on May 30, 1865 he lamented, "Soldiers, I am left a commander without an army; a general without troops." Smith went on to say, "Your present duty is plain. Return to your families. Resume the occupations of peace."

---

[645] The battle flag of the Catawba Light Infantry resides in the collection of the Museum of the Confederacy at Richmond, Va. Color Sergeant John H. Barry carried the Catawba flag until he was wounded at Gaine's Mill on June 27, 1862. The flag was sent to Barry while he was home on furlough.
Museum of the Confederacy. *Colours of the Gray: An Illustrated Index of Wartime Flags from the Museum of the Confederacy's Collection* (Richmond, Va.: Museum of the Confederacy, 1998). 15

Yield obedience to the laws. Labor to restore order. Strive both by counsel and example to give security to life and property. And may God in His mercy direct you aright, and heal the wounds of our distracted country."

Through the final days of the war, Walker's Texas Division held together remarkably well. Morale was low in the division but the remaining remnant of troops stood by their commanders. The soldiers of the 19th Texas Infantry, except for Company-K, which was assigned to guard the powder mill at Marshall, whiled away their time at Camp Groce near Hempstead, waiting and becoming more despondent with each passing day. On May 16, 1865, General John Magruder sent a letter to General Edmund Kirby Smith explaining the condition of the troops under his command in Texas. After conferring with the officers of Walker's Division, then under command of General John H. Forney, General Walker added the following postscript to General Magruder's memo, "I will say in addition, that my observation convinces me that the troops of this district cannot be relied upon. They consider the contest a hopeless one, and will lay down their arms at the first appearance of the enemy. This is the unanimous opinion of the brigade and regimental commanders of Forney's [Walker's] Division whom I have this day consulted." General Magruder pleaded with Smith in his closing, "Nothing more can be done except to satisfy the soldiers, to induce them to preserve their organization, and to send them in regiments, &c., to their homes, with as little damage to the community as possible. For God's sake, act or let me act."

The breakup of Walker's Division began at Camp Groce on May 19, 1865. The remaining soldiers were discharged and left for home in groups of squads, companies, or regiments, keeping a wagon to each company. By the evening of May 20, nothing remained of the division but memories.

Homecoming

The long journey home for Captain Wallace and his war weary company was nearly 210 miles, or about seventeen to twenty days travel[646]. The ladies of Rusk, Panola, and Nacogdoches Counties welcomed their men home with relief, but there was very little time to celebrate or rest. Like many of their fellow veterans, the soldiers of Company-H returned to neglected farms and homes, crops to work, equipment to repair, fences to mend, and hungry children to feed. As one Texas cavalry trooper put it, "I came home from the war, rolled up my sleeves, and commenced to wage war on the corn." Harvey Wallace arrived home in time to find the crops almost ready for the summer harvest. Wallace began preparations as soon as he returned. On June 19, 1865, the slaves in Texas were set free by order of General Gordon Grainger, commander of Federal occupation forces. Many slaves left their plantations soon afterward but those on the Wallace farm were given the choice to stay on as sharecroppers. Most of Harvey's slaves chose to stay, taking on the Wallace name as their inheritance. As the summer of 1865 continued, Harvey gave his all to get the crops in and the land ready for fall planting, but he was not completely over the scourge that followed him throughout the war.

A Casualty of War

Harvey Wallace arrived home in June 1865 weak and emaciated from disease, starvation, and exposure. The dysentery that Wallace suffered with through the war still inflicted him and he was worn down physically. With very little assistance on the farm and no time to rest and recuperate, Harvey's physical condition slowly deteriorated. On August 7, the Wallace's infant son, Harvey Jr., died of an unknown cause. No death records are available from that period, but it is possible that the child contracted dysentery from his father. Without a doubt, the death was an almost unbearable blow to Harvey and Achsah. Harvey's condition continued to worsen after the death of his son and on September 1, 1865, Harvey Wallace died at his home at Minden of dysentery. The grieving family laid Harvey to rest beside his son at the Shiloh Cemetery near Minden. Like so many veterans who died of their wartime illnesses or

---

[646] Blessington, 300-302.

wounds after returning home, Captain Wallace was surely a casualty of war.

Out of the Valley

Through the remaining months of 1865 and into the following year, Achsah struggled to keep the farm going and provide for the children. Times were hard for the people of the south after the close of the war. It seemed though that the worst was over for the Wallace family, but one more tragedy remained. On September 25, 1866, the Wallace's beloved "Little Matty" (Martha Margaret Rebecca Wallace) died at the age of six. The family buried Matty beside her father at Shiloh and tried to recover from their loss.

During the late 1860's, more immigrants from South Carolina arrived in Rusk County. Many came to escape the hardships placed on them in South Carolina by the reconstruction government. Like their ancestors, they sought a place where they could live in peace, tend their farms, and start a new life. Among these came Duncan Poovey[647], a young friend of the Wallace family. Duncan was a veteran of Company-E, 17th South Carolina Infantry and a farmer and carpenter by trade. He and his parents were neighbors of the Wallaces when they lived in York District. Achsah and Duncan courted and were married on March 5, 1868.

Duncan Poovey was a good husband and provider. He cared for the farm and built the family a grand, sprawling farmhouse of the finest workmanship to replace the old one. Although the couple never had children together, Duncan raised Achsah's two boys as if they were his own. The Poovey-Wallace farm prospered under Duncan and Achsah's capable leadership. William and Aaron Wallace took to farming like their father before them. They both became excellent farmers under Duncan Poovey's careful instruction. William eventually married and became a successful tomato farmer in Cherokee County, Texas. Aaron settled at Minden,

---

[647] Duncan McCallum Poovey (3/31/1844-7/26/1921), son of David and Lucretia (McCallum) Poovey of York District, S. C.

farmed, and worked as the local rural mail carrier. Harvey and Achsah's two boys produced seventeen grandchildren who kept the Poovey farm a lively place for many years.

William Thomas Wallace

Aaron Wood Wallace

Aaron Wood Wallace (seated front) delivering mail at Minden, Texas (Others in photo are unidentified)

(L-R) William and Aaron Wallace

The Sun Sets

Achsah Wallace treasured the letters sent by her husband during the trying times of the Civil War. She kept the collection safe and secure through the years. They were the family's last link to Harvey. Achsah must have turned to them for consolation many times after her husband's death. They provided encouragement and comfort through the difficult years after the war. Of most importance though, they taught her to trust in God to see her through those dark and difficult times that surely come into everyone's life. When Achsah Wallace Poovey died on June 6, 1904, she could surely say with the psalmist, "Yea though I walk through the valley of the shadow of death, I will fear no evil, for thou art with me." She was buried at Shiloh Cemetery with Harvey and her children.

The End

(L–R) Duncan Poovey, Granddaughter–Flora Darcus Wallace, Achsah Wood Wallace Poovey, Grandsons–Elias Elmer Wallace, and James Harvey Wallace, and two unidentified neighbor girls (Photo dated 1900)

Appendix-I

Deaths In Capt. H. A. Wallace's Comp. - H 19th Texas Vol. Inft.[648]

[As recorded in Capt. Wallace's Company Ledger Book]

(1) Private Rufus Irby[649], who died at Camp Waterhouse near Jefferson, Texas of measles, Aug. the 15th, 1862; aged 27 years.

(2) Private J. A. Koonce, who died September the 10th, 1862 at Rondo, Lafayette County, Arkansas of measles.

(3) Private Abner Stanley, who died September the 11th, 1862 near Rondo at Mrs. Owens, Lafayette County, Arkansas.

(4) Private Jasper Edge, who died September the 12th, 1862 at the company hospital at Rondo, Lafayette Co., Arkansas.

(5) Private Robert H. Gowens, who died September the 14th, 1862 at Mr. Hicks near Rondo, Lafayette County, Arkansas.

---

[648] Captain Wallace's record reflects a 37.5 percent casualty rate. This rate is calculated from a total of 128 men who served with the company during the war.

[649] Rufus Irby (c.1835-8/15/1862). According to descendents, Private Irby's wife, Keziah, was busy making his uniform when a messenger arrived to inform her of her husband's death.

(6) Private Thomas Easley, who died September the 15th, 1862 in camps at Camp Josaphene McDermott in Lafayette County, Arkansas.

(7) Private A. B. Barry, who died September the 17th, 1862 three miles east of Rondo at Mr. Hunt's house in Lafayette County, Arkansas of pneumonia.

(8) Private J. G. Ghentry[650], who died Oct. the 2nd, 1862 at Rondo, Lafayette Co., Arkansas of measles.

(9) Private J. C. J. Little[651], who died Oct. the 7th, 1862 at Rondo, Lafayette County, Arkansas of measles.

(10) W. R. Grimes, who died Oct. the 12th, 1862 at Arkadelphia, Arkansas of pneumonia.

(11) Sergeant J. O. Easley died at Washington, Arkansas, Oct. the 17th, 1862 of pneumonia. Was left there in the hospital the 6th with G. L. Stoveall as nurse.

(12) 1st Lieutenant D. A. McCallum, who died at Capt. Gingle's near Camp Nelson on Tuesday morning, the 11th day of Nov., 1862 of congestion.

(13) Sergt. J. R. Ray, who died at Camp Nelson Friday evening, the 14th of Nov., 1862 of congestion.

(14) Private T. P. Jones, who died in camps 7 miles from Camp Nelson the 24th of Nov., 1862 of congestion.

---

[650] J. G. Ghentry (Gentry) (c.1832-10/2/1862)
[651] James C. J. Little (c.1844-10/7/1862), son of Lewis and Elizabeth Little of Pine Hill

(15) Franklin McKnight[652], who died at the hospital in Washington, Arkansas of the effects of measles, Nov. 10th, 1862.

(16) William Acrey[653], who died at Camp Nelson, Arkansas Nov. the 24th, 1862 of pneumonia.

(17) Private J. T. Hudman[654], who died at St. Johns Hospital, Little Rock, of the effects of measles, Nov. the 22nd, 1862.

(18) Private A. L. Barry, who died at Camp Nelson Nov. the 25th, 1862 of quinsy[655].

(19) Private B. W. Thomas[656], who died at Camp Nelson of pneumonia, Dec. the 3rd, 1862.

(20) Private D. L. McCall[657], who died at Camp Nelson Dec. the 4th, 1862, of pneumonia.

(21) Private J. P. H. Reinhat[658], who died at the Little Rock Hospital Dec. the 7th, 1862 of pneumonia.

(22) Private H. F. Woods[659], who died at Camp Bayou Metre [Meto] Dec. the 11th, 1862 of pneumonia.

---

[652] Private John Franklin C. McKnight (c.1842-11/10/1862), son of Andrew and Sarah (Hudman) McKnight

[653] Private William Acrey (c.1834-11/24/1862)

[654] James T. Hudman (c.1841-11/22/1862), son of Francis and Elizabeth Hudman of Panola County

[655] Quinsy was an infection or inflammation of the tonsils and surrounding tissues, often leading to the formation of an abcess that caused massive infection and death.

[656] Burrel W. Thomas (c.1836- 12/3/1862)

[657] David L. McCall (c.1841- 12/4/1862), son of Robert and Ann (Lacy) McCall

[658] James P. Henderson Reinhat (Reinhardt) (c.1840- 12/7/1862), son of Martin F. and Mary Reinhat

[659] Henry F. Wood (c.1839- 12/11/1862)

(23) Private W. B. Whitfield, who died at Camp Nelson Dec. the 12th, 1862 of pneumonia.

(24) Private W. E. Parker[660], who died at Camp Nelson of pneumonia, Dec. the 12th, 1862.

(25) Private J. C. Drenan[661], who died at Camp Nelson of pneumonia, Dec. the 13th, 1862.

(26) Private T. J. Moseley[662], who died at Arkadelphia, Arkansas Nov. the 13th 1862.

(27) Private C. C. Hawkins died at Camp Nelson Dec. the 16th, 1862 of brain fever[663].

(28) Private J. D. Raburn[664] died in the hospital at Little Rock Dec. the 25th, 1862 of chronic diarrhea

(29) H. Gage[665], Private, died in the hospital at Little Rock Jan. the 5th, 1863.

(30) Private W. A. Kuykendall died in Pine Bluff Hospital Jan. the 26th, 1863.

(31) Corp. [James] Cook died Feb. the 17th, 1863 at Pine Bluff Hospital, Ark. of pneumonia.

---

[660] William E. Parker (c.1833-12/12/1862), son of Robert F. and Pertima (Simmons) Parker.
[661] John C. Drennan (c.1841-12/13/1862), son of William Drennan of Panola County.
[662] Thomas J. Moseley (c.1841-11/13/1862), son of Flora Moseley of the Caledonia Community, Rusk County.
[663] An inflammation of the brain or meninges, most often caused by encephalitis or meningitis.
[664] James D. Raburn (c.1828-12/25/1862)
[665] Harrison Gage (c.1836-1/5/1863)

(32) Sergt. J. Deason died Feb. the 14th, [1863] near Camp Mills, Arkansas at a private house, of pneumonia.

(33) Private G. L. Tinkle[666], who died at his home in Rusk County, Texas Feb. the 7th, 1863.

(34) Private James Parker died in the hospital at Little Rock February the 28th, 1863.

(35) Private F. M. Scott[667] died in the hospital at Pine Bluff, Ark. March the 15th, 1863.

(36) Private Wm. Nichols[668] died in the hospital at Pine Bluff, Ark. March the 31st, 1863.

(37) Private W. S. H. Burns died at his home in Rusk County, Texas Sept. the 28th, 1863.

(38) Private P. W. S. Stone died in St. Louis Hospital in New Orleans, La. whilst a prisoner of war, May the 29th, 1864.

(39) Sergt. T. J. Riley died in St Louis Hospital May the 30th, 1864 whilst a prisoner of war in New Orleans, La.

(40) Private T. P. Billingsley died at St. Louis Hospital, New Orleans, La. June the 9th, 1864, whilst a prisoner of war.

(41) Private J. M. Jones died at the St. Louis Hospital, New Orleans, La. June the 27th, 1864, whilst a prisoner of war.

(42) Private P. G. Conner died at the St. Louis Hospital, New Orleans, La. July the 2nd, 1864, whilst a prisoner of war.

---

[666] G. L. Tinkle (c.1844-2/7/1863), son of William and Sabra (Nolan) Tinkle
[667] F. M. Scott (c.1832-3/15/1863)
[668] William Nichols (c.1818-3/31/1863)

(43) Private James O. Rhodes was killed in the battle at Jenkin's Ferry on Saline River in Arkansas April the 29th, 1864.

(44) Private J. B. McCarter died at the Taylor Hospital, La. August the 22nd, 1864.

(45) Private T. J. Clark died at Camp Magruder, La. January the 12th, 1865.

(46) Private Jesse Arledge died in Rusk County, Texas January the 12th, 1865.

(47) Private T. W. Strickland died in the hospital at Shreveport, La. Feb. the 28th, 1865.

[(48) Private Joseph Akin (or Akins) died at Camp Nelson, Arkansas, November, 1862.]

Appendix-II

Muster Roll- The Catawba Light Infantry (April, 1861)

Key

DOD- Died of disease
DOW- Died of wounds
KIA- Killed in action
POW- Prisoner of war
W- Wounded

<u>Listing Order</u>- **Name; Rank; Age; Residence; Other Service; Other Ranks Held; Remarks**

Abernathy, William N. - Private; 15; Ebenezer; Co.-H, 18th S.C. Infantry; W- 6/6/64, Paroled-Appomattox

Adkins, S. Randolph - Private; 20; Fort Mill; Co.-H, 18th S.C. Infantry; W- 10/28/64, Richmond, Va.

Anderson, Joseph P. - Private; 36; Clay Hill; Co.-H, 6th S.C. Infantry

Armstrong, James S. - Private; Ebenezer; Discharged- 10/31/61

Barnes, John O. - Private; 40; Clay Hill; Co.-A, 12th S.C. Infantry; KIA- 5/12/64, Spotsylvania, Va.

Barnett, Alexander A. - 2nd Sergeant; 30; Bethel; Co.-B, 5th S.C. Infantry; Private, Teamster; Paroled-Appomattox

Barnett, David F. - Private; 22; Ebenezer; Co.-E, 17th S.C. Infantry; Surgeon; Paroled-Appomattox

Barnett, James M. - Private; 18; Bethel; Co.-B, 5th S.C. Infantry; DOD- 8/23/64, Virginia

Barnett, Joseph J. - Private; 26; Clay Hill; Co.-B, 5th S.C. Infantry; DOD- 4/6/63, Jerusalem, Va.

Barron, Archibald A. - Private; 24; Fort Mill; Co.-B & Co-H, 6th S.C. Infantry; 4th Corporal; KIA- 7/20/64, Petersburg, Va.
Barry, John H. - 3rd Sergeant; 27; Ebenezer; Co.-B, 5th S.C. Infantry; 1st & 2nd Sergeant, 2nd & 3rd Lieutenant; W- 6/27/62, Paroled-Appomattox
Bowen, William J. - Private; 43; Clay Hill; Captain
Boyd, Benjamin F. - Private; 45; Yorkville
Brison, B. P. - Private
Brown, John B. - Private; 30; Co.-B, 5th S.C. Infantry; 1st Corporal; DOW- 8/15/64, Petersburg, Va.
Campbell, Napoleon B. - Private; 22; Zeno; Co.-H, 18th S.C. Infantry
Campbell, Samuel L. - 2nd Lieutenant; 31; Clay Hill; Co.-H, 18th S.C. Infantry; 1st Lieutenant; W, POW- South Mountain, Md., Discharged
Campbell, William E. - Private; 18; New Center; 6th Corporal
Cathcart, James H. - Private; 24; Ebenezer; DOD- 8/20/61, Charlottesville, Va.
Choat, James V. - Private; 31; Clay Hill; Co.-E, 17th S.C. Infantry; 2nd Corporal; Paroled- 4/9/65 from Hospital at Danville, Va.
Choat, Robert W. - Private; 23; Clay Hill; Co.-B, 13th N.C. Infantry; Corporal; W, POW-Gettysburg, W-Spotsylvania, Va. & DOW- 5/21/64, York District, S.C.
Cook, James R. - Private; 20; Clay Hill; Co.-H, 18th S.C. Infantry; POW- 4/6/65
Cullender, William J. - Private; 25; Clay Hill
Divinny, John J. - Private; 21; Fifer
Felts, John W. - Private; 17; Co.-G, Palmetto Sharpshooters; DOD- 3/16/63, Petersburg, Va.
Fewell, Benjamin F. - Private; 21; New Center; Co.-B, 5th S.C. Infantry; DOD- 1/16/62, Richmond, Va.
Fewell, James S. - Private; 25; Clay Hill; Co.-B, 5th S.C. Infantry; Paroled-Appomattox
Finley, William G. - Private; 29; Co.-H, 1st S.C. Cavalry
Garrison, William F. - Private; 20; Ebenezer; Co.-E, 17th S.C. Infantry; POW- 10/14/64, Petersburg, Va., Paroled- 1/17/65
Glenn, James A. - 1st Sergeant, Orderly Sergeant; 32; Zeno

Glenn, James H. - Private; 41; Zeno; Co.-H, 18th S.C. Infantry; Corporal; DOW- 6/8/65, Farmville, Va.

Glenn, Robert B. - Private; 21; Bethel

Glenn, Robert Henry - Captain; 31; Clay Hill; Co.-H, 18th S.C. Infantry; Discharged- 5/5/62

Glenn, Samuel A. - Private; 21; Zeno; Co.-H, 18th S.C. Infantry; 1st, 2nd, & 3rd Corporal; Paroled-Appomattox

Glenn, Samuel L. - Private; 21; Zeno; DOD- 2/21/62, Centreville, Va.

Glenn, William R. - 5th Corporal; 28; Zeno; 5th Sergeant; DOD- 12/26/61, Culpeper, Va.

Grier, Thomas - Private; 35; Zeno; Staff-Palmetto Sharpshooters; Orderly Sergeant; Transferred to an unlisted unit- 1/31/63

Huddleston, Robert R. - Private; 27; Fort Mill; Co.-B, 6th S.C. Infantry

Huddleston, Thomas J. - Private; 31; Clay Hill; Co.-H, 18th S.C. Infantry

Hutchison, Samuel J. - Private; 18; Ebenezer; Co.-H, 18th S.C. Infantry

Jackson, Samuel W. - Private; 35; New Center; Co.-B, 5th S.C. Infantry; Paroled-Appomattox

Johnston, David M. - Private; 24; Zeno; Co.-B, 5th S.C. Infantry; 1st, 2nd, & 3rd Corporal

Johnston, William G. - Private; 21; Zeno; Co.-B, 5th S.C. Infantry; DOD- 7/3/63, Wilson, N.C.

Laney, Livingston L. W. - Private; 20; DOD- 2/9/62, Centreville, Va.

Latta, Robert - 4th Corporal; 19; Clay Hill; Co.-A, 12th S.C. Infantry; DOD- 7/9/62, Petersburg, Va.

Mason, George W. - 6th Corporal; 35; Clay Hill; DOD- 5/30/61, Columbia, S.C.

McCallum, William A. J. - Private; 22; Zeno; Co.-B, 5th S.C. Infantry; 1st, 2nd, & 4th Corporal/3rd & 4th Sergeant; W- 6/27/62, Discharged

McCarter, David A. - Private; 22; New Center; DOD- 6/15/61, Charlottesville, Va.

McCarter, John A. - Private; 26; Clay Hill

McCaw, Robert G. - Private; 38; Ebenezer; Co.-G, Palmetto Sharpshooters; DOW- 6/6/62, Seven Pines, Va.
McCully, John W. - Private; 19; New Center; Co.-B, 5th S.C. Infantry; Hospital Steward; W- 5/31/62, Detached to Petersburg Hospital
McCully, Robert H. - Private; 21; Zeno; Co.-B, 5th S.C. Infantry; Paroled-Appomattox
McKenzie, Arthur A. - Private; 51; Zeno; 1st Lieutenant; Discharged 4/62
McKenzie, Joseph S. - Private; 19; Zeno; Co.-B, 5th S.C. Infantry; 5th Corporal; Paroled-Appomattox
Mitchell, Samuel A. - Private; 18; Fort Mill
Moore, William R. - Private; 22; New Center; Co.-H, 1st S.C. Cavalry; Musician
Nesbitt, James F. - Private; 21; Co.-F, 5th S.C. Infantry; DOW- 7/15/62, Weldon, N.C.
Patrick, George A. - Private; 29; Zeno; Co.-B, 5th S.C. Infantry; 1st & 2nd Lieutenant, & Captain; Paroled-Appomattox
Patrick, Robert V. - Private; 22; DOD- 12/12/61, Culpeper, Va.
Pierce, Josiah W. - Private; 19; Ebenezer; Co.-B, 5th S.C. Infantry; Bugler; Paroled-Appomattox
Poovy, William P. - Private; 18; Clay Hill; Co.-E, 17th S.C. Infantry; POW- 4/1/65, Paroled- 6/16/65 at Point Lookout, Md.
Quinn, Leroy D. - Private; 25; Zeno; DOD- 11/21/61, Culpeper, Va.
Simril, John J. - Private; 20; Yorkville; DOD- 4/28/62, Richmond, Va.
Simril, Samuel D. - 1st Corporal; 26; Yorkville; Co.-H, 18th S.C. Infantry; Private; W- 6/30/64, Petersburg, Va., Discharged
Stewart, James A. - Private; 21; Clay Hill; Co.-B, 5th S.C. Infantry; Company Cook; W- 8/62, Paroled-Appomattox
Stewart, James C. - 3rd Corporal; 21; Zeno
Tate, James B. - 5th Sergeant; 25; Clay Hill; Co.-H, 18th S.C. Infantry; 1st Sergeant, Orderly Sergeant; Paroled-Appomattox
Thompson, John T. - 4th Sergeant; 21; Zeno; Co.-B, 5th S.C. Infantry; 3rd Sergeant

Thompson, William L. - 3rd Lieutenant; 26; Zeno; Co.-B, 5th S.C. Infantry; 2nd Lieutenant; KIA- 6/30/62, Frayser's Farm, Va.
Timberlake, John C. - Private; 43; Co.-C, Gill's Battalion, 4th S.C. State Troops; Corporal
Wallace, Harvey A. - 1st Lieutenant; 32; Clay Hill; Co.-H, 19th Tx. Infantry; Captain; DOD- 9/1/65, Minden, Tx.
Wallace, John R. H. - 2nd Corporal; 23; Clay Hill; Co.-B, 5th S.C. Infantry; KIA- 6/27/62, Gaines Mill, Va.
Wallace, Joseph F. - Private; 22; Clay Hill; Co.-B, 5th S.C. Infantry; DOD-11/24/62, Richmond, Va.
Wallace, Samuel W. - Private; 20; Clay Hill; Co.-E, 17th S.C. Infantry; 2nd Sergeant; POW- 4/6/65, Paroled 6/25/65 at Newport News, Va.
Warrant, James R. - Private; 19; Zeno
Watson, William D. - Private; 19; Clay Hill; Co.-B, 5th S.C. Infantry; DOW- 6/4/62, Richmond, Va.
Wilkerson, Robert S. - Private; 21; DOD- Unknown date, Manchester, Va.
Williams, Leroy R. - Private; 19; Clay Hill; Co.-E, 17th S.C. Infantry; 3rd & 4th Sergeant; POW- 3/25/65, Paroled 6/22/65 at Point Lookout, Md.
Wood, Chesley G. - Private; 23; Clay Hill; Co.-B, 5th S.C. Infantry; DOW- 6/30/62, Frayser's Farm, Va.
Wright, James S. - Private; 26; Clay Hill; Co.-A, 12th S.C. Infantry
Yearwood, Anderson - Private; 34; Co.-B, 5th S.C. Infantry
Youngblood, Orin N. - Private; 18; Ebenezer; Co.-E, 17th S.C. Infantry
Youngblood, Thomas W. - Private; 22; Clay Hill; Co.-H, 18th S.C. Infantry; DOD- 7/22/62, Charleston, S.C.

Sources:

Compiled Service Records Of Confederate Soldiers from the State of South Carolina: 17th Infantry. M267: 291-296. Washington D.C.: National Archives.

Eighth U.S. Census, 1860. Washington D.C.: U.S. Census Office, 1860.

Hart, Joseph E. *Supplement To Confederate Veterans Enrollment Book of York County S.C.-1902.* York, S.C.; N. p., 1984.

Hewett, Janet B., ed. *The Roster of Confederate Soldiers, 1861-1865.* 16 Volumes. Wilmington, N.C.; Broadfoot Publishing Co., 1995-1996.

Kirkland, Randolph W. Jr. *Broken Fortunes: South Carolina Soldiers, Sailors, and Citizens Who Died in the Service of Their Country and State in the War For Southern Independence 1861- 1865.* Charleston, S.C.: The South Carolina Historical Society, 1995.

Muster Rolls of The Catawba Light Infantry. *The Yorkville Enquirer.* Yorkville, S.C., February 7, 1861 & May 2, 1861.

Owens, Jo Roberts, and Ruth Dickson Thomas, eds. *Confederate Veterans Enrollment Book of York County S.C.- 1902.* Clover, S.C.; Westmoreland Printers Inc., 1983.

Salley, A.S. Jr. *South Carolina Troops In Confederate Service.* Three Volumes. Columbia, S.C.: The R. L. Bryan Company, 1913.

South Carolina Department Of Archives And History. *Roll Of The Dead: South Carolina Troops, Confederate States Service.* Columbia, S.C.: South Carolina Department Of Archives And History, 1994.

Appendix-III

Muster Roll- Company-H, 19th Texas Infantry

Key

DOD- Died of disease
KIA- Killed in action
POW- Prisoner of war
W- Wounded

<u>Listing Order</u>- Name; Rank; Age; Residence; Eyes; Hair; Height; Occupation; Birthplace; Remarks

Acrey, Cosby D. - Private; 34; Mt. Enterprise; Blue; Fair; 5'6"; Wagoner; Habersham Co., Ga.; Camp Wagoner- 5/14/63

Acrey, James - Private; 33; Mt. Enterprise; Blue; Dark; 5'5"; Wagoner; Habersham Co., Ga.; Camp Wagoner- 5/14/63, Detached to Cotton Bureau- 9/63

Acrey, William J. - Private; 28; Mt. Enterprise; Blue; Black; 5'2"; Farmer; Meriweather, Ga.; Wagoner- 9/4/62, DOD- 11/24/62, Camp Nelson, Ar.

Akins (or Akin), John D. - Private; 18; Murvaul; Grey; Light; 5'8"; Farmer; York Dist. S.C.; Transferred to Lane's Partisan Rangers (First Texas Partisan Ranger Cavalry Regiment)- 9/24/62

Akins (or Akin), Joseph F. - Private; 30; Murvaul; Dark; Brown; 5'11"; Farmer; York Dist., S.C.; Drummer, DOD- 11/62, Camp Nelson, Ar.

Anderson, J. E. - Private; 30; Murvaul; Brown; Dark; 5'8"; Farmer; Scott Co., Mo.; Promoted to 3rd Corporal- 9/13/63

Arledge, Jesse - Private; 29; Mt. Enterprise; Black; Dark; 5'8"; Farmer; Claiborne Parish, La. ; DOD- 1/12/65, Rusk Co., Tx.

Arnold, John T. - Private; 29; Minden; Dark; Auburn; 5'8"; Farmer; Green Co., Ga.

Baker, George T. - Private; 32; Mt. Enterprise; Grey; Black; 5'11"; Farmer; Company and Regimental Teamster (Wagoner)

Baker, W. H. - Private; 17; Mt. Enterprise; Blue; Black; 5'10"; Farmer; Chambers Co., Al.; Present for duty 2/64

Bane, James A. - Private; 30; Mt. Enterprise; Blue; Fair; 5'8"; Farmer; Blunt Co., Al.; W, POW- 3/14/64 at Ft. DeRussy, La.

Barksdale, William E. - 1st Sergeant; 34; Yancy; Black; Black; 6'2"; Farmer; McMinn Co., Tn.; Promoted to 2nd Lieutenant- 11/30/62; POW- 3/14/64 at Ft. DeRussy, La.

Barry, Andrew L. - Private; 28; Pine Hill; Blue; Light; 5'7"; Farmer; York Dist., S.C.; DOD- 11/25/62, Camp Nelson, Ar.

Barry, Archibald B. - Private; 28; Pine Hill; Blue; Dark; 5'2"; Farmer; York Dist., S.C.; DOD- 9/17/62, Rondo, Ar.

Bates, William J. - Private; 34; Mt. Enterprise; Grey; Fair; 5'11"; Farmer; Green Co., Ga.; Detached to Ordinance Dept- 12/2/64

Billingsly, T. P. - Private; 50; Mt. Enterprise; Dark; Black; 5'9"; Farmer; Montgomery Co., N.C.; Wagoner- 8/63, POW- 3/14/64 at Ft. DeRussy, La. & DOD- 6/10/64, New Orleans, La.

Bradford, James - Private; 16; Rusk Co.; Grey; Dark; 5'7"; Farmer; Davidson Co., Tn.; POW- 3/14/64 at Ft. DeRussy, La.

Brooks, John R. K. - 3rd Lieutenant; 30; Minden; Blue; Dark; 5'7"; Farmer; Green Co., Ga.; Promoted to 1st Lieutenant- 11/28/62, POW- 3/14/64 at Ft. DeRussy, La.

Burkhalter, William - Private; 30; Briley Town; Brown; Auburn; 5'6"; Farmer; Edgefield Dist., S.C.; Promoted to 4th Corporal- 2/1/64

Burns, Charles G. - Private; 17; Minden; Blue; Black; 5'9¾"; Farmer; Tishomingo Co., Ms.; Substitute for J. W. Hays, POW- 3/14/64 at Ft. DeRussy, La.

Burns, William S. H. - Private; 18; Minden; Blue; Black; 5'7"; Farmer; Pontotoc Co., Ms.; DOD- 9/28/63, Rusk Co., Tx.
Clark, T. J. - Private; 17; Yellow; Dark; 5'6"; Farmer; Talladega Co., Al.; DOD- 1/12/65, Minden, La.
Connally, John W. - Private; 27; Harmony Hill; Grey; Dark; 6'2"; Farmer; Madison Co., Ga.; Promoted to 5th Corporal- 11/26/62, Disability Discharge- 11-28-62
Conner, John N. - Private; 24; Yancey; Dark; Black; 5'6"; Farmer; Panola Co., Ms.; Promoted to 5th Sergeant- 12/1/62, POW- 3/14/64 at Ft. DeRussy, La.
Conner, Pleasonton G. - Private; 21; Yancey; Brown; Black; 5'9"; Farmer; Noxford Co., Ms.; POW- 3/14/64 at Ft. DeRussy, La. & DOD- 7/2/64, New Orleans, La.
Conner, William B. - Private; 30; Yancy; Black; Dark; 5'8"; Farmer; Edgecombe Co., N.C.; Present for duty- 4/65
Cook, James E. - Private; 28; Mt. Enterprise; Blue; Auburn; 5'10"; Farmer; Wilcox Co, Al.; Promoted to Corporal- 12/1/62, DOD- 2/17/63- Pine Bluff, Ar.
Deason, Jeremiah - 4th Sergeant; 32; Pine Hill; Dark; Dark; 6'5"; Tanner; Pike Co., Ga.; DOD- 2/14/63, Camp Mills, Ar.
Deason, Joseph C. - Private; 34; Minden; Grey; Dark; 6'1½"; Farmer; Pike Co., Ga.; POW- 3/14/64 at Ft. DeRussy, La.
Doherty, R. J. - Private; 32; Briley Town; Black; Black; 5'7½"; School Teacher; Henderson Co., Tn.; Deserted to the enemy- 4/21/64
Drennan, John C. - Private; 23; Rusk County; Blue; Dark; 5'10"; Farmer; Talbert Co., Ga.; DOD- 12/11/62, Camp Nelson, Ar.
Dulin, Daniel - Private; 37; Minden; Blue; Auburn; 5'10"; Farmer; York Dist., S.C.; Substitute for G.W. Rhodes, Discharged- 2/22/63
Duncan, Simeon S. - Private; 34; Pine Hill; Blue; Fair; 5'10"; Farmer; Lexington Dist., S.C.; Promoted to 2nd Corporal- 9/20/62, POW- 3/14/64 at Ft. DeRussy, La.
Easley, James O. - Private; 34; Caledonia; Blue; Dark; 5'8"; Farmer; Marion Co., Tn.; DOD- 10/19/62, Washington, Ar.
Easley, Thomas F. - Private; 24; Caledonia; Black; Black; 5'9"; Farmer; Jackson Co., Tn.; DOD- 9/15/62, Rondo, Ar.

Edge, Jasper - Private; 25; Mt. Enterprise; Blue; Light; 5'6"; Farmer; Chambers Co., Al.; DOD- 9/12/62, Rondo, Ar.

Ferguson, Augustus - Private; 30; Minden; Blue; Dark; 6'0"; Farmer; Monroe Co., Ga.

Gage, Harrison - Private; 26; Minden; Blue; Auburn; 5'3"; Farmer; Cherokee Co., Al.; DOD- 1/3/63, Little Rock, Ar.

Ghentry, J. G. - Private; 30; Minden; Black; Black; 5'8"; Farmer; Franklin Co., Tn.; DOD- 10/2/62, Rondo, Ar.

Ghentry, John T. - Private; 18; Mt. Enterprise; Dark; Dark; 5'7"; Farmer; Jackson Co., Al.; POW- 3/14/64 at Ft. DeRussy, La.

Giles, John; Private - 33; Pine Hill; Dark; Black; 6'0"; Wood Workman; Bibb Co., Al.; Promoted to 4th Corporal- 6/1/63; On furlough- 2/64

Golden, Newton A. - Private; 21; Pine Hill; Blue; Fair; 5'7"; Farmer; Yalobusha Co., Ms.; Present for duty- 2/64

Golden, W. M. - Private; 16; Dark; Dark; 5'5"; Farmer; Phillips Co., Ar.

Gowens, Robert H. - Private; 34; Minden; Blue; Dark; 5'7"; Farmer; Jefferson Co., Al.; DOD- 9/14/62, Rondo, Ar.

Grimes, James K. - Private; 23; Briley Town; Black; Black; 5'6"; Farmer; York Dist., S.C.; Present for duty- 2/64

Grimes, Marion H. - Private; 31; Briley Town; Blue; Fair; 5'11"; Farmer; Talbert Co., Ga.; POW- 3/14/64 at Ft. DeRussy, La.

Grimes, W. R. - Private; 32; Briley Town; Brown; Dark; 6'0"; Farmer; Talbert Co., Ga.; DOD- 10/12/62, Arkadelphia, Ar.

Guthrie, Thomas C. - Private; 18; Minden; Black; Black; 5'4"; Farmer; Cherokee Co., Al.; POW- 3/14/64 at Ft. DeRussy, La.

Hallum, Robert B. - Private; 20; Pine Hill; Brown; Dark; 5'9"; Farmer; Rusk Co., Tx.; Present for duty- 4/65

Harper, John H. - Private; 29; Henderson; Grey; Auburn; 5'10"; Farmer; Pike Co., Ga.; POW- 3/14/64 at Ft. DeRussy, La., Discharged 5/65 at Hempstead, Tx.

Harris, Peter J. - Private; 19; Briley Town; Grey; Fair; 5'6"; Farmer; York Dist., S.C.; Sick at Rusk, Tx.- 3/21/65

Harris, W. D. - 4th Corporal; 34; Pine Hill; Brown; Dark; 6'2"; Mechanic; Franklin Co., N.C.; Promoted to 4th Corporal- 8/4/62

Hawkins, Columbus C. - Private; 30; Mt. Enterprise; Blue; Black; 5'10"; Farmer; Lawrence Co., Al.; DOD- 12/6/62, Camp Nelson, Ar.

Hays, Benjamin F. - 3rd Sergeant; 26; Minden; Blue; Sandy; 6' 3"; Tanner; Murray Co., Tn; POW- 3/14/64 at Ft. DeRussy, La.

Hays, Cunningham S. - 2nd Lieutenant; 28; Yancy; Blue; Dark; 6' 0"; Farmer; Williamson Co., Tn.; Resigned 10/30/62, Camp Nelson, Ar.

Hays, Daniel M. - 2nd Corporal; 27; Minden; Blue; Brown; 5' 0"; Farmer; Williamson Co., Tn.; POW- 3/14/64 at Ft. DeRussy, La.

Hays, William H. H. - Private; 22; Grand Bluff; Blue; Red; 5'10"; Harness Maker; Murray Co., Al.; Absent without leave- 2/64

Healton, R. R. - Private; 41; Blue; Dark; 6'0"; Farmer; ? Co., Tn.; Agriculturist attached to the company by order of General McCulloch

Hellum, H. - Private; 33; Rusk Co.; Black; Dark; 6'0"; Farmer; Troup Co., Ga.; Transferred to Engineer Corps.- 1/9/64

Holleman, Green W. - Private; 40; Mt. Enterprise; Blue; Light; 5'7"; Farmer; McNary Co., Tn.; Substitute for G. W. Stegall, POW- 3/14/64 at Ft. DeRussy, La.

Holley, J. M. - Private; 17; Blue; Light; 5'5"; Farmer; Tuscaloosa Co., Al.

Holley, Richard R. - Private; 21; Mt. Enterprise; Grey; Sandy; 5'4½"; Farmer; Tuscaloosa Co., Al.; Promoted to 3rd Corporal- 2/22/63

Holley, Sion - Private; 32; Mt. Enterprise; Blue; Fair; 5'7"; Farmer; Tuscaloosa Co., Al.; Present for duty- 2/64

Hudman, James T. - Private; 21; Murvaul; Blue; Auburn; 5'9"; Farmer; Chambers Co., Al.; DOD- 11/22/62, Little Rock, Ar.

Hull, John L. - 5th Sergeant; 19; Mt. Enterprise; Grey; Auburn; 5'3"; Painter; Newton Co., Ga.; Promoted to 5th Sergeant- 8/4/62, Promoted to 1st Sergeant- 12/1/62, POW- 3/14/64 at Ft. DeRussy, La.

Hull, Thomas J. - Private; 18; Mt. Enterprise; Grey; Dark; 5'8"; Farmer; Newton Co., Ga.; POW- 3/14/64 at Ft. DeRussy, La.

Hunt, Thomas J. - Private; 27; Henderson; Blue; Black; 6'0"; Farmer; Blunt Co., Tn.; On detached duty making soap for the regiment- 4/65

Irby, Rufus - Private; 27; Yancy; Blue; Dark; 5'9"; Farmer; Green Co., Ga.; DOD- 8/15/62, Jefferson, Tx.

Jones, H. P. - Private; Transferred from Lane's (First Texas) Partisan Rangers- 9/20/62, Detailed as gunsmith at Little Rock, Ar.- 11/11/62, Disability discharge- 11/3/63

Jones, James M. - Private; 19; Mt. Enterprise; Blue; Fair; 5'11"; Farmer; Rusk Co., Tx.; POW- 3/14/64 at Ft. DeRussy, La. & DOD- 6/27/64, New Orleans, La.

Jones, Joseph H. - Private; 27; Mt. Enterprise; Grey; Black; 5'8"; Farmer; Madison Co., Ga.; On medical leave- 3/65

Jones, Thomas P. - Private; 22; Mt. Enterprise; Blue; Fair; 5'10"; Farmer; Rusk Co., Tx.; DOD- 11/24/62, on the march, 7 miles from Camp Nelson, Ar.

Koonce, John A. - Private; 30; Mt. Enterprise; Black; Dark; 6'0"; Farmer; McNary Co., Tn.; DOD- 9/10/62, Rondo, Ar.

Kuykendall, G. M. - Private; 18; Dark; Dark; 5'6"; Rusk Co., Tx.; POW- 3/14/64 at Ft. DeRussy, La.

Kuykendall, William A. - Private; 21; Yancy; Grey; Dark; 5'8"; Farmer; Desoto Co., Ms.; DOD- 1/26/63, Pine Bluff, Ar.

Lee, W. W. - Private.; 20; Mt. Enterprise; Brown; Fair; 5'9"; Farmer; Bledsoe Co., Tn.; POW- 3/14/64 at Ft. DeRussy, La.

Leslie, John A. - Private; 34; Mt. Enterprise; Blue; Black; 5'11"; Farmer; Monroe Co., Ga.; Promoted to 1st Corporal- 9/13/62

Little, James C. J. - Private; 18; Murvaul; Blue; Fair; 5'8"; Farmer; ? Co., Tn.; DOD- 10/7/62, Rondo, Ar.

Mabry, John F. - Private; 20; Hazel; Light; 5'8"; Marshall Co., Tn.; Transferred from Co.-B, 11th Tx. Infantry- 11/1/62

McCall, David L. - Private; 21; Mt. Enterprise; Black; Black; 6'1½"; Farmer; Dallas Co., Al.; DOD- 12/4/62, Camp Nelson, Ar.
McCallum, Duncan A. - 1st Lieutenant; 30; Pine Hill; Blue; Dark; 6' 0"; Farmer; York Dist. S.C.; DOD- 11/11/62, Camp Nelson, Ar.
McCarter, Joseph B. - Private; 28; Mt. Enterprise; Dark; Dark; 5'10"; Farmer; York Dist., S.C.; Transferred from Co.-E, 10th Tx. Cavalry, POW- 3/14/64 at Ft. DeRussy & DOD- 8/22/64 at the Taylor Hospital, ?, La.
McCrary, Neal D. - Private; 18; Mt. Enterprise; Blue; Dark; 5'1"; Farmer; Jackson Co., Al.; Promoted to 4th Corporal- 9/13/63
McKnight, John Franklin C. - Private; 20; Mt. Enterprise; Black; Black; 5'9"; Farmer; Chambers Co., Al.; DOD- 11/10/62, Washington, Ar.
Moseley, Thomas J. - Private; 21; Caledonia; Grey; Dark; 6'0"; Farmer; Green Co., Al.; DOD- 11/13/62, Arkadelphia, Ar.
Nall, John M. - Private; 29; Mt. Enterprise; Blue; Auburn; 6'0"; Farmer; Henry Co., Ga.; W, POW- 3/14/64 at Ft. DeRussy, La., On detached service-Marshall, Tx.- 4/65
Nichols, William - Private; 44; Mt. Enterprise; Blue; Black; 5'1"; Farmer; Abbeville Dist., S.C.; DOD- 3/31/63, Pine Bluff, Ar.
Nix, T. L. - Private; 21; Mt. Enterprise; Blue; Black; 5'6"; Farmer; Newton Co., Ga.; Detached to Cotton Bureau in Jefferson, Tx.- 9/3/63
Osburn, George W. - Private; 33; Mt. Enterprise; Grey; Black; 5'8"; Farmer; Troup Co., Ga.; Detailed as Wagoner- 9/1/62, Present for duty- 2/64, W- 4/30/64 at Jenkins Ferry, Ar.
Owens, William J. - Private; 27; Mt. Enterprise; Blue; Dark; 6'0"; Farmer; Bledsoe Co., Tn.; Detailed as Wagoner- 8/11/62; Promoted to 4th Sergeant- 2/22/63
Parker, Asa J. - Private; 33; Mt. Enterprise; Grey; Brown; 5'4½"; Farmer; Taliaferro Co., Ga.; Promoted to 4th Sergeant- 4/63, POW- 3/14/64 at Ft. DeRussy, La.
Parker, Franklin J. - 3rd Corporal; 34; Minden; Blue; Sandy; 5'8"; Farmer; Green Co., Ga.; Promoted to 2nd Sergeant- 11/26/62
Parker, James - Private; 37; Mt. Enterprise; Blue; Black; 6'0"; Farmer; Lincoln Co., N.C.; DOD- 2/28/63, Little Rock, Ar.

Parker, William E. - Private; 28; Mt. Enterprise; Blue; Grey; 5'8"; Farmer; Green Co., Ga.; DOD- 11/12/62, Camp Nelson, Ar.

Patrick, John C. - Private; 18; Blue; Dark; 5'8"; Farmer; York Dist., S.C.; Previous service in Co.-F, 17th Tx. Cavalry; POW- 3/14/64 at Ft. DeRussy, La.

Peterson, James F. - Private; 22; Mt. Enterprise; Blue; Light; 6'1"; Farmer; Limestone Co., Al.; POW- 3/14/64 at Ft. DeRussy, La.

Peurifoy, Amos J. - Private; 29; Mt. Enterprise; Brown; Dark; 5'5"; Farmer; Monroe Co., Ga.; Detached to Quartermasters Dept.- Shreveport, La.- 4/65

Raburn, James D. - Private; 34; Mt. Enterprise; Black; Dark; 5'6"; Farmer; Giles Co., Tn.; DOD- 12/25/62, Little Rock, Ar.

Ray, John R. - 2nd Sergeant; 30; Mt. Enterprise; Blue; Black; 5'10"; Farmer; Henderson Co., Tn.; DOD- 11/14/62, Camp Nelson, Ar.

Reid, John M. - Private; 32; Mt. Enterprise; Dark; Black; 6'0"; Farmer; DeKalb Co., Ga.; Absent without leave 8/19/62 & 9/4/63

Reinhart (or Reinhardt), James P. H. - Private; 22; Murvaul; Grey; Black; 5'5"; Wagoner; Nacogdoches Co., Tx.; Detailed as Wagoner- 5/11/62, DOD- 12/7/62, Little Rock, Ar.

Rhodes, James O. - Private; 33; Murvaul; Blue; Black; 6'1"; Farmer; Walton Co., GA.; KIA- 4/30/64, Jenkin's Ferry, Ar.

Riley, Thomas J. - Private; 27; Mt. Enterprise; Grey; Dark; 6'0"; Farmer; Green Co., Ga.; POW- 3/14/64 at Ft. DeRussy, La. & DOD- 5/30/64, New Orleans, La.

Robertson, E. T. - Private; 30; Pine Hill; Dark; Dark; 6'0"; Farmer; Humphries Co., Tn.; Discharged- 12/3/62

Scott, F. M. - Private; 30; Yancy; Dark; Dark; 5'7"; Farmer; Pike Co., Ga.; DOD- 3/15/63, Pine Bluff, Ar.

Singletary, Robert - Private; 34; Mt. Enterprise; Grey; Auburn; 5'10"; Farmer; Blaten Co., N.C.; On detached duty in Medical Dept.- 4/65

Smith, Charles A. - Private; 50; Mt. Enterprise; Dark; Black; 5'10"; Carpenter; Buckingham Co., Va.; Transferred to Co.-B, 11th Tx. Infantry- 11/1/62

Smith, Jerome D. - Private; 30; Mt. Enterprise; Blue; Light; 5'9"; Farmer; Greenville Dist., S.C.; POW- 3/14/64 at Ft. DeRussy, La.
Stanley, Abner - Private; 30; Mt. Enterprise; Blue; Light; 5'8"; Farmer; Green Co., Ga.; DOD- 9/11/62, Rondo, Ar.
Stone, Peter W. S. - Private; 20; Yancy; Blue; Fair; 6'0"; Farmer; Tippah Co., Ms.; W-1863, POW- 3/14/64 at Ft. DeRussy, La. & DOD- 5/29/64, New Orleans, La.
Stovall, George L. - Private; 27; Concord; Brown; Dark; 5'6"; Farmer; Madison Co., Ga.; Present on sick call- 2/64
Strickland, Thomas W. - Private; 28; Mt. Enterprise; Black; Black; 5'9"; Farmer; Spartanburg Dist., S.C.; DOD- 2/28/65, Shreveport, La.
Strickland, William A. - Private; 23; Mt. Enterprise; Black; Light; 5'10"; Farmer; Spartanturg Dist., S.C.; POW- 3/14/64 at Ft. DeRussy, La.
Thomas, Burrel W. - Private; 26; Concord; Blue; Dark; 5'8"; Farmer; Bedford Co., Tn.; DOD- 12/2/62, Camp Nelson, Ar.
Thompson, John R. - Private; 18; Blue; Dark; 5'6"; Farmer; Franklin Co., Mo.; POW- 3/14/64 at Ft. DeRussy, La.
Tinkle, G. L. - Private; 18; Mt. Enterprise; Grey; Dark; 6'0"; Farmer; Panola Co., Ms.; DOD- 2/7/63, Rusk Co., Tx.
Treadwell, William L. - Private; 19; Mt. Enterprise; Black; Black; 5'7"; Farmer; Caldwell Co., Ky.; Absent without leave- 2/64
Turner, Rice R. - 1st Corporal; 31; Mt. Enterprise; Blue; Black; 5'5"; Farmer; Meriweather, Ga.; Promoted to 1st Corporal- 2/1/64, POW- 3/14/64 at Ft. DeRussy, La.
Turner, Romulus G. W. - Private; 35; Mt. Enterprise; Grey; Fair; 6'1½"; Farmer; Henry Co., Ga.; Present for duty- 2/64
Walker, James L. - Private; 20; Rusk Co.; Farmer; Left without permission and joined Co.-I, 18th Tx. Infantry
Wallace, Harvey A. - Captain; 33; Minden; Blue; Fair; 5'10"; Farmer; York Dist. S.C.; POW- 3/14/64 at Ft. DeRussy, La., DOD- 9/1/65, Minden, Tx.
Wallace, William M. - Private; 35; Mt. Enterprise; Blue; Sandy; 6'0"; Farmer; York Dist., S.C.; Promoted to 2nd Lieutenant- 11/30/62

Welch, Joseph A. H. - Private; 18; Minden; Blue; Sandy; 5'1"; Farmer; Chambers Co., Al.; Disability discharge- 2/6/63

West, Houston - Private; 33; Mt. Enterprise; Blue; Black; 5'10 ¼"; Farmer; Ray Co., Tn.; POW- 3/14/64 at Ft. DeRussy, La., Escaped from prison-1864, New Orleans, La. & present for duty- 4/65

Whitfield, William B. - Private; 31; Mt. Enterprise; Black; Black; 5'9"; Farmer; Troup Co., Ga.; DOD- 12/12/62, Camp Nelson, Ar.

Wood, Henry F. - Private; 23; Mt. Enterprise; Brown; Black; 5'10"; Farmer; Franklin Co., Ga.; DOD- 12/11/62, Camp Bayou Meto, Ar.

Wood, Leonard T. - Private; 18; Minden; Dark; Dark; 5'6"; Farmer; Mecklenburg, Co., N. C.; POW-3/14/64 at Ft. DeRussy, La.

Wright, James C. - Private; 29; Mt. Enterprise; Blue; Dark; 6'6"; Wagon Maker; Monroe Co., Ga; Previous service in Co.-D, 14th Tx. Cavalry

Sources:

Compiled Service Records of Confederate Soldiers From The State of Texas: 19th Texas Infantry. Washington D.C.: National Archives.

Davis, Kathryn, and Carolyn Ericson, eds. *Rusk County Rebs*. Nacogdoches, Tx.; Ericson Books, 1998.

Farmer, Garland R. *The Realm of Rusk County*. Henderson, Tx. : The Henderson Times, 1951.

Hewett, Janet B., ed. *The Roster of Confederate Soldiers, 1861-1865*. 16 Volumes. Wilmington, N.C. ; Broadfoot Publishing Co., 1995-1996.

LaGrone, Leila Stone. *This Very Unreasonable War- A History of Panola County During the Civil War*. Carthage, Tx.: Private Printing, 1972.

Moore, Colonel J.B. "List of Prisoners Captured at Fort DeRussy, La. March 14th, 1864". Washington D.C.: National Archives; N.p., 1864.

U.S. Census Office. *Seventh U.S. Census, 1850*. Washington D.C.: U.S. Census Office.

U.S. Census Office. *Eighth U.S. Census, 1860*. Washington D.C.: U.S. Census Office.

Wallace, Harvey A. "A Descriptive Book of Capt. H. A. Wallace's Co.-H, 19th Regiment of Texas Inf. CSA, Rusk County, Texas". Wallace Papers. N.p., 1862-1865.

Bibliography

Primary Sources

Anderson, John Q. *A Texas Surgeon in the C.S.A.* Tuscaloosa, Al.: Confederate Publishing Company, Inc., 1957.

Barnes, Joseph K., and J. J. Woodward. *The Medical and Surgical History of the War of the Rebellion, 1861-65.* Washington D.C.: U.S. War Department, 1870-88.

Blessington, Joseph Palmer. *The Campaigns Of Walker's Texas Division.* 1875. Reprint, Austin: State House Press, 1994.

Boyd, Colonel David F. Letter to General Richard Taylor, 14 April 1864. Copy located in the Friends of Fort DeRussy Collection. Marksville, La.

Brown, Norman D., ed. *Journey To Pleasant Hill: The Civil War Letters of Captain Elijah P. Petty; Walker's Texas Division CSA.* San Antonio, Tx.: The University Of Texas Institute Of Texan Cultures, 1982.

Byrd, William. "The Capture Of Fort De Russy, La.". *The Land We Love* 6, no. 3 (January, 1869).

Campbell, Lieutenant Samuel Leroy Papers. York, S.C.: Historical Center of York County.

Compiled Service Records Of Confederate Soldiers from the State of South Carolina: 17th Infantry. M267: 291-296, (Microfilm, Washington D.C.: National Archives).

Compiled Service Records of Confederate Soldiers From The State of Texas: 19th Infantry. (Microfilm, Washington D.C.: National Archives).

Coward, Asbury. *The South Carolinians: Colonel Asbury Coward's Memoirs*. Edited by Natalie Jenkins Bond and Osmun Latrobe Coward. New York: Vantage Press Inc., 1968.

Cutrer, Thomas W., ed. " An Experience in Soldier's Life: The Civil War Letters of Volney Ellis, Adjutant, Twelfth Texas Infantry, Walker's Texas Division, C.S.A." *Military History of the Southwest* 22 (Fall, 1992), 109-172.

―――. " Bully for Flournoy's Regiment, We Are Some Punkins, You'll Bet: The Civil War Letters of Virgil Sullivan Rabb, Captain, Company I, Sixteenth Texas Infantry, C.S.A." *Military History of the Southwest* 19 (Fall, 1989), 161-190; 20 (Spring, 1990), 61-96.

Davis, Major George B., et al. *The Official Military Atlas of the Civil War*. New York: Gramercy Books, 1983.

Fairbanks, Henry N. "The Red River Expedition of 1864". *Military Order of the Loyal Legion of the United States- Maine, Vol. I*. Wilmington, N.C.: Broadfoot Publishing Co., 1992.

Fremantle, Arthur James Lyon. *The Fremantle Diary: Being the Journal of Lieutenant Colonel Arthur James Lyon Fremantle, Coldstream Guards, on his Three Months in the Southern States*. Edited by Walter Lord. Boston: Little Brown and Company, 1954.

Gibbs, Dr. R. T. Letter to Maj. Gen. Richard Taylor, 16 April 1864. *Official Records of the Union and Confederate Armies- Series 2, vol. 7, no. 120, Union & Confed. Correspondence, Orders, Etc., Relating to Prisoners of War and State from April 1, 1864 to December 31, 1864*. Washington D.C.: Government Printing Office, 1880-1901.

Hardee, Lieutenant Colonel W.J. *Rifle and Light Infantry Tactics; for The Exercise And Manoeuvres of Troops When Acting As Light Infantry Or Riflemen: Vol. II, School Of The Battalion*. Philadelphia: J. B. Lippincott & Co., 1861.

Hart, Joseph E. Collection. York, S.C.: Historical Center of York County.

Hewett, Janet B., Noah Trudeau, and Bryce Suderow, eds. *Supplement to the Official Records of the Union and Confederate Armies; Part-I: Reports.* Wilmington, N.C.: Broadfoot Publishing Co., 1998.

Hewett, Janet B., ed. *Supplement to the Official Records of the Union and Confederate Armies; Part-II: Record of Events.* Wilmington, N.C.: Broadfoot Publishing Co., 1998.

―――. *The Roster of Confederate Soldiers, 1861-1865.* 16 Volumes. Wilmington, N.C.: Broadfoot Publishing Co., 1995-1996.

Holcomb, Brent H. *York, South Carolina Newspapers Marriage and Death Notices 1823- 1865.* Spartanburg, S.C.: The Reprint Company, Publishers, 1989.

Joiner, Henry C. "Requesting information on the battle flag of the 19th Tx. Infantry". *Confederate Veteran* 13, no. 11 (November, 1905).

Kight, L. L. *Their Last Full Measure: Texas Confederate Casualty Lists.* 3 vols. Arlington, Tx.: GTT Publishing, 1997.

King, Captain E.T. "E.T. King Papers". Edited by Steve Mayeux. Lafayette, La.: Dupre Library, USL. 1910.

Moore, Colonel J.B. "List of Prisoners Captured at Fort DeRussy, La. March 14th, 1864". Washington D.C.: National Archives.1864.

Moore, Dr. Maurice. *Reminiscences Of York.* Edited by Elmer Oris Parker. Greenville, S.C.: A Press Inc., 1981.

Murray, John C. "Diary of John C. Murray- Crescent Artillery". Civil War Manuscript Series No. 52. New Orleans: Howard Tilton Memorial Library, Tulane University. 1864

Owens, Jo Roberts, and Ruth Dickson Thomas, eds. *Confederate Veterans Enrollment Book of York County S.C.- 1902.* Clover, S.C.: Westmoreland Printers Inc., 1983.

Page, D. D. " Reminiscences". *Confederate Veteran Magazine* 33, no. 7 (July, 1924).

Ray, Sergeant John R. (Co.-H, 19th Texas Infantry). Letter to wife, 16 September 1862. East Texas Research Center Collection, Stephen F. Austin State University. Nacogdoches, Tx.

Schorb, John R. Collection. York, S.C.: Historical Center of York County.

Smith, Zadok Darby Papers. York, S.C.: Historical Center of York County.

South Carolina Department Of Archives And History. *Roll Of The Dead: South Carolina Troops, Confederate States Service.* Columbia, S.C.: South Carolina Department Of Archives And History, 1994.

Stevens, Mrs. Ruby Lee (Beall). Interviews with the editor, 1997-2003.

Taylor, General Richard. *Destruction And Reconstruction: Personal Experiences Of The Late War.* 1879. Reprint, New York: Bantam Books, 1992.

The Carolina Spartan. May 16, 1861.

The Yorkville Enquirer. Yorkville, S.C., 1861-1865.

U.S. Bureau of the Census. *Seventh U. S. Census, 1850.* Washington D.C.: U.S. Census Office.

U.S. Bureau of the Census. *Eighth U. S. Census, 1860.* Washington D.C.: U.S. Census Office.

U.S. Bureau of the Census. *Ninth U. S. Census, 1870.* Washington D.C.: U.S. Census Office.

United States War Department. *The War of the Rebellion: A Compilation of the Official Records of the Union and Confederate Armies.* 128 Vols. Washington D.C.: Government Printing Office, 1880-1901.

Wallace, Harvey A. Papers. Jacksonville, Tx.: Ruby Lee (Beall) Stevens Collection.

Waterhouse, Colonel Richard Jr. Papers, 1862-65. Hillsboro, Tx.: Richard Waterhouse file. Hill College Confederate Research Center.

Secondary Sources

Baldwin, James J. III. *The Struck Eagle: A Biography of Brigadier General Micah Jenkins, and a History of the 5th South Carolina Volunteers and the Palmetto Sharpshooters.* Cambridge: White Mane Publishing, 1996.

Barr, Alwyn. " Confederate Losses in the Red River Campaign, 1864." *Texas Military History* 3 (Summer, 1963), 103-110.

Bearss, Edwin C. *Steele's Retreat from Camden and the Battle of Jenkin's Ferry.* Little Rock: Arkansas Civil War Centennial Commission, 1967.

―――. *The Campaign for Vicksburg.* 3 vols. Dayton, OH: Morningside House, Inc., 1991.

Brooks, Stewart. *Civil War Medicine.* Springfield, Ill: Charles C. Thomas Publisher, 1966.

Bullard, Lucille Blackburn. *Marion County, Texas 1860-1870.* Jefferson, Tx.: N. p., 1965.

Casey, Powell A. *Encyclopedia Of Forts, Posts, Named Camps And Other Military Installations In Louisiana, 1700-1981.* Baton Rouge: Claitor's Publishing Division, 1983.

Cawthon, Juanita Davis. *Some Early Citizens of Marion County, Texas.* Jefferson, Tx.: N. p., 1996.

Cunningham, H.H. *Doctors In Gray: The Confederate Medical Service.* Baton Rouge: Louisiana State University Press, 1958.

Davis, James Henry. *Texans In Gray: A Regimental History of the Eighteenth Texas Infantry, Walker's Texas Division, in the Civil War.* Tulsa, Ok.: Heritage Oak Press, 1999.

Davis, Kathryn, and Carolyn Ericson, eds. *Rusk County Rebs.* Nacogdoches, Tx.: Ericson Books, 1998.

Denny, Robert E. *Civil War Prisons & Escapes: A Day-by-Day Chronicle.* New York: Sterling Publishing Co. Inc., 1993.

Dougan, Michael B. *Confederate Arkansas: The People and Policies of a Frontier State in Wartime.* Tuscaloosa: University of Alabama Press, 1976.

Fairey, Wade B., and Iva Jean Maddox. *Making Money: Early Occupations In York County, S.C.* York, S.C.: York County Historical Commission, 1994.

Farmer, Garland R. *The Realm of Rusk County.* Henderson, Tx.: The Henderson Times, 1951.

Fehrenbach, T. R. *Lone Star: A History of Texas and the Texans.* New York: American Legacy Press, 1983.

Gibson, Charles Dana, and E. Kay Gibson. *Assault and Logistics: Union Army Coastal and River Operations 1861-1866*. The Army's Navy Series, vol. 2. Camden, Maine: Ensign Press, 1995.

Gremillion, Nelson. "Fort De Russey." *The Avoyeles Journal*. Tuesday, May 20, 1980.

———. "Fort De Russey: The Confederate Side". *The Avoyeles Journal*. Tuesday, May 27, 1980.

Hart, Joseph E. *Supplement To Confederate Veterans Enrollment Book of York County S.C.- 1902*. York, S.C.: N. p., 1984.

Hauptman, Laurence M. *Between Two Fires: American Indians in the Civil War*. New York: The Free Press, 1995.

Henderson, Colonel Harry McCorry. *Texas In The Confederacy*. San Antonio, Tx.: The Naylor Company, 1955.

Hendrickson, Robert. *Sumter: The First Day of the Civil War*. Chelsea, Michigan: Scarborough House Publishers, 1990.

Ingmire, Francis T. *Confederate Officers of Texas*. Signal Mountain, Tn.: Mountain Press, 1983.

Johansson, M. Jane Harris. "Peculiar Honor: A History of the 28th Texas Cavalry (Dismounted), Walker's Texas Division, 1862-1865." Doctor of Philosophy Dissertation, University Of North Texas, 1993.

Johnson, Ludwell H. *Red River Campaign: Politics and Cotton in the Civil War*. Baltimore: Johns Hopkins University Press, 1958.

Kerby, Robert L. *Kirby Smith's Confederacy: The Trans-Mississippi South, 1863-1865*. 1972. Reprint, Tuscaloosa: University of Alabama Press, 1991.

Kirkland, Randolph W. Jr. *Broken Fortunes: South Carolina Soldiers, Sailors, and Citizens Who Died in the Service of Their Country and State in the War For Southern Independence 1861- 1865.* Charleston, S.C.: The South Carolina Historical Society, 1995.

Klein, Maury. *Days Of Defiance: Sumter, Secession, and the Coming of the Civil War.* New York: Alfred A. Knopf, Inc., 1997.

Krick, Robert K. *Lee's Colonels: A Biographical Register of Field Officers of the Army of Northern Virginia.* Dayton, Ohio: Morningside Bookshop, 1979.

LaGrone, Leila Stone. *This Very Unreasonable War- A History of Panola County During the Civil War.* Carthage, Tx.: N. p., 1972.

Leet, William D. *Texarkana: A Pictorial History.* Texarkana, Tx.: Texarkana Historical Museum, 1982.

Long, E. B. *The Civil War Day By Day: An Almanac 1861-1865.* Garden City, N. Y.: Doubleday, 1971.

Lowe, Richard G., and Randolph B. Campbell. *Planters & Plain Folk: Agriculture in Antebellum Texas.* Dallas: Southern Methodist University, 1987.

Lowe, Richard. *The Texas Overland Expedition of 1863.* Fort Worth, Tx.: Ryan Place Publishers, 1996.

McCarthy, Carlton. *Detailed Minutiae of Soldier Life in the Army of Northern Virginia 1861- 1865.* Lincoln, Ne.: University of Nebraska Press, 1993.

McPherson, James M. *For Cause and Comrades: Why Men Fought in the Civil War.* New York: Oxford University Press, 1997.

Mendenhall, Samuel Brooks. *Tales Of York County.* N. p., 1989.

Miles, Jim. *A River Unvexed: A History and Tour Guide of the Campaign for the Mississippi River.* Nashville, Tn.: Rutledge Hill Press, 1994.

Museum of the Confederacy. *Colours of the Gray: An Illustrated Index of Wartime Flags from the Museum of the Confederacy's Collection.* Richmond, Va.: Museum of the Confederacy, 1998.

Pettus, Louise, ed. *The Quarterly- A quarterly journal of information relating to York County, S.C. History and genealogy.* Rock Hill, S.C.: The York County Genealogical and Historical Society.

Plummer, Alonzo H. *Confederate Victory at Mansfield: Including Federal Advance From and Retreat to Natchitoches.* Mansfield, La.: Kate Beard Chapter No. 397 United Daughters Of The Confederacy, 1969.

Phares, Ross. *The Governors Of Texas.* Gretna, La.: Pelican Publishing Company, 1976.

Reed, Germaine M. *David French Boyd: Founder of Louisiana State University.* Baton Rouge: Louisiana State University Press, 1977.

Rusk County Genealogical Society. *Remembering Rusk County.* Dallas: Curtis Media Corporation, 1992.

Rusk County Historical Commission. *Rusk County History.* Dallas: Taylor Publishing Company, 1982.

Salley, A. S. Jr. *South Carolina Troops In Confederate Service.* 3 vols. Columbia, S.C.: The R. L. Bryan Company, 1913.

Shankman, Arnold, E., et al. *York County South Carolina: It's People and It's Heritage.* Rock Hill, S.C.: Rock Hill Area Chamber of Commerce, 1983.

Sherer, Palmer Grier. "A Partial History Of Some Of The Early Schools And Educational Movements Of York County." Master's thesis, University Of South Carolina, 1929.

Silverstone, Paul H. *Warships Of The Civil War Navies.* Annapolis, Md.: Naval Institute Press, 1989

Silverthorne, Elizabeth. *Plantation Life In Texas.* College Station, Tx.: Texas A&M University Press, 1986.

Speer, Lonnie R. *Portals To Hell: Military Prisons of the Civil War.* Mechanicsburg, Pa.: Stackpole Books, 1997.

Stauffer, Michael E. *South Carolina's Antebellum Militia.* Columbia, S.C.: South Carolina Department of Archives & History, 1991.

Steiner, Paul E. *Disease In The Civil War: Natural Biological Warfare in 1861-1865.* Springfield, Ill: Charles C. Thomas Publisher, 1968.

Tabors Cyclopedic Medical Dictionary, Edition 18. Philadelphia: F.A. Davis Co., 1997.

Tarpley, Fred. *Jefferson: Riverport to the Southwest.* Austin: Eakin Press, 1983.

Teal, Harvey S., and Robert J. Stets. *South Carolina Postal History And Illustrated Catalog Of Postmarks 1760-1860.* Lake Oswego, Or.: Raven Press, 1989.

Thomas, Samuel N. Jr. and Jason H.Silverman, eds. *A Rising Star of Promise: The Civil War Odyssey of David Jackson Logan, 17th South Carolina Volunteers, 1861-1864.* Campbell, Ca.: Savas Publishing Company, 1998.

Thomas, Samuel N. Jr., and Paul C. Whitesides. *Under The Leaves Of The Palmetto: York County's Confederate Veterans.* York, S.C.: Historical Center Of York County, 1994.

Warner, Ezra J. *Generals in Gray: Lives of the Confederate Commanders*. Baton Rouge: Louisiana State University Press, 1959.

Weymouth, T. Jordan Jr., and Louis H. Manarin. *North Carolina Troops 1861-1865: A Roster*. 13 vols. Raleigh, N.C.: North Carolina Department Of Archives And History, 1979.

White, William W. "The Disintegration Of An Army: Confederate Forces In Texas, April- June, 1865". *East Texas Historical Journal* 26, no. 2 (1988).

Wilcox, Arthur M., and Warren Ripley. *The Civil War At Charleston*. Charleston, S.C.: Evening Post Publishing Company, 1998.

Wiley, Bell Irvin. *The Life Of Johnny Reb: The Common Soldier Of The Confederacy*. 1948. Reprint, Baton Rouge: Louisiana State University Press, 1986.

Winfrey, Dorman H. *A History Of Rusk County, Texas*. Waco, Tx.: Texian Press, 1961.

Winters, John D. *The Civil War In Louisiana*. Baton Rouge: Louisiana State University Press, 1963.

Wooster, Ralph A., and Robert Wooster. "Rarin for a Fight: Texans in the Confederate Army". *Southwestern Historical Quarterly* 84, no. 4 (April, 1981).

Wooster, Ralph A. "Life In Civil War East Texas". *East Texas Historical Journal* 3, (1965).

Wright, Marcus J. *Texas In The War 1861-1865*. Edited by Harold B. Simpson. Hillsboro, Tx.: Hill Junior College, 1965.

Electronic Sources

Cutrer, Thomas W. "Baylor, George Wythe (1832-1916)." *The Handbook of Texas Online*.
[http://www.tsha.utexas.edu/handbook/online/articles/view/BB/fbaar.html]

———. "Magruder, John Bankhead (1807-1871)". *The Handbook of Texas Online*.
[http://www.tsha.utexas.edu/handbook/online/articles/view/MM/fma15.html]

Maberry, Robert Jr. "Wharton, John Austin (1828-65)". *The Handbook of Texas Online*.
[http://www.tsha.utexas.edu/handbook/online/articles/view/WW/fwh4.html]

Pettus, Louise. "Catawba Indians in the Civil War".
[http://www.rootsweb.com/~scyork/louise.htm].

———. "Downtown Yorkville, 1858".
[http://www.rootsweb.com/~scyork/louise.htm]

Sultzman, Lee. "Catawba History".
[http://www.dickshovel.com/Catawba.html].

Index

A

Abernathy, William N. 327
Acrey, Abner n425; Cosby D.n523, 333; James n425, n523, 333; Martha (Jackson) n425; William, J. n653, 333
Adams, Rev. James M. H. n53
Adkins, James S. n149; Jane n149; S. Randolph n149, n221, 327
Akin (or Akins), John n456, n458; John Durham n456, n457, 333; Nancy T. (Wallace) n456, n457, n458; William Davis n458; Jo 45; Joseph F. n373, 201, 326, 333
Alexander, Moses n133
Allen, Capt. Augustus C. n462, n587, 284, 298; Col. R. T. P. n416
Allison, William Barry n289
Anderson, J. E. n418, 333; Joseph Pendle n165, 116, 327; Maj. Richard Clough n33; Maj. Robert n33, 12, 14; Mary V. n165, n242; Sarah E. n242; William n242; William ("Billy") n165, n242, n245, 167
Arledge, Jesse n562, 299, 304, 326, 334
Armstrong, James S. 327
Arnold, John Thomas n540, 334

B

Baker, Capt. B. A. n600; George T. 334; W. H. 334
Ball, Lt. George J. n605
Bane, James A. n584, 302, 334
Banks, Gen. Nathaniel P. n582, n593, 283, n602

Barksdale, Lt. William E. n525, 239, 244, 262, 282, 285, 298, 307, 334
Barnes, John O. n62, 130, 327; Miles n369, 185
Barnett, Alexander n119; Alexander Albert n87, 327; Alexander Hamilton n119, n476; David F. 327; Eliza (Currence) n86, n87, n471; James n86, n87, n471; James M. 327; Jane Meek (Adams) n476; Joseph Arthur 223; Joseph Josiah n471, 327; Martha Minerva (Stowe) n475; Rachel Jane (Adams) n119; Robert A. n86, 57; Sally n303, 163; William Amzi ("Bill") n284, n303, n475
Barron, Amelia n412; Archibald n440; Archibald A. 328; Bill n412, 197; Margaret (Watson) n440; Samuel Watson n440
Barry, Andrew L. n343, n395, 196, 197, 201, 323, 334; Archibald B. n343, n395, 322, 334; Eliza (Watson) n196; James Hanna n259; John n259; John Henderson n196, n645, 328; Violet (Moore) n259; William A. n196
Bates, William J. n415, n639, 334
Baxter, Bill n177, 97
Baylor, Col. George W. n573
Beard, Andrew n172
Beauregard, Gen. Pierre Gustave n90, 136
Becton, Dr. Edward P. n347, 177, 192, 197; Emeline n347; Rev. J. M. n347
Bigger, Alexander M. n285; Erixeny (Barnett) n285; Matthew n285

Billingsley, T. P. n568, 288, 303, 325, 334
Birdwell, George n453
Black, Eliza n297, n308; Emily n297; John D. n297, n308; Susan R. iv; Turentine M. n308; W. C. n191
Blackstock, Cassandra (Wright) n430; Daniel K. n430; Richard n430
Blair, Lt. Col. James Douglas n565, 287
Bowen, Andrew n46; Mary J. n137; Col. William James n46ff, 328
Boyd, Benjamin Franklin n224, 328; Capt. David French n597; Elizabeth n224; James D. n327; Thomas ("Tommy") 45, n224; William n306
Bradford, James 334
Bragg, Gen. Braxton 254
Brandon, Edwin T. n185, 139; Susannah n185, 98
Bratton, Dr. James Rufus n79
Brison (or Bryson), B. P. 328
Brooks, Lt. John Reece King n335, 193, 199, 240, 244, 254, 259, 262, 267, 281, 289, 291, 334; Martha (Wilson) n335; Price n576; William III n335
Brown, George W. n454; John B. 328; Capt. Phil n628
Buckner, John S. n321; Mariah n321
Burbank, Lt. F. G. n605
Burbridge, Gen. Stephen n547
Burkhalter, William 334
Burns, Charles George n372, 238, 334; William S. H. ("Billy") n345, 180, 185, 238, 325, 335

C

Campbell, Elizabeth (Waller)n44; Isaac A. n44; Margaret Rebecca (Wallace) n15, n128, n315; Napolean B. 328; Samuel Fair n128, n194, 126, n315; Lt. Samuel Leroy n15ff, n44, n128, 141, 153, n315, 205, n437, 222, 224, 328; William E. 328
Canby, Gen. Edward R. S. n602
Carothers, Hugh n125
Carter, Col. George Washington n643
Cathcart, James H. 328
Choate (or Choat), Augustine D. n99ff, n102, 103, 159, n295; Dorcas (Garrison) ("Nancy") n99, n103, n295; James Van Buren n99, 48, 130, 157, 328; Josina Madison n103; Robert Walker n102, n217, 132, 139, 158, 328; William n295
Churchill, Gen. Thomas J. n624
Clark, Gov. Edward n21; T. J. n640, 325, 335
Clinton, Mary (Barnett) n461; Peter n461; Peter Minor n461, 213
Connally, John W. n424, 335
Conner, Elizabeth n560, n610; John N. 335; Nelson n560, n610; Pleasonton G. n610, 290, 299, 303, 325, 335; William B. n560, n561, 335
Cook, Ann n367, n408; Dempsey n17, n97, n157, 150, n274, n310, 164; Dempsey Tresvan n17, 14, 48, 60, 166; Elijah G. n381; James E. n631, 324, 335; James Robertson n97, 151, 157, 161, 162, 328; Jethro G. n310, 163; John n367, 186, 189, n408, 195, 196, 197; John R. n381 Mary (Gibson) ("Polly") n17, n97, n157, n274, n310, 163; Mary E. n408; William L. n381
Corbey, Lt. Thomas J. n535
Coward, Col. Asbury xvii, n50, n56, n68, 311
Craven, Dr. Alfred n85, 63
Crawford, Capt. William L. n538, 246, 250, 252

Croxton, Rev. John S. n75
Cullender, Lawrence n96, n314; Sarah n96, n112; William John n96, 70, 114, n314, 328
Currence, John N. n478; Martha Patrick (Barnett) n478

D

Davis, Pres. Jefferson 70, 108, n353
Deason, Jelico (Cates) n397; Jeremiah n397, 295, 299, 325, 335; Joseph n397; Joseph Collinsworth 248, 335
DeMorse, Col. Charles n642
Deshler, Col. James n624
Divinney (or Divinny), Aaron n216; John J. n309, 328; John McFarland n216, 132; Rachel n216
Doherty, R. J. n534, 335
Dole, Polly n186
Douglas (or Douglass), Mary n402; James Logan n363
Draper, James Madison. Jr. n433; James Madison Sr. n433, 216; Marion W. n433
Drennan, John C. n661, 335; William n661
Dulin, Daniel n431, n632, 335; Frances (Durham) n632; James n632
Duncan, Simeon S. 335
Dunovant, Gen. John n89, 48
Durant, Rev. H. H. n152

E

Eakins, Joseph n178, 97
Easley, James O. n359, 295, 322, 335; John n342, n359; Nancy n342, n359; Thomas F. n342, 177, 322, 335
East, William W. n219
Edgar, Capt. William n589
Edge, Jasper n340, 321, 336

Erwin, Capt. Albert A. n179; Randolph n182; Sarah n182
Estarge, Dr. Joseph L. n597

F

Fairbanks, Lt. Henry n618
Faris, Miles n266; Samuel Thomas n266; Sarah G. n266
Fauntleroy, Capt. Thomas K. n595
Felts, Hilliard J. n264, 161, 162; John W. 328; Miriam (Cook) n274; Sarah n264; William Sr. n264
Ferguson, Augustus 336; Capt. L. M. n375
Fewell (or Fewel), William n364; Benjamin F. 328; James S. 328
Finley, Robert n43, n146; William Green n43, 328
Flournoy, Col. George M. n394, n623
Fogarty, Lt. M. n605
Forney, Gen. John H. n574, 304, 313

G

Gadberry, Col. James M. n288
Gage, Harrison n665, 336
Garrison, William F. 328
Ghentry (or Gentry), J. G. n650, 336; John T. n418, 336
Gibbs, Dr. R. T. n597
Gibson, Eleanor ("Nelly") n17, n41, 152, 167; Harriet n17, 86; Mahala ("Haley") n17, 60, 166; Nancy (Mayhew) n157; Ruebin n157
Giles, John n414, 198, 336
Gingles, Andrew J. n409, 195, 196, 197; Eliza n409
Gist, Gen. States Rights n225
Glenn, Christine (Wood) n317, 166; E. L. n198; Eliza (Boyd) n10, n109, n262; James A. n93, 134,

n318, 328; James H. n60, 329; John F. n60, n109, 95, 151, 154, n317, n318, 166; Robert B. 329; Capt. Robert Henry n10ff, n46, n256, 329; Samuel A. 329; Samuel L. 329; Sarah (Johnston) n60; William n10, n109, n262; William R. n262, 151, 154, 329
Golden, Newton A. n418, n464, 336; Ruben n464; W. M. 336
Gowens, Robert H. n341, 321, 336
Grainger, Gen. Gordon 314
Grant, Gen. Ulysses S. n512, n601, n604, 309
Green, Gen. Thomas n547, n555, 253, 254
Gregg, Col. Maxcy n226
Grier, Mary Catharine (Barnett) n477; Thomas H. n67, 55, n477, 329
Griffin, Dr. H. n597
Grimes, James K. 336; Marion H. n399, 198, 336; W. R. n619, 322, 336
Guthrie, Nelson n495; Panina n495; Thomas C. n495, 238, 336
Guynes, Capt. John n638

H

Hallum, Robert B. 336
Harper, John H. 336; Robert J. n83
Harris, Peter J. n543, 336; W. D. n418, n506, 244, 337
Hawes, Gen. James M. n509
Hawkins, Columbus C. n513, n622, 324, 337; Sarah O. n513
Hays, Benjamin Franklin n349, n527, 262, 287, 288, 289, 291, n637, 337; Cunningham S. n349, n410, 337; Daniel Matterson ("Matt") n349, n528, 267, 269, 337; James William n455; Mary (Wilson) n349, n410, n527, n528, n544; William C. n349, n410, n527, n528, n544; William Henry Harrison n349, n544, n552, 337
Healton, R. R. 337
Hellum, H. 337
Henry, Malancton n136
Hindman, Gen. Thomas C. n387, 194, n419, 296
Holleman, Green W. 337
Holly (or Holley), J. M. 337; Richard R. 337; Sion n418, 337
Holmes, Gen. Theophilus H. n419
Horsley, David Richard n195; Rees (or Reece) n313; Robertus n329
Houston, Gov. Sam 8, n20
Howe, David n254; Jane (Horsley) n254; Richard Oates n254, 151, 157, 161
Huddleston, Nancy n107, n115; Robert R. 329; Stephen n107; Thomas J. n115, 329; William Henry n107, n115
Hudman, Elizabeth n621, n654; Francis n621, n654; James T. n418, n621, n654, 337
Hulender (or Hullender), I. n278
Hull, James n494, n530; John L. 237, n530, 240, 288, 289, 337; Sarah n494, n530; Thomas Jefferson n494, 237, 240, 289, 338
Hunt, James Samuel n578, 272; Joseph J. n578; Lucy n422; Thomas J. Jr. n422, 338; Thomas J. Sr. n422
Hutchison, Samuel J. 329

I

Irby, Keziah n649; Rufus n649, 338

J

Jackson, Gen. Andrew xiv; John McClain n482; Robert P. n479, n482; Samuel W. 329; Gen. Thomas J. ("Stonewall") n173,

230
Jenkins, Gen. Micah xvii, xviii, n48ff, n50, n51, n68, 34, 47, n601
Johnston (or Johnson), Samuel C. n187, 141, 149, 160; David n151; David M. 329; Gen. Joseph E. n501; Mary (Glenn) n151; William Glenn n151, 329
Jones, Gen. David Rumph n138; Ellen n352; H. P. 338; James M. n337, n352, n567, 287, 288, 289, 303, 325, 338; Joseph H. 338; , Capt. Robin A. P. Cadwallader n258; Thomas n337, n352; Thomas P. n337, n352, n620, 322, 338

K

Kelly, Joseph n100
King, Gen. Wilburn H. n641
Knapp, Virginia iv
Koonce, John Alexander n338, 321, 338
Kuykendall, G. M. 338; Marian (Branch) n630; Middleton n630; William Asher n630, 324, 338

L

Lacy, Andrew n451; Calvin n451; Margaret (Akin) n451; William n452
Landrum, Rev. John Gill n154
Laney, John n118; Livingston L. W. n118, 329; Rachel n118
Latham, Elizabeth n243; John W. n243
Latta, Robert 329
Leake, Col. J. B. n555
Lee, Gen. Robert E. n51, 145, 240, 246, 254, n601, n604, 309, 311, 312; W. W. 338
Leslie, John A. 338
Lewis, J. N. 136
Lincoln, Pres. Abraham 72

Little, Elizabeth n651; James C. J. n651, 338; Lewis n651
Logan, David Jackson n296; John B. n296; John Randolph n296; Lois (Rainey) n296
Long, G. W. n518; J. E. n518; Nancy n518; W. D. n518
Longstreet, Gen. James n601
Loverett (or Leverich), Emma n580
Loving, Capt. William C. n376
Lubbock, Gov. Francis n21

M

Mabry, Hester n532; John F. n532, 266, 338; Joseph n532
Magruder, Gen. John Bankhead n571, 269, 270, 313
March, Dr. S. W. n427
Mason, George Washington n32, 40, 73, n211, 329; Nancy A. (Pegram) n32, n184; Nancy Hannah (Stowe) n84, 67, 87, 97; William n32, n72
Matthews, Dr. Y. A. n505, 236
Mayeux, Steve iv
Mayhew, Charity n6, n8; Reason ("Uncle Reese") n6ff; William n6, n8
McCall, Ann (Lacy) n657; David L. n657, 338; Robert n657
McCallum, Aaron ("Ren") n28; Lt. Duncan A. xx, n23, n36, 195, 295, 322, 339; Infant ("Buddy") n28; James n28, n193; Matilda Jane (Wood) n22, n23, 10, 195, 204, 208, 213, 219; Peter ("Cousin Peter") n23ff, n36, 213; Violet n23, n36; William n28; William Augustus J. n36ff, n55, n77, 329
McCarter, David A. n208, 329; Elias n207, n208, n449; Elizabeth Olivia (Patrick) n207, n208, n449; John A. 329; Joseph Bredner n449, n556, 325, 339
McCaw, Robert G. 330

McCay, James n160; Jane (Mayhew) n160
McCorkle, Jane (Hart) n132; Stephen n132; Col. William Hart n132, 140, 153;
McCrary, Neal D. 339
McCulloch, Gen. Henry E. n353, n360, n394, n396, 198, 297, n634
McCully, John W. 330; Robert H. 330
McDermott, Josaphine 284, 294
McElhaney, Elias n263; Lucinda n263
McElwee, James n120; Nancy (Wright) n120; Samuel Anderson n120, 66
McKenzie, Arthur Armstrong ("Uncle Arthur") n111ff, n143, 330; Joseph n111; Joseph Stanhope n143, 330; Rachel (Barnett) n111, n143
McKnight, Andrew n652; John Franklin C. n652, 339; Sarah (Hudman) n652
McLean, Joseph A. n131
McLester, Lt. H. n600
Meacham, Dr. Thomas Boyd n265
Meade, Gen. George Gordon 246
Mitchell, Dawson N. n299; James Thomas n299, 162; Nancy (Carothers) n299; Samuel A, 330; William R. n299, 162
Moore, Lee n389; Mary H. n302; Samuel E. n54; William R. n116, 134, n302, 330
Moseley, Flora n662; Thomas J. n662, 339
Mower, Gen. J. A. n582, n589

N

Nall, John M. n583, 302, 339
Neal, Eliza C. n24; Neal, Mary F. n24
Neely, Jim n365, 193
Nesbitt, James F. 330

Nichols, Sally 187; William n668, 339; William ("Bill") n368, 187
Nix, T. L. 339
Northrop, Capt. A. R. K. n548

O

Ochiltree, Col. William B. n463
Orr, Nic n74
Osburn, George W. n636, 339
Owens, Rev. William C. n110; William J. 339

P

Page, D. D. n354
Parker, Asa J. n514, n520, 242, 290, 307, 339; Franklin J. 339; James n370, 185, n418, 325, 339; Jeremiah n629; Pertima (Simmons) n629, n660; Robert F. n629, n660; Susan M. A. (Bates) n514; William E. n660, 339
Partlowe, David n164; David Theodore n164; Mary (Barnett) n164
Patrick, Elias n141, n142; Frances n328; George Anderson n141, 83, 330; John C. 340; Robert Vaughn n142, 149, 154, 330; Susannah (Anderson) n141, n142
Patton, T. L. n145, 121
Pegram, Winchester n269
Pegues, Capt. James A. n579; O. H. n579
Peterson, James F. 340
Peurifoy, Amos J. n533, 340
Pickens, Gov. Frances xi, xviii, 70, n214
Pierce, Josiah W. 330
Pinckney, Charles n57
Poovey, David n647; Duncan McCallum n647; Lucretia (McCallum) n647; William P. 330

Porter, Adm. David n582, n593;
  Sgt. John C. n586, n596, n609,
  n611
Price, Gen. Sterling n599, n635

Q

Quinn, Elizabeth (Denham) n260;
  Leroy D. n260, 154, 330;
  Walter n260

R

Raburn, James D. n418, n664, 340
Randal, Gen. Horace n377, n498,
  n511, n635; Lt. John Leonard
  Jr. n498
Ray, Eleanor (Templeton) n350,
  n572; John R. n350, 185, n411,
  197, n572, 295, 322, 340;
  Robert T. n572; William D.
  n350, n572
Redwood, Maj. William H. n507,
  300
Reid (or Reed), John M. n25, n542,
  340
Reinhart (or Reinhardt), James P.
  Henderson n423, n658, 340;
  Martin F. n423, n658; Mary
  n423, n658
Rettig, Dr. Conrad n333, 177;
  Frederic n333; Lucie n333
Rhodes, Elizabeth n390; Elizabeth
  (Thompson) n351; George W.
  n431, n632; James Olen n351,
  185, n390, 194, 201, 219, 302,
  326, 340; Nancy (Whitfield)
  n390; Nathaniel n351
Riley, Anna n356, 263; Len n504;
  Thomas J. n356, n357, n466,
  227, 237, 254, 260, 262, 287,
  303, 325, 340
Robertson, E. T. n417, 340
Robinson, John W. n439; Larkin B.
  n439; Mary (Clark) n439
Roper, Rev. Jonathan M. n167

S

Sartor (or Sarter), Capt. Jacob W.
  n222, 133
Schorb, John R. n130; Mary n130
Scott, F. M. n667, 340
Scurry, Gen. William R. n353, n635
Shepard, Col. James E. n627
Simril, Frank n293; Franklin M.
  n238; Hugh H. n16, n148,
  n238; John J. n16, 330; Nancy
  (Partlowe) n148, n238; Samuel
  Davidson n16, n148, 77, n238,
  330
Singletary, Nancy n503; Robert
  n503, 237, 340
Skelton, Pam (Burns) iv
Slaves- Adline n190; Aunt Cintha
  n39, 38, 64, 207; Candis n134,
  207, 224; Caroline n127, 207;
  Dave n180; Jack n180; John
  n168, 207; Letty n491;
  McCallum, Mary n27;Nelly
  n117; Sally 224; Sam n444,
  n553, 254, 270; Simril, Lawson
  n292, 173, 177, 199, 267;
  Thaddeus n180; Wallace,
  Edward n171, 224; Wallace,
  Frank n40, n114; Wallace,
  Green n429; Wallace, Miles
  n88, 52, 59, 76, 81, n286, 157;
  Wood, Addison ("Add") n4,
  n114, 63, 64, n245, 144, 145,
  154, 155, 167, 224; Wood,
  Andrew ("Andy") n14, 64, 80;
  Wood, Mack n4, n245, n246
Slemmer, Lt. Adam n34
Smith, Gen. Andrew J. n585; Col.
  Ashbel n558; Charles A. 340;
  Gen. Edmund Kirby n501,
  n536, n574, 270, 302, n635,
  312, 313; Jane (Darby) n71;
  Jerome Decatur n529, 341;
  Capt. John n508, 307; Martha
  Jane (Glenn) n71, n301, 166;
  Rev. Martin V. n539; Samuel

D. n71; Zadoc Darby n71, 35, n183, n301, 224
South, Heather iv
Stanley, Abner n339, 321, 341
Starnes, Feriba n307; Joseph n307; Thomas R. n307
Steele, Gen. Frederick n599, n635
Stevens, Ruby Lee (Beall) iv, vii; Tommy Dean iv
Stewart, Eliza (Tate) n98, n279; James A. n98, 53, 55, 57, 70, 239, 330; James Calhoun n201, 127, 128, 330; James M. n201; Jimmy 207; John Andrew Martin Luther n279; Joseph B. n98, n126, 61, n279; Margaret (Rooker) n201
Stillwell, Alfred n54
Stone, Peter Wynn Stovall n566, 287, 303, 325, 341
Stoveall, George L. n420, 201, 237, 240, 295, 341
Stowe, White n188
Strickland, Thomas W. n546, 304, 326, 341; William A. 341

T

Talbert, Jim n361
Tappan, Gen. James C. n510
Tate, Hugh n139, n147; James B. n139, 161, 330; Jane (Patrick) n139
Taylor, Col. Enos Ward n626; Gen. Richard n499, n536, 253, 259, n574, n597; Pres. Zachary n536
Thomas, Burrel W. n656, 341; Sam iv
Thompson, Ephraim D. n45; John R. n612, 341; John T. 330; Mary (Gingles) n45; Dr. T. C. n597; Maj. W. T. n80; William Lawson n45, 331
Timberlake, John C. n92ff, 47, 73, 120, 331
Tinkle, G. L. n666, 341; Sabra (Nolan) n666; William n666
Treadwell, William L. 341

Turner, George R. n235; Rice Ross n531, 341; Romulus G. W. n541, 341; Samuel n531; William n235

U

Upshaw, Lt. R. L. n598

V

Vallandigham, Clement L. n500

W

Walker, James L. 341; Gen. John George xxi, n396, n499, 239, 253, 259, n574, 270, 298, 306, 313; Capt. Joseph n192
Wallace, Aaron Wood xiv, n5ff; Achsah (Wood) xiv, ff; Ann n234; Bartley n515; David G. n234, 148, 151; Ellen Adaline n240, n467; George Franklin n240, n438, n467; Harriet (Cook) n95; Capt. Harvey Alexander vi, ff, 331, 341; Harvey Alexander Jr. xiv, n577, 314; James xi, n11ff, 92, 145, 155; James Adams n22ff, n66, n203, 167, n558; John Rufus H. ("Ruff") n55, n64, 136, 331; Joseph n468; Joseph F. n240, n438, n467; 331; Joseph Franklin n22, n175, 124, 153, n469; Josephine G. (Ray) n176, n350, n428, n434; Margaret Ann n203; Margaret Elizabeth (Farris) n66, n203, 167; Margaret Ewart (Barnett) xi, ff; Martha Adeline n435, n492; Martha C. (Wood) n18, n210, n426; Martha Margaret Rebecca ("Matty") xiv, n7ff, 315; Matilda Jane xiv; Samuel Watson n55ff, n95, 331; Thomas Stanhope n18ff, n210, n558; Lt. William Marcellus

xx, n176ff, 341; William
    Thomas xiv, ff
Waltom, Tillis n616
Ward, Martin n161; Nancy (Wood)
    n161,
Warrant, James R. 331
Waterhouse, Gen. Richard Jr.xx,
    n353, n512, 243, 304
Watkins, Archibald H. n323
Watson, Elizabeth (Currence)n241;
    John L. n65, 141, 149; William
    n241; William D. n241, 331
Welch, James W. n388, 254; John
    n443; Joseph Alexander
    Hamilton n443, n545, 342;
    Larissa (McKnight) n443
Wells, Lt. Col. John W. n642
West, Houston n611, 342; Martin
    n366
Wharton, Gen. John A. n573
Whitaker, T. Morrison n230
Whiteside, Billy 140
Whitfield, Bryan n398; Emily
    (Bailey) n398; William B.
    n398, 198, 234, 324, 342
Wilkerson, Robert S. 331
Williams, Leroy R. 331
Wilson, Dorcas 151, 186, 193; Elias
    C. n406; Jesse n405, n406; Jim
    n121, 75; Margaret n405, n406,
    n407; Robert n380, 193;
    William n380, 193; Capt.
    William Blackburn n249
Witherspoon, Ann (Reid) n94; Isaac
    n94; John Alfred n94, 78, 98
Wolverton, Elijah H. n557;
    Greenville n550, n557;
    Parmelia (Guinn) n557;
    Thornton B. n557; William T.
    n557
Wood, Aaron xiv; Lt. Charles A.
    n605; Chesley G. n218, 132,
    331; Daniel Marion n13ff, 16,
    n61, n108, 49, 63, 81, n317;
    David Johnston n236;
    Elizabeth (Bailey) n236;
    Elizabeth (Johnston) n484;
    Henry F. n659, 342; James A.
    n400, 197; Joseph n484;
    Leonard Thomas Mason xx,
    n236, 168, 204, 209, 238, 245,
    246, 267, 268, 288, 289, 342;
    Mariah n13; Martin Ward n13,
    n70, 49, 81; Mary (Harper)
    n13, n70, 49, 81; Matilda
    (Mayhew) xiv, n8ff, 163;
    Newton L. n484; Rachel (Hall)
    n400; Rezin n13
Wright, James n496; James C. 342;
    James L. n12ff, 11, n140;
    James Spratt n140, 331; Martha
    (Spratt) n140

Y

Yearwood, Anderson 331
Youngblood, Eliza (Faris) n255;
    Henry n255; Orin N. 331;
    Samuel C. n104, n441; Thomas
    W. n255, 151, 157, 161, 162,
    331

Z

Zuber, Mariah (Brooks) n450;
    William n450; William M.
    n450, n516

About The Author

Steve Skelton is a research historian and historical consultant specializing in local, Texas, U. S. military, and U. S. Civil War history. Specific areas of concentrated Civil War research include Texas and Texas units involved in the war, the Trans-Mississippi Department and region, and the Red River Campaign in Louisiana. Other interests include archaeology and historic preservation.

Steve is a Texas unit consultant with the University of Tennessee's Civil War Units File Project and has consulted on various research, writing, and genealogical projects. He also has extensive experience in historic site research and investigation, as well as artifact recovery and preservation. Steve holds degrees from Houston Community College, Charter Oak State College, and the University of Texas at Tyler.

As a Christian, Steve believes that human history originates with God and reveals His nature and relationship with man through time. As a result, the best reason to study and record history is to show how God works in our world in the past to bring us to the future.

Steve Skelton and his wife Pam reside in Rusk County, Texas. He welcomes all comments or enquiries and may be contacted through Heritage Books.

www.ingramcontent.com/pod-product-compliance
Lightning Source LLC
Chambersburg PA
CBHW050428240426
43661CB00055B/2308